East West Central

East West Central
Re-Building Europe, 1950–1990

Edited by Ákos Moravánszky, Torsten Lange,
Judith Hopfengärtner, Karl R. Kegler

Ákos Moravánszky, Judith Hopfengärtner (Eds.)

Re-Humanizing Architecture

New Forms of Community, 1950–1970

East West Central
Re-Building Europe
1950–1990
Vol. 1

Birkhäuser
Basel

Editors
Prof. Dr. Ákos Moravánszky
Department of Architecture, ETH Zurich, Switzerland

Judith Hopfengärtner
Department of Architecture, ETH Zurich, Switzerland

Editors' proofreading: Alan Lockwood, PL-Warsaw
Publishers' proofreading: Alun Brown, A-Vienna
Project and production management: Angelika Heller, Birkhäuser Verlag, A-Vienna
Layout and typography: Ekke Wolf, typic.at, A-Vienna
Cover design: Martin Gaal, A-Vienna
Printing and binding: Holzhausen Druck GmbH, A-Wolkersdorf

Library of Congress Cataloging-in-Publication data
A CIP catalog record for this book has been applied for at the Library of Congress.

Bibliographic information published by the German National Library
The German National Library lists this publication in the Deutsche Nationalbibliografie; detailed bibliographic data are available on the Internet at http://dnb.dnb.de.

This publication is also available as an e-book (ISBN PDF 978-3-0356-0811-3).

P.O. Box 44, 4009 Basel, Switzerland
Part of Walter de Gruyter GmbH, Berlin/Boston

Printed on acid-free paper produced from chlorine-free pulp. TCF ∞

Printed in Austria

ISBN 978-3-0356-1015-4 Volume 1
ISBN 978-3-0356-1016-1 Volume 2
ISBN 978-3-0356-1017-8 Volume 3
ISBN 978-3-0356-1014-7 Set Volume 1–3

9 8 7 6 5 4 3 2 1

www.birkhauser.com

Contents

Ákos Moravánszky

Foreword

East West Central: Re-Building Europe

The Iron Curtain stood for the static immutability of the status quo. "From Stettin in the Baltic to Trieste in the Adriatic, an iron curtain has descended across the Continent" – Winston Churchill told his audience in a famous speech on March 5, 1946. Like most metaphors, the term Iron Curtain has imprinted itself into the perception of reality and was associated with the fortified border, erected to block the movement of people and information between East and West. Architectural historiography followed suit, presenting the history of modernization and modernism in Europe from a perspective determined – and limited – by this political boundary. The imagery produced by the dissolution of the Soviet Union: the "fall," the "lifting" or the "raising" of the curtain, the "breaching" of the wall, is a sign of confusion – regarding not only metaphors, but also underlying assumptions, methods and categories of architectural historiography.

Writing in the 1920s, art historian Erwin Panofsky famously referred to the perspective as a symbolic form. By this he meant that representing reality by means of a cohesive set of rules and symbols would give shape to a specific worldview. The exchange of views between cultures can therefore be studied using examples of visual representations, based on differing concepts of the relationship between observer and reality. When Panofsky gave his seminal lecture on Western perspective, Russian philosopher-physicist-inventor-priest Pavel Florensky wrote a study on the "reverse perspective" used in icon painting. He compared it to Renaissance representations of space in order to point out the differences between the two types of visual representation and their respective philosophical and theological underpinnings.

The exchange of glances as expressed in the German word *Blickwechsel* is a suggestive image: we are invited to switch between the viewpoints of the observer and the observed, so that our image of the world is suddenly no longer taken for granted. The metaphor of the Iron Curtain, however, suggests that after WWII the boundary between the two halves of Europe was hermetic and impermeable, even to the gaze. Western and Eastern Europe regarded each other as their own dark "others": communism and capitalism, divided by the Iron Curtain, were the "Twin Empires" on the mythical map of Europe. Yet, the perfect symmetry of the image eschewed the evidently more complex reality. As an image, the Iron Curtain was able to trigger both Western fear and desire, but actually it was far from being impenetrable. Rather, the Iron Curtain's semi-permeability, which turned it into an osmotic membrane, refuted the supposed symmetry of the East-West division. Contrary to the widespread identification in the West with the concept of Western Europe and its corresponding values, the idea of a shared Eastern European identity has never been popular among the inhabitants of this region. Architects in the East were generally very well informed about the latest developments in Western architecture. One could hardly survive as an architect without having browsed the latest issues of *L'Architecture d'Aujourd'hui, The Architectural Review* or the magazines from Scandinavian countries, all of which were available in the libraries of the large state-owned design offices. The optical metaphor, however, held true: images were floating around but remained disembodied signifiers, as they weren't grounded in personal experience. At the same time, travels of architects and professional organizations from the West to the East intensified during 1970s and 1980s. The lessons that participants drew from such exchanges more often than not depended on their respective viewpoints of the perspective.

The discrepancy between the bipolarity of block-thinking and the more complex and heterogeneous civilizational and political reality of Europe has led historians to develop different concepts to describe the historical identity of European regions more adequately than the East-West dichotomy. The term *Mitteleuropa* has never been merely a geographical term. It was a political one as well, just as East and West were connected with distinct political ideas or concepts. With the active support of intellectuals from the United States and England in the 1980s, Central Europe became a program to affirm a particular identity of the region: politically part of the Eastern Bloc, but without losing its Western cultural orientation – a result of the region's specific historical development and its political affiliations before the war. "The phrase, a peculiar one, a hybrid of sorts, hearkened back to the Cold War period; while it reflected a certain deference to the ideas of Milan Kundera and others, it avoided the outright suggestion that the notion of Eastern Europe was outmoded, essentially a fabrication of the age of Stalin, that it brought together in a single category societies that remained significantly different" – wrote Stephen R. Graubard, editor of *Daedalus*, the journal of the American Academy of Arts and Sciences in 1990, in his introduction for the issue "Eastern Europe... Central Europe... Europe." The title suggested a development of concepts: the first term referred to the Cold War period, the second was the "preferred word of certain individuals and groups in the 1960s, 1970s, and 1980s," while the third was the "word of the moment." From the contemporary perspective of more than two decades later, the question about what might be further stages in this progression is at the heart of heated debates.

Ironically, it was exactly the abolishment of state socialism and the new freedom of movement that have lessened the urgency to cross borders intellectually. In 1987, the idea of a joint international exhibition to take place in Budapest and Vienna in 1995 was embraced with much enthusiasm, only to be abandoned in its advanced stage. The "bridges into the future" – the motto of Expo'95 – literally lost their appeal after the Pan-European Picnic in August 1989.

Today, as block-thinking and block-politics are reemerging, the category of the Central promises to be a useful tool for investigating European architecture between two moments of "re-building": the postwar reconstruction and the start of shifting the "curtain" (which is not less "irony" today than before) more and more toward the East. We decided to use the word Central not only because it was a buzzword during the decades that are the focus of our investigation, but because the "thirding" that is implicit in the term opposes a bipolar narrative that regards modernization and globalization as Westernization and regards Eastern European developments as secondary or non-authentic, never questioning the constructs that legitimate these interpretations.

An investigation into issues such as housing, the exporting of knowledge to the Third World, building for education and for leisure between the two re-buildings of Europe would be impossible if one resorted to the narrative of the Iron Curtain. Rather than this dualistic concept, we have to consider among others competitions, cooperation, critical transformation, and knowledge transfer as more adequate frameworks for investigating these more dynamic conditions. The critique of self-serving dichotomizations of cultural phenomena in line with the East/West dispositive (marginal/central, modern/traditional, authentic/copy etc.) does not mean that, in this process of explaining the changing urban and architectural conditions over the course of the last seventy years, the diverse cultural landscape of Europe needs to be flattened.

The re-mapping of the European historiography of the postwar decades is an urgent task in the face of the paradoxical perpetuation of the Cold War discourse. One of the reasons behind its endurance is the imbalance between the ongoing institutionalization of archives of postwar architectural production in Western Europe vis-à-vis the disappearance of archival sources in the East. To lend visibility to the architectural discourse in former socialist countries, it is important to give voice to protagonists and witnesses. The failure to do this would not only reinforce already existing blind spots in the architectural historiography of the postwar period, but would also distort the perception of Western-European architecture culture from the 1960s onward. This includes the concept of the welfare state as being restricted to the Western social-democratic project and posited in contrast to state socialism, rather than recognizing parallel development in the post-Stalinist socialist countries and its architecture revolving around issues of consumption, leisure, mass housing and the emergence of new collective subjectivities such as "users," "inhabitants," or "consumers." Another example could be the reduction of current processes of globalization to their earlier stages, presenting globalization as "Americanization," thus forgetting the multiple, vibrant and heterogeneous processes of the internationalization of architecture and planning practices between socialist and post-colonial countries.

Three international conferences organized by the Chair of Architectural Theory at the ETH Zurich prepared the ground for this re-mapping. The topic of our first East West Central conference in May 2014 was *Re-Humanizing Architecture: New Forms of Community, 1950–1970*. Our intention was to show that the rhetoric of humanism provided an ideal common ground for liberal and socialist positions in the postwar years. With the second conference *Re-Scaling the Environment: New Landscapes of Design, 1960–1980*, held in November 2014, we abandoned the metaphor of the "human scale" as the natural way of viewing the world for a larger, superhuman, geographic or territorial scale. The theme of the third conference in *Re-Framing Identities: Architecture's Turn to History, 1970–1990* in September 2015 shows another overlap by a decade. This does not mean that the themes of humanism and scale disappear; even postmodernism is regarded by some historians as a project of re-humanization. While we investigate these altogether four decades from three different perspectives, the themes of humanism, scale and identity remain relevant categories throughout the entire time period 1950–1990.

We could not have gotten started on this project without the generous and long-term support of the Department of Architecture of the ETH Zurich and its Institut gta (Institute for the History and Theory of Architecture). The Swiss National Science Foundation (SNF) has provided us with financial assistance for the organization of the conferences. The book has been made possible only by the contributions of our authors; we owe them all a debt of gratitude. We would also like to thank the persons and institutions who gave their permission for the illustrations. We owe a considerable debt to everybody at Birkhäuser Verlag who helped in the production of the book; most of all David Marold and Angelika Heller. We also would like to express our gratitude to our student assistants Josephine Eigner and Laure Nashed for their help.

Judith Hopfengärtner

Introduction

What does it mean to "humanize" architecture? The notion of re-humanization has been a vehicle to connect a series of debates and discussions from around the middle of the twentieth century which employ the term in relation to architecture and urban planning. The conspicuous frequency of this usage clearly indicates a perception of crisis, while the term itself is hardly defined and the claim of humanization bears so many positive/affirmative associations/connotations it is also seldom to be rejected. Indeed, the possible meanings behind the phrase of (re-)humanization bear an undeniable kinship and usually trigger associations of sensitivity to (human) scale, experience and perception; to human needs and dignity; also fragility; and they often come with an ethical allusion.

Even though the possible translation of these values into the architectural is manifold, architectural currents which have been connected to efforts to humanizing often share similar characteristics; as modesty in scale and expression, diversity in the organization of spaces and volumes, the usage of traditional and regional motives, and a concern for the everyday, the banal, the playful. Via proponents of an architectural avant-garde these flirtations with ordinary taste have repeatedly raised harsh criticism – against an architecture strolling in the fields of mediocrity and blandness, and dangerously balancing on the edges of the picturesque and kitsch.

Where re-humanization is asked for, some sort of de-humanization must have taken place. Many of the ideas underlying the strategies and conceptions of humanization had their roots in discussions about problems of identity and alienation associated with modernization and modern civilization, as well as with the rigid functionalism of the modern movement. Around 1940, the so called "New Empiricism" [1] developed in Sweden; a realist tendency associated with the ideals of the welfare state which was influential in Britain and found support in the US where Lewis Mumford advocated an "organic" humanism. At the same time, Giedion, Leger and Sert proposed their "Nine Points on Monumentality" (1943), arguing for new kinds of monuments for people "that represent their social and community life to give more than functional fulfillment."[2]

After 1945, the call for a humanization of architecture received an acute and existential dimension. The Second World War, with its unprecedented devastation and with the horrors of oppression and the Holocaust, made restoration feel as necessary on the social and moral levels as on the physical one. Beyond the urgency of meeting basic needs, the re-building of large parts of the European continent triggered fundamental questions about how to build new, better societies – and how to build *for* them

Architecture and urbanism were key disciplines in giving shape to these new environments – on a map that from the late 1940s onward displayed a stable divide between the two blocs and their ideological systems of capitalism and state-socialism. Eager to both demonstrate their economic and political superiority and to succeed in the Cultural Cold War[3], a period of intense competition but also of cooperation and mutual influences between the capitalist, socialist, and non-aligned states of Europe set in. As different as the political ambitions in the two blocs and as opposing as the views about the relations between individual and collective were, there was a general agreement on the need to improve and "humanize" people's living conditions in terms of everyday life.

"The problem is one of forging a taste, a technique, a morality, as different manifestations of the same problem: the problem of building a society," Ernesto Nathan Rogers formulated as newly elected editor of *Domus* in 1946 in his lead column titled "The House of Man."[4] He saw the comprehensive task of a profound reassessment of the conditions of modern architecture in relation to life in a community. The close connection between formal, social and ethical questions is emblematic of a series of architectural debates during this period.

In the Eastern Bloc, architects were to be confronted in the early 1950s with the short-lived period of socialist realism, which engaged a decisively humanist rhetoric in its aim of addressing the people by means of familiar aesthetics and a realistic imagery, intending a sharp contrast to capitalist ("cosmopolitan") architecture. When de-Stalinization started in 1954, the return of modernism would connote the humanizing spirit of the Thaw, symbolizing the rejection of Stalinist oppression.

The biographies of modern architects illustrate the complexity of their social and political motivations. Many Western protagonists of CIAM had already worked in the USSR during the Nazi regime, like Ernst May, Hans Schmid and Hannes Meyer. In the years after the war significant exchange and mutual transfer across the "Iron Curtain" went on – as the pro-communist attitude of a significant part of Western European intellectuals continued and many dreamed of contributing to the building of socialism in the new people's democracies – until their disillusionment through Stalinist terror.

In the West, the focus redirected itself at the beginning of the 1950s onto alternative strategies of humanization within the capitalist system, criticizing the functionalist principles of urbanism propagated by CIAM. Debates on identity and community peaked at the eighth CIAM conference in Hoddesdon 1951 ("The Core of the City," published as *The Heart of the City*).[5] There, Sigfried Giedion repeated his visions for a New Monumentality and a "humanization" through the reorganization of community life and the planning and design of civic centers. Younger CIAM participants – many of them later to be known as part of Team 10 – didn't feel comfortable with the somewhat heroic gestus of Giedion's vision. They were looking for alternative ways to break up the painful limitations of an almost exclusively rationalist orientation of modern architecture. For the following decades, Aldo van Eyck, the Smithsons, Giancarlo De Carlo, Ernesto N. Rogers, and, of "Team 10 East",[6] f. e. Oskar Hansen and Charles Polónyi among many others established a network that kept on pushing the boundaries of modern architecture, urging for a re-establishment of traditional and regional patterns in order to "humanize" environmental design. Taking inspiration from spatial structures, local materials and anonymous architecture in different climates and cultural zones, and from the human habitat; building in Third World countries, emphasizing the individual and subjective – the spectrum of interests and forms of expression widened significantly, also reflecting the growing possibilities for travel and communication.

The call for humanism and re-humanizing temporarily lost its urgency around the 1960s, when the accelerated economic growth on both sides of the Iron Curtain resulted in a relative material wellbeing and – in large areas of the West, but also in Eastern Bloc states like Hungary – the fascinations of consume and leisure entered daily life. The one-sided dominance of the technological and rational aspects of modern architecture soon showed its consequences in the "inhospitality" (*Unwirtlichkeit*) and monotony of urban sprawl and raised anew the call for a more human environment. This time the critique wasn't mainly an avant-garde phenomenon but would join in the big social movements of the 1970s, fighting for ecological and emancipatory concerns.

Many aspects of humanism combined well with the goals of the welfare state, as with socialist ideas of equality and safety. On a more comprehensive level, facets like individual choice and responsibility – as highlighted in Jean-Paul Sartre's[7] Existentialism – or the anti-heroism and persistence with the lasting absurdity of the condition of man according to Albert Camus, stood in clear tension with the very nature of (any) systems and their institutions. This can explain why many strategies of re-humanization have been developed – and continue to be so – on the periphery, and outside or at the edges of institutions.

The book is structured in four parts, each of which puts emphasis on specific aspects within the field of humanization strategies in Eastern and Western European countries. The first part focuses on the term "humanization" and on related discourses on humanism, the second on humanizing aspects in concepts for building new societies. The third part discusses efforts for a re-humanization of public space in the urban context, while the last part deals with questions about attempts to reconcile notions of rural and urban in the field of housing as well as in leisure and tourism.

Part1: Discourses on Humanism

The intense and diverse debates on humanism, or what it means to be human in the middle of the twentieth century, are the subject of the first part. The vagueness of the term and its predominantly positive connotations made it accessible and easy to take up from different sides and disciplines in an effort of reconciliation, or in order to make political allies. Ákos Moravánszky describes how the notion of humanism unfolded a strong persuasive aura in the early postwar years. For a short period, opposite positions like that of Western (French) communists or Christian humanists could find common ground (not least mediated by Sartre's atheist Existentialism) and built alliances for political action. The hidden ambiguities in understanding the term however wouldn't take long to surface again, though, and to trigger controversy; as was the case with architectural concepts of humanism. Annie Pedret takes a close look at the likewise vague and rather undefined term "spiritual," which was used by CIAM members in relation to efforts of humanization in architecture in the period 1950–1970 in an almost synonymous sense, which tried to understand human reality in a more complete way by emphasizing psychological aspects and reaching beyond the physical. She argues that, probably due to its esoteric overtones, the term has been neglected in historiography, but should be taken into account to fully understand the concept of humanization in postwar modernist discourse. "Socialism with a human face" was a popular phrase in Hungary. Béla Kerékgyártó traces the often failed attempts at reform before and after the Prague Spring. When after 1968 the belief in the possibilities of fundamental political change had diminished, the regime concentrated on material wellbeing to improve the population's sense of satisfaction and invested in big scale housing production, thus leaving a troublesome legacy for the built environment and for the architectural profession. Polish artist, intellectual and writer Mieczysław Porębski found himself in a similar situation. Wojciech Bałus describes his search for a new kind of poetics as an individual strategy for freedom. Porębski's book *Man and Architecture in the Iconosphere* addresses the culture of the twentieth century in general, trying to mentally cross borders and keeping in touch with intellectual debates in the West.

Part 2: Building New Societies

The second part takes a closer look at postwar reconstruction, which in Europe's Eastern half went parallel with the constitution of peoples' democracies. The new socialist societies, under a strong Soviet influence, strived to represent themselves with a "human face" as opposed to the so-called inhuman alienation and exploitation of the capitalist world. While many built ensembles of the socialist-realist era and early examples of the subsequent modernist period express a strong personal involvement of architects, planners, workers and artists, from 1960 on large-scale mass-housing, prefabrication and standardization dominated the building production, causing heavy criticism from inhabitants and from the researchers of newly established sciences like environmental psychology. Marcela Hanáčková looks at the period shortly after the war, when the reconstruction plan for the heavily destroyed city of Warsaw became part of a vivid East-West discussion. The plan can be seen as an attempt to build up an ostentatiously social(ist) city virtually from scratch in the few years before the division of the world into "socialist" and "capitalist" manifested. A few years later, the American architecture critic Sibyl Moholy-Nagy, widow of László Moholy-Nagy, shares under a pseudonym her impressions and insights about the new constructions mainly in Berlin East (Stalinallee) and West (Hansaviertel) in American architectural records. In comparing these two texts, Hilde Heynen shows how the Cold War context informs Moholy-Nagy's way of highlighting contrasts and stresses another point of view of perceiving the continuities and similarities of the architecture of the 1960s in both German states. Nikolas Drosos confronts Le Corbusier's concept of *chantier de synthese* (collaborative construction sites), as a means of "humanizing" architecture and of providing it with meaning, with different forms of collaborations between architects and architects in Poland and Yugoslavia, from the highly symbolic socialist-realist construction site of Constitution Square in Warsaw, to the experimental Art Research Workshops and the Yugoslav group EXAT 51. Marijke Martin and Cor Wagenaar compare concepts of community and neighborhood in the Netherlands and Czechoslovakia around 1960, finding striking similarities and parallel developments in the way community life has been valued, and in their development towards participation and psychological approaches towards the late 1960s. This phase of humanization abruptly stopped in Czechoslovakia with the Prague spring. In Romania, the period until the early 1970s can be seen as the most "humane" period, paralleling the Khrushchev Thaw. Dana Vais discusses the fact that in Romania it is precisely modernism that is associated with a time of humanization; while Karin Hallas-Murula describes how in Estonia, in parallel to the majority of European countries, new human-centered sciences such as urban sociology and environmental psychology aimed to inform architectural practice with a critical attitude toward Soviet mass housing and lifestyle.

Part 3: The Urban Context

In an attempt to reform and develop CIAM's principles, the planners, architects and intellectuals of Eastern and Western Europe tried to develop alternative strategies to deal with the challenges of modernity and to try and give form and meaning to urban space. Vladimir Kulić introduces the Serbian-Yugoslav architect, writer, and politician Bogdan Bogdanović. Known mainly for his memorials to the Second World War, Bogdanović's writings on the city focus on human scale, experience, and the meaning attached to urban space. For Bogdanović, architecture was "applied anthropology," and in his view the modern city required symbolic identification as much as technical rationality in order to sustain itself as a social space. Elke Beyer traces the pathway of the NĖR group – an informal group that formed itself in late Soviet Modernism and was active in the 1960s and 1970s searching to "define the parameters of an ideal urbanism on the road to Communism." Via research and design projects, they investigated spaces of community within a socialist urbanity and based on human scale, privacy and individual freedom. Their work caught the attention of Giancarlo De Carlo, and they were able to present it in 1968 at the XIV. Triennale in Milan. The seminal work of De Carlo in Urbino and Terni is subject of Luca Molinari's chapter, together with the attempts of his mentor Ernesto N. Rogers to redefine a humanized vision of modern architecture in close connection with modern art and culture. The editor of *Domus*, and later of *Casabella-continuità*, used his influence to inform a generation of young Italian architects. Sven Sterken and Eva Weyns bring the focus onto a figure who challenged the technocratic and ahistorical character of the modern movement by safeguarding tradition and cultural differences: French urban theoretician Gaston Bardet, who aimed to establish forms of spatial planning in the service of a moral and spiritual regeneration of post-war society. Despite his peripheral position, he exerted a major influence in his day. Susana Constantino examines the student center at the Coimbra University Campus, commissioned at the end of the 1950s by the authoritarian Portuguese regime. She interprets the building as a counterimage within the master-plan characterized by classic monumentality, putting function and expression of this multipurpose building in the context of the debates about the New Monumentality. The "monumentality of the matchbox" is the subject of Stanislaus von Moos' chapter as he discusses the iconic power of the (highrise office) "slab" as a paradigm of the postwar visual culture. Apart from the emblematic Rockefeller Center and the Lever House in New York, he discusses examples which in East and West-Berlin have almost simultaneously been added to the skyline of the city: The Haus des Lehrers on Alexanderplatz (Hermann Henselmann 1961–64,) and the Europa-Center (Helmut Hentrich und Hubert Petschnigg, 1963–65).

Part 4: The Inhabited Nature

While the main focus of modern architecture has always been the city and the urban environment, diverse attempts of humanization have suggested nature and the countryside as places of unspoiled unity in opposition to urban fragmentation. Members of Team 10, like Charles Polónyi or Oskar Hansen, pledged for a re-establishment of tradition and regional patterns in order to "humanize" environmental design and develop spatial strategies of community building in urban and rural situations as well as in the contexts of work and leisure. Juliana Maxim looks at the first postwar decades in Romania with its decisively modern architecture culture, and detects a simultaneous interest in tradition and in vernacular art. Exhibitions and fairs with folkloric music and dance, rural craftwork or peasant artifacts became for the urban population as commonplace as modernist mass housing estates. The tension between the rural and the urban was the theme at the tenth CIAM Congress in Dubrovnik in 1956. Nelson Mota presents projects which seem to create a "middle landscape" in an attempt to reconcile the domus and the megalopolis. Domonkos Wettstein portrays the Balaton development plan (1957–68) as a legendary episode in Hungarian architecture and planning, free from ideological pressure and unfolding major impact. The development was meant for the recreation of society after the revolution had failed, providing an illusion of freedom, while the planning of small collective facilities and the creative adaptation to local conditions led architects onto a new regional path of modernism. In contrast to the small scale of the Balaton project, postwar Yugoslavia faced international mass tourism and found itself "in between" East and West due to Third Way policies. Michael Zinganel points out that in the self-management system of Tito's Yugoslavia, tourism operations were conceived as monuments of modernization; combining avant-garde-architecture, cosmopolitanism, design and lifestyle to serve as meeting points for national and transnational reconciliation, thus contributing to a re-humanization of modernist planning doctrines.

As the different contributions in this volume show, efforts for re-humanization typically re-act to situations which are experienced as not suiting the needs of (a specific group of) men or women anymore (be it as individuals, or as part of a collective). While, as can be seen in many examples portrayed in this book, in the specific period of 1950 –1970 the term has been of prominent use, the urge for a re-centering, a re-orientation towards human basic needs, is a timeless concern in architecture and urban planning where strategies have to be developed anew due to an ever changing context.

Endnotes

1 Stanford Anderson, "The 'New Empiricism: Bay Region Axis': Kay Fisker and Postwar Debates on Functionalism, Regionalism, and Monumentality," *Journal of Architectural Education* (1984–), Vol. 50, No. 3 (Feb. 1997), 197–207.

2 J. L. Sert, F. Léger, S. Giedion, "Nine Points on Monumentality," in Sigfried Giedion, *Architecture You and Me. The Diary of a Development* (Cambridge, Massachusetts: Harvard University Press, 1958), 48–51.

3 Frances Stonor Saunders, *The Cultural Cold War: The CIA and the World of Arts and Letters*, New York: The New Press, 2000.

4 Ernesto Nathan Rogers, "The House of Man," *Domus* (1946), quoted in Vittorio Gregotti, New Directions in Italian Architecture (New York: George Braziller, 1981), 38.

5 See Konstanze Sylva Domhardt, *The Heart of the City. Die Stadt in den transatlantischen Debatten der CIAM 1933–1951*, Zurich (gta Verlag) 2012.

6 Lukasz Stanek (ed.), *Team 10 East: Revisionist Architecture in Real Existing Modernism*, Warsaw: Museum of Modern Art in Warsaw, 2014.

7 Jean-Paul Sartre, *L'existentialisme est un humanisme* (Paris: Éditions Nagel, 1946).

I
Discourses on Humanism

Ákos Moravánszky

Re-Humanizing Architecture: The Search for a Common Ground in the Postwar Years, 1950–1970

Humanism as a program that places the human being in the center of the universe was embraced by all sides during the Second World War and in the years of reconstruction. The great appeal of the term lies in its persuasive aura. Humanism entails a wide range of ideas regarding the individual and society throughout history; therefore in the postwar years it provided an ideal common ground for liberal and socialist positions. No matter if serving Stalinist, socialist, communitarian, liberal capitalist or Catholic agendas, their respective protagonists believed that they could engage their counterparts as potential allies in the name of humanism. Not only intellectuals living in the war-destroyed cities but also those who escaped this cataclysm in New York or Switzerland felt a sense of loss and shared a longing for *community* – another "warmly persuasive" word, to quote Raymond Williams; that is, unlike state or nation, never used unfavorably.[1]

The political climate nourished such conciliatory, inviting gestures. For instance Pope Pius XII, who had excommunicated Communist party members for persecuting Catholic clerics in Eastern Europe before, called for an agreement banning the use of the atomic bomb in April 1954 – and the French communist Gilbert Mury called for a "Unity of action with Catholic workers", while "Christian humanism is not alien to us".[2] Roger Garaudy's Humanist Marxism served the goal of a Socialist-Communist alliance and of a Socialist government. But large parts of their respective constituencies, understandably, were afraid that such advances would blunt the clarity of their specific goals and compromise their struggle. Such differences between fractions and predominant personalities fueled the so-called Humanist Controversy in France.

Humanism was even regarded as a component of existentialism. Jean-Paul Sartre argued in his famous 1946 lecture *Existentialism as Humanism* that the absence of God from his philosophy does not condemn us to despair since it is our actions, our decisions, and not God that will enable us to realize ourselves as humans and to unfold our full potential.[3] Sartre exploited the tensions of a postwar political debate, positioning himself between the French Communist Party and the Catholic Social Democrats, the main division of the time. With his optimistic plea for collective action, aiming to avoid both Marxist accusations of bourgeois individualism and Christian critique of pessimism and nihilism, Sartre successfully established the political value of his philosophy. With existentialism as a basically atheist program, he tried to claim humanism from Christians like Abbé Pierre, who in 1954 launched very effective appeals in the French media to build emergency shelters. Architects like Le Corbusier supported Abbé Pierre, and Jean Prouvé developed the prototype for the *Maison des Jours Meilleurs* for his organization in 1956.[4]

Not all sides of the Communist party agreed on the value of humanism. For another wing of the party headed by Louis Althusser, embracing humanism meant abandoning class struggles and subscribing to a bourgeois ideology. Althusser maintained that appeals to the "human spirit" negates or weakens the class struggle.[5] In 1947 the Communists decided to leave a government that was interested in Marshall Plan money – the humanist persuasion lost its appeal and was soon discarded by French communists. Henri Lefebvre and Roger Garaudy published critical articles emphasizing the danger of the humanist label to divert attention from the current historical context. Similarly, Catholic thinkers started to pull away from the notion of humanism. Martin Heidegger's text *Über den Humanismus*, known as *Letter on Humanism* played a major role in this respect for French Catholics: "seeking to recover God, one has to dispense with the pretensions of man: the concept of the sacred can only be grasped when humanistic suppositions are put aside."[6]

This troubled relationship with the term humanism also applies to the debates about modern architecture during and after the war. Kenneth Frampton has pointed out that Sigfried Giedion's stance during the war and the postwar years was strangely apolitical.[7] A look at Giedion's notion of "humanization" shows, however, that this stance is not so surprising, since it was driven by the intention of creating a broad basis for the modern move-

fig. 1 The Bellevue bridge in Zurich at the Zürifäscht, July 1951. Photo from *Werk* 10 (1951).

ment, which essentially resulted in the *Congrès Internationaux d'Architecture Moderne* (CIAM).

What were the sources of this program? Lewis Mumford and his Swiss ideological ally, architect and architectural critic Peter Meyer, were the "oldest" source with roots going back to English socialism (William Morris), the German theory of the *organische Gemeinschaft* (organic community, by Ferdinand Tönnies) and Werkbund aesthetics. Mumford was the American correspondent of the Werkbund journal *Die Form*. Another possible source was Alvar Aalto's call for the humanization of architecture. Aalto's organicism had similar connections to turn-of-the-century National Romanticism and Frank Lloyd Wright's thoughts and aesthetic. Contributions by Paul Zucker, a German émigré architect, historian and theorist, influenced the debate as well. He was the editor of *New Architecture and City Planning*,[8] which includes an essay on New Monumentality by Sigfried Giedion, the most important early contribution to the American discourse on this topic.[9]

Monumentality as Humanism in Switzerland

In July 1951, Zurich celebrated the 600th anniversary of the city's joining the Swiss Confederation with a festival that has been annually repeated ever since as *Zürifäscht*. The intention of the organizing committee was to create a "quatorze Juillet" for the city's population. Alfred Roth, in his review of the *Zürifäscht*, drew the conclusion that participants could realize how much their "right to the street and to urban space" is diminished or annihilated by the "moloch of traffic."[10] The task, stressed Roth, was to find out how the latent needs of the population for strolling, informal gathering, and even such "explosive expressions" as the Zurich festival could be satisfied within the boundaries of the city. He noted that just two weeks after the *Zürifäscht*, a CIAM conference in England (the one in Hoddesdon) discussed the question of the social and cultural cores of the city. "The right of the pedestrian to freedom of movement and gathering, that in Zurich has been turned into reality for a few days, was emphatically claimed and concretized on the conference," he added[11] (fig. 1).

In the coming year, 1952, Sigfried Giedion wrote again about the *Zürifäscht* in his essay "Die Humanisierung der Stadt" (The Humanization of the City), published in the November issue of *Werk*, and he included "The Humanization of Urban Life" in the volume *Architecture, You and Me* in 1958. He emphasized "[...] the suppressed demand for social contact, which has lived on imperishably in the human soul ever since men first met in caves during the ice ages [...] breaks out spontaneously when man is shaken by some great event."[12] Speaking about the Zurich festival, he stressed "spontaneity" as the key to its success: "To be actor and spectator in one person is what we wanted! Clearly the public is ready. The question is whether we are! Let us not wait for a structurally well-defined society to arise. Let us ask what is alive in the bare and naked man that needs to be given form and expression. Let us ask what there is that lives in the bare and naked man, who is not just a symbol but is you and me."[13] Here, Giedion almost literally repeated Lewis Mumford's description of church rituals as the ideal civic sphere in his *Culture of Cities* (1938) – in which Mumford wrote: "[...] the city itself was the stage for [...] separate scenes of the drama, and the citizen himself was an actor"[14] (fig. 2).

Spontaneity, the heart of the city, artists and the role of symbols: these were the main ingredients of Giedion's program for a New Monumentality, announcing a stronger relationship between society and architectural form. This program was first outlined in the manifesto "Nine Points on Monumentality" by Giedion, Josep Lluís Sert and Fernand Léger, written in 1943.[15] It was a more or less direct response to Lewis Mumford's critique of Josep Lluís Sert's book *Can Our Cities Survive?* (1942) for its lack of attention toward the "civic realm". The arguments forwarded in Mumford's *Culture of Cities* are echoed in countless texts written by CIAM-affiliated architects afterwards.[16]

Giedion has successfully appropriated the positions of his opponents. One of them, Swiss architectural historian, critic and editor Peter Meyer, suggested that modern architects could begin to explore a New Monumentality

November 1952 **WERK** 39. Jahrgang Heft 11

Spanische Treppe in Rom. Ungestörter Aufenthaltsort der Anwohner / Escalier d'Espagne à Rome. Lieu de séjour public / Spanish Staircase in Rome serving as a gathering place
Photo: L. von Matt SWB, Buochs

DIE HUMANISIERUNG DER STADT

Von S. Giedion

Betrachtet man den Weg, den die Architektur in diesem Jahrhundert durchschritten hat, von einem menschlichen Standpunkt, so zeichnen sich deutlich zwei Stufen ab.

Die Entwicklung begann weit zurück im 19. Jahrhundert als «ein Kampf gegen die verpestete Atmosphäre und als eine moralische Revolte gegen die Verfälschung der Formen» (Henry van de Velde). Diese Reinigung der nächsten Umgebung des Menschen, die vor allem darauf ausgeht, den Gegenständen des täglichen Gebrauchs wieder formale Würde zu verleihen, ist seit William Morris in stetigem Fluß. Um 1900 ergriff sie auch die Architektur, wo sie sich am ausgesprochensten geltend machte bei den von Frank Lloyd Wright und andern in den Vorstädten von Chicago erbauten Einfamilienhäusern. Der Funke sprang von Amerika nach Europa über. Die Bauten der Stijl-Gruppe in Holland, Mies van der Rohes Pläne für ein Landhaus, Le Corbusiers erstes Pariser Haus in Eisenbeton, all diese, früh im Jahrhundert entstanden, waren Einfamilienhäuser. Ihren Höhepunkt hatte diese Entwicklung später in Kalifornien.

Die «Familienzelle» liegt den verschiedenen Formen vielstöckiger Wohnbauten zu Grunde, die gleichzeitig entstanden, darunter vielstöckige Zeilenbauten und Wolkenkratzer. Einen Kompromiß zwischen hohen und niederen Wohnbauformen stellen die «Turmhäuser» dar, die in Schweden zuerst zur Entwicklung kamen.

345

fig. 2 Sigfried Giedion, "Die Humanisierung der Stadt," page from *Werk* 11 (1952).

as long as they reserved it for particularly significant public building programs. Meyer, who wrote on the German translation of Mumford's *Sticks and Stones* in 1926 with great enthusiasm, sympathized with Mumford's distanced view of the modern movement. They both supported what Mumford called the "native form" of modern architecture; in America, the "The Bay-Region Style," exemplified by William Wurster in California; in Scandinavia or Switzerland the use of local materials such as wood. "I look for the continued spread [...] of that native and humane form of modernism one might call the Bay Region style, a free yet unobtrusive use of terrain, the climate, and the way of life on the coast."[17] – wrote Mumford.

The emblematic type of program that Peter Meyer had in mind for sparking the search for this New Monumentality was the 1939 Swiss National Exhibition (*Landi*) in Zurich, in many respects a predecessor to the 1951 *Zürifäscht*: "The buildings of the National Exhibition make an important contribution exactly to the dominant problem of monumentality," Meyer wrote. He was convinced that to properly express the republican traditions of Switzerland a less formal layout was required, without the symmetry, axiality, and grand gestures of entrance pavilions common in exhibition architecture.[18]

Giedion first rejected this – just as Meyer ridiculed functionalism's renunciation of style and its obvious attempts to codify a formal vocabulary. But as the debate over modern architecture's capacity for expression intensified, he increasingly warmed up to such concepts. In the "Nine Points", Giedion, Sert

figs. 3a, b Cover of *The Technology Review* 1 (1940) and Alvar Aalto's article "The Humanizing of Architecture."

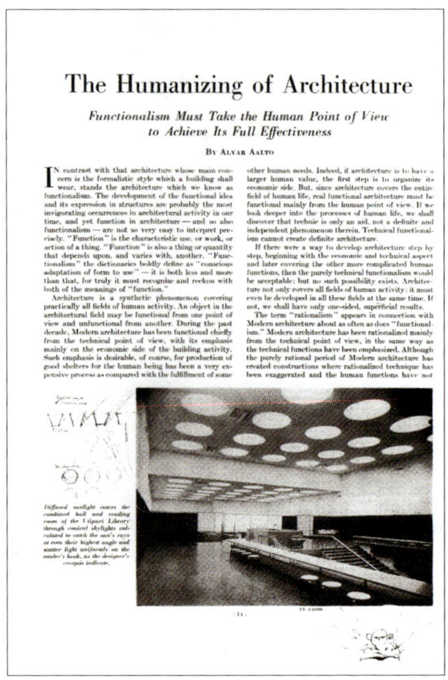

The Humanizing of Architecture

Functionalism Must Take the Human Point of View to Achieve Its Full Effectiveness

By Alvar Aalto

In contrast with that architecture whose main concern is the formalistic style which a building shall wear, stands the architecture which we know as functionalism. The development of the functional idea and its expression in structures are probably the most invigorating occurrences in architectural activity in our time, and yet function in architecture — and so also functionalism — are not so very easy to interpret precisely. "Function" is the characteristic use, or work, or action of a thing. "Function" is also a thing or quantity that depends upon, and varies with, another. "Functionalism" the dictionaries boldly define as "conscious adaptation of form to use" — it is both less and more than that, for truly it must recognize and reckon with both of the meanings of "function."

Architecture is a synthetic phenomenon covering practically all fields of human activity. An object in the architectural field may be functional from one point of view and unfunctional from another. During the past decade, Modern architecture has been functional chiefly from the technical point of view, with its emphasis mainly on the economic side of the building activity. Such emphasis is desirable, of course, for production of good shelters for the human being has been a very expensive process as compared with the fulfillment of some other human needs. Indeed, if architecture is to have a larger human value, the first step is to organize its economic side. But, since architecture covers the entire field of human life, real functional architecture must be functional mainly from the human point of view. If we look deeper into the processes of human life, we shall discover that technic is only an aid, not a definite and independent phenomenon therein. Technical functionalism cannot create definite architecture.

If there were a way to develop architecture step by step, beginning with the economic and technical aspect and later covering the other more complicated human functions, then the purely technical functionalism would be acceptable; but no such possibility exists. Architecture not only covers all fields of human activity; it must even be developed in all these fields at the same time. If not, we shall have only one-sided, superficial results.

The term "rationalism" appears in connection with Modern architecture about as often as does "functionalism." Modern architecture has been rationalized mainly from the technical point of view, in the same way as the technical functions have been emphasized. Although the purely rational period of Modern architecture has created constructions where rationalized technique has been exaggerated and the human functions have not

Diffused sunlight enters the combined hall and reading room of the Viipuri Library through conical skylights calculated to catch the sun's rays at even their highest angle and scatter light uniformly on the reader's book, as the designer's croquis indicate.

and Léger mentioned "those who govern and administer a people," but only to criticize them for their lack of artistic judgment. This political detachment can be traced to Swiss neutrality, not just as a "mentality" but as a necessary prerequisite for somebody who wishes to organize and administer the "modern tradition" and also be as inclusive as possible; to connect and distribute information, persons, conferences on a global scale.[19]

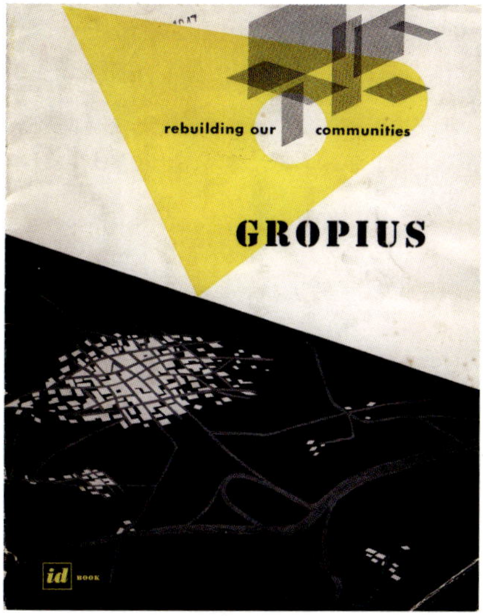

fig. 4 Walter Gropius, *Rebuilding Our Communities*, Chicago 1945, cover.

Alvar Aalto and the Humanizing of Architecture

Another important document that might have contributed to Giedion's widening of the ideological basis of modern architecture was Alvar Aalto's article "The Humanizing of Architecture," published in November 1940 in the Massachusetts Institute of Technology's *The Technology Review* – just weeks after Aalto's research professorship at MIT began. In this text, Aalto maintained that modern architecture in its new phase "tries to project rational methods from the technical field out to human and psychological fields."[20] He insisted that architecture "is to have a larger human value," and that sheer "technical functionalism" cannot create "definite architecture". He demonstrated with the example of his Paimio Sanatorium that space for patients lying in a bed requires a different approach than space for a standing person; and criticized tubular steel furniture as only being rational in a technological – but not in a psychological – sense.[21] "Functionalism is correct only if enlarged to cover even the psychophysical field. That is the only way to humanize architecture"[22] (fig. 3).

This position differed significantly from the one represented by Walter Gropius. He gave a lecture titled *Rebuilding Our Communities*, held on February 23, 1945 in Chicago (fig. 4). László Moholy-Nagy, his host at the Institute of Design, lauded him in the introduction as an "architect of humanistic departure."[23] Indeed, Gropius addressed right away the difficult task of "rebalancing the life of the community and humanizing the impact of the machine. The key for a successful rebuilding of our postwar communities [...] is our determination to let the human element become the dominant factor."[24]

He illustrated his statement with a "pictorial comparison": a New York street scene "showing a bewildering chaos of competing individual stunts; a disorderly riot of styles, materials and color" and Pieter Brueghel's painting of a Dutch village where the "streets and squares still serve as fitting receptacles for social intercourse of the whole community".[25] He mentioned further ingredients for humanizing the community: the human scale of organic social structures, with consequences for the size of the neighborhood unit and the building of new civic and cultural centers, the rationalization of the house and household (including pre-cooked and quick-frozen food in plastic containers that Gropius calls "wife-saving devices"), and standardization with new building techniques.[26] Aalto's earlier critique of this "technical functionalism" targeted exactly this position. Giedion, the chief ideologist of CIAM, had to use a few rhetorical tricks to present them as a consistent program. He was eager to point out to Aalto that he had given him the most pages in the new edition of *Space, Time and Architecture*. The chapter on Aalto would bear the remarkable title "Alvar Aalto: Irrationality and Standardization." The inclusion of a new chapter in *Space, Time and Architecture* was not simply an extension of the book; it showed, rather, that the history of architectural modernism took a new turn. Giedion claimed that "the combination of standardization with irrationality" intends to fulfill the moral imperative of the avant garde, "to reestablish a union between life and architecture."[27]

In 1940, at the time his article "The Humanizing of Architecture" was published, Aalto had to abandon his work in the United States and return to Finland because of the Winter war. In April 1941, he travelled to Switzerland, hosted by Sigfried Giedion and Alfred Roth, to deliver a lecture known as "Aalto's Swiss Sermon on the Mount".[28] Its topic was the reconstruction of Europe after the war ("Der Wiederaufbau Europas stellt die zentralen Probleme der Baukunst unserer Zeit zur Diskussion").[29] In the lecture, he criticized the practice in the United States of basing standardization in architecture on car-manufacturing models, despite the fundamental difference in the way the objects relate to their environment and to nature. He stressed that standardization in architecture should be based on biological models. "If the character of the landscape is such – should we really build this way?" – he asked rhetorically, not only showing images of the Finnish landscape and standardized houses, but also pictures of "life starting anew": a woman baking bread in the oven of a destroyed home, and the re-use of bricks taken from the rubble. "And so life goes on. Despite its primitive character, it slowly and touchingly takes on ever richer forms."[30] He spoke of blossoms as examples of the standardization in nature.[31] Aalto's lecture in Zurich and six other cities made an enormous impact on Swiss architects; on the Swiss CIAM group first

fig. 5 Alfred Roth, "Civitas: The Human City Collection." Page from *Werk* 1 (1944).

of all. Alfred Roth has summoned the members – Hans Bernoulli, Max Bill, Ernst Friedrich Burckhardt, Hans Schmidt and Rudolf Steiger – for "reconstruction efforts". Roth immediately decided to start the publication series CIVITAS, and asked Le Corbusier in Vichy for his cooperation to which he responded favorably[32] (fig. 5).

Paul Zucker and the Humanistic Approach

Finally, the third possible source for Giedion's program for a new humanism came from the émigré architect and architectural historian Paul Zucker – who worked as a lecturer at the New School for Social Research, a "university in exile" for German émigré scholars in New York – and published his "The Humanistic Approach to Modern Architecture" in *The Journal of Aesthetics and Art Criticism*, Vol. 2, No. 7 (Winter 1942–1943). He wrote: "Let us consider functionalism as the architectural expression of and the stage setting for this our contemporary file. Does not this functionalism mean precisely the triumph of materialism, emphasizing technical construction, material, and practical functions? And are *these* values not contradictory to both human and humanistic values?"[33]

Zucker, who wrote his doctoral dissertation at the *Technische Hochschule* in Berlin in 1912 on the representation of space in Florentine renaissance painting, commented here – and in other essays published in scholarly magazines in the United States – on the changing perception of space as also reflected in modern art: "Construction changes into expression. In this way modern architecture becomes a subject of humanism. […] Based on the expression of rational conditions and functional needs, it became as independent, free and even emotional as any work ever created by man – therefore approachable from the humanistic point of view."[34] Zucker's book *New Architecture and City Planning* (1944) contains next to Giedion's "The need for a New Monumentality" a series of other important texts contributing to the discourse on monumentality, among them Louis I. Kahn's "Monumentality," Philip L. Goodwin's "Monuments" (discussing the issue of memorials) and Ernest Fiene's "Figurative Arts and Architecture: Mural and Architectural Sculpture." Zucker, like Werner Hegemann whose work he used and appreciated, connected the American civic center movement with the success of the pageantry of the World Fairs, the World's Columbian Exhibition in Chicago in 1893 being particularly important and a source of influence for Giedion and Meyer.

The Austrian émigré architect Richard Neutra, who started his American career working for Frank Lloyd Wright, was similarly interested in the psycho-physiological interpretation of humanism, connecting it with new insights into the process of the human perception of space. In his text *Turn to a Humanistic Renaissance in Architecture* written on August 12, 1957, he argues that – like in the Italian Renaissance – new scientific insights into the physiology and psychology of the "self-knowing and free man" will result in spaces with multiple possibilities for perception and unobstructed views and movement.[35] Neutra was a CIAM member and he responded to Giedion's call for humanizing architecture by drawing attention to American, or more precisely, Californian reality. He warned that the enthusiasm for spontaneity and community might end in a "tyranny of common sense". It seems that this was a concern for Giedion as well. In his introduction to the book *A Decade of New Architecture* (1951) that summarized the results of the Bridgwater conference (1947), he wrote: "Sweden, though very social-minded and not at all averse from adventures in town planning, is nevertheless endangered by sentimental trends such as the 'new empirism' which, under cover of 'humanizing' architecture leads only into another cul-de-sac. Switzerland, supreme in the detailed finish and technique of its architecture, is moving under a similar cloud of 'coziness' for its housing schemes, while sterile and desiccated business blocks are destroying the organic kernel of its largest city."[36]

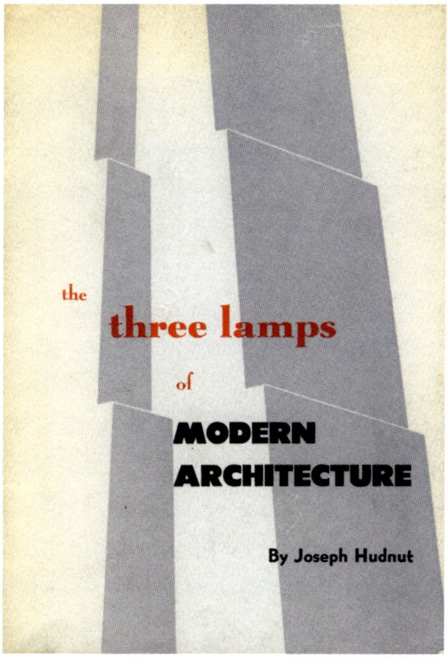

fig. 6 Joseph Hudnut, *The Three Lamps of Modern Architecture*, Cambridge, Mass. 1952, cover.

Joseph Hudnut's Post-Modern Humanism

So far we have looked at some of the differences between concepts of humanism and humanization inside the CIAM group. But humanism as a program for postwar architecture was also flourishing outside the CIAM, with Joseph Hudnut as perhaps its most important protagonist. Hudnut was founding professor of Harvard Graduate School of Design (GSD) in 1936 and its dean until 1953, even if during those years he was overshadowed by Walter Gropius. He brought Gropius to the GSD and supported him, but increasingly Gropius thought that Hudnut wanted to anchor architecture and architectural education in the "humanistic tradition" as opposed to what he called "the Bauhaus tradition."[37] For Hudnut, New Humanism was first of all a program in architectural education that embraced modern architecture (not uncritically, however) but insisted on the lessons of history and was open to popular culture as well. With Werner Hegemann as his mentor it was no wonder that "Civic Design" was at the very center of his thought: "emotional content," spontaneity, symbolic values and expression were at the heart of his creed. It comes as no surprise that a fight evolved between Hudnut and Gropius regarding the goals of modern architecture. Hudnut published his *Three Lamps of Modern Architecture* in 1952: instead of Ruskin's seven sources of good architecture, he kept only three; Progress, Nature and Democracy[38] (fig. 6).

In his *Architecture and the Spirit of Man*, in the chapter "The Post-Modern House," Hudnut wrote: "Space, structure, texture, light – these are less the elements of a technology than the elements of art. They are the colors of the painter, the tones of the musician, the images out of which poets build their invisible architectures. Like color, tone, and image they are the most serviceable when they are so used as to make known the grace and dignity of the spirit of man."[39] Hudnut's ideas resonated well in Europe, particularly in Italy, searching for the fundamentals of postwar urbanism. The Italian translation of Hudnut's *The Post-Modern House* was published in Bruno Zevi's journal *Metron* in 1945 along with articles by Enrico Tedeschi, who soon started to develop Argentina's architectural education on the basis of "New Humanism" with Gino Calcaprina and Ernesto N. Rogers.[40]

New Deal, New Humanism

An omnipresent example in the European architectural magazines of this period was the Tennessee Valley Authority's (TVA) giant project, the first and most important result of Franklin D. Roosevelt's New Deal policy, starting in 1933 and praised in the catalogue of the 1944 MOMA exhibition as "one of the monuments of our civilization."[41] Such American attempts at integrating ecological, engineering, landscaping, architectural, and aesthetic concerns to realize a socio-economical vision were followed with enormous interest in Europe – before and after the war, in both West and East – and applauded by different political systems. For instance, in the first issue of the German journal for the research and organization of space, *Raumforschung und Raumordung* (October 1936) with a clearly national socialist program, the Tennessee Valley project was presented. It was praised as the first effort to a scientific research of space in the USA and an example for the world, as it demonstrates the tasks and potentials of the research and organization of space.[42] The TVA project also served as a model for the development plan of the Aosta Valley, supported in 1937 by the industrialist Adriano Olivetti, who published the results six years later as *Studi e proposte preliminari per il piano regolatore della Valle d'Aosta*.[43] Luigi Figini and Gino Pollini, Antonio Banfi, Enrico Peressutti and Ernesto N. Rogers participated as architects, conducting demographic studies and presenting data on public health, hygiene or climate (fig. 7).

Adriano Olivetti's *Comunità* movement was originally inspired by French personalism – a Christian line of thought, critical of materialism and liberalism – that stressed the person's communitarian dimension, and therefore resonated well with Lewis Mumford's ideas. Olivetti had already established this cultural group during the war years and only afterwards did it commence political activity at a local level, becoming involved in municipal and provincial elections. The *Comunità* fought against party rule and centralism, aiming

fig. 7 G. L.Banfi, E. Peressutti, E. N.Rogers, Winter view of the Stazione Pila, from Adriano Olivetti, ed., *Studi e proposte preliminari per il Piano regolatore della Valle d'Aosta*, Ivrea: Nuove Edizione Ivrea, 1937, p. 179.

fig. 8 Julian Huxley, *TVA: Adventure in Planning*. Cheam 1943, cover.

to replace them with a federal union of local communities. The movement tried to merge both liberal and socialist ideas, opposing both conservatives and communists. Olivetti and his circle and publishing house *Comunità*, publishing the international journal of modern architecture *Zodiac*, were all interested in American models.[44]

A widely-read account of the project with the title *TVA: Adventure in Planning* was published in 1943 by Julian Huxley, a British evolutionary biologist who became the founding director of UNESCO three years later (fig. 8). In his book he wrote that during the first decade of its existence, the TVA will have definitely established the validity of overall, regional, democratic planning; and this is an achievement of first-class importance in the evolution of human society."[45] In his next book, *The Humanist Frame*, Huxley gathered ideas that served as a basis for UNESCO. In Western countries, stated Huxley, art reflects the nihilism of the postwar period, the fragmentation of its life between frustration and hope, its intellectual chaos and moral disillusionment. In Communist countries, dogmatic ideology operates by authoritarian methods. But in both camps "the spread of Humanist ideas would tend to heal the split between creative art and its social environment," he stressed.[46] As for architecture, the task is to express "human ideas and aspirations. Good architecture can enrich human life, especially urban life, while bad architecture can impoverish it, as is all too obvious in the many ugly towns and drab city fringes and subtopian sprawls of our age. To the humanist, the importance of architecture's social function is obvious: the problem is to persuade officials and taxpayers to recognize its importance in practice."[47] Evolutionary humanism "could bridge the gap between Sir Charles Snow's 'two cultures' [within Western societies, the sciences and the humanities] and heal the split between the two sides in the ideological cold war."[48]

The example of the New Deal and in particular the TVA was regarded as a model for triggering development in many other countries after the Second World War. The Swiss architect, artist and designer Max Bill in his publication *Wiederaufbau* (Reconstruction) compared the TVA project with regional planning in the Soviet Union as described by Hans Schmidt. Bill's book, also, took Switzerland's central position and neutrality as the basis for an exchange of ideas between East and West[49] (fig. 9). The important architectural magazine of the Hungarian avant garde *Tér és Forma* likewise emphasized the significance of the project to European cooperation: "The work in the Tennessee Valley is particularly important from a Hungarian point of view, since it has proven that the regulation and development plan of a river valley cannot be dissected along administrative borders. The Danube crosses six countries, the river changes its name six times until it is swallowed by the Black Sea, but the development of its valley is only possible with the cooperation and peaceful joint work of all countries involved."[50] The editor of *Tér és forma* was József Fischer, the leader of the Hungarian CIAM group; at this time in regular contact with Giedion. He traveled to Zurich to the CIAM conference on May 26–29, 1947 with his wife, the engineer Eszter Pécsi and

fig. 9 Max Bill, *Wiederaufbau*. Erlenbach-Zurich 1945, cover.

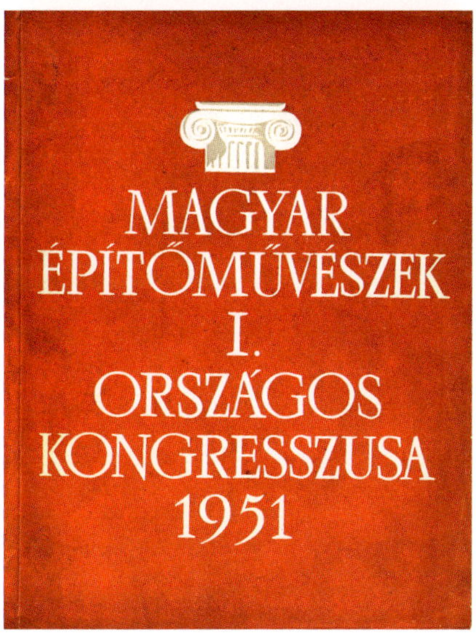

fig. 10 Papers of the First National Congress of Hungarian Architects, 1951, cover.

with architect-writer Pál Granasztói, and reported on this event in his journal.[51] However such renewed East-West contacts soon came to a grinding halt. On March 2, 1949 Fischer sent a telegram to Giedion, canceling his participation in the CIAM meeting in Bergamo (July 23–30, 1949): "On account of passport difficulties unable to join council meeting – Good work."[52] This message announced the end of the East European participation in the CIAM movement.

figs. 11a, b, c *Le Carré bleu 2* (1958), with the article by Aulis Blomstedt, "La deshumanización de la arquitectura."

At the time when Giedion wrote his article on the humanization of the city, in October 1951, the first national congress of Hungarian architects took place in Budapest (fig. 10). It was a big event that acknowledged architects, now employed by the state, as an important part of socialist society. Humanization was an issue here as well, as part of an assault on functionalism, building on the results of the so-called "big debate on architecture" in the previous year that was organized by the Communist Party to pave the way for socialist realism. György Kardos, one of the first speakers at the conference, ridiculed the claims of functionalism for serving human needs, pointing out that this claimed humanism was in reality a "machine aesthetic of *Sachlichkeit*" while disregarding the "human principle."[53]

The interest in humanism and its use as a point of connection between Western Europe and the Eastern Bloc waned in the late 1950s. While postwar humanism provided the conditions for the rise of existentialism, allowing it to mold phenomenology to its subjective and atheistic purposes, its passing freed the philosophical work of Husserl and Heidegger to be reconsidered in new contexts. Instead of Sartre's death of God, Foucault would now declare the end of man. The journal *Le Carré bleu* was founded in Helsinki in 1957 and strongly supported the goals of Team 10, distributing the contributions of its members internationally. In the second issue of the year 1958, editor Aulis Blomstedt published his manifesto *La deshumanizacion de la arquitectura* (the Spanish title is a reference to the essay *Deshumanizacion del arte* by the philosopher José Ortega y Gasset), stressing the importance of the formal, geometrical means of architecture[54] (figs. 11a, b, c).

The call for humanism and re-humanizing was a common stomping ground for protagonists of the Monumental, the Symbolic, the Spontaneous, the Collective and the Communal in the postwar years. The fading of such ideals in the 1960s allowed for a re-focusing on questions of form, technology, the machine and the environment. However, the term and the program of humanism did not disappear altogether, but periodically reemerged as the recognition of the role of human agency in history or a postmodernist emphasis on multiculturalism and individual difference.

Endnotes

1 Raymond Williams, "Community," in *Keywords. A Vocabulary of Culture and Society* (New York: Oxford University Press, 1983), 75–76.

2 G. Michael Goshgarian, "Introduction," in Luis Althusser, *The Humanist Controversy and Other Writings* (London: Verso 2003), XXV.

3 Jean-Paul Sartre, *L'existentialisme est un humanisme* (Paris: Éditions Nagel, 1946).

4 Laura Pandelle, "Quand le design passe à l'acte. Project-performance et demonstration," in *Jean Prouvé* (Nancy: Musée des Beaux-Arts, Paris: Somogy Éditions d'Art, 2012), 373–381.

5 Goshgarian, "Introduction," XXVff.

6 Martin Heidegger, *Über den Humanismus* (Frankfurt am Main: Vittorio Klostermann, 1949), 13. Author's translation.
7 Kenneth Frampton, "Giedion in America. Reflections in a Mirror," *Architectural Design* 51:6–7 (1981), 44–51, p. 46.
8 Paul Zucker (ed.), *New Architecture and City Planning. A Symposium*, (New York: Philosophical Library, 1944).
9 Ákos Moravánszky, "Das Monumentale als symbolische Form. Zum öffentlichen Auftritt der Moderne in den Vereinigten Staaten," in *Mythos Monument. Urbane Strategien in Architektur und Kunst seit 1945*, ed. Carsten Ruhl (Bielefeld: transcript, 2011), 37–61.
10 Alfred Roth, "Der städtebauliche Rahmen der 600-Jahrfeier Zürichs," *Werk* 38:10 (1951), 289–291, p. 291.
11 Ibid., 291. Author's translation.
12 Sigfried Giedion, "The Humanization of Urban Life," in *Architecture You and Me*. The Diary of a Development (Cambridge, Massachusetts: Harvard University Press, 1958), 125–137, p. 126. Original edition: Sigfried Giedion, "Die Humanisierung der Stadt," in *Werk*, 39/11 (1952), 345–352, p. 346.
13 Ibid., 130.
14 Lewis Mumford, *The Culture of Cities* (San Diego, New York, London: Harcourt Brace, 1970), 64 (First Edition: New York: Harcourt Brace, 1938).
15 Josep Lluís Sert, Fernand Léger, Sigfried Giedion, "Nine Points on Monumentality," in Giedion, *Architecture You and Me*, 48–51.
16 Eric Mumford, *The CIAM Discourse on Urbanism 1928–1960* (Cambridge, Massachusetts: The MIT Press, 2002), 130–142.
17 Lewis Mumford, "Bay Region Style," *The New Yorker*, 22, 11. 10 (1947), 104–110.
18 Peter Meyer, "Die Architektur der Landesausstellung – kritische Besprechung," *Das Werk*, 7 (1939), 321–352.
19 Sert, Léger, Giedion "Nine Points on Monumentality," 50.
20 Alvar Aalto, "The Humanizing of Architecture," *The Technology Review*, 43/1 (1940), 14–16, p. 15.
21 Ibid., 16.
22 Ibid.
23 László Moholy-Nagy, "Introduction", in Walter Gropius, *Rebuilding our Communities*, (Chicago: Paul Theobald, 1945), 11–12, p. 12.
24 Gropius, *Rebuilding our Communities*, 13–17.
25 Ibid., 17.
26 Ibid., 27.
27 Sigfried Giedion, *Space, Time and Architecture. The Growth of a New Tradition* (Cambridge, Massachusetts: Harvard University Press, 1967), 618.
28 Göran Schildt, *Alvar Aalto. The Mature Years* (New York: Rizzoli 1991), 41ff.
29 Alvar Aalto, "Der Wiederaufbau Europas stellt die zentralen Probleme der Baukunst unserer Zeit zur Diskussion," in *"Der Magus des Nordens." Alvar Aalto und die Schweiz*, ed. Teppo Jokinen, Bruno Maurer (Zurich: gta Verlag 1998), 177–187.
30 Alvar Aalto, "The Reconstruction of Europe is the Key Problem for the Architecture of Our Time" (1941), in *Alvar Aalto in His Own Words*, ed. Göran Schildt (New York: Rizzoli 1997), 149–157.
31 Ibid., 154.
32 Mumford, *The CIAM Discourse on Urbanism*, 154.

33 Paul Zucker, "The Humanistic Approach to Modern Architecture," *The Journal of Aesthetics and Art Criticism*, 2:7 (1942–1943), 21–26, pp. 21–22.
34 Ibid., 26.
35 UCLA Library Special Collections, Charles E. Young Research Library, Richard and Dion Neutra Papers, Box 158, Folder 18.
36 Sigfried Giedion, "Introduction," in *A Decade of New Architecture*, ed. Sigfried Giedion (Zurich: Editions Girsberger, 1951), 2.
37 On Hudnut and Harvard Graduate School of Design see: Jill Pearlman, *Inventing American Modernism: Joseph Hudnut, Walter Gropius, and the Bauhaus Legacy at Harvard* (Charlottesville, Virginia: University of Virginia Press, 2007).
38 Joseph Hudnut, *The Three Lamps of Modern Architecture. Lectures Delivered at College of Architecture and Design, University of Michigan, May 12–16, 1952* (Ann Arbor, Michigan: University of Michigan Press, 1952).
39 Joseph Hudnut, *Architecture and the Spirit of Man* (Cambridge, Massachusetts: Harvard University Press, 1949), 118.
40 Noemi Adagio, "Mass Culture at Mid-Century. Architecture under a 'New Humanism,'" in *Latin American Modernities. Ambiguous Territories*, ed. Patricio del Real, Helen Gyger, (New York, London: Routledge, 2013), 75–89.
41 *Built in USA. 1932–1944*, ed. Elizabeth Mock (New York: Museum of Modern Art, 1944), 111.
42 Günter Schmölders, "Probleme der Raumordnung in USA," *Raumforschung und Raumordnung*, 1/1 (1936), 29–36.
43 *Studi e proposte preliminari per il piano regolatore della Valle d'Aosta*, ed. Adriano Olivetti (Ivrea: Nuove Edizioni Ivrea, 1943).
44 Paolo Scrivano, *Building Transatlantic Italy. Architectural Dialogues with Postwar America* (Burlington, Vermont: Ashgate, 2013).
45 Julian Huxley, *TVA: Adventure in Planning* (Cheam: Architectural Press, 1943), 136.
46 Ibid., 32.
47 Ibid., 34.
48 Ibid., 6.
49 Max Bill, *Wiederaufbau. Dokumente über Zerstörungen, Planungen, Konstruktionen* (Erlenbach-Zurich: Verlag für Architektur AG, 1945).
50 László Dölle, "Építőmunka a Tennessee völgyében," *Tér és Forma* 5 (1947), 105–107.
51 József Fischer, "Dokumentum," *Tér és Forma* 6 (1947), 119–121.
52 ETH Zurich, gta Archiv, CIAM collection, Fischer's telegram to Giedion, March 2, 1949.
53 Magyar Képzőművészek és Iparművészek Szövetsége Építőművészeti Szakosztály, *Vita építészetünk helyzetéről* (Budapest 1951) 37–42.
54 Aulis Blomstedt, "La deshumanizacion de la arquitectura," *Le Carré Bleu. Feuille internationale d'architecture*, 1–2 (1958), 2–8.

Annie Pedret

CIAM: From "Spirit of the Age" to the "Spiritual Needs" of People

To be human means to be spiritualized.
Ludwig Mies van der Rohe,
quoting Romano Guardini's *Briefe vom Comer See*[1]

The language of modern architecture includes various terms that refer to the spiritual or non-physical reality of people: referred to by Mies van der Rohe as "spiritual existence," "spiritual position," "spiritual order," "spiritual being," "spiritual nature of the epoch," "spiritual ideas," "spiritual aim," "spiritual center," "spiritual decisions," "spiritual schooling," "spiritual person," "spiritual problems," "spiritually speaking," "spiritualized economy";[2] by Louis Sullivan as "spiritual quality," "spiritual idea," "spirituality," "infinite creative spirit or what I call God"[3]; Adolf Loos, "spiritual strength"[4]; Hermann Muthesius, "more important than the material aspect is the spiritual"[5]; Sant'Elia and Marinetti, "spiritual attitude"[6]; De Stijl, "spiritual plane"[7]; Bruno Taut, "spiritual forces,"[8] "spiritual flowering"[9]; Erich Mendelsohn, "spiritual will"[10]; Gropius/Taut/Behne, "spiritual descent," "spiritual unity"[11]; Arthur Korn, "spiritual realm"[12]; Hugo Häring, "spiritual life"[13]; Buckminster Fuller, "spiritual progress," "spiritual being," "spiritual consideration"[14]; CIAM, "spiritual needs," "spiritual values," "spiritual growth,"[15]; Alfred Roth "intuitive existence"[16]; Walter Gropius, "spiritual content," "spiritual guidance," "spiritual aims," "spiritual implications," "spiritual direction," "spiritual functions," "spiritual meaning," "spiritual aspirations," "spiritual possibilities," "spiritual world," "spiritual achievements," "spiritual growth"[17]; Joseph

Hudnut "human spirit," "the ethereal things"[18]; J.P. Oud, "spiritual base"[19]; and Sigfried Giedion "spirit," "life of the spirit," "inner development," "inner states," "inner being," "inner significance," "inner life" and "inner reality."[20] However, this is not language one finds in histories of modern architecture. There is, as Karla Britton acknowledges, "a stronger narrative of concern for the spirit to be traced within the history of modern architecture than many critics have observed."[21] Nevertheless, the spiritual lies at the margins of scholarship, and in architecture schools it is heretical to use the term "spiritual" and "modern architecture" in the same sentence.

When architecture students' theses address the subject of the spiritual in architecture, it is largely done by specifying a kind of formal "pattern language," which they argue is conducive to spiritual experiences. Practicing architects also address the spiritual in formal terms and refer to it as the transcendental dimension of architecture,[22] relegating it almost exclusively to religious building types: temples, churches, mosques, synagogues, sites of occult practices such as Stonehenge, or prehistoric caves and memorials. The word "spiritual" in architecture is synonymous with a religious vocabulary of the "sacred," "Absolute Unitary Being"[23] and "divine awe," or as a kind of non-physical reality of the "immaterial," "ineffable," "numinous" and "immeasurable."[24] Historians, with a few exceptions, do not address the subject of the spiritual unless it is in terms of sacred and religious building types. However, there is an indication that historians are taking a more critical turn.[25] It is encouraging that Vincent Scully addresses the subject by posing the question, "What do we consider sacred today?"[26] The more pertinent question however, is, "What do we consider spiritual today?"[27] Kenneth Frampton places a concern with the spiritual in modern architecture within a cultural shift that resulted from the loss of traditional faith at the end of the nineteenth century and that was "followed by the need to develop a new anthropocentric, universal religion."[28] More recently, the spiritual has expanded from religious building types to include the art gallery or thermal baths as sites of "spiritual" experience.[29]

This chapter examines the spiritual in modern architecture: not in theological terms or in terms of religion or religious buildings, but on its own terms. It focuses on how the word "spiritual" was introduced and used in a particular way by CIAM (the International Congress for Modern Architecture) – the bastion of the functionalist, rationalist approach to modern architecture and town planning – after the Second World War. In CIAM, this discourse about the spiritual was not framed in terms of the "sacred," limited to religious building types, or approached in terms of the formal qualities of architecture. Instead, it was discussed as a kind of secular, intangible need that modern architects were obliged to satisfy as much as any physical need. The CIAM use of the word spiritual was more closely aligned to Foucault's definition of the word as a way of gaining access to a fuller range of human needs – both physical and spiritual – and where human needs can take many forms, and change with time and circumstance. For Foucault, this was the way towards the "truth," which in the case of CIAM, meant acknowledging the fullness of human reality beyond the physical realm.[30]

The requirement that modern architecture address the "spiritual needs," "spiritual values," "spiritual life," of people, in addition to their "intellectual" and "material demands," was necessary for a "new conception of architecture," one that could address the problem of the "deep disturbances of the social structure brought about by machines."[31] Although CIAM stated this as an ethical requirement of modern architecture in their founding document, the "La Sarraz Declaration" in 1928, their work over the course of the four subsequent congresses before the Second World War focused on satisfying the physical needs of people. This included setting minimum housing standards, comparing the economic efficiencies of low-, medium- and high-rise building types, and promoting the "functional city" as a rational way of organizing four functions of living: work, dwelling, recreation and transportation. The functional city emphasized the providing of inhabitants with the basic physical needs of hygiene, fresh air and sunlight as a means of counteracting the chaos and poor sanitary conditions of the nineteenth-century city.

The word "spiritual" surfaced in the discussions at CIAM 6, where members argued that modern architects were now required to not only work towards creating physical environments that "satisfy man's emotional and material needs," but also "stimulate his spiritual growth."[32] This emphasis of the spiritual after the war was CIAM's solution to what they feared was an "all-too-mechanized" and "rationalist world," and the "standardization and the mechanistic quality of the spirit of modern architecture."[33] For Le Corbusier the contemporary problem was the "dispiriting absence of soul/spirit from which mechanized society was suffering," and "the disgrace, unspeakable ugliness, a defeat of grace, of smiles, the evasion of happiness" brought about by the "disaster" and "chaos" of the "scientific, moral and spiritual conquests" of the first machine age.[34] Sigfried Giedion perceived society as suffering from the effects of an excessively "mechanistic view of the world" inherited from the nineteenth century, in which thinking was dissociated from feeling.[35] Among the younger modern architects, Peter Smithson considered that "the mechanics of urbanism in the functional city" had "nothing to do with spirit."[36] Van Eyck perceived the current ills as being the result of "spiritual isolation" caused by the century-old "spiritual bankruptcy" of "false" and "worn-out" values that belonged to an "outworn world" where the mind triumphed over imagination.[37] He raised the question of how architects would grapple with the "material and spiritual implications" of what he considered the primary problem of the postwar period – "multiplicity" and "quantity."[38] As far as he was concerned, the underlying work of his generation was how, in the face of having to solve the technical problem of building millions of dwellings, architects were going to maintain the identity of anything: the parts of something, the whole, individuals and their communities and cultures.[39]

The context of CIAM's aim to "humanize"[40] and promote a "more humane approach"[41] to modern architecture that developed "in sympathy with the aspirations of the people it serves"[42] and was the organization's reaction to the "de-humanizing techniques,"[43] "mechanical speeds,"[44] "mechanical tools,"[45] "mechanical efficiency,"[46] "mechanical analysis" of urbanism,[47] "mechanical concepts of order,"[48] endless expansion and prefabrication,[49] and the excessively rationalist state of modern architecture at mid-century.[50] According to Jacob Bakema, the aim of postwar architecture was "to humanize the spatial needs of people"[51]; for Giedion, it was to provide a "truly human aspect" to communities by integrating the "ideological and aesthetic problems" of the "core" of the city[52]; J.M. Richards thought they ought to develop their current idiom in a "more human direction" by introducing "human qualities" of contrast, variety and individuality[53] to architecture and town planning; Ernesto Rogers argued in favor of steering away from the "appearance of a humane ambience" towards "integrity"[54]; Aldo van Eyck argued that the movement towards "complete reality" was the means "to manifest for humanity, and through humanity"[55]; J.H. van den Broek proposed that "human values" be introduced at every scale in community planning – from the dwelling to the region – which the Dutch CIAM Group thought was possible by providing the "human values" through guaranteeing "work and rest for the individual, family life and community spirit" in every case[56]; and the Dutch CIAM group questioned whether the evolutionary trend toward technical construction would be "determined primarily by economy mechanics and calculation? or toward a more intensive investigation and evaluation of human life, human reactions, human happiness, in order to stimulate and enrich human society?"[57] (See Table 1.). The tool or the means to achieve their aim of humanizing modern architecture lay, according to CIAM, in recognizing the "spiritual worth" and satisfying the "spiritual needs" of people. They affirmed that the "new architecture" could take for granted imaginative spatial and aesthetic concerns and the technical, material, and economic considerations of building that had been the focus of modernism. Now modern architecture should aspire to creating "certain significance to human life."[58]

NEW AIMS OF MODERN ARCHITECTURE

HUMAN/-E/-IZE	human aspect[1] human direction, more[2] human ends[3] human happiness[4] human life[5] human life, daily[6] human qualities[7] human reactions[8] human values[9] humane ambience, appearance of vs. integrity[10] humane approach[11] humane, more[12] humanization[13] humanize[14] humanize, spatial needs of people[15]
HUMAN/-ITY	humanity[16] children "common man" "la people" "le public" "l'homme" "man-in-the-streets" masses working class
SPIRITUAL	aspirations[17] aspiration of the masses[18] inner life[19] inner states[20] inner reality[21] life of the spirit[22] religion [23] soul/spirit, dispiriting absence of[24] souls, state of our own[25] spirit of modern architecture, the mechanistic quality of[26 27] spiritual aberration[28] spiritual activities[29] spiritual bankruptcy[30] spiritual conquests[31] spiritual demands of present-day life[32] spiritual evolution[33] spiritual facts[34] spiritual factors[35] spiritual growth[36] spiritual implications[37] spiritual isolation[38] spiritual life[39] spiritual moments[40] spiritual needs[41] spiritual plane[42] spiritual transformation[43] spiritual worth[44]

Table 1 CIAM's new aims for modern architecture and town planning, 1947–59

SPIRITUAL NEEDS DEFINED

EMOTION/-AL	psychical requirements of mankind desires emotion emotional life emotional needs emotional needs of life, basic emotional satisfaction feelings and emotions wonder, joy, excitement
EXPRESSION	expression, architectural expression, architectural as an emotional outlet expression, individual and family expression, spiritual and racial traditions expression of ancestral traditions expression through form expression, means of expression, regional expression, social expressions, manifold
GROWTH & CHANGE	change and move every day constant transformation of the centers of community life communities conceived in a dynamic state ever-changing needs of social life evolutionary shifting needs, aspirations, and stages in life
IDENTITY	identity individuality "identifying device" character "cluster" local character local culture particular cultures regional unit regionalism regionalism, new "visual group"

Hence, in the postwar period, CIAM stated that they should turn their attention away from addressing physical factors – that is, "the life of the body," which "had already been studied" – and turn to the life of the spirit.[59] For Giedion, "the outstanding task of the period [was] to humanize – that is, to reabsorb emotionally – what has been created by the spirit."[60] For the Dutch group De8, "economy and industrialization must not merely be accepted, but subjected to human ends."[61] The English MARS and French Bâtir groups argued that modern architecture should construct a framework that would allow social and spiritual activities to develop unhindered. MARS members were clear in their priorities stating that these "extra amenities" were "just as essential as floor space or bathrooms."[62] Modern architecture had not only

RELATIONSHIPS	belonging, sense of, through social contacts with family and community community community centers community life collective mind collective enterprise collective action collective life including education children cooperation communal character "Hierarchy of Association" human association, groupings human associations, fundamental "neighborhood units" relationships, between building and environment relationships, between individual and the collective relationships, between man and man, and man and thing i.e., "doorstep" as the primary contact relationships, between man and things relationships, between people relationships, human relationship, of particular things to one another "Scale of Association" significant relationships
	social hierarchy social intercourse social imagination social life social righteousness "unities" of social life – "living unit," "social unit," "neighborhood unit"

Table 2 Definitions of the spiritual needs of people in CIAM discourse, 1947–59

proved itself capable of satisfying the physical needs of people – but now demanded that architects also meet the aspirations, spiritual and emotional needs of the "common man," "man-in-the-street," "the masses," "*le peuple,*" "*le public,*" "*l'homme,*" the working class, and children. Although satisfying the spiritual needs of people was the means by which CIAM would achieve its postwar aim of humanizing modern architecture, the task was left for each member to define in their own terms, which the members consistently did in non-religious terms. Among them was Bakema who described "spiritual" as those moments in life that occur when "the isolation between people and things disappears and we discover the wonder of the relationship between man and things and between men and men."[63] Other Dutch CIAM members considered social life as being a component of a spiritual life, by which they meant the relationship between man and man, between individuals in the community, and between "man and cosmos."[64] The Bâtir group's undefined notion of "individual and family spiritual life" also made reference to the spiritual in collective terms, which for them included the education of children.[65] Others also defined spiritual life as being equated with different kinds of social life defined as the relationships between people (See "relationships" in Table 2). The only time the word "religion" appeared in postwar CIAM discourse was in Louis Kahn's keynote address at the last CIAM congress, in Otterlo in 1959. But even here it was not defined in theological terms, but in experiential terms. Kahn referred to "religion" as being "feeling at its greatest moment … religion from which we derive such feelings as nobility," which he made a point of distinguishing from "ritualistic religion."[66] Nowhere in the CIAM discourse was the spiritual associated with theology or the "sacred," nor did they think that the spiritual needs of people would be satisfied by a religious building type. The spiritual in CIAM referred to the intangible needs of people – their emotions, desires, aspirations and need to grow and change.

There were myriad architectural means for satisfying the spiritual needs of people and thus humanizing modern architecture, but the means that were discussed the most collectively were the "core" of the city, the theme of CIAM 6 in 1951, and "habitat," discussed at length at the meeting held at Sigtuna in 1952. The "core," also referred to as the "civic center" or "heart of the city," was conceived as the site of spontaneous social encounters, the site where "integration" through "synthesis of the plastic arts" was possible, where the New Monumentality could manifest itself, where wonder, joy, excitement evidenced during fireworks, and where the emotions that bound communities together were expressed.[67] "Habitat" represented the more humane approach to modern architecture – one that would accommodate the spiritual and emotional development of the people for whom they were building. Habitat, defined by the committee responsible for determining the theme of CIAM 9, was defined as the natural or created environment established with a view to man's total and harmonious spiritual, intellectual, and physical fulfillment.[68] They thought that when applied to man, habitat embraced "all the aspects of taking possession of land and space for organizing in view of his biological, sociological and spiritual life."[69] For Bakema, the "totality" of habitat took into consideration essential needs comprising of "physical activities such as eating, dressing, relaxing, washing and procreating; spiritual activities; the freedom to choose from a wide range of ways of living"; and the opportunity to grow and change as required by the dynamism of both life and the age.[70] The members of the Norwegian CIAM group PAGON acknowledged the dual nature of habitat: there were physical, biological and spiritual facts that influenced dwelling, and there was also the question of the individual and the collective. Although these were generally valid principles, the Norwegian members thought that different cultural patterns in different regions, communities, and environments required different forms and compositions.[71]

In addition to the core and habitat, the spiritual and emotional demands of people could also be satisfied by other architectural means. These included organizing the city into the four functions of living, dwelling, recreation, and transportation developed by CIAM before the Second World War; to which they now added aesthetics, art, poetry, historical continuity, identity, belonging, community and collective life, local character, integration, relationships, the "identifying group," and "cluster." For the French CIAM group, satisfying the spiritual and material needs of people would be accomplished "through the creation of a milieu true to social, ethical, aesthetic and scientific concepts of urbanism and architecture," and "to tender to the development of the individual harmoniously integrated into collective life."[72] The Dutch members thought they ought to adopt an attitude that considered the task of design as a "whole social process" that would be arrived at through an analysis of material and spiritual factors. While material and construction had a technical function, form making, they argued, ought to be a direct expression of social function.[73] For van Eyck the problem was that conventions and outward appearances dominated instead of stimulating "a universal revaluation of the basic elements" and turning to "complete reality," "simplicity" and "approaching the real sense of things" as a means for achieving a more desirable state of "grace," or "healthy vitality."[74] Giedion proposed a more organic conception of the world and the city and "integration" to remedy the effects of excessive mechanization in everyday life.[75] For Roth, significance in human life was to be achieved by creating relations between things. The relation between things was the innermost essence of the new architecture that differentiated "real value from external form" and lent "certain significance to human life."[76] The members of sub-commission Ic at CIAM 9 articulated the necessity "to recreate the harmony between the individual and the collective to organize the extension of dwelling in a way that favors the full blossoming of the spiritual and material life of the individual and the collective"[77] (See Table 3.).

To ignore the discourse of the spiritual in modern architecture is to ignore the dialectic between the spiritual and the scientific method in modern architecture. However, according to Foucault, unraveling the conflict between the spiritual and the scientific method is not as important an historical issue as the conflict between spirituality and theology.[78] To continue to frame the discourse of the spiritual in theological terms and as a function that pertains to

ARCHITECTURAL MEANS

aesthetics	aesthetics aesthetic language of architecture aesthetic expressiveness art culture grace harmony imagination poetry *"Style"* symbols visual satisfaction
functions of living	fifth function of the Core fifth function of "totalities" that embrace the other four functions *four functions of living – work, dwelling, recreation & transportation* functions, considered in their totality
integration	aesthetic integration in the "heart of the city" aesthetic unity harmony between the works of man and his environment "in-between," "threshold" integrated atmosphere integrated unities integration in aesthetics integration of contemporary reality and inherited experience integration of dualism between imagination & common sense integration of independent and articulated parts into a totality "reciprocity" social cohesion, first principle for integration of four functions social integration spatial coherence "synthesis of the arts"
history	archaic historical continuity history as human interaction on a site over time history, as continuity of human experience history as a dynamic development and continuous process history of a place history, living inherited experience traditional forms

religious building types – and not on its own terms, as was discussed by modern architects each in their own way – keeps us from a fuller understanding of modern architecture.

The failure to discriminate between the spiritual and religion is problematic for the historiography of modern architecture. Although the spiritual, theology and religion are similarly related, they are different. Theology is

particular/-ity	*milieu* particular climate and physical conditions "particular total complex" specific behavior extended into built form, i.e. "form" & "counterform" specific social, territorial and spiritual conditions "visual group"
"totalities"	total, habitat as man's harmonious spiritual, intellectual & physical fulfillment totalities, as the abstract quality that describes the nature of life totalities, as settlement types totalities, whole entities totality, implications of whole, city as a whole, clarity and fitness of whole, community center as a whole, consider regions as a whole, ever-changing whole, identifiable whole, integrating differentiated parts into a whole, modification of any one part changes whole, new kind of whole, organic whole, non-dichotomy, part-whole whole, individual parts that make up a whole, relation of differentiated parts to whole, separate identity in relation to the whole whole, social whole, social process whole, special obligation towards whole things in a network of whole things wholeness wholes, comprehensible wholes, comprehensive wholes, difficult wholes, entities wholes, integrated

Table 3 Architectural means for satisfying the spiritual needs of people in, CIAM discourse, 1945-59

strictly a discourse about God, which when rightly understood embraces spirituality. Religion and the spiritual are also related, but different. One can be spiritual without being religious, and religious without being spiritual. Religion is tangible. It refers to a set of beliefs about the universe, the practices of one's belief, and it usually defines a creed and code of ethics. Religion is about *believing*, the spiritual is about *being*. The spiritual refers to becoming more attuned to the world, and the interior world of personal experience. It also refers to a nebulous kind of experience, the reason for one's existence, the meaning and values to which one ascribes, and more recently as a reaction against purely material ways of viewing the world.[79] The spiritual defined in this way, by contrast to the universalism of religion, is variegated by cultural, historical, sociological, theological, linguistic and philosophical orientations.

The spiritual defined by CIAM members referred to *being*, which they articulated in terms of one's personal relationship to everything except a supernatural power – including how to *be* with oneself – through the need for individuality, identity, and growth and change – how to *be* with others through the need for relationships between people, between people and things, people and their environments, and between things. The spiritual, as it was used in CIAM, referred to the non-tangible qualities of an interior life that exist in the matrix of everyday life and are necessary components for a human and humane life. For CIAM members, addressing the spiritual needs of people gave more power to the socially transformative ideals of prewar modern architecture. Thus, conflating the spiritual with "God," "otherworldliness" or "holiness," taking the functionalist view and confining spiritual needs to only being satisfied in religious building types, and framing the spiritual as antithetical to modernization is not only an incomplete account of modern architecture, but it prevents us from recognizing that implicit in this ethic of postwar modern architecture – which is even more evident today – is the role that the spiritual plays as a force for personal *and* societal transformation.

Endnotes

1 In Fritz Neumeyer, The Artless Word: Mies van der Rohe on the Building Art (Cambridge, Mass,; London, England: The MIT Press, 1991), 281.

2 Ludwig Mies van der Rohe, "Inaugural Address as Director of Architecture at Armour Institute of Technology"; "Principles for Education in the Building Art"; "Preconditions of Architectural Work," in *The Artless Word: Mies van der Rohe Building Art*, Fritz Neumeyer (Cambridge, Mass.: MIT Press, 1991), 316, 336, 301, 273, 276; Mies van der Rohe, quoted by Joan Ockman in *Architecture Culture 1943–1968: A Documentary Anthology* (New York: Columbia Books of Architecture, Rizzoli, 1993), 163; "The New Era" [1930], in *Programs and Manifestoes on 20th-Century Architecture*, ed. Ulrich Conrads, (Cambridge, Mass.: MIT Press, 1971), 123; "Notes for Lecture," in Fritz Neumeyer, *The Artless Word: Mies van der Rohe on the Art of Building* (Cambridge, Mass.: MIT Press, 1991), 268.

3 Louis Sullivan, "Function and Form," *Kindergarten Chats* (New York: Dover, [1934] 1979), 42–48, 162–64.

4 Adolf Loos, "Ornament and Crime" [1908], in *Programs and Manifestoes*, ed. Conrads, 24.

5 Hermann Muthesius, "The Aims of the Werkbund" [1911], ibid., 27.
6 Antonio Sant'Elia and Tommaso Marinetti, "Futurist Architecture" [1914], ibid., 35.
7 De Stijl, "Manifesto I," [1918], ibid., 39.
8 Bruno Taut, "A Programme for Architecture," [1918], ibid., 41.
9 Bruno Taut, "Frühlicht [Daybreak]," [1921], ibid., 63.
10 Erich Mendelsohn, "The Problem of a New Architecture," [1919], ibid., 54.
11 Walter Gropius, Bruno Taut, Adolf Behne, "New Ideas on Architecture," [1919], ibid., 46.
12 Arthur Korn, "Analytical and Utopian Architecture," [1923], ibid., 77.
13 Hugo Häring, "The House as an Organic Structure," [1932], ibid., 126.
14 Buckminster Fuller, "Universal Architecture," [1932], ibid., 135.
15 CIAM, "Charter of Athens," [1933], in Programs and Manifestoes, ed. Conrads, 138, 142; "Re-affirmation of the Aims of CIAM [1947]," in Sigfried Giedion, ed. A Decade of New Architecture (Zurich: Girsberger, 1951), 16–19; Le Corbusier & CIAM, The Athens Charter (New York, NY: 1973), 100.
16 Alfred Roth, *A New Architecture* (Zurich: Girsberger, 1940), 9.
17 Walter Gropius, *The Scope of Total Architecture* (New York: Collier, 1943), 29, 47, 142, 51, 67, 126, 128, 141, 157, 158.
18 Joseph Hudnut, "Post-modern House [1945]," in *Architecture Culture*, ed. Ockman 73.
19 J. J. P. Oud, "Mr. Oud Replies [1947]," ibid., 103.
20 Sigfried Giedion, "The Need for a New Monumentality," in *New Architecture and City Planning*, ed. Paul Zucker (New York: Philosophical Library, 1944), 551, 553; *Mechanization Takes Command: A Contribution to Anonymous History* (New York, London: W. W. Norton, 1948), 720; *Space, Time and Architecture: The Growth of a New Tradition* (Cambridge, Mass.: Harvard University Press; London: Oxford University Press, 1949), 651, 17, 363.
21 Karla Britton, "Concern for the Spirit: A History of Modern Church Architecture," *Sacred Architecture*, 22 (2012), 33.
22 Julio Bermudez (ed.), *Transcending Architecture: Contemporary Views on Sacred Space* (Washington, D.C.: Catholic University of America Press, 2015).
23 William C. Helm II, "Numinous Space: Exploring the Spiritual Dimension of Architecture" *306090* 12 (2008), 101–111.
24 Thomas Barrie and Julio Bermudez (eds.), "Immateriality in Architecture," *Journal of Architectural Education*, 62:2 (2008), 4–5; Giedion, *The Eternal Present, a Contribution on Constancy and Change: the Beginnings of Architecture,* 2 (New York: Bollingen Foundation, 1964), xix.; Giedion, *Space, Time and Architecture: The Growth of a New Tradition* (Cambridge, Mass.: Harvard University Press; London: Oxford University Press, 1949), 17.
25 Britton, "Concern for the Spirit," 27–33; Britton and Jaime Lara, organizers, Constructing the Ineffable: Contemporary Sacred Architecture Symposium, School of Architecture, Yale University, October 2007; Britton, ed., *Constructing the Ineffable: Contemporary Sacred Architecture* (New Haven: Yale University School of Architecture, 2010); Randall Ott, review of Constructing the Ineffable: Contemporary Sacred Architecture Symposium, *Journal of Architectural Education* 62:2 (March 2008):

73–4; Ayla Lepine, review of Britton ed., Constructing the Ineffable: *Contemporary Sacred Architecture, The Architects' Journal* (September 1, 2011), http://www.architectsjournal.co.uk/constructing-the-ineffable-contemporary-sacred-architecture/8619285.article; Kenneth Frampton, "The New Spirituality and the Cathedral of the Future," paper presented at the Middle Ground/Middle East: Religious Sites in Urban Contexts Conference; Ott, "Foreward," in Bermudez, *Transcending Architecture*, xiii–xvi; Vincent Scully, quoted in Britton, "Concern for the Spirit," 33.

26 Vincent Scully, keynote address, Middle Ground/Middle East: Religious Sites in Urban Contexts Conference, School of Architecture, Yale University, January 2011, cited by Britton, "Concern for the Spirit," 29.

27 Michel de Certeau, Spiritual Spaces: History and Mysticism in Michel de Certeau, Leuven: Walpole, Mass.: Peeters, 2013.

28 Kenneth Frampton, "The New Spirituality and the Cathedral of the Future," paper presented at the Middle Ground/Middle East: Religious Sites in Urban Contexts Conference, cited by Britton, "Concern for the Spirit," 29.

29 Kyle Chayka quoting Peter Zumthor, "Contemporary Architecture Goes Spiritual," Hyperallergic, March 11, 2011, accessed September 26, 2016, http://hyperallergic.com/20763/contemporary-architecture-spiritual.

30 "Spirituality," accessed January 22, 2015, http://www.michel-foucault.com/concepts.

31 CIAM, "La Sarraz Declaration," in *Programs and Manifestoes on 20th-Century Architecture,* ed. Ulrich Conrads (Cambridge, Mass.: MIT Press, 1970), 109.

32 CIAM, "Re-Affirmation of the Aims of CIAM," in Giedion, *A Decade of New Architecture* (Zurich: Girsberger, 1951), 17.

33 Ibid.

34 Le Corbusier, "Discourse de Le Corbusier au VIème Congrès CIAM. Séance de l'Assemblée Générale sur l'expression architectural," September 15, 1947 Bakema Archive, Nederlands Architectuurinstituut, Rotterdam, BAK OR97, hereafter the Bakema Archive.

35 Giedion, Mechanization Takes Command, 717–721.

36 Peter Smithson, "Notes of Meeting of MARS Group CIAM 10 Sub-Committee," London, April 23, 1954, written by John Voelcker and Trevor Dannatt, May 1954, Bakema Archive, BAK, or 97.

37 Aldo van Eyck, "Report Concerning the Interrelation of the Plastic Arts and the Importance of Cooperation," 1947, CIAM Archive, ETH/gta, Zurich, 42-SG-9-87/88, hereafter the CIAM Archive.

38 Aldo van Eyck (Commission II), "The Role of Aesthetics[s] in the Habitat," July 1953, CIAM Archive, SG-37–85.

39 Aldo van Eyck, "Conclusion of Sub-Commission Meetings on 20th and 21st of July 1953," in "Le Logis dans l'untité d'habitation," Bakema Archive, BAK, a12[21].

40 Sigfried Giedion, Mechanization Takes Command, 717–21.

41 Report of Commission I, "Re-Affirmation of the Aims of CIAM," 1947, CIAM Archive, 42-JT-X-3; "MARS Group Proposal for CIAM 9," in "Les Documents de Sigtuna"; Commission Ib, "Le Logis dans l'unité d'habitation."

42 CIAM, "Re-affirmation of the Aims of CIAM," CIAM Archive, 42-JT-X-3.

43 J. M. Richards, "Architectural Expression," (paper presented at CIAM 6, Bridgwater, England, September 1947), in "CIAM 6 Documents," CIAM Archive, 42-JT-X-3, 25.
44 Programme du 7ème Congrès CIAM. Mis en application de la Charte d'Athènes; The Athens Charter in Practice. CIAM 7, Bergamo, Italy (Boulogne-sûr-Seine: Architecture d'Aujourd'hui, 1949), 24.
45 Untitled typewritten transcript of discussion from CIAM 8, CIAM Archive, 42-JT-9-370/372.
46 Peter Smithson, "Notes of Meeting of MARS Group CIAM 10 Sub-Committee," London, April 23, 1954, Bakema Archive, BAK, or97.
47 Minutes of Meeting, London, August 28–29, 1954, Bakema Archive, BAK, a30, 2.
48 Alison and Peter Smithson, "Draft Framework 3. CIAM X. Instructions to Groups," [c. September 1954] Bakema Archive, BAK, vd4.
49 Commission Ib, "Le Logis dans l'unité d'habitation."
50 Commission II, "Final Report of Commission II" 12 September 1947, CIAM Archive, 42-RV-X-6-30, 14; Report of Commission I, "Re-affirmation of the Aims of CIAM," 1947, CIAM Archive, 42-JT-X-3; "MARS Group Proposal for CIAM 9," in "Les Documents de Sigtuna," CIAM Archive, 42-AR-X-4; CIAM, "Re–affirmation of the Aims of CIAM," in Ockman, *Architecture Culture*, 102; Cornelis van Eesteren, Helena Syrkus and Sigfried Giedion, "Séance plénière de la 2ème Commission," in *CIAM 7 Bergamo 1949: Documents* (Nendeln: Kraus Reprint, 1979); J. M. Richards, "Architectural Expression," paper given at CIAM 6, 1947, in "CIAM 6 Documents," CIAM Archive, 42-JT-X-3.
51 Commission 1b "Le Logis dans l'unité d'habitation."
52 Giedion, "Proposed Program of the Seventh Congress," June 1947, CIAM Archive, 42-JLS-11-53.
53 J. M. Richards, "Contemporary Architecture and the Common Man," in Giedion, *A Decade of New Architecture*, 33.
54 Ernesto N. Rogers, "Minutes for Full Session, 5:30pm, September 9th 1955," in "La Sarraz 1955," CIAM Archive, JT-13-169.
55 Van Eyck, "We Discover Style, Journal of the Royal Architectural Institute of Canada" (July 1950), 216.
56 J. H. van den Broek, handwritten note, "Aims of CIAM, Trial to Precise 4 & 5," CIAM Archive, 42-JLS-7-17.
57 De 8 (Dutch Group), untitled, document submitted to the Secretary of CIAM, Amsterdam, May 19, 1947. BAK OR94, p. 4.
58 Alfred Roth, The New Architecture, 8.
59 ASCORAL, "Project de Programme pour le 9e Congrès CIAM 1953," January 10, 1952, in "Les Documents de Sigtuna."
60 Sigfried Giedion, Space, Time and Architecture: the growth of a new tradition (Cambridge, Mass.: Harvard University Press; London: Oxford University Press, 1949, 651.
61 Ben Merkelbach for Dutch CIAM group, "Dutch Report," May 19, 1947, Bakema Archive, BAK, or94.
62 Report of Commission I, "Re-affirmation of the Aims of CIAM," 1947, CIAM Archive, 42-JT-X-3; Roth, *The New Architecture*, 8; ASCORAL, "Projet de Programme pour le 9e Congrès CIAM 1953," January 10, 1952, in "Les Documents de Sigtuna"; Giedion, *Space, Time and Architecture*, 17, 651; "Dutch Report," [CIAM 6] n.d., Bakema Archive, BAK OR94; Bâtir (with

the approval of the Moroccan group), "A Note on the Proposed Habitat Charter," CIAM Archive, 42-JT-10-54/66.

63 Jacob Bakema, "Relationship between Men and Things," in Heart of the City: Towards the Humanisation of Urban Life, eds. J. Tyrwhitt, J. L. Sert, E. N. Rogers (New York: Pellegrini and Ducahy, 1952), 67–68.

64 Ben Merkelbach, "Dutch Report."

65 Jacob Bakema, "Relationships between Men and Things," in "Report of Hoddesdon Conference," 1951, CIAM Archive, AR-X-3; "Dutch Report," [CIAM 6], Bakema Archive, BAK or94; Ben Merkelbach, "Dutch Report"; Bâtir, "Project of Grid for the Habitat," CIAM Archive, 42-JT-10-91; ASCORAL, "Projet de Programme pour le 9e Congrès CIAM 1953," January 10 1952, and E. R. (unknown author for the Norwegian group), "The Dwelling Charter. Some Remarks," in "Les Documents de Sigtuna."

66 Louis Kahn, "Talk at the Conclusion of the Otterlo Congress," in *CIAM '59 at Otterlo*, by Oscar Newman (London: Alec Tiranti, 1961), 215.

67 Giedion, "The Need for a New Monumentality," 552; similar statement by Sert, Léger and Giedion, "Nine Points on Monumentality," in Ockman, *Architecture Culture*, 29.

68 "Rapport de la Commission sûr la thème du CIAM 9," June 28, 1952, "Les Documents de CIAM," CIAM Archive, 42-AR-X-4.

69 Ibid.

70 Dutch CIAM group, "Introduction à la contribution CIAM-Holland, Statut de Logis," in "La Sarraz, 1955," CIAM Archive, 42-JT-13-226/227.

71 Norwegian Group, "The Dwelling Charter. Some Remarks," May 30, 1952, in "Les Documents de Sigtuna."

72 CIAM, Commission I, "Re-Affirmation of the Aims of CIAM," 1947, French version, CIAM Archive, 42-JT-X-3.

73 Ben Merkelbach, "Dutch Report."

74 Aldo van Eyck, "We Discover Style," 216.

75 Sigfried Giedion, "Report Concerning the Interrelation of the Plastic Arts and the Importance of Cooperation, CIAM 6, Bridgwater, 1947," CIAM Archive, 42-SG-9-85/90; Mechanization Takes Command, 717–721.

76 Alfred Roth, The New Architecture, 8.

77 Commission Ic, untitled, CIAM 9, July 22, 1953, in "CIAM 9. Aix-en-Provence, July 19–26 1953, Rapports des Commissions," CIAM Archive, JT-X-1.

78 Clare O'Farrell, "Spirituality," Key Concepts, 2007, http://michel-foucault.com, accessed August 13, 2016.

79 Alister E. McGrath, "Theological Foundations for Spirituality: Basic Issues," in *Christian Spirituality: an introduction* (Hoboken, NJ: Wiley-Blackwell, 1999), 25.

Endnotes/Table 1

1 Sigfried Giedion, "Proposed Program of the Seventh Congress," June 1947, translated by Stamos Papadaki, July 12, 1947, CIAM Archive, ETH/gta, Zurich, 42-JLS-11-53; Arthur Ling, "Satisfying Human Needs at the Core," in *Heart of the City*, eds. J. L. Sert et al. (London: Lund Humphries, 1952), 96.

2 J. M. Richards, "Architectural Expression," paper given at CIAM 6, 1947, "CIAM 6 Documents," 1947, CIAM Archive, 42-JT-X-3.

3 De 8 (Dutch CIAM Group), manuscript, May 19, 1947, Bakema Archive, hereafter cited as BAK, Nederlands Architectuurinstituut, Rotterdam, BAK or94. "Dutch Report," n.d. [c. CIAM 6], BAK or94, 10.

4 De 8, [untitled], document submitted to the Secretary of CIAM, Amsterdam, May 19, 1947, BAK or94.

5 Ibid.; Alfred Roth, The New Architecture, (Zurich: Girsberger, 1940), 8; J. M. Richards, "Contemporary Architecture and the Common Man," in *A Decade of New Architecture*, ed. Sigfried Giedion (Zurich: Girsberger, 1951), 33.

6 English translation of the minutes of the Working Congress of CIAM, July 30, 1949, CIAM, 42-JT-8-134; Dutch Group, "Remarks of the Dutch Group Concerning Theme of CIAM 9," in "Les Documents de Sigtuna 1952," CIAM Archive, 42-ARX-4.

7 J. M. Richards, "Contemporary Architecture and the Common Man," *A Decade of New Architecture*, ed. Giedieon, 33; J. H. van den Broek, handwritten note, "Aims of CIAM. Trial to Precise 4 & 5," [of Draft. Reaffirmation of the Aims of CIAM] n.d., CIAM, JLS-7-17; J. M. Richards, "Contemporary Architecture and the Common Man," in *A Decade of New Architecture*, ed. Giedieon, 33.

8 De 8, untitled, document submitted to the Secretary of CIAM, Amsterdam, May 19, 1947. BAK or94.

9 Van den Broek, handwritten note, "Aims of the CIAM. Trial to precise 4 & 5 [of Draft. Reaffirmation of the Aims of CIAM]. n.d., CIAM, JLS-7-17; [untitled], [CIAM 6] 42-RV-X-6-27.

10 Rogers, "Minutes for Full Session," 5:30 p.m., September 9, 1955, in "La Sarraz 1955," CIAM, JT-13-169.

11 "MARS Group Proposal for CIAM 9," in "Les Documents de Sigtuna," CIAM 42-AR-X-4.

12 Report of Commission I, "Re-affirmation of the Aims of CIAM," 1947, CIAM, 42-JT-X-3; "MARS Group Proposal for CIAM 9," in "Les Documents de Sigtuna," CIAM 42-AR-X-4; Van Eesteren, Syrkus, and Giedion, "Séance plénière de la 2ème Commission," in "Les Actes officiels du VIIème CIAM," Metron n. 33–34 (September–October 1949): 59, 53, 60.

13 CIAM, "Outline for the reports to be submitted to the Congress by the national groups." CIAM 6, CIAM, 42-JLS-11-35; Le Corbusier to André Wogenscky, 3 May 1947, CIAM, 42-HMS-297/298.

14 Sigfried Giedion, *Space, Time and Architecture: the growth of a new tradition* (Cambridge, Mass.: Harvard University Press; London: Oxford University Press, 1949), 651; Commission Ib (presided over by Bakema), "Le Logis dans l'unité d'habitation," Bakema Archive, BAK, a12[21]; J. M. Richards, "Architectural Expression," paper given at CIAM 6, 1947, in "CIAM 6 Documents," 1947, 42-JT-X-3, 28.

15 Commission Ib (presided over by Bakema), "Le Logis dans l'unité d'habitation," Bakema Archive, BAK, a12[21].

16 Aldo van Eyck, We Discover Style, *Journal, Royal Architectural Institute of Canada* 27 (July 1950): 216.

17 Alison Smithson, *Team 10 Primer* (London: Standard Catalogue, 1966), 30; Alison and Peter Smithson, "Open letter to Sert and Team 10. Commentary on 'Preparation for CIAM X of Team 10 Nov '55 and CIAM

Secretariat Dec '55'," January 30, 1956, Smithsons Office Archive, London, Team 10 box; Alison and Peter Smithson, "Open letter to Sert and Team 10. Commentary on 'Preparation for CIAM X of Team 10 Nov '55 and CIAM Secretariat Dec '55'," January 30, 1956, Smithsons Office Archive, London, Team 10 box; CIAM, "Re-affirmation of the Aims of CIAM," CIAM, 42-JT-X-3; Alison Smithson to John Voelcker, Jacob Bakema, Shadrach Woods, and Aldo van Eyck, January 8, 1961, Francis Strauven Papers; J.M. Richards and MARS Group, "The Impact of Social Developments," September 1947, in "Commission 2 Report. The Collaboration of the Architect, Painter and Sculptor," July 24–26, 1949, CIAM, 42-JT-2-468/469, 4; Jacob Bakema, "Relationship between man and things," July 11 1951, BAK, or90.

18 J.M. Richards, "Report on MARS Group: war and postwar," May 1947, CIAM 42-HMS-305/307.

19 Sigfried Giedion, "The Need for a New Monumentality," in *New Architecture and City Planning*, ed. Paul Zucker (New York: Philosophical Library, 1944), 552–3.

20 Sigfried Giedion, *Space Time and Architecture*, 363.

21 Sigfried Giedion, *Mechanization Takes Command: a contribution to an anonymous history*, (New York; London: W. W. Norton, 1948), 720; Van Eyck, "A Tribute to Carola Giedion-Welcker," *Forum*, n. 9 (1957): 322.

22 [ASCORAL] "Rapport pour l'Assemblée Génerale des CIAM, Londres, 7/15 Septembre 1947," Fondation Le Corbusier, Paris, D3-16/112-126. Hereafter cited as LeC.

23 Louis Kahn, "Talk at the Conclusion of the Otterlo Congress," in *CIAM '59 at Otterlo*, ed. Oscar Newman (London: Alec Tiranti, 1961), 215.

24 J.L. Sert, "Centers of Community Life," in *Heart of the City: Towards the Humanisation of Urban Life*, (New York: Pelligrini & Cudhay, 1952), 4, 11.

25 Sigfried Giedion, *Space Time and Architecture*, 364.

26 J.M. Richards, "Architectural Expression," paper given at CIAM 6, 1947, in CIAM 6 Documents, 28–9.

27 Ibid.

28 Van Eyck, "Report Concerning the Interrelation of the Plastic Arts and the Importance of Cooperation, CIAM 6, Bridgwater, 1947," CIAM, 42-SG-9-85/90.

29 Dutch CIAM group, "Introduction à la contribution CIAM-Holland. Statut de Logis," in "La Sarraz, 1955," CIAM, 42-JT-13- 226/227; CIAM Netherlands (De 8 and OPBOUW), "Summary of aims and program for 'le logis' (extract and compilation from the result of studies by prominent Dutch architects, made during and after the war)," in "La Sarraz, 1955," CIAM, 42-JT-13-225; Bâtir (with the approval of the Moroccan group), "A Note on the Proposed Habitat Charter," CIAM, 42-JT-10-54/66.

30 Aldo van Eyck, "Report concerning the Interrelation of the Plastic Arts and the Importance of Cooperation," CIAM 6 (1947), CIAM, 42-SG-9-85/90; "We Discover Style," 216.

31 Le Corbusier, "Discourse de Le Corbusier au VIème Congrès CIAM. Séance de l'Assemblée Générale sur l'expression architectural," September 15, 1947, BAK or97.

32 CIAM, "La Sarraz Declaration," [1928], in *Programs and Manifestoes on 20th-century Architecture*, ed. Ulrich Conrads (Cambridge, Mass.: MIT Press, 1970), 109.

33 Romke de Vries, "The Aim and the Task of C.I.A.M." Forum 11, n.4 (1956): English summ*ary.*
34 Norwegian Group, "The Dwelling Charter. Some Remarks," May 30, 1952, in "Les Documents de Sigtuna," CIAM, 42-AR-X-4.
35 Ben Merkelbach, "Dutch Report," [CIAM 6] n.d., BAK or94.
36 CIAM, "Re-Statement of the Aims of CIAM," in *A Decade of New Architecture*, ed. Giedion, 17; [untitled Timeline], attached to the "Statement on Habitat" and circulated to CIAM members by Jacob Bakema, March 1, 1954, LeC, D2 B16.
37 Aldo van Eyck, (Commission II), "The Role of Aesthetic[s] in the Habitat," July 1953, CIAM Archive, Sigfried Giedion Papers, ETH/gta SG-37-85.
38 Aldo van Eyck, "We Discover Style," 216.
39 Bâtir, "Project of Grid for the Habitat," CIAM 42-JT-10-91; ASCORAL, "Projet de Programme pour le 9è Congrès CIAM 1953," January 10, 1952, and E. R. [unknown author for the Norwegian group], "The Dwelling Charter. Some Remarks," in "Les Documents de Sigtuna," CIAM, 42-AR-X-4; Commission Ic, untitled, CIAM 9, July 22, 1953, in "CIAM 9. Aix-en-Provence, July 19–26, 1953, Rapports des Commissions," CIAM, JT-X-1; "Rapport de la Commission sur la thème du CIAM 9," June 28, 1952, "Les Documents de Sigtuna" CIAM, 42-AR-X-4.
40 Jacob Bakema, "Relationships between Men and Things," in "Report of Hoddesdon Conference," 1951, CIAM, AR-X-3; Ben Merkelbach for Dutch CIAM group, "Dutch Report" [1947], BAK, or94.
41 Helena and Szymon Syrkus, "Statement by the CIAM," October 16, 1946, CIAM, 42-JLS-11-25; Sigfried Giedion, "The Need for a New Monumentality," 552.
42 ASCORAL (with Le Corbusier), *The Athens Charter*. Translated by Anthony Eardley (New York: Grossman, 1973), 95.
43 [ASCORAL] "Rapport pour l'Assemblée Génerale des CIAM," LeC, D3-16/112-126; Aldo van Eyck, in *A Decade of New Architecture*, ed. Giedion, 37; J. M. Richards, "Contemporary Architecture and the Common Man," ibid., 33.
44 CIAM, "Regulations for Joining CIAM," CIAM 6, 42-JT-2-10.

Béla Kerékgyártó

Was Humanized Socialist Modernism Possible After All? The Promise and Failure of Mass Housing in Hungary[1]

> What I called in this lecture the Kádár era coincided with "the 60s" – with an era of liberation (and libertinism) and of hope throughout the developed world. It still seemed possible to hope for a more fair, equal, free and democratic future where the roads of the East and the West could meet (since that time people have hardly believed in the possibility of reconciliation of these aims without a trade-off).[2]
>
> –Iván Szelényi

The call for a new kind of humanism, or humanization, was an important trend in public and intellectual life after the Second World War, affecting disciplines from political theory to philosophy, from anthropology to sociology and architectural theory.[3] It was based on a consensus among the Allies that rejected racism, war and the Holocaust. This new humanism was at the same time an answer to the challenges of modern, technological civilization, striving for reinforcement and expansion of the humanist heritage of the European Enlightenment and following egalitarian and emancipative ideals while rejecting exploitation and coercion. The human condition and relations between individual and community were common yet controversial subjects of existentialism, phenomenology, anthropology and Marxism.

The definition of this new humanism soon became a battlefield between former allies, the West and the East. The promise of material equality and well-being versus that of freedom and of material versus formal democracy were contrasting, colliding principles in the postwar world. Socialist countries in Central and Eastern Europe came into being on Soviet-occupied territories and remained subject to Soviet politics and influence. The Stalinist era was characterized by totalitarian indoctrination, manifested in architecture and art in official socialist realism. The supposedly human face and scale of this art opposed the so called inhuman alienation, coercion and exploitation in the capitalist or imperialist world.

In these countries, in the late 1950s and 1960s, humanization also came to mean the rejection of the Stalinist heritage of brute force and oppression. Two of Nikita Khrushchev's doctrines were of fundamental importance from the point of view of architecture. The first was formulated in his famous speech "On the Extensive Introduction of Industrial Methods, Improving the Quality and Reducing the Cost of Construction" at the National Conference of Builders, Architects and Workers in Construction Materials on December 7, 1954.[4] This speech rejected unnecessary, expensive representation in socialist-realist architecture and promoted the industrialized mass production of housing. As Khrushchev put it: "We are not against beauty, but we are against superfluities. [...] In order to build quickly and successfully, we must use standard designs in our building [...]."[5]

The second doctrine envisioned peaceful economic competition between capitalism and socialism, which opened the way to mutual contacts and influences. In the "Kitchen Debate" between Khrushchev and Vice President Richard Nixon, the former declared that in peaceful competition the Soviet Union would catch up with or overtake America in the near future: "We have existed not quite forty-two years and in another seven years we will be on the same level as America. When we catch up, in passing you by we will wave to you."[6]

Snapshots from a New Beginning: The Reorganization of Professional Discourse in Hungarian Architecture after 1956

In Hungary in 1956, János Kádár (1912–1989), "Khrushchev's best pupil" came to power with the help of Soviet tanks. Kádár oversaw the restoration of fundamentals of the Soviet model: the single-party system, a monopoly on power and ideology and the state-ownership of property. A surprisingly rapid consolidation allowed him to reinforce his power. While taking cruel revenge on participants in the revolution, he rejected the dogmatic left and strove to make a compromise with Hungarian society. His slogan, "He who is not

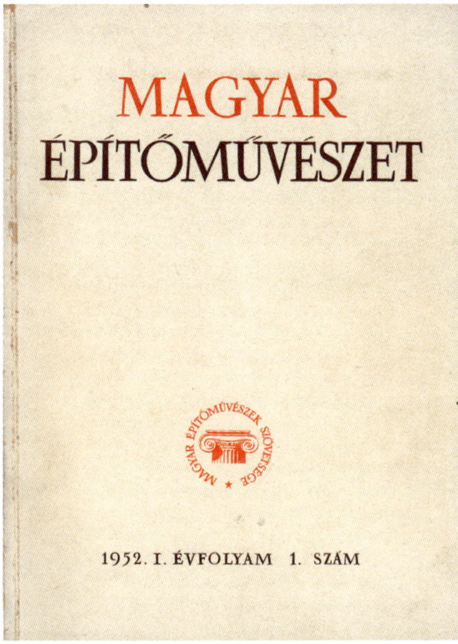

fig. 1 The "socialist-realist" cover of the periodical "Magyar Építőművészet" (Hungarian Architecture, MÉ). 1:1 (1952).

fig. 2 Detail of the "humanized" cover of the MÉ, 7:1–3 (1958)

against us is with us," reversed the Stalinist-era practice of "he who is not with us is against us." At the eighth party congress, in 1962, it was declared that by 1980, as in the Soviet Union, per-capita consumption in Hungary would be higher than in the developed capitalist countries. Like Khrushchev, the Hungarian Socialist Worker's Party placed great emphasis on the construction of housing. In the early 1960s, it passed a resolution to construct one million flats within the next fifteen years.[7]

In parallel with the political developments, the public sphere was reorganized, including cultural institutions and periodicals. Even in cases where continuity formally existed, as with *Magyar Építőművészet* [*Hungarian Architecture*], journals changed both outlook and content (figs. 1, 2). Architects and theorists (or ideologists) of architecture had to find a new orientation. The central question in this new era of peaceful competition was "the struggle for the people."

In the next part I will focus on three aspects of the discourse on identity. First, explanations offered for the switch from socialist realism to socialist modernism; second, the nature of socialist modernism, particularly differences between socialist and capitalist architecture. Finally, I will examine the reception of and response to contemporary Western architecture during this period by architects in Hungary.

(1) When examining the transition from the socialist realism to socialist modern architecture, it may be instructive to compare the positions of two architectural theorists (or ideologists), Máté Major (1904–1986) and János Bonta (*1921). They were participants in the famous – or infamous – "great architectural debate" of 1951, when the obligatory line of socialist realism was approved. They took opposite sides in the debate, with Major, as main representative of new or modern architecture within the Party, playing the role of scapegoat while Bonta was adjutant of the main representative of socialist realism, György Kardos (1902–1953).[8]

After 1956, changes in politics and the profession put Bonta in an embarrassing situation, resolved with his maintaining a simple argument that both changes in approach were necessary in their own times. He drew parallels between ideological-aesthetical shifts in the Soviet Union in the 1930s and those in Hungary in the 1950s. The rejection of modernism and the turn to socialist realism was necessary, in his opinion, because of avant-garde elitism and its distance from the masses' elementary needs, means and tastes. His second argument emphasized the dangers of cosmopolitism opening the gates to "imperialist" Western influences. To Bonta, the error of socialist realism lay in its one-sided accentuation of architecture's political and artistic sides, and its corresponding neglect of the technological side. The socialist system now possessed a more developed industrial base and more advanced technology, however, making industrialized mass production of housing a real alternative. A new generation, meanwhile, had grown up with a more

fig. 3 The portrait of Máté Major on the cover of the periodical "Magyar Technika" [Hungarian Technology], 2:12 (1947).

developed taste for abstract forms. The main question, in his opinion, would become the relationship between architecture and industrial mass production. No wonder Bonta became an advocate of mass-produced housing, about which he published a book in 1963.[9]

For his former opponent Máté Major, socialist realism with its neglect of technological development and return to historical or archaic forms was a pure anachronism (fig. 3). Major reacted to the return of modernism with relief and new hope: "Now, at a time of great clarifications and orderings, changes and improvements, in the era of the splendidly increasing dynamism of the construction of socialism, we have to fight to put architecture, in every aspect, in its rightful place."[10]

(2) In order to find this "rightful place," Major had to define the identity of modernist *and* socialist architecture. Socialist realism had aimed to differ at all costs from capitalist architecture, Major claimed, but this was a fundamental mistake – many parallels and similarities resulted from convergent natural conditions, modern technology and lifestyles.[11] Major nevertheless identified three main differences to capitalist architecture. One was the opposition between self-interest and the common interest, central to Socialism, which required the socialist system to ensure a continuous improvement in the standard of living for all. This improvement included the mass construction of housing that led – inevitably, in Major's opinion – to functional and formal shortcomings in quality. The second difference was the lack of competition, a mechanism which stimulated the capitalist economy to greater

efficiency. Major naturally distanced himself from the competition of private interests aimed at profit, but admitted the lack of a corresponding source of stimulation in (state) socialism. The third difference derived from public ownership – that is, the state – of land and building plots in socialism, which opened the way for the realization of projects on a large scale. Major continued to believe in the collectivist-utopian promise of ideology, at the same time considering questions of professional identity and the artistic or creative autonomy of architects to be equally important. He tried to believe in the advent of a new era with magnificent new prospects for the profession, and to see the difficulties as only transitional phenomena.[12]

(3) The return to modernism was closely connected with renewed attention toward the contemporary international (Western) architecture in the journal *Magyar Építőművészet*. Two large ensembles built for major architectural "exhibitions" afforded an overview of current trends, the Interbau in West Berlin in 1957 and the Brussels World's Fair in 1958, with accounts of both published in detail. With the Hansaviertel estate built as a counterpoint to the socialist-realist Stalinallee in East Berlin, coverage of it could also be understood as an indirect polemic against socialist realism. The overview on the Interbau was written by two architects from the Planning Office for Industrial Buildings, the most progressive studio in Hungarian architecture, and did not include ideological allusions.[13]

An issue of *Magyar Építőművészet* was devoted to the Brussels exhibition pavilions of Expo 58, with a matter-of-fact introductory overview classifying and evaluating types of exhibition buildings and pavilions (fig. 4). Designs such as the Philips Pavilion by Le Corbusier were criticized for their extravagance, while pavilions whose form and construction were in harmony with each other were preferred (being the West-German, Yugoslavian, Austrian, Finnish and Norwegian ones). The Hungarian pavilion was deemed a modernist statement that presented Hungarian culture and Hungarian cuisine.[14]

A polemical article by Bonta attempted to differentiate between progressive and retrograde tendencies in modern architecture and referred explicitly though briefly to the discourse of humanization in architecture. He referenced examples of old masters: the cool neutral "technicism" of Mies van der Rohe and sculptural forms of late Le Corbusier, or the technological acrobatics of new designs with cable and shell construction. His ultimate argument remained ideological: Bonta accused modern (Western) architects of showing interest in the development and humanization of architecture only on a formal level; therefore they supported the irrationalism of capitalism, whether directly or indirectly.[15]

fig. 4 The cover of the special issue of the *MÉ* about the World Fair in Brussels, 8:1–2 (1959).

Architects of the younger generation were less dogmatic. For them, the central dilemma was how to adapt the architecture of the developed countries, which they knew mostly from professional journals, to local cultural and technological conditions. Elemér Nagy (1928–1985), later the editor of *Magyar Építőművészet*, felt Bonta's article lacked a sufficiently precise, current definition of modern architecture, and criticized his dualistic and reductionist approach. Nagy argued for a more pluralistic, expanded notion of modern architecture, which would include different regional variations.[16] Another important architect, Károly Polónyi (1928–2002), took part in Team 10 meetings from the beginning and tried to mediate the group's concepts and projects to Hungary. Polónyi was chief architect of Budapest for a period, then spent years in the Third World working on major development projects in Ghana, Nigeria and other African countries.

Public Debates about Consumerism, Dwelling and Lifestyle

In accordance with the second of Khrushchev's doctrines, material wellbeing became increasingly important for the peaceful coexistence of and competition between socialist and capitalist political systems, or rather for the legitimation of the respective regimes. From the late 1950s, Hungary saw a steady increase in wages, loans and the purchase of consumer durables. Typical 1950s examples were furniture, bicycles and motorbikes, ovens, ranges and radios; in the 1960s, Hungarians began to buy TVs, electronics, refrigerators, washing machines, and dryers; then from the 1970s private cars came within the reach of ordinary citizens.[17]

The appearance of early forms of consumerism created tension with the ascetic, collectivist ideals of official ideology, and "Frigidaire socialism" was subject to widespread debates in this period.[18] Advocates of collectivist ideals sharply criticized "egoistic philistine individualism" and the immediate pleasures of consumerism. A leftist poet asked whether "the relaxing, happy coasts of communism" wouldn't be perverted "to enervating beaches of material wealth?"[19]

Party leader János Kádár took a stance in favor of a pragmatist position: in his opinion, material goods for individual use such as private houses along with holiday travel were means of self-fulfillment, which could therefore be judged positively. Kádár rejected acquisition as an end in itself, however, and condemned the "hamster-like" accumulation of money and goods as alien to "socialist man."

A special debate was organized in the literary journal *Kortárs* [*Contemporary*] on proper lifestyle and its relationship to forms of housing. In the opening article, a novelist argued against island-dwelling, meaning the individual dwelling unit, whether a house or a flat with all the modern conveniences. He opted for collective houses combining individual dwelling with collectivized household services.[20]

Major was definitely against single-family houses, from both an economic and an aesthetic point of view: "Every room is bigger than needed for economical furnishing and rational use." Family houses were in his opinion morally and aesthetically bad, the embodiment of kitsch culture ("a kitsch-man in a kitsch-house").[21] Major wanted to reform the floor plan and living style in houses – instead of a large kitchen and an "elegant" sitting room which did not see daily use, he proposed spacious rooms for everyday life and a small kitchen (or kitchenette). This form could be a transitional stage on the way to the collective house and architecture could thus contribute to the transformation of the lone individual to a man of collectivity: "This is the right way for the man of socialism who knows the propelling force of development and knows the magnificent possibilities offered by and through the collective."[22]

Even the journal *Műszaki Tervezés* [*Technical Planning*] dealt with the problem of the dwelling, emphasizing that the construction of housing is "not only a technical question." One author considered the mutual relationship between economic and technical factors and the needs and lifestyles of potential residents. This author aligned himself with the opinion of Máté Major that the individual should be educated to become a collectivist person and that the built environment could play an important role in this process. On the basis of statistical data, he compared the timetable of a housewife with that of a working woman; results indicated that the emancipated working woman had less time for housework and leisure. The solution, according to the author, could be the mechanization of individual households or the delegation of these tasks to external services. He preferred the latter and mentioned three forms of similar experiments: the hotel-like apartment house, the collective house of Le Corbusier and the socialist neighborhood, known as *mikroraion* where dwelling units of different types shared a common service center.[23]

Toward Industrialized Housing Production

The postwar period saw a definitive shift toward mass-housing production in both West and East, partly due to the demands of reconstruction and partly as a result of prevailing egalitarian and emancipative ideals. As a Hungarian architect of the period put it: "the key realm of our new architecture is mass housing built by new building methods and in new materials. [...] The essential tasks of architect-designers are closely connected to the satisfaction of the subjective needs of man."[24] Nationalization was also on the agenda in parts of the West, but this was not identified with the almost total elimination of private property. Ideologically driven development and extreme centralization in the form of the nationalization of institutions, properties and professions was seen in the East as the most effective way to catch up with Western development levels, including the housing sector. Initially aiming at the quantitative reduction of the housing shortage, in the longer term this sought to attain a higher level of societal development than what prevailed in the capitalist West. Architectural design work was concentrated in large state-owned planning offices throughout the existence of state socialism. A crucial task of these offices was the categorization and standardization that would make mass production possible.

The mass production of housing from the late 1950s until the 1970s went through three phases, which can be considered as a sort of progression from the minimal dwellings of the modern "model estates" of the 1920s and 1930s through the mainstream estates built in prefabricated construction in the 1960s, to later efforts to correct the perceived problems of the earlier phases in the reformed or humanized housing estates. In the following, I will briefly describe a typical example of each period.

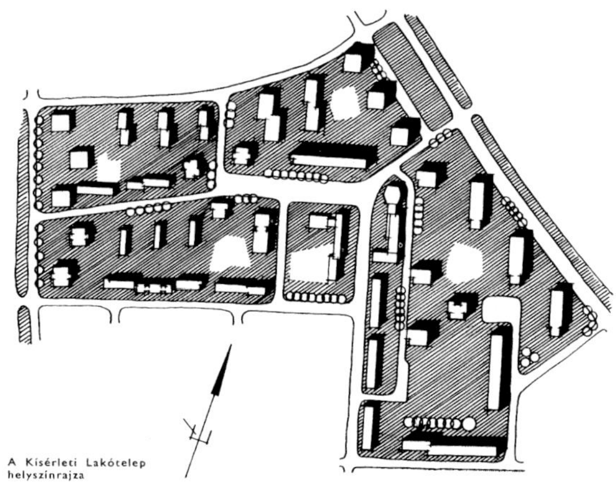

fig. 5 Site plan of the experimental housing estate in Óbuda. Source: MÉ 10:1 (1961), p. 4.

During the preparation of the major housing program in Hungary in the late 1950s, a complex experimental and innovational process was initiated to address the questions of housing. This campaign concerned not only the architectural design of buildings and flats but also their furnishing. The organizer of the program summarized it thus: "First we announced a competition for new ceiling structures, built-in kitchen arrangements and wardrobes, and door and window systems. [...] we then announced a National Competition on Dwelling. The third National Competition aimed at the design of varied furniture to equip selected dwellings. This was followed by competitions of carpets, textiles and lighting equipment for interiors"[25] (fig. 5).

Some one hundred eighty projects were submitted to the housing-prototype competition. Unusual for such competitions, the winning plans were actually built, and some were even furnished. The resulting model estate was opened to the public as an exhibition propagating and educating about the new, economical and at the same time aesthetically pleasing type of dwelling and lifestyle. A film was produced and many articles were published in journals and newspapers. Visitors were asked to fill out a questionnaire to assess the general opinion concerning these new dwellings.

The buildings were mostly medium-sized and varied in typology, including tower blocks, ribbon buildings and some terraced houses. They were constructed using mixed technologies and structures, mainly traditional materials and building techniques but also some standardized elements produced *in situ*.

The flats were arranged around staircases, along central corridors or exterior galleries and the most important aspects of the design were the rational organization of floor plans and the standardized range of mass-produced kitchen furniture and built-in wardrobes. The floor plans were designed to

fig. 6 The building No. 527. Three floors with four flats on each. The flats are for four persons. Architect Olga Mináry. Source: MÉ 10:1 (1961), p. 11.

fig. 7 Ground plan with furniture and photo with dining recess between the kitchen and the living room. Ibid.

fit the furnishing and were mostly organized around a large living room with smaller sleeping rooms attached. The kitchen was typically small, a rationally organized workplace with modular built-in furniture. An important feature was the connection between the kitchen and dining room or area. The housing types and the size and arrangement of the flats provided an appropriate setting for families of different sizes and lifestyles (figs. 6, 7).

As far as the future perspective was concerned, the organizer of the experimental estate stipulated that "a healthy compromise should be found between the constructional scale of up-to-date technology and the differentiated floor plans."[26] In practice, however, the politically motivated requirement of mass production overrode the qualitative aspects. The scale and realization already seemed to be anachronistic. One leading architect formulated the following *bon mot*: "The only thing which is true about the experimental housing estate in Óbuda is that it is in Óbuda."[27]

After the government's resolution to construct a million dwellings within fifteen years, attention turned increasingly to industrialized mass production. Before the advent of prefabrication, planning offices first used local standards, adapted to specific sites. The so-called medium and large blocks could be produced *in situ*. According to a Party resolution of June 1960, 60 to 70 percent of housing and public buildings were to be erected by 1965 on the basis of standardized plans.[28] In 1961, a new super-planning office was founded, the Institute for Standardization, which merged similar divisions from different planning offices. The new institution was tasked with devising a uniform scale- and construction system and was empowered with special authority.[29] At the same time, in the periodical *Magyar Építőipar* [*Hungarian Building Industry*], a series of reports and evaluations appeared on international industrialized construction systems. An overview article with the ambitious title "Prefabricated Housing in Hungary and the World Standard" compared and evaluated the systems, and the Danish Larsen-Nielsen system was found to be the best.[30] Officials nevertheless then bought only one Larsen-Nielsen housing factory and five Soviet ones. This made prefabricated housing production even more rigid in the following decade. An overview of postwar housing-estate production summarizes the situation as follows: "The planning of urban housing estates occurred in the form of obligatory planning guidelines. […] In the economy of the building industry the endowment by the state played a crucial role. […] It ensured the co-ordination of the enterprises of the building industry and was the basis for the expansion of housing factories and prefabricated building construction."[31]

The first large estate constructed was Kelenföld, largely built between 1967 and 1975 and by applying the products of the first housing factory – allegedly a personal present from Khrushchev to Hungary. Kelenföld is a typical example of a postwar, mono-functional housing estate: mechanically arranged slab buildings or medium-height tower blocks floating in a wide green area without any connection to each other. The center for commercial and cultural services was only built in the 1970s (figs. 8, 9).

In the late 1960s, one housing factory after another was opened and the construction of prefabricated-housing estates boomed. Mechanically repeated configurations of building blocks and orthodox dogmas of functional separation, with the resulting monotonous environment lacking in scale, drew ever

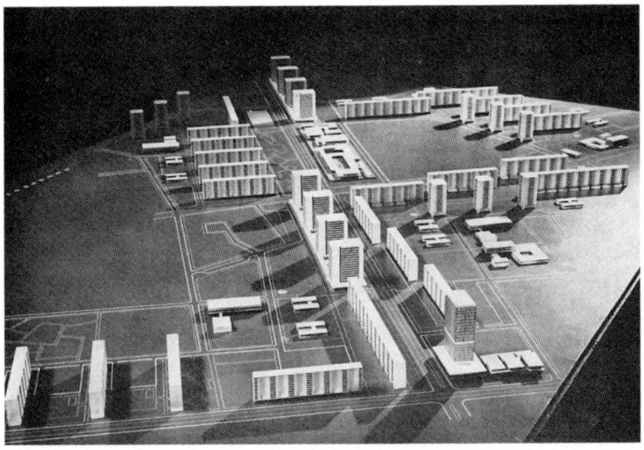

fig. 8 Model photo of the prefabricated housing estate in Kelenföld. Source: József Katona et al., Építésiparosítás, műszaki tervezés, tipizálás. Budapest: Típustervező Intézet 1969, 33.

fig. 9 View of the estate. Source: MÉ 17:5 (1968), p. 22.

stronger criticism. This then stimulated different experiments and efforts to produce new or corrected designs.

Among the experiments worth mentioning is the visionary plan of a three-kilometer ribbon house by Elemér Zalotay, which launched the idea of mass-produced housing into the absurd. Parallels can be drawn with other utopian megastructures of the 1950s and 1960s (including those by Yona Friedman, Constant, Superstudio). With his superblock, Zalotay aimed to combine urban complexity and closeness to nature. From the point of view of construction and functional order, however, his plan remained rather vague. Zalotay fought desperately for its realization with the planning offices and bureaucratic institutions. Purported conflicts between such progressive, active, innovative and productive personalities and the retrograde, passive, unproductive bureaucracy was a widely discussed topic among the intelligentsia. A series of film portraits, *Nehéz emberek* [*Difficult People*], was produced about these "heroes of the everyday." Zalotay's case was so well known and controversial among the intellectual public that a separate, longer film was made about him.[32]

Vision and Reality: The Reform Estate in Újpalota

It can be asserted that the mass-produced industrialized housing estate reached its peak in Hungary with the reform estate in Újpalota. This project reflected on the (negative) experiences of realized estates such as Kelenföld while taking international developments into consideration. Újpalota is an example of the last major wave of reformed housing estates throughout Europe, along with Le Mirail in Toulouse, Märkisches Viertel in Berlin and Bijlmermeer in Amsterdam. At the time, system theory, structuralism, participation and spontaneous or vernacular influences were on the agenda of the design discussions. The planners of these estates intended to produce a more urban, lively and humane environment with the organic configuration of different elements and functions. The scale was bigger than ever: new cities were planned for 50,000 to 100,000 inhabitants.

In the case of Újpalota, the design team came mainly from the Institute for Standardization, where research, design and planning were closely connected. Their competition proposal for developing the Asúa valley near Bilbao can be seen as a forerunner of the Újpalota project. It aimed at the expansion of Bilbao outside of the city borders creating a new city for 100,000 to 150,000 inhabitants. The large-scale plan distributed the built units in clusters, with each housing almost 12,500 people.[33] Similar principles came to the fore in the Újpalota plans, hailed by an enthusiastic colleague as a turning point in Hungarian urban planning. The same team began the project in 1966, but with a leading role for the architect Tibor Tenke. Tenke believed in the modernist credo of an egalitarian society for which the architecture had to create a framework. He was convinced that traditional building practices should make way for industrialized building methods, with prefabrication in factories and construction at the building site. "I strongly believe," Tenke said, "that human needs and the requirements of machinery can be synchronized in our new housing estates."[34]

Újpalota was constructed not as a typical housing estate, but as a city consisting of a center of greater concentration and a large green area around it flowing uninterrupted into the adjacent landscape (fig. 10). The center was

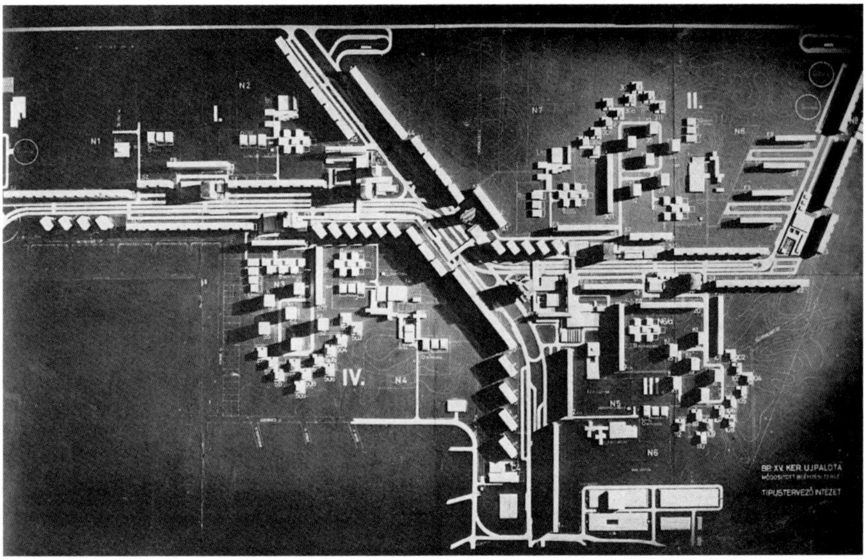

fig. 10 Model photo of the housing estate in Újpalota.
Source: Katona et al., 47.

organized around the crossing of two main traffic arteries, which divided the territory into four parts. Around this main area, lower housing ensembles and educational institutions were laid out, connected by pedestrian paths and service roads. Parts embedded in green were traffic-free. The crossing of the main traffic arteries at the center of the estate was to be surrounded by medium-high slabs and ten-story tower block buildings. By placing the buildings parallel to the main roads, the planners wanted to form an urban street. "It would be desirable," suggested Árpád Mester, one of the architect-planners of the estate in a surprisingly tentative tone, "for colorful shop windows, intimate terraces, cafes and restaurants to be placed on both sides of the roads, so that the street lighting would be provided by the shop windows and advertisements and not only by street lamps. And – equally important – the shops should stock consumer goods of high-street quality. This and many further elements make the city urban."[35]

The reality was far from the concept. Problems were caused by external factors commonly associated with the construction of large housing estates in the East and West: postponed or canceled plans for communal institutions; lack of appropriate public-transport connections to the city center, which served to increase the isolation of the estates. In both East and West, the monotony and abstract character of the mass-produced prefabricated elements created an unfriendly environment, worsened in the East by the rigid,

fig. 11 View from the elevated deck in Újpalota. Source: Collection Fortepan No. 38941. http://www.fortepan.hu/?view=query&q=&lang=hu&img=25150&tags=budapest+xv

uniform production of elements in Soviet housing factories and by the centralized command economy. The types of products and the rhythm of production prescribed the distribution, size and timetable of the building process, and the eventual appearance of the buildings. As one housing-factory engineer complained, the obligation to use the products of a designated housing factory became a real burden.

In the name of cost efficiency the original Újpalota plans were often reduced, with some parts simply omitted. Although plans foresaw the separation of the pedestrian from motorized traffic in the form of elevated sidewalks and bridges, only a small part of the elevated decks was realized (fig. 11). Due to the wide road, heavy traffic and car parks in front of buildings, there is almost no connection between the two sides of the road. It was an illusion from the start that this combination could produce a livable environment. Planners, as part of a large centralized organization, were far removed from residents' daily life and needs. "The helicopter view" of planning, as Tenke mentioned in an interview, could hardly be experienced by inhabitants. The architect furthermore believed in the modernist aesthetics of rhythm, "exactness, subtle edges, the logical order, and the clear constructive expression,"[36] which was experienced by people on the ground as monotone and depressing. The ground level of houses was mostly closed, with few places where shops or services could be found.

Contemporary Critiques of Mass Housing and the End of Hopes of Possible Humanization

It is unsurprising that around 1970, parallel to the construction of the Újpalota estate, standardized housing production and its urban consequences were subject to criticism from several disciplines. I would like to mention three of these critiques; from an architect, an urbanist and from urban sociologists.

fig. 12 Factory for prefabricated panels in Budapest, Szentendrei út in Óbuda. Photo Tibor Kádas 1974. Source: Collection Fortepan No. 84856. http://www.fortepan.hu/?view=all&lang=hu&img=84856&tags=%C3%93buda

The first was formulated by a charismatic architect Jenő Szendrői, who was for some time chief architect of the legendary Planning Office for Industrial Buildings. In his introductory essay to a volume about Hungarian architecture between 1945 and 1970, Szendrői struck a note that was very critical, even self-critical: he warned that the advantages of industrialized architecture should be taken into consideration but so should its limits and dangers. He saw a very serious problem in the uniformity and the loss of architectural or artistic quality and stressed that the order of scale of standardized elements and the number produced in each series were especially sensitive and critical. "Beyond a certain limit," he said, "the economic advantages of the series are no longer evident, and greater numbers could even be a hindrance to further development." Szendrői gave an almost classical formulation of the phenomenon of alienation, which was so often referred to at this time: "Standardized products are the products of man and it should not be permitted that, either for economic reasons or as a result of impotence or misunderstanding, the product gain the upper hand over the producer"[37] (fig. 12).

The urbanist Pál Granasztói stressed the importance of long-term considerations. Most solutions in a given social and housing situation were significant, according to Granasztói, but their further development seemed doubtful because of the small size of flats and the inflexible use of interior

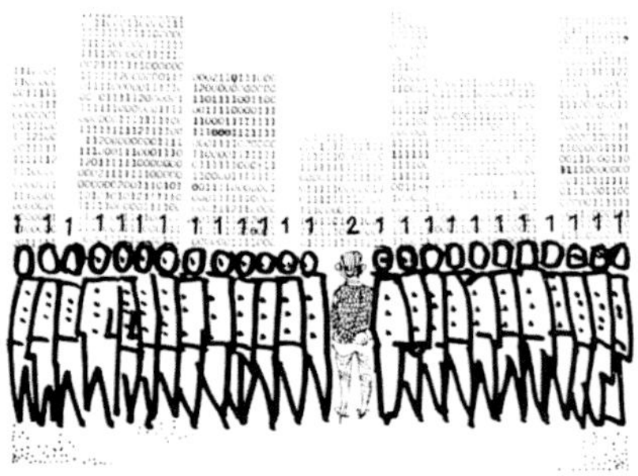

fig. 13 Drawing from the periodical "Városépítés" ("City Building") accompanying the text "Social problems in the urban architecture in Budapest" written by Iván Szelényi. 8:1 (1971), p. 10.

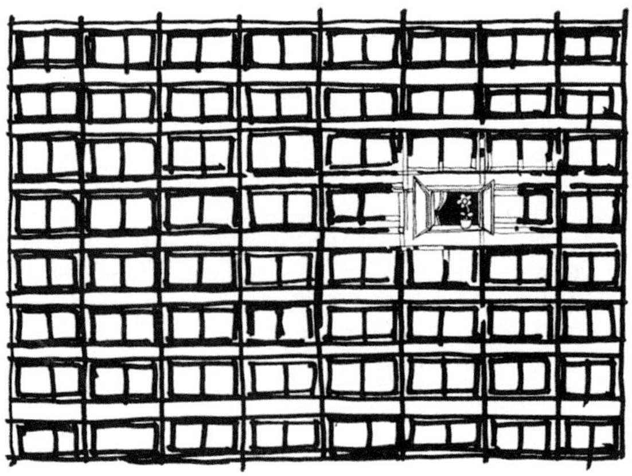

fig. 14 Drawing from the periodical "Városépítés" ("City Building") accompanying the text "Housing construction in Budapest", 8:6 (1971), p. 7.

space, along with the unalterable appearance of buildings. Similarly, housing estates built almost simultaneously on the scale of entire city districts hindered both further development and any adaptation to changing needs and circumstances. He argued for a more variable and flexible building practice, which made some changes necessary even in the methods of industrialized housing production[38] (figs. 13, 14).

The third critique came from the urban sociologist Iván Szelényi and the well-known novelist György Konrád, who worked together in the 1960s, criticizing both the ineffective economic and political model of "socialist" urbanization and the negative social consequences of mass-housing estates. Szelényi and Konrád refuted the official line and general belief about the "excessive urbanization" of socialist urban development. They demonstrated statistically that the degree of urbanization was actually lower than at the outset of the twentieth century. Forced – and ineffective – industrialization under the socialist system demanded a great amount of resources and hindered the appropriate development of infrastructure and housing.[39] Szelényi and Konrád conducted empirical research on housing estates in Hungarian cities

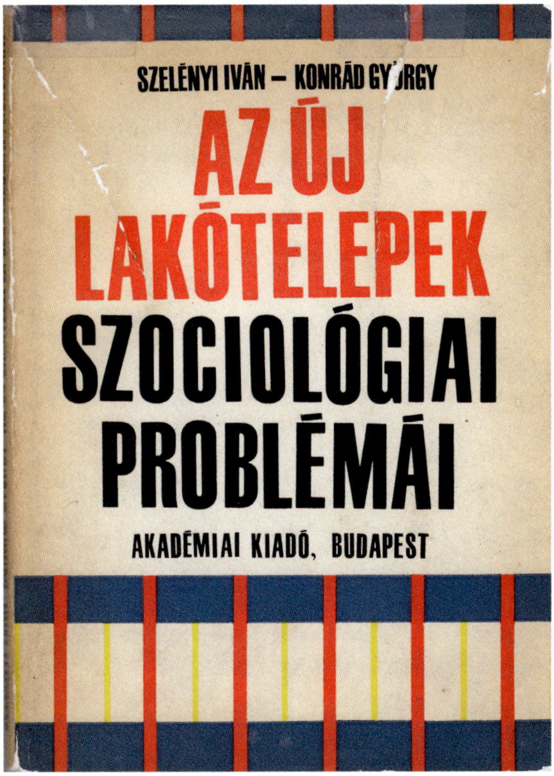

fig. 15 Cover of the book *Sociological Problems of New Housing Estates* written by György Konrád and Iván Szelényi (Budapest: Akadémiai Kiadó 1969).

as early as the late 1960s. Their profound analysis addressed the system's social vision and promises. The housing shortage triggered competition for relatively scarce new flats from which white-collar workers and the intelligentsia benefited – in opposition to state ideology. Standardized, expensive housing production resulted in a homogeneous and inflexible housing stock without the necessary differentiation: without the construction of cheaper flats for first-time buyers, for example, in order to foster mobility[40] (fig. 15).

The newly built city districts were, according to these urban sociologists, neither urban nor rural in character. These highly subsidized, territorially concentrated housing developments had other undesirable consequences: neglected old-city districts declined, the middle class moved away (to new housing estates, for instance) and slums arose. Their final conclusion was as follows: "when the differentiation in architecture does not match the real differences in society in an appropriate manner, it fosters the increase of social differences and inequalities and causes new segregation."[41]

The efforts towards pluralism, social control and autonomy ran against the very principles of the existing centralized system and its institutions. The defeat of the Prague Spring heightened doubts about the possibilities of fundamental reform and regarding the notion of "socialism with a human face" in general.[42] Instead of embarking on a necessary change of course, the rigid political regime increased the quantity of housing production in number and scale until the economic and systemic crisis of the late 1970s and early 1980s, leaving a troublesome legacy for the built environment, its inhabitants and the architectural profession alike.

Endnotes

1 The title alludes to a system-critical work from the early 1970s, not to be published until the collapse of the regime: György Bence, János Kis and György Márkus, *Hogyan lehetséges kritikai gazdaságtan? [Is Critical Economics Possible After All?]* (Budapest: T-Twins Kiadó, Lukács Archívum, 1992 [1970–1972]). All translations from Hungarian by the author.

2 Iván Szelényi: "A Kádár-korszak lehetőségei és korlátjai. Útinapló a hatvanas évek Magyarországából," http://*egyenlito.eu*/szelenyi-ivan-a-kadar-korszak-lehetosegei-es-korlatjai-utinaplo-a-hatvanas-evek-magyarorszagabol-1/, http://*egyenlito.eu*/szelenyi-ivan-a-kadar-korszak-lehetosegei-es-korlatjai-utinaplo-a-hatvanas-evek-magyarorszagabol-2/. Iván Szelényi (1938) is a Hungarian-American Sociologist who had to leave Hungary because of political reasons in 1974.

3 E. g., the famous debate about humanism between Sartre and Heidegger in 1945 and 1946. Cf. Thomas Baldwin: "The Humanist Debate," Brian Leiter – Michael Rosen eds.), *The Oxford Handbook of Continental Philosophy*, (Oxford, New York: Oxford University Press 2008), 671–710; related to architecture: Paul Zucker: "The Humanistic Approach to Modern Architecture," *The Journal of Aesthetics and Art Criticism* Vol. 2, No. 7 (Winter, 1942–1943), 21–26, or the resolution of the first postwar Congress of CIAM in Bridgwater 1947. Sigfried Giedion (ed.), *A Decade of New Architecture* (Zurich: Editions Girsberger, 1951), 22–23.

4 See English version of Khrushev's speech in *Architecture Culture 1943–1968: A Documentary Anthology*, ed. Joan Ockman (New York: Columbia Books of Architecture / Rizzoli, 1993), 184–188.

5 Ibid., 188.

6 http://www3.sympatico.ca/robsab/debate.html; http://www.foia.cia.gov/sites/default/files/document_conversions/16/1959-07-24.pdf

7 Resolution of the Council of Ministries 1002/1960 (10. 01. 1960). Zsuzsa Körner – Márta Nagy, *Az európai és a magyar telepszerű lakásépítés története 1945–től napjainkig* (Budapest: Terc Kiadó, 2006), 162.

8 *Vita építészetünk helyzetéről* (Budapest: Magyar Képzőművészek és Iparművészek Szövetsége, 1951).

9 János Bonta, "Tanulságok és prognosis," *Magyar Építőművészet*, 9:2 (1960), 16–23; Bonta, *Építészet és tömegtermelés* (Budapest: Műszaki Kiadó, 1963).

10 Máté Major, "Negyven esztendő," *Magyar Építőművészet* 8:1–2 (1959), 3 (p. 3).

11 Major, "A kultúra forradalma hassa át építészetünket!", *Magyar Építőművészet* 6:5–6 (1957), 115–116 (p. 115).
12 Major, "Kapitalista építészet – szocialista építészet," *Társadalmi Szemle* 9:8–9 (1964), 77–83.
13 Dr. Jenő Szendrői and József Schall, "Interbau 1957," *Magyar Építőművészet*, 7:13 (1958), 1–10.
14 *Magyar Építőművészet*, 8:1–2 (1959), 5–77.
15 Bonta, "Új vonások a modern építészetben," *Magyar Építőművészet*, 8:7–8 (1959), 253–258.
16 Elemér Nagy, "Gondolatok az építészet új vonásairól," *Magyar Építőművészet* 8:7–8 (1959), 260.
17 Tibor Valuch, *Magyarország társadalomtörténete a XX. század második felében* (Budapest: Osiris, 2001), 293.
18 Mariann Simon, "'Taste Must Arise from the Doctrine': Architecture in the Hungarian Cultural Media in the 1960s," *sITA. studies in History & Theory of Architecture*, 1 (2013), 30–42.
19 Mihály Váci, "Se az atombomba, se az isten," *Új Írás*, 1:9 (1961), 579–580 (p. 580).
20 Gyula Sipos, "Kinek építkezünk?", *Kortárs*, 6 (1960), 920–925.
21 Major, "'Sziget'– ház, 'sziget'– lakás vagy kollektív otthon?", *Kortárs*, 11 (1960), 749–754 (p. 753).
22 Ibid, 756.
23 Endre Koltai, "Új igények a lakástervezésben," *Műszaki Tervezés*, 9 (1962), 1–5.
24 Dezső Cserba, "Esztétika a mai építészetben," *Magyar Építőművészet* 9:2 (1960), 60.
25 Imre Egressy, "Kísérleti lakások, új berendezések az óbudai lakótelepen," *Magyar Építőművészet*, 10:1 (1961), 4–13 (p. 4). For a comprehensive overview and catalogue of the estate, see Márta Branczik and Márkus Keller, *Korszerű lakás 1960. Az óbudai kísérlet* (Budapest: Terc Kiadó, 2011).
26 Egressy, "Kísérleti lakások," 5.
27 See Elemér Zalotay, "Egy 'nehéz ember," *Új Írás* 5:6 (1965): 67–77 (p. 69).
28 See Zsuzsa Körner – Márta Nagy, *Az európai és a magyar telepszerű lakásépítés története 1945–től napjainkig*, 281.
29 József Katona, ed., *Építésiparosítás, műszaki tervezés, tipizálás* (Budapest: Típustervező Intézet, 1969).
30 István Csekma and Bálint Pethe, "Hazai paneles lakóházak és a világszínvonal," *Magyar Építőipar*, 13 (1963/11), 689–706.
31 Zsuzsa Körner – Márta Nagy, *Az európai és a magyar telepszerű lakásépítés története 1945–től napjainkig*, 244.
32 Péter Haba and Mariann Simon, "A Difficult Person for Socialism: Elemér Zalotay and His Strip Building," in *Architecture and the Paradox of Dissidence*, ed. Ines Weizman (Abingdon, Oxford: Routledge, 2013), 45–58.
33 Árpád Mester, "Az Asua völgy – Bilbao," *Magyar Építőművészet*, 12:2 (1963), 4–5.
34 Tibor Tenke, "Gondolatok 'Az ember és a gazdaságosság az építésiparosításban' c. tanulmányhoz," *Magyar Építőművészet*, 10:5 (1961), 48–50 (p. 49).
35 Árpád Mester, "Budapest XV. Páskomliget – Újpalota részletes a terve," *Magyar Építőművészet*, 17:5 (1968), 32–33 (p. 32).

36 Tibor Tenke, "Ismételt felhasználás formalakítási kísérletei," *Magyar Építőipar* 15:4–5 (1966), 226–232 (p. 232).
37 Jenő Szendrői, et al., *Magyar építészet 1945–1970* (Budapest: Műszaki Kiadó, 1972), 9.
38 Pál Granasztói, "A hazai urbanisztika problémáiról," *Társadalmi Szemle*, 23:3 (1968), 30–39 (pp. 36–39).
39 Iván Szelényi and György Konrád, "A késleltetett városfejlődés társadalmi konfliktusai," *Valóság*, 12 (1971), 19–35.
40 Szelényi, Konrád, *Az új lakótelepek szociológiai problémája* (Budapest: Akadémiai Kiadó, 1969).
41 Szelényi, Konrád, "A késleltetett városfejlődés," 35.
42 The fate of Iván Szelényi and György Konrád illustrates the end of all hope. Arrested in 1974 because of their system-critical manuscript *The Road of Intelligentsia to Class Power*, Szelényi was expelled from the country, while Konrád chose to remain in Hungary although publication of his works was officially prohibited.

Wojciech Bałus

Mieczysław Porębski: Man and Architecture in the Iconosphere

I.

> A complete renewal and transformation of the architectural image of the world that surrounds us already seems to be a necessity and it appears to be quite easy to implement today. Automation and miniaturization of production, the shifting underground of excessively burdensome industrial transport and its warehouse and refuse base, the liberation of the surface of the earth from superfluous and cancerous developments, a reconstruction on the broadest possible scale of the natural landscape and the historical substance of urban centers, a new conception of linear settlement that piles up in open spaces – constitute but one, maybe even the easiest side of the problem. The other side is infinitely more difficult, as it can neither be solved by the introduction of new technology, nor by new organization. It may only be attained by new spatial poetics which will restore sense and dignity to the place of every man and, at the same time, of the whole of mankind on this devastated though still living planet.[1]

The above was written in 1972 by Mieczysław Porębski, an art critic, theoretician and art historian, one of the pioneers of research on twentieth-century art in Poland[2] (fig. 1). Born in 1921, this ex-prisoner of the concentration camps in Gross-Rosen and Sachsenhausen had graduated from the department of art history in Kraków after the war. Since the time of the German occupation of Poland, Porębski had been closely associated with Tadeusz Kantor, a painter and subsequently the creator of the influential theater Cricot II. In 1949, Porębski left Poland for France, where he became acquainted with surrealist circles and familiarized himself with the publications of Georges Bataille and

fig. 1 Mieczysław Porębski, Photo: Adam Rzepecki, Institute of Art History of the Jagiellonian University in Krakow.

Roger Caillois. After a short socialist-realist episode in the early 1950s, during the post-Stalin political thaw (that is, after 1955), he once again became interested in the modern world as well as in Polish art (in the works of painters grouped around Kantor, among others). Porębski's successive scholarship in Paris (1960–1961) brought about his fascination with semiotics, structuralism and information theory; it also aroused his interest in the writings of Norbert Wiener, Claude Lévi-Strauss, Roland Barthes and archaeologist André Leroi-Gourhan.[3] Yet he remained totally impervious to existentialism.[4] From his return until 1970, Porębski resided in Warsaw, where he worked as a lecturer at the Academy of Fine Arts. Afterwards, he obtained the post of professor of art history at the Jagiellonian University in Kraków, where he continued to work until his retirement. He was a member of the Communist Party until 1981. He died in 2012 at the age of 91.

The quotation at the start of this chapter has been taken from Porębski's book *Ikonosfera* [*Iconosphere*] (fig. 2). In this publication, he tried to create the foundations of a complex theory of art that would combine into a coherent whole all symptoms of human creative activity from the first Palaeolithic rock paintings to pop art, *Nouveau réalisme* and happenings. The book not only explained the causes of the changes that art had undergone over the course of its existence, it also diagnosed its contemporary condition.

The excerpt quoted was incorporated in *Iconosphere* to sum up the chapter devoted to architecture. It has a particularly "prophetic" overtone that is not present with such intensity in other parts of the book. One is struck not only by the author's care for the endangered earth, but above all by a certain visionary eloquence stripped of all criticism. Porębski oversteps his professional competence. In a book devoted to the theory of art and culture, he writes without any reference to scientific prognoses or architectural theories about "shifting underground the entire industrial transport" system, doing

fig. 2 Mieczysław Porębski, *Ikonosfera* (Warsaw, 1972), cover of the book.

away with "cancerous housing developments" and implementing new urban conceptions characterized by "linear settlement." At the same time, he talks of the need to "renew the architectural image of the world" and of restoring to man his dignity and sense of life; according to the author, these goals can only be implemented with the help of a "new spatial poetic," that is, artistic activity.

II.

If Porębski's bold visions of the future – in which the entire industrial transport system was to be moved underground and "cancerous developments" as well as warehouses and refuse-storage sites were to disappear entirely from the surface of the planet – may be regarded as influenced by futurology, which was fashionable in the 1960s, his conception of linear settlement is quite a different story. Ignoring at this point the obvious references to utopian ideas, which – as shown by Colin Rowe – were reborn at that time among architects, the concepts of linear cities originated in the thinking of various architects during the Cold War period.[5] In postwar Poland, the most well-known project was the Linear Continuous System (LCS), proposed by architect Oskar Hansen, a professor at the Warsaw Academy of Fine Arts.[6]

In 1968, Porębski participated in a debate that was published in the journal *Projekt*; it is worth mentioning here that at that time he worked together with Hansen at the same academy.[7] Porębski was not an uncritical enthusiast of Hansen's concept. If in this vision of the future he saw some hope for humanity in the realization of a "band settlement that piled up in the open spaces," it was because he regarded the uncontrolled growth of the existing metropolises as a greater threat.[8] In his novel *Z.*, published in 1989, which constituted a literary attempt to sum up his many years of long reflections on the essence of history, he described his view of what a historian would see in the year 2045, repeating his well-known metaphor of cancer:

> up until now, the entire multi-billion growth of world population has been absorbed by the continually expanding cities, or rather, to be more precise, by these urbanized slums, which the former metropolises, perishing in this encirclement, have had accumulating around them. There was no chance to [...] control the tightening grip; the conurbations surrounded by this living, cancerous tissue became rapidly devalued; the increasingly obsolete and non-renewable industry abandoned these places, whereas the social and cultural facilities crumbled and disintegrated.[9]

III.

In the opening quotation from Porębski's writings, the author summoned a renewal of the architectural image of the world. He did so not only in response to the notion of the "cancerous tissue" of cities that could have posed a threat to mankind in the future, but also because the architecture arising right in front of the eyes constituted, as he put it, "only a vast amorphous housing, an anonymous multi-segment macro-shell which gave no possibility of self-definition."[10]

Porębski defined urban design and architecture as a "*technique* and *a system of communication* which speaks about *space with the language of space* with respect to its natural and arbitrary divisions and peculiarities, and to the significance it has for the man who lives and works in it."[11] This definition was a consequence of the author's conception of culture as a system of communication.[12] For Porębski, human creativity carried, above all, a message which allowed both old and new societies to exist and function together. At the same time, though relying strongly on the achievements of semiotics and information theory, he vehemently opposed the tendency to limit all forms of human communication to a linguistic model. Hence he emphasized that architecture speaks with the "language of space." This language has a completely different structure than the language of words. The latter consists of "particles," distinguished and isolated through a system of differences. In the language of space, there are no individual particles combined with each other to form sensible bigger units, like sounds, syllables, words, or sentences and complex narrations. Architecture is defined in turn by "boxlike" structures.

Buildings enclose a certain space and, at the same time, they themselves are located in a spatial environment. This environment usually consists of more than one building. This way, there arises a conglomerate of separate internal spaces, enclosed and filled with human artifacts, and with continuous and empty external spaces which flow between the external shapes of buildings, leading out of the urban organism to rural areas, fields, forests and, subsequently, to other human communities.

As a "system of communication" mentioned in the definition, architecture transcends its physical localization. According to Porębski, buildings may acquire their sense as either metaphors or metonymies: "The saying: 'My home – my world' constitutes an architectural metonymy, whereas the saying: 'My home – my castle' is an architectural metaphor."[13] A prototype of an architectural metonymy is a prehistoric cave, a "symbol of a life-giving Mother's womb, from which everything takes its origin and to which everything returns to renew its strength and resources."[14] In the nineteenth century, an apartment in a tenement building fulfilled this role and, in particular, its living room, that public space in the middle of a private space: "a separate, fragmentary world of a middle class interior with the mandatory private shrine – the salon: grand piano or piano, music scores, a glass cabinet, a whatnot with books, patriotic prints, a portrait, a watercolor landscape on the wall, a lamp with a shade, a Columbine and Pierrot in the corner on the sofa, an album with family photos and artistic postcards and another one brought from abroad, and a third one brought from the latest world exhibition."[15]

While metonymy often treats a part as a whole (a cave isolated from a vast massif as a synecdoche of the womb of the Great Mother, a middle-class salon as *pars pro toto* of the world), metaphor "becomes like or distinguishes itself in relation to analogous wholes." Metonymy "has a share in the mysteries of the entire universe which is concentrated in it" – that is, in the building – whereas metaphor "protects one's own mysteries against this universe; it informs and misinforms, teaches and deludes."[16] The architectural metaphor reveals itself in the shape of a building or on its facade. Sumerian ziggurats rise up to the skies like great mountains, whereas decorations of abutments on Greek temples, Romanesque portals and Gothic churches reveal theophanic religious truths.

According to Porębski, since early modern times the metaphoric properties of architecture had begun to shrink, while its former suggestive power has moved on to the technical and architectural equipment of transport:

> It is no longer the ancient and mediaeval city walls, the church or fortified castle towers rising up to the skies and not even the border defense structures such as the Roman limes or the Chinese wall together with the

> internal network of land and sea routes, but the caravels, galleons and frigates, the nineteenth-century steamship, the steam train engine, the twentieth-century car and airplane, and finally the space ship with the entire necessary equipment, port facilities, a system of railways and thoroughfares, railway stations, airports and cosmodromes, that constitute the proper metaphoric and metaphorizing facade of contemporary man and his world. The latter is far more powerful and more suggestive than what is still commonly regarded as architecture today.[17]

Although in his speculations concerning the language of architecture Porębski called external space – into which boxlike buildings have been inserted – an "empty space," he at the same time emphasized strongly that since time immemorial the human experience of space had had axiological character. In one of his subsequent articles, he distinguished a continuous and empty physical space from the axiologically marked, anthropological, symbolic space.[18] In *Iconosphere*, he remarked that:

> *from the beginning* and *by the very nature of things* the human habitat is a qualified, functionally and emotionally heterogeneous space. This habitat has always possessed its own natural, more or less visible and discernible borders beyond which everything that is familiar, acquired, expected and everyday comes to an end. It possesses its own natural orientation, clear-cut directions […] It also possesses from the very beginning what can be described as top and bottom.[19]

Following French anthropologists, Porębski subsequently referred to this primal diversification of symbolic space as the spheres of *sacrum* and *profanum.* Similarly to Stefan Czarnowski, a Polish disciple of Emile Durkheim, he wrote that there exists an internal sacrum where organized rituals and customs predominate, as well as an external sacrum which is unbridled, demonic and wild. Symbolic space has a concentric structure (fig. 3). At its center, one finds the city with a temple in the middle (*temenos, templum*); the city is surrounded with walls (*pomoerium*). Beyond city walls, one finds a hostile, alien world, which is unspecified and divided into zones which are less and less cognized and more and more wild: *ager effatus* (zone of agricultural produce), *ager peregrinus* (zone intersected by the routes of neighborly peregrinations), *ager hosticus* (alien and principally hostile zone) and *ager incertus* (zone where unknown powers hold sway). Wanderers from this external world sometimes do find their way to the city; they are, for the most part, merchants, prophets and jugglers who appear and perform in the agora, which is a specific outpost of the external sacrum in the area enclosed by city walls.[20]

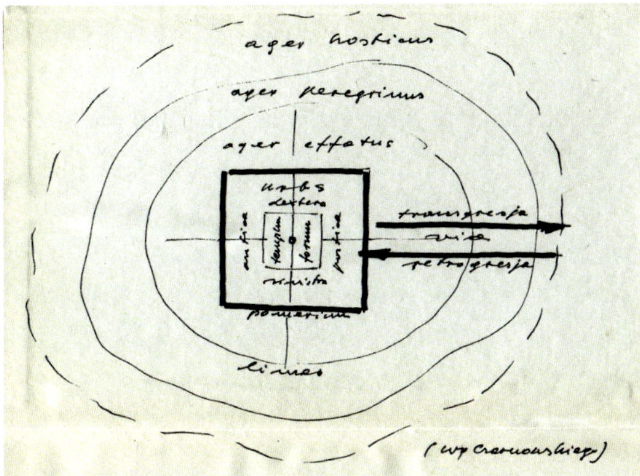

fig. 3 Mieczysław Porębski, diagram of the internal and external *sacrum*, drawing published in his book *Sztuka a informacja* (Kraków, 1986).

As a consequence of Europe's expansion onto other continents, this experience of space began to change. Caravels, steamships, cars and spaceships have shifted the boundaries of the known and tamed world beyond the earth's borders right up to the moon (Porębski published *Iconosphere* three years after the Apollo 11 mission). In this way, it was the technical means of transport that became the modern-day *pomoerium* – the boundary and outpost of human culture. Naturally, it was a metaphorical boundary that took over the meanings which had earlier been anchored in architecture. Airports, railway stations, airplanes and cars began to express not so much the power of a deity but the might of man, his glory and greatness.

However, if there is no more room for a city surrounded by walls and for *ager effatus, peregrinus, hosticus* and *incertus* in modern-day space, the only sensible new urban proposition for the future becomes a linear development which takes into consideration a system of highways and express trains, one that treats the entire territories of states and continents as an axiologically uniform, internal, controlled and tamed area of social activity. Yet this did not mean that the author excluded altogether the so-called focal points within the individual stretches, as he described them during the *Projekt* debate on Hansen's LCS project; for the need to organize spatial centers was "archetypically" rooted in human nature.[21]

IV.

When on February 1, 1972, Porębski had finished writing *Iconosphere*, Europe had just emerged from a series of serious social and political upheavals. The year 1968 had changed the social and mental order of the Western world, whereas the events in Poland and Czechoslovakia had revealed the imperialist, nationalistic and anti-Semitic faces of the communist system.[22] December

1970 had brought strikes along the Polish coast as well as demonstrations in Gdańsk that were brutally suppressed by the militia (the Communist police). The era of utopian faith in the possibility of creating a "socialist system with a human face" had come to an end.

Porębski was a witness to the tragic events in Poland. Although he must have seen the student demonstrations and the brutal militia interventions of on the streets in Warsaw in March 1968, he wrote no word about the political dimension of the public sphere. In *Iconosphere*, we find no passage about the relation between the urban space and state or ideological power.

Porębski's strategy was dictated not so much by his awareness of the presence of censorship, which surely would not have allowed obvious allusions to the inconveniences of life under communism, but rather by a conscious decision to ignore political barriers so as to incorporate his reflection into the main current of the arguments and debates taking place in the West at that time. It was a rather typical attitude among Polish intellectuals at that time; despite the cold war and the difficulties in foreign travel, most tried not to lose touch with Western civilization.[23] But the decision not to comment on political differences illustrated the author's tacit agreement to the existing order in Europe, which could not be changed and in which one had to continue living, whether one wanted to or not.

After the Stalinist period in Poland, one of the ways to go beyond the opposition of the two major political systems was modernization. This gave a feeling of participation in the main current of world development. Porębski also thought along these lines. In *Iconosphere,* modern technology – cars, airplanes, ships and space rockets – clashed with amorphous contemporary architecture as well as with meticulously depicted middle-class nineteenth-century interiors, echoing the contrastive juxtapositions found in Le Corbusier's *Vers une architecture* [*Towards a New Architecture*]. In the Swiss architect's words, "Tail pieces and garlands, exquisite ovals where triangular doves preen themselves or one another, boudoirs embellished with 'poufs' in gold and black velvet, are now no more than the intolerable witnesses to a dead spirit."[24] And he adds: "If we forget for a moment that a steamship is a machine used for transportation and look at it with a fresh eye, we shall feel that we are facing an important manifestation of temerity, of discipline, of harmony, of a beauty that is calm, vital and strong."[25] Nearly fifty years separated the publication of *Towards a New Architecture* and the first edition of *Iconosphere.* Through studying the products of technology, Le Corbusier had shown modern architects a way out of historicism and past academic rules. But Porębski came to the conclusion that the experiment had not succeeded. In the second half of the twentieth century, technology continued to retain its avant-garde character, whereas architectural modernism only replaced the former insincerity of historical styles and of middle-class interiors with a "completely amorphous architecture, characterized by an anonymous, multi-segment macro-shell, which gave no chance of a self-definition." Modern buildings were not capable of fulfilling their informative function because modernists were incapable of turning their creations into metonymies or metaphors. In this respect, there was no difference between the capitalist and socialist worlds.

But the informative function, this semantic surplus, had not disappeared from the world altogether. It had only moved away from architecture to the products of modern technology and civilization, Porębski wrote. "The only ways of escape which allow it [contemporary architecture] to move beyond its own territory are TV, cinema, one's own 'four wheels' of appropriate class and character."[26] The first two were for the author a modern-day embodiment of metonymy, which gave the possibility of "collective initiations and metonymic participations."[27] The car, on the other hand (most probably following Roland Barthes' *Mythologies*), was becoming a metaphor that mythologized the owner's status. As Barthes noted: "I think that cars today are almost the exact equivalent of the great Gothic cathedrals: I mean the supreme creation of an era, conceived with passion by unknown artists, and consumed in image if not usage by a whole population which appropriates them as a purely magical object."[28]

V.

In *Iconosphere,* Porębski tried to describe a new cultural formation arising out of technological progress right before his eyes. He observed that the civilization of print was coming to an end while the civilization of mass communication, in which images would fulfill the fundamental informative role, was taking its place. These images ceased to belong to the sphere of art and began to lead a life of their own:

> The man of the second half of the twentieth century no longer looks for the first information and initiations that are important for him in books or in what may be referred to as literature of artistic or musical images. [...] He looks for the *first, initiating* information on the radio, on television, in the cinema, in a shop window, on advertisements or propaganda posters, in a magazine richly illustrated with colored photographs, in publications which have glossy covers and which can easily be folded and put in one's pocket.[29]

As a result of the expansion of new media, the urban-architectural external space of cities began to change, as did the internal space of homes and apartments. Advertisements, neon signs, shop windows, posters, traffic lights and TV sets in homes created an environment permanently filled with images the author referred to as the iconosphere. The reality of the iconosphere had shaped the world of man then to such an extent that even the forms for expressing prestige had shifted from traditional media, such as architecture and visual arts, to images such as the car; contact with what was important was now supplied by a TV set.

Porębski did not have a critical view of the changes taking place in culture. He noticed and described them, leaving critical commentary on these phenomena to art itself. Yet he concluded that Dadaism, surrealism, pop art, happening and hyper-realism did not became immersed in the new reality for the purpose of creating a new mimesis: "A pop picture is an image of a new, superior type, an image of the image, not its copy, replica or amplification. Its object is not the reality of modern man, for this we know from elsewhere, but its specific language, the language of iconic stereotypes, conventions and symbols."[30] The essence of the new art became "*the portrayal of the portrayal* – an evolution of all transformations, a realization of their effects and determination of its scope."[31]

In the section devoted to architecture from which the opening quote of this chapter is taken, Porębski postulated the need for a "complete renewal and transformation of the architectural image of the world that surrounds us" while at the same time pointing to the decisive role of a "new spatial poetics, restoring sense and dignity to every man's place," in this respect. However, we do not learn from *Iconosphere* what this new poetics should look like. Porębski's article about the multiplicity of space, published a few years later, does not explain this issue either. We learn from it that:

> creating space within a space [...] may be effected in various ways: either directly through shaping our architectural, urban, or landscape surroundings; through closing and extending, or through opening windows onto other spaces in this surrounding, through suggesting by various means a scenic or artistic illusion. It may also be created through placing in it three-dimensional images of residents (or envoys) of the other spaces – idols, silhouettes, monuments or statues.[32]

The author made diagnoses, but did not specify which roads to follow in the future.

Porębski's approach strikes one particularly when juxtaposing his presentation of iconosphere with the slightly earlier analysis by Guy Debord's of the society of the spectacle. For the French situationist, the contemporary primacy of sight and the transformation of the world into a visual representation were not simple facts belonging to the sphere of culture. "The spectacle," Debord wrote, "is the ruling order's nonstop discourse about itself, its never-ending monologue of self-praise, its self-portrait at the stage of totalitarian domination of all aspects of life."[33] In Porębski's writings, we shall not find an equally critical approach (Debord's book is regarded as one of the revolutionary fuses that had helped ignite the events of 1968 in France).[34] According to Porębski, the world should also solve burning issues associated with protection of the environment, urban design and humanization; and yet he does not indicate by what means these goals should be achieved. Where Debord treated Marxism as a call for revolution, Porębski in fact announced the end of history.

The author of *Iconosphere* explained the former festive, political and artistic negations of the social and political order by referring not only to the conception of the internal and external sacrum but also to Bataille's *Accursed Share*, where the need to destroy the surplus of accumulated goods is explained by means of the category of transgression.[35] While analyzing twentieth-century reality, Porębski concluded that all revolutionary movements had a transgressive character. They had assumed the function of instruments helping to relieve accumulated social tension. The victory of the Bolshevik revolution, aided by avant-garde art that was subversive in character and that targeted existing, ritual academic art, had led to ultimate transgression. "For if," he wrote, "the essence of every revolution, likewise of every holiday, is *transgression – a spectacular contravention* of the normal, socially sanctioned order of things, festive transgression should be looked upon as temporary and recurrent, while revolutionary transgression as permanent and irreversible."[36]

In a reality encapsulated by the victorious revolution, no new transgression could have taken place. Naturally, the author was aware of the existence of both capitalist and socialist states, but he treated this condition as a permanent one. In his analysis, he consciously ignored political motifs, as he did not take into consideration a change of the post-Yalta political order. Thus, in his conception of architectural space, there were no references to the political sphere. He regarded the streets as empty spaces, not as zones of social argument or places marked by domination of power. Hence, in his presentation, the Iron Curtain did not assume the shape of a new *pomoerium*, but neither had it disappeared altogether in favor of conviction about the unbounded expansion of a tamed, uniform world stretching off as far as the moon.

For Porębski, contemporary man was a consumer of the iconosphere, someone who accepted technological modernization and who discovered in the products of modern technology materials for the creation of up-to-date metaphors and mythologies. This man, who had been evicted from middle-class interiors, now lived in lackluster interiors, or even in houses that reminded one of cancerous growths accumulated around the historical tissue of former cities. But his problem consisted of not so much a lack of his own, separate and tamed space in the form of an internal home sacrum, but exclusively in the general nondescript character of architecture and "the inability to organize space in city centers."[37]

The juxtaposition of Porębski and Debord illustrates effectively the conditions in which intellectuals behind the Iron Curtain had to work and live. For them, history had been a closed chapter. The victorious revolution we read about in *Iconosphere* involves both the events of 1917 and the metaphor of Yalta. The political reality was seen as determined once and for all by the stranglehold between the US and the USSR. Thus, one could not appeal for change, as had been done by the situationists, as this would not bring about any results. It would not bring change in the future as one could not hope to alter the political system, and it would not bring changes in the present as one could easily lose one's personal freedom by upholding subversive political views.

At the same time, intellectuals behind the Iron Curtain tried not to lose touch with the West. Porębski's conceptions concerned the culture of the twentieth century in general, as if the unity of Europe could easily become a fact. In the communist camp, the road to this much-dreamed-of unity was to lead through modernization – the local variety of a modernist regeneration myth.[38] In the sphere of technology, it was to bring a development of the iconosphere, and in art, an acceptance and assimilation of current artistic trends. Meanwhile in architecture, which was being criticized for its amorphous, anonymous, lackluster character and cancerous urban development, it was to lead to a realization of more interesting and sounder conceptions of linear development. Yet all of this could only be implemented on the condition that modernization received a more "human dimension"; in other words, that new, humanistic poetics were found for the development of the future. As repeated above, Porębski did not specify what this new poetics should look like. It was supposed to simply be better, more convenient and more people-friendly; it was also supposed to be more humane in the midst of the political reality, which in the existing circumstances appeared impossible to change…

Endnotes

I would like to express my thanks to Carolyn Guile, PhD, for checking and correcting language in the present paper. –W.B.

1 Mieczysław Porębski, *Ikonosfera* (Warsaw: PIW, 1972), 169. All translations, unless otherwise indicated, are from the author. The last chapter of the book was published in English as "The Iconosphere," *Polish Perspectives*, 6:11 (1973), 10–20; the book appeared in Yugoslavia as: Mječislav *Porempski, Ikonosfera*, trans. Peter Vujičič (Belgrad: Prosveta, 1978).

2 Krystyna Czerni, "Mieczysław Porębski (1921–2012)," *Biuletyn Historii Sztuki*, 75:3 (2013), 591–605.

3 Porębski, *Granica współczesności 1909–1925* (Warsaw: WAiF, 1989), 416.

4 Porębski, *Pożegnanie z krytyką* (Kraków: WL, 1983), 63.

5 Colin Rowe, "Die Architektur Utopias," in *Die Mathematik der idealen Villa und andere Essays*, trans. Christoph Schnoor (Basel/Berlin/Boston: Birkhäuser Verlag, 1988), 209–226 (pp. 221–225); Andrzej Szczerski, "LSC, or What Is a City?", in *Oskar Hansen: Opening Modernism. On Open Form Architecture, Art and Didactics*, eds. Aleksandra Kędziorek, Łukasz Ronduda (Warsaw: Museum of Modern Art, 2014), 91–113.

6 Tadeusz Zaleski, "Polish Plans for Linear Cities," *The Architect*, 1:3 (1971), 71–72; Łukasz Stanek, "Team 10 East: The Socialist State as an Architectural Project," in *Oskar Hansen*, 61–88; Piotr Juszkiewicz, *Cień modernizmu* (Poznań: Wydawnictwo Naukowe UAM, 2013), 84–126.

7 "Linearny System Ciągły/The Linear Continuous System/Le Système Linéaire Continu," *Projekt*, 64 (1968), 37–51.

8 Ibid., 49.

9 Porębski, *Z. Po-wieść* (Warsaw: PIW, 1989), 457.

10 Porębski, *Ikonosfera*, 168.

11 Ibid., 153–154.

12 Wojciech Bałus, "'Der verfemte Teil'. Die polnische Kunstgeschichte und der kommunistische Diskurs nach dem Tod Stalins," *Kunsttexte.de/Ostblick. E-Journal für Kunst- und Bildgeschichte*, 4 (2015), accessed April 20, 2016, http://edoc.hu-berlin.de/kunsttexte/2015-4/balus-wojciech-6/PDF/balus.pdf.

13 Porębski, *Ikonosfera*, 163.

14 Ibid., 164.

15 Ibid., 167; see also Jürgen Habermas, *The Structural Transformation of the Public Sphere*, trans. Thomas Burger (Cambridge, Mass.: MIT Press, 1991), 45.

16 Ibid., 164.

17 Ibid., 167–168.

18 Porębski, "Wielość przestrzeni," in *Sztuka a informacja* (Kraków: WL, 1986). 215–224 (p. 217).

19 Ibid., 152–153.

20 Porębski, *Ikonosfera*, 126–127; also "Wielość przestrzeni," 217–218.

21 "Linearny System Ciągły," 46, 49, 50.

22 *Rewolucje 1968*, ed. Hanna Wróblewska, et al. (Warsaw: Agora SA, 2008).

23 See Bałus, "Die Sigismundkapelle in Krakau – oder die Renaissanceforschung zwischen dem wissenschaftlichen Diskurs der Stalinzeit und dem Venezianischen Spiegel des Eisernen Vorhangs," *Ars*, 48:2 (2015), 145–159 (pp. 156–157).

24 Le Corbusier, *Towards a New Architecture,* transl. Frederick Etchells (New York: Dover Publications, 1986), 91.
25 Ibid., 102–103.
26 Porębski, *Ikonosfera,* 168.
27 Ibid., 167.
28 Roland Barthes, "The New Citroën," in *Mythologies,* trans. Annette Lavers (New York: The Noonday Press, 1991), 88–90 (p. 88).
29 Porębski, *Ikonosfera,* 110.
30 Porębski, "The Iconosphere," 20; Porębski, *Ikonosfera,* 285.
31 Ibid., 20; 285.
32 Porębski, "Wielość przestrzeni," 220.
33 Guy Debord, *The Society of the Spectacle,* trans. Ken Knabb (Canberra: Treaston Press, 2002), 9 (para. 24).
34 Jarosław Lubiak, "Sytuacje rozkoszy. Sytuacjonistyczna rewolucja życia codziennego," *Rewolucje 1968,* 21–26 (pp. 21–22).
35 Bałus, "'Der verfemte Teil.'"
36 Porębski, *Ikonosfera,* 120–121.
37 Porębski in the discussion "Formy przestrzenne w krajobrazie miasta / Spatial Forms in an Urban Landscape/Les formes spatiales dans le paysage de la ville," *Projekt,* 66 (1968), 33–44 (p. 43).
38 Juszkiewicz, *Cień modernizmu,* 67–71.

II
Building New Societies

Hilde Heynen

Continuity or Discontinuity? Narratives on Modern Architecture in East and West Germany during the Cold War

In 1930, Alexander Schwab, a communist critic, diagnosed the "Janus face" (*Doppelgesicht*) of modern architecture: according to Schwab, the *Neues Bauen* – New Building, the German name for modern architecture – was both bourgeois and proletarian, high capitalist and socialist, autocratic and democratic. The same formal language, he argued, was in use for programs that were serving commerce and industry, as well as for emancipatory projects of social housing or educational institutions.[1] Given this Janus face, the different trajectories of the Weimar Republic's modern architects, some of whom ended up "East" and others "West," should come as no surprise. The trajectories of modern architects illustrate that their political allegiances were very diverse indeed. Some of the protagonists of CIAM were looking eastwards when it became impossible for them to continue their profession in Nazi Germany or its neighboring countries: Ernst May left Frankfurt for the Soviet Union in 1930, where his "May Brigades" planned and started constructing entire cities, among them Magnitogorsk; the Swiss, Hans Schmidt, was with May and continued working in the USSR until 1937, then afterwards cofounded the Swiss Communist Party in 1944 and held the Chair of Theory and History of Architecture in East Berlin from 1958; Hannes Meyer worked in the USSR as well, between 1930 and 1936, before leaving for Mexico.[2] Hence the choice of Walter Gropius, Mies van der Rohe, Ludwig Hilberseimer and Marcel Breuer, who rekindled their careers in the US, was not the only possibility. When conventional historiography tells the story of modern architecture it usually has its heroic stage playing out in Western Europe, then its postwar resurrection mainly happening in the US – but this outlook does not do justice to what was an extremely diversified constellation of socially motivated yet politically diverging architects. In particular, the way that modern architecture's evolution towards the "International Style" and an Americanized high modernism has been naturalized should be questioned. It is not, after all, as if all traces of modernism and its ideas were immediately vanquished in the parts of Europe that found themselves behind the Iron Curtain. During the postwar period there were still many artists, architects and intellectuals who had spent their formative years absorbing modernist culture and who hoped to realize their ideals in the newly-shaped countries of the East. It is therefore instructive to take a closer look at the two Germanies immediately after the war. We will do so by observing through a lens provided by Sibyl Moholy-Nagy.

Sibyl Moholy-Nagy on East and West Germany

Sibyl Moholy-Nagy (1903–1971) was an American architectural historian and critic, who had a very ambivalent relationship with her native Germany. She had left Germany in 1935, following her husband László first to London and then to Chicago, where she had tried to forge a career for herself as a writer, all the while assisting him in running the Institute of Design.[3] After László Moholy-Nagy's death in 1946, she became a teacher and an academic, publishing first his biography (*Experiment in Totality,* 1950) and later many articles and some other books (among them *Native Genius in Anonymous Architecture,* 1957, and *Matrix of Man,* 1968). Sibyl Moholy-Nagy's first trip back to Europe took place in 1950, when she delivered a series of lectures on her husband's work in several West German cities. Francesca Saunders assumes that these lectures were part of the cultural program financed by the CIA, meant to foster the image of America as the country where modern art could flourish because of the favorable circumstances offered by capitalism and democracy.[4] The lectures in Munich and Stuttgart were delivered in the so-called Amerikahaus, which is consistent with Saunders's assumption.[5] At this time, Moholy-Nagy was prohibited by the Russian and East German authorities from entering the eastern part of Germany, where she wanted to visit her father – the architect Martin Pietzsch – in her native Dresden. In a letter to Ilse Gropius, she mentions that she nevertheless managed to enter the GDR for two days with false papers, visiting an old school friend in Prenzlau.[6] Moholy-Nagy's next trip was made in 1955 and financed by securing lectures in different cities in West Germany (Stuttgart, Munich, Ulm, Braunschweig,

Berlin).[7] This time she did visit Dresden and she used her time well. Thus, upon her return she was able to publish two well-documented articles in the American architecture press: "Architecture of East Germany," anonymously published in *Architectural Forum* in July 1956, and "Berlin's International Building Exhibition 1957" in *Progressive Architecture* in August 1956.[8] It is worth comparing the articles, because they tell us on one hand something about Moholy-Nagy and her ideas about architecture and the city, but also about the Cold War context in which both texts were written.

The article on East Germany came out first. The editors of *Architectural Forum* introduce it by quoting one sentence as a baseline: "If West German architecture is bad, it is by default; in East Germany it is so by decree." They further frame it by telling readers to expect "a critical appraisal of the Communists' fanatical but narrow rebuilding program by a recent visitor behind the Iron Curtain who prefers to remain anonymous." Thus Moholy-Nagy's choice not to attach her name to this article, probably inspired by earlier difficulties in getting a visa, is presented as initially significant and proof of the ominous character of the Communist regime. Moholy-Nagy sets this article up in a comparative way: she contrasts what she finds in East Germany with what she saw in West Germany. She starts by highlighting the contrast between the "prosperous normal appearance of the western half of the city" of Berlin with "pauperism, depopulation and acres of ruins in the East Sector." The Stalinallee – the centerpiece of East German urbanism and architecture of the 1950s (renamed the Karl-Marx-Allee in 1961) – is denounced as showing a "startling resemblance to the *Mietskasernen*" in the old Berlin, with "uniform, eclectic clichés" for elevations. She also points out, however, that neoclassical, unimaginative architecture is also prominent in West Germany. "The difference," according to Moholy-Nagy, "lies in the rare exceptions that are possible in the West but unthinkable in the East" – referring to buildings by F. W. Kraemer in Braunschweig and Freimuth in Munich.

She then recalls her train ride to Dresden, accompanied by "Big Brother's loudspeaker," which continuously broadcasted biased news bulletins. The train ride also allowed her to see some of the worker settlements near factories and trade centers. These she found "less depressing than the miserable little *Eigenheim*" – the sprawl of single-family houses in West Germany. In Dresden, she is inevitably struck by the gigantic destruction and the vast openness of the historic center, where there were only a few islands of reconstruction (Moholy-Nagy doesn't mention that American and British bombs destroyed Dresden). She laments the "lifeless and mechanical" character of these reconstructions, which, she adds, are no better or worse than many similar examples in the West. "The natural aging of buildings," she observes, "is obviously more than structural survival [...]. It is a settling into environment, and a fusion of compatible building elements, that age as harmoniously as a good husband and wife."

Seeing few building, she wonders about the architects: where were they? She was told that both architecture schools in Dresden were turning out architects "at top speed," and that the focus for the moment was on rationalization and education. Her informant – a Dresden professor of architecture whose name isn't mentioned in the article – explained to her that "Typenprojektion"[9] (type projection) was the new task of German architecture. He referred to the instructions of "Comrade Khruschev [sic], first secretary of the [Russian] Communist Party," who called for the industrialization of building. Standardization was thus the motto of the day, reducing the wide variety of building elements to only a limited amount that could be produced much more efficiently; a system also advocated by Walter Ulbricht, the First Party Secretary of the GDR, in a speech delivered in April 1955 and quoted by Moholy-Nagy. She comments that this focus on rationalization, standardization and type projection sounds eerily familiar, since these concepts had been advocated by the German Werkbund before the First World War. Evoking the discussion between Muthesius and van de Velde, which dates back to 1914, and the Bauhaus book by Adolf Meyer from 1924, she claims that the excessive regimentation of East German architecture has its origin in the German past.

Whereas the article on East Germany is full of comparisons between East and West, "Berlin's International Building Exhibition 1957" is far less framed as such. It lacks the polemic tone and the aggressive introduction of its counterpart, and reads rather as a very informative piece, documenting and discussing urban plans for the Berlin Hansaviertel. These plans were already well developed in summer 1955, in preparation for the International Building Exhibition two years later. The article starts by evoking the "irreverent and indomitable" character of Berliners, which brought them to pursue such a large project in less than favorable circumstances (Moholy-Nagy mentions Berlin's geographical isolation as an urban enclave in Russian-dominated territory, its poor economic conditions and the lack of raw materials). She then discusses the competition for an urban plan, which was won by Kreuer, Jobst and Schliesser, with what she calls a "free-form" plan: "Building groups are emphatically isolated, with an average height of eight stories and astonishingly uniform plan patterns." Protests against this award came from both "the *schematic* forces" (with this term she refers to those adhering to traditional and uniform patterns) and from "the *organic* forces" (those rallying around Scharoun and opting for looser configurations). Otto Bartning was then commissioned "to coordinate both principles in a compromise scheme." She carefully compares Bartning's final scheme with the one originally awarded, blaming him for neglecting to provide well-defined neighborhoods or a civic center. She also quotes Scharoun criticizing Bartning's plan for "its lack of a carrying idea." The most important feature of the whole plan, however, should be that it provides ample opportunity for international architects to participate in the design of specific buildings. Moholy-Nagy mentions how both Mies and Le Corbusier were invited but declined (the latter not without making a great "show of acceptance and rejection" and managing to get a commission for another site in Berlin). Other projects however were well underway, such as the Z-shaped seventeen-story tower by Müller-Rehm & Siegmann, which encountered some difficulties because of the instability of the Berlin soil close to the Spree river. She further positively discusses Gropius's eight-story apartment house and Niemeyer's project, which promised to become the most impressive edifices of the whole. The article closes with a sober enumeration of all architects contributing to the Hansaviertel and by mentioning the dates of the exhibition (July 6 to September 29, 1957).

The Cold War Setting

By the time of Sibyl Moholy-Nagy's 1955 visit, the Cold War was well under way (although the Berlin Wall would only be built in 1961), and the two Germanies had increasingly consolidated their structures. In 1949, the two new states had been established: the Federal Republic of Germany on the Western side – a parliamentary democracy with a capitalist economy, benefitting from the Marshall Plan – and the German Democratic Republic on the Eastern side, a one-party state under the leadership of the SED (Socialist Unity Party of Germany) with a communist economy, firmly aligned with the Soviet Union. Architectural developments in both states thus began to diverge. Reconstruction in the West was tackled by larger subsidized projects, but also by giving room to private initiatives. There were a lot of competing tendencies and a lot of discussions, but many of the commissions for larger urban plans were given to modernist architects. In the East, everything was managed by the state; hence building guidelines came from state institutions. The close alliance with Moscow meant that these guidelines closely followed directives from there.

Thus, in the initial phase "socialist realism" was the catchphrase of the GDR: architects had to build with a socialist content and a national form.[10] Socialist realism had emerged in the 1930s as an alternative to Russian constructivism and modernism, because the Party did not consider new forms that were too radical the best way to impress the people: well-established "national" forms and formal languages were much more capable of producing art and architecture that meant something to the majority of workers.[11] The implementation of such ideas in the People's Republics of postwar Eastern Europe encountered some difficulties, but generally these instructions were taken seriously. For the GDR, this meant that "Sixteen Principles of Urban Reconstruction" were formulated in 1950 by a group of high-ranking architects and urban planners after a study trip to the Soviet Union.[12] The period of socialist realism however was short–lived, because in 1954 Khrushchev announced a reorientation. Embarking upon a process of de-Stalinization and the Thaw, he first signaled the changes to come through a remarkable initiative that focused completely on architecture and planning. In 1954, he delivered a speech to the All–Union Conference of Builders and Architects in Moscow, denouncing the practice of squandering money on excessive decoration and calling for an industrialization of construction.[13] This meant the end of socialist realism. From that point, socialist-realist architecture, which in East Germany was unofficially labeled *Zuckerbäckerstil* (confectioner style), was on its way out and *Plattenbau* (prefabricated construction) on its way in.

The Stalinallee, that centerpiece of East German architecture and urban planning, embodies this history in built form (fig. 1).[14] The Stalinallee comprises a large part of what is now the Karl-Marx- and Frankfurter Allees in the eastern part of Berlin. It was built between 1952 and 1958, providing five thousand dwellings in seven- to nine-story apartment buildings lining the wide avenue, with shops, restaurants and cafés on the ground floors. It was punctuated with tower-like structures at the corners of squares, thus forming clearly enclosed and well-defined urban spaces. The very first apartment buildings erected 1949–1950 along this avenue were two five-story modernist blocks designed by Ludmilla Herzenstein, an architect who had been a collaborator of Scharoun. These first buildings were designed in a functionalist way, before the "Sixteen Principles" had acquired legal status, and were afterwards severely criticized for being too "cosmopolitan" (a code word denouncing modernist architecture). The next group of buildings therefore would be the result of a competition, meant to ensure the socialist and monumental character of the Stalinallee. Walter Ulbricht, the Party leader, played an important role in setting up guidelines for this competition. These required that "the architecture of the housing blocks should critically value and process the best examples of the Berlin architectural tradition," among other criteria.[15] The jury awarded five different architects' collectives, which were each commissioned for one of the stretches. The collective around Hermann Henselmann built the most prominent parts, including the twin dome-crowned towers at the Frankfurter Tor (1953). The last parts that were

fig. 1 The Stalinallee under construction in 1960. This photograph shows the last stretch designed by Henselmann, which is somewhat more sober and rectilinear in its volumes. © Nico Jesse. Source: Nederlands Fotomuseum

built, however, were already showing a simpler tendency, favoring industrialized building and avoiding ornamentation.

The construction of the Stalinallee presented a huge effort from the still young GDR and was widely publicized. Professional journals such as *Deutsche Architektur* (the official architects' journal) discussed it as an excellent example of a socialist architecture that was built for people and not for profit. In the general press it was heralded as a magnificent place to live, where comfort and community as well as modern conveniences were abundantly available. It was portrayed in pamphlets, posters and books contrasting the reconstruction of East Berlin with the still war-torn neighborhoods in West Berlin. Special bus tours were organized to give West Berliners the chance to see what was being realized in the East.[16] These were the conditions which provoked West Berlin to answer with an equally ambitious scheme to show how a free society dealt with urban reconstruction. The project for the Hansaviertel thus started as a response to the Stalinallee – the idea allegedly took hold when an unnamed American official casually observed that West Berlin needed something like the Stalinallee (fig. 2).[17] The Hansaviertel indeed became in many ways the opposite of the Stalinallee: freestanding buildings in a green landscape, modernist architecture, technologically savvy construction methods, abstract art and modern furniture in the model apartments, showcasing the architectural individualities of its different, international designers. The Hansaviertel, states Francesca Rogier, "was thus presented to the world as a product of the free market, symbol of the cornerstone of western policy" – and this regardless of the fact that the project necessitated a lot of subsidies from both the city and the state.[18]

This is the setting against which one should read both articles by Sibyl Moholy-Nagy. In taking this context into account, it becomes clear that both were moves as part of the "Cultural Cold War," as Frances Saunders dubbed it. This is most clearly the case with the article on East Germany. The editorial introduction already sets the tone, alluding to the ominous totalitarian character of the GDR. This is reinforced by anecdotal evidence woven through the text – the story about the train ride and "Big Brother's" broadcasting; the reference to how only children of workers now have access to higher education; the absence of visible building activities. In this article, which proves to be very well informed with its references to both Khrushchev and Ulbricht and its announcement of the industrialization that is underway, developments in architecture and urban planning are very much presented as bound up with the political system of communism. Hence the defects that the author detects are presented as flaws in the political system or, even stronger, as evidence of the sinister character of the regime. The fact that Moholy-Nagy nevertheless also sees some good things, and that the contrast between East and West sometimes turns out to be favorable to the East rather than the West, makes the article all the more effective, because it seems to be impartial and objective.

A similar assessment can be made of the article on the Hansaviertel. Only here and there, between the lines as it were, does the reader possibly become aware that the construction of the Hansaviertel formed West Berlin's answer to the Stalinallee. Its role in the Cold War cultural competition barely registers in Moholy-Nagy's article. While she mentions "the isolated existence of Berlin as an enclave in Russian-dominated territory," the rest of the article doesn't make any explicit reference to this geopolitical context. The scheme is presented as "the most ambitious replanning and rebuilding project of postwar Germany" – leaving it to the reader to silently assume that in East Germany nothing comparable is happening. Moholy-Nagy doesn't pay a lot of attention to matters of policy and finance, focusing instead on professional rivalries and critical assessments of the different plans and buildings. In doing so, she subtly enhances her own announcement of the "ambitious" character of the project, while its connection to a political and economic system remains unsaid – silently reinforcing the assumption that such a project could only be realized in a free, democratic and capitalist society.

fig. 2 The Hansaviertel as built. © Karl-Heinz Schubert. Source: Landesarchiv Berlin, F Rep. 290 Nr. 0083467

For the American readers of *Architectural Forum* and *Progressive Architecture,* she thus fulfills a role which is completely in line with the cultural Cold War conducted by the CIA. A central feature of the CIA's secret program of cultural propaganda was, according to Saunders, "to advance the claim that it did not exist."[19] Both these articles by Moholy-Nagy very subtly but effectively align innovation and cultural ambition with what is happening in the West, while the East is represented as oppressive and retarded. She thus underscores the idea that American and Western values are superior to their counterparts in the East, without explicitly articulating this as a politically informed position.

Continuities and Discontinuities

The cultural choices of East Germany however were not obvious from the beginning. In the short period between the end of the Second World War and the establishment of the GDR in 1949, there were various attempts to revive the tradition of the Bauhaus. Hermann Henselmann, the architect who later built the most important stretch of the Stalinallee, wanted to rename the Weimar Academy of Art, of which he was the director, for the Bauhaus; while there were similar plans in Dessau.[20] There were initiatives for exhibitions, and articles in several journals called for a renewed connection with modernist movements from the Weimar Republic, which had been oppressed by the fascist regime.[21] The lively and open discussions about the future orientation of architecture and urbanism were cut short in 1950, however, once the "Sixteen Principles" had been adopted as part of legislation. It was immediately made clear that these "Sixteen Principles" should be understood as in opposition to CIAM doctrines of zoning and new urban patterns based upon loose, organic configurations. Politician Lothar Bolz elucidated in 1951 that these principles constituted "a firm statement against the resolution of the city, since the center holds it together; against a dreary sameness and falsely understood 'democracy,' [...] against 'formalism,' 'constructivism' and 'cosmopolitanism.'"[22] Within communist discourse, "democracy" had to be put between quotation marks when referring to Western democracies, which supposedly misunderstood what real democracy was about – "GDR" after all meant "German Democratic Republic." Likewise "formalism," "constructivism" and "cosmopolitanism" all became code words in the language from the regime to denounce modernism, which was increasingly identified with the architecture of the West.[23]

This ideological framing of ideas and practices seen as not compatible with a socialist state culminated in the official condemnation of anything related to the Bauhaus. This was to be found, for example, in an article in 1950 in *Neues Deutschland*, the official Party newspaper, which clearly stated that "the so-called Bauhaus-style was not at all German and national [...] but rather antinational and cosmopolitan. [...] The Bauhaus-style is an authentic child of American cosmopolitanism and our victory over it is indispensable if we want to develop a new national German architecture."[24] One year later, Walter Ulbricht declared the Bauhaus-style to be "inimical to the people" – the worst insult one could inflict upon an opponent.[25] The East German ideological positioning of the Bauhaus was certainly helped along by the moves of its erstwhile director, Walter Gropius, who now had a prestigious Harvard position and who did everything he could to align the Bauhaus with American cultural politics.[26] Hence it seemed that many prominent figures in East and West agreed around 1950 that the Bauhaus was somehow bound up with Western values, and that its legacy was not at all valid for Eastern Europe – an assessment that clearly belied the Janus face that contemporaries had detected in the 1920s and 1930s and that did not take into account the many remnants of Bauhaus teachings and influences that remained active behind the Iron Curtain.[27]

The writing of the history of architecture in East and West Germany in the postwar period as one of diverging tendencies is itself, as Greg Castillo suggests, a Cold War artifact.[28] This artifact can be made very easily credible by a lot of material from the early 1950s, when both sides in the Cold War conflict were eager to point out differences between the First and the Second World. In the case of East Germany this artifact was certainly stimulated further by the efforts of the new state to establish itself as a credible institution. As Virag Molnar argues, architecture and urban reconstruction received heightened significance in this context, as each served to affirm the political sovereignty of the newly founded state.[29] As of the 1960s, however, after the turn toward industrialization, this effect gradually faded and modernism was allowed to be the dominant tendency in Eastern European architecture – even if its practitioners were reluctant to label it such, in order to not call attention to similarities with international phenomena in the West.[30] Throughout the 1950s, however, continuities with the prewar *Neues Bauen* were certainly there. Some prominent modernists had no qualms, for example, about working in the GDR. Mart Stam was invited to become the head of an art institute in Dresden and moved there in 1948 (he remained in East Germany until 1953); Grethe Schütte-Lihotzky acted as a regular consultant, especially for the design of daycare centers; Hans Schmidt occupied an important post at the Deutsche Bauakademie between 1956 and 1969.[31] It was only later, however, when industrialization and standardization got the upper hand, as decreed by Khrushchev, that modernism really became a self-evident architectural idiom.

In 1968, the Austrian critic Günther Feuerstein wrote the following:

> When one inquires how such a socialist society finds tangible expression in its architecture, one immediately experiences considerable difficulty in discerning any fundamental differences from the architecture of the West. Certainly East German planning lacks the commercial exuberance typical of a capitalist economy, but the elements of business, consumption, and even advertising are present nonetheless. In particular, there is a surprising affinity with the latest Western ideas towards sociological requirements. Community centers, open spaces, government complexes and recreational facilities are needs felt equally in East and West.[32]

Anders Aman also stresses how, after the Stalinist period of socialist realism, modernism is obviously the dominant formal language of architecture in the GDR and in the other countries of Eastern Europe.[33] Similarly, Paul Betts states that "on the whole, in fact, German industrial design did not change very much from 1925 to 1965; and this goes for both West and East Germany."[34] Adrian Forty, in his seminal work on the material history of concrete, comments upon the remarkable similarities in international housing typologies in the 1960s and 1970s, which were very much based on modernist schemes and concrete construction systems. He also points out the strange counter-symmetry that accompanies the choices for modernist concrete and for prefabricated housing typologies in East and West:

> In the communist East, normally regarded as the home of ideology, one might have expected the preference for concrete as a building material to have been primarily *ideological,* while in the West, driven by market forces, one would expect the use of concrete to have been economically driven. But the situation turns out to have been quite the reverse. In the Soviet bloc, it was the *economic* incentive, to create surpluses to fund the armaments program, that was primarily responsible for the wide use of concrete, while in the West the incentives were above all ideological, the need for social democratic governments to maintain their electoral advantage by keeping the scenery moving, even if life stood still. In Western Europe, precast concrete systems lasted only as long as the state was prepared to subsidize them; when the subsidies were removed, contractors stopped using them.[35]

One thus sees a gradual waning of ideological battles that had been so prominent in the 1950s. Indeed, after the seemingly clear-cut divergences and discontinuities that were the product of Cold War discourses in the 1950s, it is difficult not to recognize a growing convergence in architectural typologies and formal languages in the decades thereafter. This might mean that, amidst all the Cold War rhetoric that informs Sibyl Moholy-Nagy's two articles, her hypothesis about continuity at work in East Germany's focus on standardization and industrialization was essentially correct.

Endnotes

1 Alexander Schwab, *"Das Buch vom Bauen:" Wohnungsnot, neue Technik, neue Baukunst, Städtebau, aus sozialistischer Sicht* (Düsseldorf: Bertelsmann, 1973, written in 1930).

2 Koos Bosma, "New Socialist Cities: Foreign Architects in the USSR 1920–1940," *Planning Perspectives*, 29:3 (2014), 301–328.

3 She published one fiction book: S.D. Peech, *Children's Children* (New York: Bittner and Company, 1945).

4 Francesca Stonor Saunders, *The Cultural Cold War: The CIA and the World of Arts and Letters* (New York: The New Press, 1999), 22–23.

5 The papers of Sibyl Moholy-Nagy are available on microfilm in the Archives of American Art, Smithsonian Institute, Washington, D.C. For the announcements of the lectures in Munich and Stuttgart, see AAA 948–914; AAA 948–871.

6 Letter from Sibyl Moholy-Nagy to Ilse Gropius, September 3, 1950, Walter Gropius Papers, Houghton Library, Harvard University.

7 AAA 948–563; AAA 948–881; AAA 948–917; AAA 948–569.
8 Anonymous (Sibyl Moholy-Nagy), "Architecture of East Germany," *Architectural Forum*, 105 (July 1956), 152–155; Moholy-Nagy, "Berlin's International Building Exhibition 1957," *Progressive Architecture*. 37 (August 1956), 89–93.
9 The more common expression is "Typenprojektierung," see f.e. the "Institut für Typenprojektierung" led by Hermann Henselmann from 1964 to 1967.
10 Anders Aman, *Architecture and Ideology in Eastern Europe during the Stalin Era: An Aspect of Cold War History* (London: MIT Press, 1992).
11 Catherine Cooke, "Beauty as a Route to 'the Radiant Future': Responses of Soviet Architecture," *Journal of Design History*, 10:2 (1997), 137–160.
12 Virag Molnar, *Building the State: Architecture, Politics and State Formation in Post-war Central Europe* (London: Routledge, 2013), 32–37; Andreas Schätzke, *Zwischen Bauhaus und Stalinallee* (Braunschweig: Vieweg, 1991), 40–42.
13 Molnar, *Building the State*, 53–55; Adrian Forty, *Concrete and Culture: A Material History* (London: Reaktion, 2012), 150–159.
14 Bruno Flierl, "Die Stalinallee in Berlin," in Flierl, *Gebaute DDR. Über Stadtplaner, Architekten und die Macht* (Berlin: Verlag für Bauwesen, 1998), 12–33.
15 Ibid., 19.
16 Francesca Rogier, "The Monumentality of Rhetoric: The Will to Rebuild in Postwar Berlin," in *Anxious Modernisms: Experimentation in Postwar Architectural Culture*, eds. Sarah Williams Goldhagen and Réjean Legault, (London: MIT Press, 2000), 165–190 (p. 181).
17 Ibid., 178.
18 Ibid., 181.
19 Saunders, *The Cultural Cold War*, 1.
20 Schätzke, *Zwischen Bauhaus und Stalinallee*, 32.
21 Ibid., 33; Rixt Hoekstra, "Thinking about the Bauhaus from the Other Side: the History of the *Bauhaus Kolloquium* in Communist Germany," in *Studies in History and Theory of Architecture*, 1 (2013), 54–68.
22 Lothar Bolz quoted in Schätzke, *Zwischen Bauhaus und Stalinallee*, 41.
23 Aman, *Architecture and Ideology*, 25–47.
24 "Im Kampf um eine neue deutsche Architektur. Eine Diskussion im 'Neuen Deutschland,'" in Schätzke, *Zwischen Bauhaus und Stalinallee*, 132–137, (p. 137).
25 Walter Ulbricht, "Kunst und Wissenschaft im Plan. Rede vor der Volkskammer (31. Oktober 1951)," in Schätzke, *Zwischen Bauhaus und Stalinallee*, 143–145, (p. 144).
26 Wolfgang Thöner, "Deutschland, USA und das Bauhaus. Vom 'Exportschlager' zum Medium des kulturellen Austauschs," in *Amerika und Deutschland. Ambivalente Begegnungen*, eds. Frank Kelleter und Wolfgang Knöbl (Göttingen: Walstein, 2006), 155–170; Greg Castillo, "The Bauhaus in Cold War Germany," in *Bauhaus Culture from Weimar to the Cold War*, ed. Kathleen James-Chakraborty, (London: University of Minnesota Press, 2006), 171–193; Paul Betts, "The Bauhaus as a Cold War Weapon," in Philip Oswalt, et al., *Bauhaus Conflicts, 1919–2009: Controversies and Counterparts* (Ostfildern: Hatje Cantz, 2009), 190–211.
27 Simone Hain, "A Failed Rebirth: The Bauhaus and Stalinism, 1945–1952," in Philipp Oswalt, *Bauhaus Conflicts*, 106–127, (p. 122).

28 Castillo, "The Bauhaus in Cold War Germany," 171.
29 Molnar, *Building the State,* 64.
30 Radu-Alex Rauta, Hilde Heynen, "Shifting Meanings of Modernism: Parallels and Contrasts between Karel Teige and Cesare Lazarescu," *Journal of Architecture,* 14:1 (2009), 27–44.
31 Hain, "A Failed Rebirth"; Mary Pepchinski, "Feminist Utopia or Instrument of Ideology? Women Architects and the Planning of Standard Childcare Facilities in the First Decade of the GDR (1949–1959)," paper presented during the Leipzig conference on "Architecture and the Woman Question," Leipzig, April 7–9, 2016; Ursula Suter, et al., *Hans Schmidt 1893–1972. Architekt in Basel, Moskau, Berlin-Ost* (Zurich: gta, 1993).
32 Günther Feuerstein, *New Directions in German Architecture* (New York: George Braziller, 1968), 103.
33 Aman, *Architecture and Ideology,* 215–229.
34 Paul Betts, *The Authority of Everyday Objects: A Cultural History of West German Industrial Design* (London: University of California Press, 2007), 11.
35 Forty, *Concrete,* 164.

Nikolas Drosos

Building Together: Construction Sites in a Divided Europe During the 1950s

In 1952, Le Corbusier gave a short lecture at the closing session of the UNESCO-sponsored International Conference of Artists in Venice, entitled "The Relations Between Artists: Synthesis of the Plastic Arts."[1] He proposed the establishment of "*chantiers de synthèse*," construction sites where creative collaborations between artists and architects could take place, thus allowing art to imbue the built environment with poetic qualities (what he called *présences*) and incite emotional responses from the inhabitants. Conversely, architecture was to provide art with a context from which it could operate in the social realm (the "*terrain de la réalité*"). In this scheme, art and architecture were joined by a supplementary relation: architecture was to help art regain a social function that mobile, gallery-bound artworks seemed to have forgone; on the other hand, art was to "humanize" architecture, to provide it with meaning and an emotional resonance that it had lost through mechanized, large-scale construction.

These were leitmotifs in the growing discourse on the synthesis of the arts that called for the integration of art into modern architecture and had reached its apex at the time.[2] Despite its limited circulation, the speech represented Le Corbusier's effort to take the lead in this discussion, which he himself had helped shape since the late 1940s.[3] By focusing on the space of the construction site, he attributed a tangible form to the problem of synthesis, transposing the discussion onto the physical space. Ubiquitous at a time of ongoing reconstruction further fueled by a rapid population growth, the construction site was thus charged with symbolism: it was the place where a new, better society was being built.

Such parallels were particularly pronounced in Europe's eastern half, where postwar reconstruction coincided with the new constitution of Peoples' Democracies closely aligned with Moscow. Drawing on Soviet precedents from the 1930s, such as photographs in the widely circulated journal *USSR in Construction*, collaborative building became a central trope in both architectural and artistic practice, as well as in official political discourse. While for Le Corbusier the *chantiers de synthèse* were visions that still remained to be realized, images of existing, "socialist" construction sites were constantly conjured in different media as potent stand-ins of the new political system being "built" from the ground up.

Warsaw, which underwent tremendous destruction during the final stage of the war, became iconic in that respect. In July 1949, the Stalinist President of the People's Republic of Poland, Bolesław Bierut, presented a six-year plan for the reconstruction of Warsaw, a significant component of which was the Marszałkowska Housing District (Marszałkowska Dzielnica Mieszkaniowa, known by its Polish initials MDM), the Warsaw equivalent to the contemporaneous Stalinallee in Berlin (fig. 1).[4] Designed in socialist-realist style by a team of architects lead by Józef Sigalin and Stanisław Jankowski, the project was intended to provide housing for 45,000 people, along with communal facilities such as schools and kindergartens, clinics, theaters and shops. It was developed along the prewar axis of Marszałkowska Street, which was significantly widened to accommodate colossal ionic colonnades of boxy pilasters in grey granite. The monumental Constitution Square was placed at the center of the ensemble; it was named for the new Polish constitution, which had been modeled on the Soviet one and was inaugurated in 1952 on the annual Holiday of Rebirth, when the first section of the MDM was opened with a grand procession through the square. This double inauguration of new political and architectural structures marked the apex of Stalinization in Poland – a process that had already begun in 1948.

On the north side of Constitution Square, a series of six limestone reliefs prominently placed above arches depict the process of the project's creation, from its conception and design to its construction (figs. 2, 3). As in the other reliefs of the MDM, men and women are equally represented, reflecting the greater belief that socialism ought to be built through the equal participation of genders. This rhetoric of equality governs the entire series: equal space is given to different professions, from the administrators, architects and engineers, through artists and craftspeople responsible for the decorations, to the welders and bricklayers.

As works of art integrated into architecture, the Constitution Square reliefs are an example of the synthesis of the arts; at the same time, they give concrete

fig. 1 Józef Sigalin, Stanisław Jankowski and others, Marszałkowska Housing District (*Marszałkowska Dzielnica Mieszkaniowa* – MDM), Warsaw, 1950–52. Photograph: Edmund Zdanowski.

fig. 2 J. Chojnacki, Stone relief from Constitution Square, 1952. Photograph: Tomasz Kubaczyk.

fig. 3 J. Chojnacki, Stone relief from Constitution Square, 1952. Photograph: Tomasz Kubaczyk.

form to the discourse on synthesis by depicting the process of the concept's materialization. Their focus on the community of the construction site encapsulates the equivalence between artistic synthesis and social harmony that was the driving force behind the phenomenon. Adorning an architectural complex that emerged from one of the largest construction sites in the Polish capital, they represent an idealized version of such a site, devoid of the divisions between classes and genders that governed the Western *chantiers*. This rhetoric was also transposed onto the photographs that were published soon thereafter in propaganda publications that accompanied large-scale projects such as MDM.[5] These depicted the collaboration between intellectual and manual laborers, as seen in the image of an engineer talking to a foreman over blueprints (fig. 4). The published photograph appears retouched so that the engineer's sleeves are rolled up above his elbows, thus signifying his proximity to the manual laborers on the site.

After MDM's inauguration, many of the artists responsible for its ornamentation relocated to Warsaw's Old Town Square, which had been destroyed during the war and was being reconstructed. There they applied the same forms, such as stone reliefs and *sgraffito*, to the new facades (fig. 5). The painter Bohdan Urbanowicz, who participated in the restoration, wrote that the aim of the polychrome facades was to return a "human" character to the buildings, which had been robbed of such by the mechanical means and modern materials that were employed in their reconstruction.[6] The aim of the painting was thus to "enliven" the architecture, to humanize it. Yet these handmade forms could not fulfill their task unless they were executed in a spirit of collaboration. In describing the teamwork and greater sense of social responsibility of the project that he was part of, he contrasted it to the restoration of the 1920s and 1930s. He considered his predecessors to be too individualistic, failing to work with the existing architecture and with each other. Each concentrating on a different facade and driven by their own whims, the artists of the prewar era could not create a harmonious ensemble. By comparing the two approaches to polychromy, Urbanowicz was in fact comparing two different types of construction site; a failed capitalist one, driven by individualism, and a successful socialist one that is collaborative and collective.

During the early years of the People's Republic of Poland, the construction sites of MDM and the Old Town were not just emblems of the destroyed capital's rebuilding; above all, they were envisioned as microcosms of the new social order, where a supposedly harmonious, classless community of different yet equal people would collaborate to construct a better future. Yet in the context of the construction site, the crucial question was one of power and, at its core, of politics: Who would coordinate the labor of so many different constituents? What would be the parameters of their collaboration?

Le Corbusier's answers to such questions, delivered on the other side of the Iron Curtain, were telling. He outright rejected interventions by the

fig. 4 Page from Stanisław Jankowski, *MDM: Marszałkowska, 1730–1954* (Warsaw: Czytelnik, 1955). Photograph: Władysław Piotrowski.

fig. 5 Unidentified artist, *Sgraffito* façade from the Old Town Square, Warsaw, 1953. Photograph by the author.

state or any other external factor in the formation of the *chantiers de synthèse*, insisting that they should be "spontaneous, self-organized and self-managed groupings."[7] He thus purged the construction site from its associations with forced labor that it had acquired under fascism, but also repudiated the top-down imposition of collaboration that defined state socialism. Yet this was surely not an anarchist vision. Above all, Le Corbusier sought to defend the primacy of architecture, emphasizing the "architectural conditions" that should first be established before any synthesis of the arts could take place. In addition, he took it upon himself to instigate such a creative community by assuming the leading role and even having a number of artists and critics sign his lecture, which thus became a sort of declaration of synthesis. Finally, recognizing that such collaborations should be premised on a shared set of principles, he recommended his own "Modulor": a system of proportions that he had devised in the preceding years and that was based on those of his own, significantly above average in height, body. The universal adoption of the "Modulor" would allow for a global network of *chantiers de synthèse* (construction sites of synthesis) with mobile works and itinerant artists, which would thus ensure the ongoing expansion of synthesis to an infinite variety of locations and social contexts. In this model, Le Corbusier reserved for himself the position of the architect as *archi-tekton*: the master builder of this new, global construction site.

Le Corbusier's hierarchical structure reflects a democratic yet paternalistic system, not unlike the one of Christian Democracy that defined much of Western European politics during the period in question. The Warsaw model, on the other hand, is a corollary of state socialism: the construction sites have no apparent author; despite having been designed by architects, a project like the MDM housing was presented as the product of a greater collectivity, as seen on the aforementioned photos and reliefs. At least on the level of official rhetoric, this was a "spontaneous and self-managed" grouping like the one Le Corbusier had mentioned. Obviously, this was not entirely the case, as these sites were set up by executive fiat, issued by a centralized and authoritarian government. It is telling, in that respect, that the only listed author of the extensive and multi-faceted six-year plan for the reconstruction of Warsaw was none other than president Bierut, whose only professional experience was as a bookkeeper.[8] Whereas Le Corbusier's model calls for singular projects led by the architect whose position is *analogous* to that of a political leader of subordinate yet willing participants, in the case of Stalinism the architect / master builder *is* in fact the totalitarian leader, who is the final author of buildings, cities and the society as a whole.[9]

In 1956, a wave of political change swept through the Eastern Bloc. Khrushchev's denunciation of Stalin in his famous "Secret Speech" of that year initiated the process of de-Stalinization, gradually introducing more civil liberties and curbing the centralization of power. Poland played a key role in the process: the so-called "Polish October" of 1956, a bloodless revolt that called for a more open form of government, presaged the violently quashed Hungarian Revolution which followed soon thereafter.[10] De-Stalinization in Poland also translated into reforming the aesthetics of Stalinism into a freer "socialist modernism," which would preserve the social aspirations of art and architecture but also allow for more freedom and experimentation. The discussion on the synthesis of the arts was a significant component of this process. As a rather vague term, it could be used to refer to many different periods and styles: thus, as socialist realism was abandoned, the desire to integrate art and architecture, and the collaborative impetus that was associated with it remained as strong as ever. Towards the end of the decade, the meaning of synthesis was so expanded that it was used to describe even industrial and interior design as well as experimental, neo-avant-garde practices that transcended the traditional divisions between art and architecture.

One of the practitioners that pushed the agenda for synthesis in postwar Poland was Jerzy Sołtan. Having worked at Le Corbusier's office in the 1940s, Sołtan briefly visited Warsaw in 1948 and delivered a speech on the synthesis of the arts at the National Museum.[11] During the height of socialist realism, Sołtan mostly worked as an exhibition designer, while also being actively involved at the *Congrès Internationaux d'Architecture Moderne* (CIAM) and the international community, eventually becoming one of the founding members of Team 10.[12] With the onset of the Thaw, he began teaching at the Warsaw Academy of Fine Arts, where other important figures such as Oskar Hansen and Lech Tomaszewski were also active. This became a hotbed of neo-avant-garde activity, a place of intense collaboration between artists and architects.

During this period of reformism, the construction sites of the previous period were themselves adapted into interdisciplinary associations of artists and architects that redefined the synthesis of the arts as a more experimental practice, one that could go beyond the traditional use of frescos, reliefs and mosaics in architecture. One of the most important associations was the Art Research Workshops (Zakłady Artystyczno-Badawcze), founded by Sołtan, Tomaszewski and others within the Academy's department of Interior Architecture.[13] In the second half of the 1950s, the Workshops produced an impressive array of projects – from exhibition installations to temporary architecture – that were all driven by this new, revised concept of synthesis between art and architecture.

The Polish pavilion for the Brussels World Fair of 1958 was the most iconic project to emerge from this creative environment.[14] Eventually shelved due to financial difficulties – not to mention the growing unease of Polish officials with its experimental nature – the 1956 design consisted of a transparent roof made of modular prismatic trusses that covered most of the allotted plot, including all the trees that would be left intact (figs. 6, 7). A long undulating wall ran the length of one side, decorated with a double-sided polychrome mural. Unlike most world fair pavilions, the exhibits were to be very sparse and, in fact, immaterial: experimental films would be projected on four curved screens and electronic music would fill the rest of the covered space, thus completely omitting the machinery and the industrial products that were commonplace in world fairs. The pavilion was a product of an interdisciplinary team led by Sołtan and Lech Tomaszewski, who was an engineer, and included painter Wojciech Fangor – who made the central mural – and Stanisław Skrowaczewski, who composed the electronic music, as well as other important figures of the Polish neo-avant-garde. The Polish pavilion was thus conceived as a composite work where art and architecture met on equal terms, producing an altogether new category which would soon be called an "environment." Still inscribed within the official state culture, the pavilion turned the conventional discourse on the synthesis of the arts into a radical proposition: the integration of art and architecture led to the abolition of medium-specific categories; the collectivism of the previous construction sites had become an interdisciplinary collaboration within a research laboratory.

A similar type of experimental synthesis also developed in socialist Yugoslavia during the 1950s. Due to the Tito-Stalin split of 1948, the country was never Stalinized, and as a result the dogma of socialist realism never became as dominant as in the Soviet Union and its satellites. Already in 1951, a number of artists, architects and critics had formed the group EXAT 51, with the explicit goal of fostering collaboration between artists and architects and undoing the disciplinary boundaries between them.[15] As stated in their 1953 manifesto, this was to take place in "real space," and solely rely on abstract forms.[16] For EXAT 51, the synthesis of the arts was the *telos* of modernism, a fulfillment of its utopian aims, an idea that was disseminated to a wider audience with the 1957 "Didactic Exhibition of Abstract Art," which was organized by members of EXAT 51 and toured in many Yugoslav cities.[17] It consisted of cardboard panels with reproductions of works of modern art and architecture accompanied by explanatory texts. Starting with a Serbo-Croatian translation of Alfred Barr's famous diagram on the development of abstract art, the exhibition sketched out the well-established narrative of modernism's development, through Cezanne, cubism, futurism, constructivism etc., all the way to the postwar period, which was represented by International-style architecture and abstract painting and sculpture. The last six panels were dedicated to the

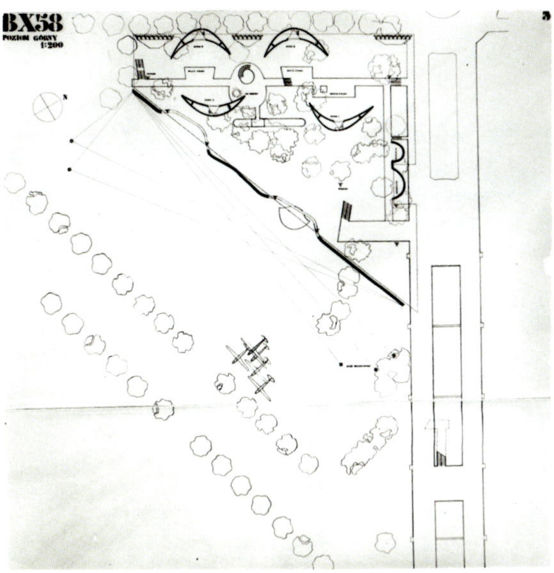

fig. 6 Jerzy Sołtan and Zbigniew Ihnatowicz, Plan of the Polish Pavilion for the Brussels World Fair, 1956. The four curved film screens are visible at the top. Courtesy of Muzeum Akademii Sztuk Pięknych, Warsaw.

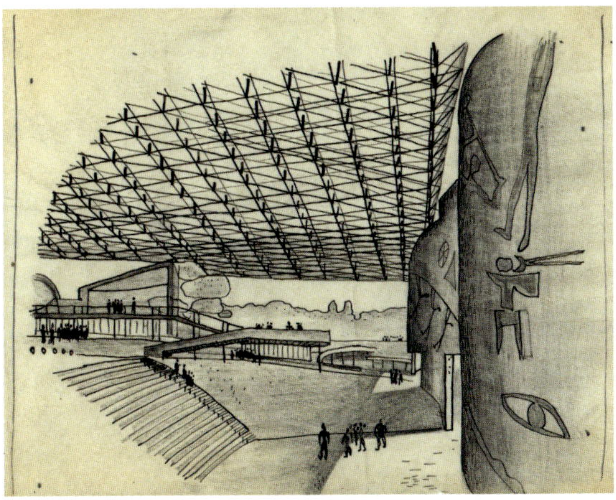

fig. 7 Jerzy Sołtan, sketch of the Polish pavilion project, 1956, depicting Lech Tomaszewski's roof and Wojciech Fangor's mural. Courtesy of Muzeum Akademii Sztuk Pięknych, Warsaw.

synthesis of the arts, depicting iconic *chantiers de synthèse* culled from the pages of *L'Architecture d'Aujourd'hui*, such as Carlos Raúl Villanueva's Ciudad Universitaria in Caracas, which featured works by Fernand Léger, Alexander Calder, Victor Vasarely and others. The message was clear: the synthesis of the arts was posited as the last – and perhaps final – step in the development of modernism.

Despite all this activity, EXAT 51's ideas did not find the widespread application in society that its members had hoped for. One of the few built projects to emerge from their activities was the Yugoslav pavilion for the 1958 World Fair in Brussels (fig. 8). It was designed by EXAT 51 member Vjenceslav Richter, who a few years prior had written an extensive essay on

fig. 8 Vjenceslav Richter, Yugoslav Pavilion at the Brussels Expo, 1958. The base of Richter's sculpture, *Nada*, is visible on the left. Photo: Archives of Yugoslavia, Belgrade.

the synthesis of the arts, relating it to the anti-individualistic ethos of socialism.[18] The pavilion was a light construction of steel and glass that appeared gently suspended over reflecting pools. The open-plan interior was organized along split-levels connected with staircases and contained exhibits ranging from machinery to historical artifacts, folk crafts and contemporary art, all complemented with sparse texts and photo murals that extolled the Yugoslav brand of socialism.[19] The extensive display of contemporary art was curated by Aleskandar Srnec, an abstract painter and also an EXAT 51 member.

The synthesis of the Yugoslav pavilion consisted of the rather conventional integration of distinct artworks, such as reliefs and free-standing sculptures into the architecture, not unlike Western examples of the time. The most striking feature was the abstract welded sculpture that stood tall near the entrance to the pavilion. It consisted of interlocking steel arches held together with tensile cables, in a repetitive arrangement that gave the impression of infinity.[20] While it did not deliver on EXAT 51 promises of non-hierarchical, experimental collaboration between artists and architects, the Yugoslav pavilion was still driven by the desire to serve as a symbol of socialist ideas. In

fig. 9 Workers constructing a preliminary mockup of Vjenceslav Richter's *Nada* in Zagreb, 1958. Photograph: Tošo Dabac. Courtesy of Muzej Suvremene Umjetnosti, Zagreb.

the photographs of the sculpture (fig. 9), the iconography of the construction site resurfaced and, with it, its utopian associations. Taken obliquely from below and depicting workers in the process of assembling the sculpture, the photo reflects Soviet examples from the 1920s and 1930s. Much like them, it symbolizes a revolutionary society in construction. Appropriately for a country that saw itself as the vanguard of word socialism, the *chantier* of the Yugoslav pavilion is no longer a conventional building site: unmoored, it is thrust towards the sky.

At a time of vast sociopolitical changes set against the ideological divisions of the Cold War, the problem of the synthesis of the arts seems to have distilled the tensions and anxieties of an era. While most parts of Europe where being rebuilt, different types of synthesis and the different collectivities they sought to produce tested out competing social visions for the new, postwar world. From Le Corbusier's *chantiers* to the scaffolds of the MDM, the experimental laboratories of the Warsaw Academy and the activities of EXAT 51, artists and architects operating in distinct political contexts sought to collaborate and contribute to the postwar reconstruction, which went beyond the brick-and-mortar rebuilding of cities and into the building of a new, and hopefully better, society.

Endnotes

1 The lecture survives in two slightly different typewritten versions at the Fondation Le Corbusier in Paris, U3–7–317 and U3–10–318.

2 For an overview published in the 1950s, see Paul F. Damaz, *Art in European Architecture / Synthèse des arts* (New York: Reinhold Publishing, 1956); More recent studies of the phenomenon include Nicola Pezolet, "Spectacles Plastiques: Reconstruction and the Debates on the 'Synthesis of the Arts' in France, 1944–1962," PhD Dissertation, MIT, 2013; Joan Ockman, "Plastic Epic: The Synthesis of the Arts Discourse in France in the Mid-Twentieth Century," in *Architecture and Art: New Visions, New Strategies*, ed. Eeva-Liisa Pelkonen and Esa Laaksonen (Helsinki: Alvar Aalto Academy, 2007), 30–61; Romy Golan, "Italy and the Concept of the Synthesis of the Arts," in *Architecture and Art: New Visions, New Strategies*, 62–83 and *Muralnomad: The Paradox of Wall Painting, Europe 1927–1957* New Haven: Yale University Press, 2009), 181–248.

3 See Christopher E. M. Pearson, "Le Corbusier's 'Synthesis of the Major Arts' in the Context of the French Reconstruction," in *The Built Surface, vol. II: Architecture and the Pictorial Arts from Romanticism to the Twenty-First Century*, ed. Karen Koehler (Farnham, Surrey; Burlington, VT: Ashgate, 2002), 222–23; also Golan, "Italy and the Concept of the Synthesis of the Arts," 62–64.

4 *Sześcioletni plan odbudowy Warszawy: Szatę graficzną, wykresy, plany i perspektywy opracowano na podstawie materiałow i projektów Biura Urbanistycznego Warszawy* (Warsaw: Książka i Wiedza, 1950); Jan Mucharski, *MDM: Marszałkowska Dzielnica Mieszkaniowa* (Warsawa: Spółdzielczy Instytut Wydawniczy "Kraj," 1952); for a comparison between the Stalinallee and the MDM, see Maria Wojtysiak and Monika Kapa-Cichocka, *KMA-MDM: Warschau: das architektonische Erbe des Realsozialismus in Warschau* (Warsaw: Dom spotkań z historią: 2011).

5 The most prominent example is the oversize clothbound folio Stanisław Jankowski, *MDM: Marszałkowska 1730–1954* (Warsaw: Czytelnik, 1955).

6 Bohdan Urbanowicz, "Dwie polichromie Starego Rynku," *Ochrona Zabytków* 6:2/3 (December 1953), 142–156.

7 Fondation Le Corbusier, U3–7–317, 3.

8 See *Sześcioletni plan odbudowy Warszawy.*

9 See the interpretation of Stalin as the ultimate demiurge – author of the totality of Soviet society in Boris Groys, *The Total Art of Stalinism: Avant-Garde, Aesthetic Dictatorship, and Beyond*, trans. Charles Rougle (London: Verso, 2011).

10 On the history of the Polish October, see Paweł Machcewicz, *Rebellious Satellite: Poland, 1956* (Stanford, CA: Stanford University Press, 2009).

11 Printed invitations to the lecture are preserved in the Jerzy Sołtan papers at the archives of the Warsaw Academy of Fine Arts.

12 For more on the Eastern European involvement in Team 10, see Łukasz Stanek, ed., *Team 10 East: Revisionist Architecture in Real Existing Modernism* (Warsaw: Museum of Modern Art, 2014).

13 Jola Gola, *Jerzy Sołtan: A Monograph*, (Warsaw; Cambridge, MA: Muzeum Akademii Sztuk Pięknych w Warszawie; Graduate School of Design, Harvard University, 1995), 144–153. For a detailed account of the activities of the Art and Research Worskhops, see Wojciech Włodarczyk, *Akademia*

Sztuk Pięknych w Warszawie w latach 1944–2004 (Warsaw: Wydawnictwa Szkolne i Pedagogiczne Spółka Akcyjna; Akademia Sztuk Pięknych, 2005), 234–48.

14 On the pavilion, see Jola Gola, "BX 58: Le projet inabouti du pavillon polonais," in *L'architecture moderne à l'Expo 58: "Pour un monde plus humain,"* ed. Rika Devos, Mil De Kooning and Geert Bekaert (Antwerp: Mercatorfonds, 2006): 307–17; Jola Gola, *Jerzy Sołtan: A Monograph*, 168–79; Aleksandra Kędziorek, "Jerzy Sołtan and the Art and Research Unit's Project for the Polish Pavilion at Expo 58," in *Team 10 East: Revisionist Architecture in Real Existing Modernism*, 109–114; Jerzy Sołtan, "Bruksela 1958," *Architektura* 2 (March–April 1957), 34–45.

15 See Ješa Denegri and Želimir Koščević, *Exat 51: 1951–1956* (Zagreb: Centar za kulturnu djelatnost; Galeria Nova, 1979); Jerko Denegri, *Umjetnost konstruktivnog pristupa: Exat 51 i Nove Tendencije* (Zagreb: Horetzky, 2000); Ješa Denegri, "Inside or outside 'Socialist Modernism'? Radical Views on the Yugoslav Art Scene, 1950–1970," in *Impossible Histories: Historical Avant-Gardes, Neo-Avant-Gardes, and Post-Avant-Gardes in Yugoslavia, 1918–1991* ed. Dubravka Djurić and Miško Šuvaković (Cambridge, MA: MIT Press, 2003), 178–183.

16 The manifesto was reproduced in the pamphlet *EXAT 51: Experimentalni atelier*, published on the occasion of an exhibition of Kristl, Picelj, Rašica and Srnec at the Gallery of the Graphic Collective in Belgrade (March 29 – April 5, 1953). An English translation of the manifesto has been published in *Impossible Histories*, 539.

17 See Ljiljana Kolešnik, "Conflicting Visions of Modernity and the Post-war Modern Art," in *Socialism and Modernity: Art, Culture, Politics: 1950–1974*, ed. Ljiljana Kolešnik (Zagreb: Museum of Contemporary Art; Institute of Art History, 2012), 116–19. For a contemporary reappraisal of the exhibition, see the essay by the Croatian artists' collective What, How, and for Whom, "Didactic Exhibition on Abstract Art," in *Political Practices of (post-) Yugoslav Art: RETROSPECTIVE 01*, ed. Jelena Vesić and Prelom Kolektiv (Belgrade: Museum of 25 of May, 2010), 64–79.

18 Vjenceslav Richter, "Prognoza životne i likovne sinteze kao izraza naše epohe," in *Sinturbanizam* (Zagreb: Mladost, 1964), 15–82.

19 Vladimir Kulić, "An Avant-Garde Architecture for an Avant-Garde Socialism: Yugoslavia at Expo '58," *Journal of Contemporary History* 47, no. 1 (January 2012): 170; Mil De Kooning, "La Navette spatiale de Vjenceslav Richter: Le pavillon yougoslave," in *L'architecture moderne à l'Expo 58*, 288–305; Jasna Galjer, *Expo 58 and the Yugoslav pavilion by Vjenceslav Richter* (Zagreb: Horetzky, 2009).

20 The sculpture derives its form from Richter's initial project for the pavilion, which involved the suspension of the building from a single central mast, which he called "foundations in the air." See Kulić, ibid. Seen as too daring or even unfeasible, the mast was scrapped in favor of a more conventional structural solution, becoming instead a free-standing sculpture.

Marcela Hanáčková

Building a New Warsaw, Building a Social Warsaw: The First Reconstruction Plans and Their International Review

The Second World War turned Warsaw into a ruin. Though the destruction was more extensive than in any other European city, it was also interpreted by some, especially by modernist architects such as Helena and Szymon Syrkus, claiming their allegiance to CIAM modernism and to social(ist) ideas, as an opportunity to raise a new city for a new society and to leave behind the burdens of the historical, capitalist city. Only a year after the war ended, the Bureau for the Reconstruction of the Capital (BOS)[1] introduced the first reconstruction plans[2] (fig. 1), which were indeed very much in keeping with CIAM discourse and social ideas, and which were then given the blessing of the leftist government in power in Poland. It was apparently a matter of such strategic importance for the early postwar state that the authorities decided to invite representatives from the international architectural community to review the plans. The socialist-realist plans that were eventually realized as a rebuilt Warsaw would be introduced only after the Communist coup in late 1948 and the rejection of modernism as a state ideology representing socialism in mid-1949.

Half a year after the public introduction of the first plans (at the end of 1945), international architects from East and West were invited to Warsaw to

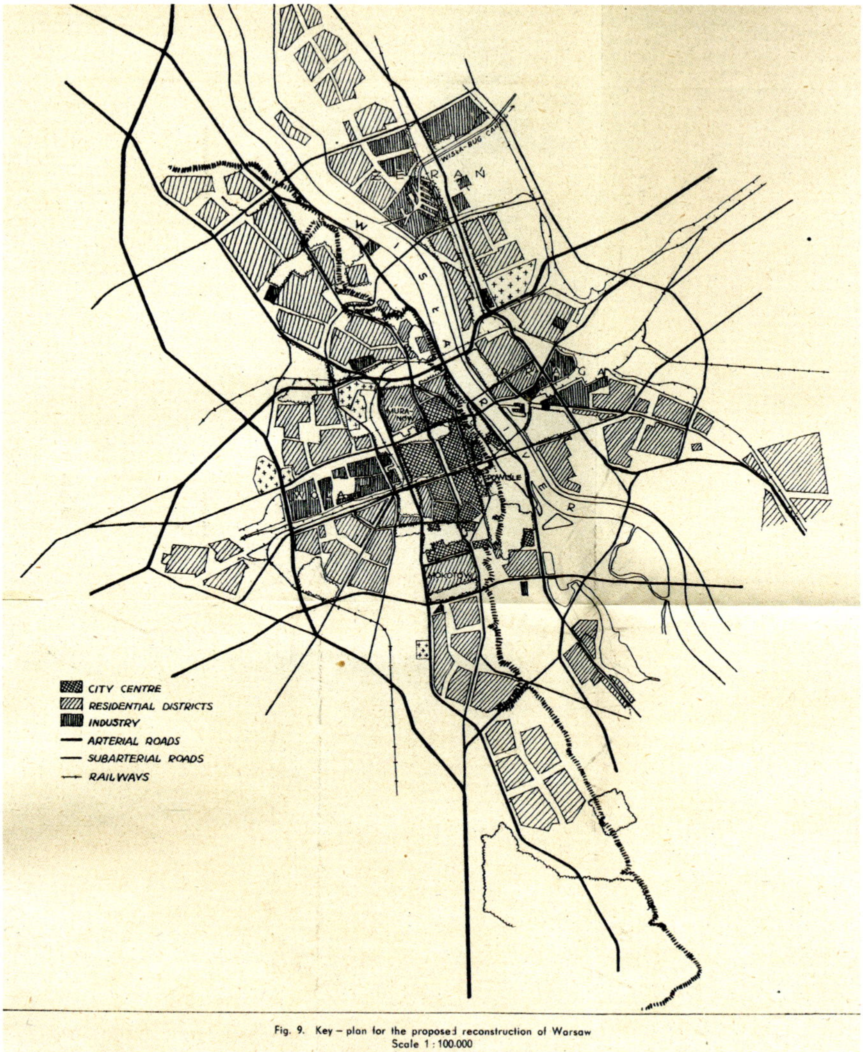

fig. 1 Functional division of postwar Warsaw as presented in the text: Replanning of the Central Districts of Warsaw, in *Physical Planning and Housing in Poland 1946*, ed. Ministry of Reconstruction (Warsaw: Trzaska, Evert & Michalski, Ltd. And E. Kuthan, 1946).

review the work of BOS. The "committee" was made up of Sergey Chernyshev and Viktor Baburov (USSR), Hans Schmidt and Hans Bernoulli (Switzerland), André Lurçat (France) and Paul Nelson (France, US). This list of the architects and their professional backgrounds implies that these candidates may have been selected for their presumed attachments to the original plans, to social ideology and possibly also to the government in power.

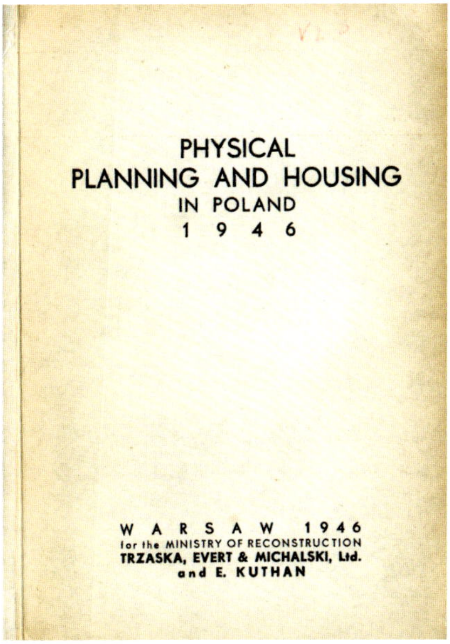

fig. 2 The book *Physical Planning and Housing in Poland 1946*, ed. Ministry of Reconstruction (Warsaw: Trzaska, Evert & Michalski, Ltd. And E. Kuthan, 1946).

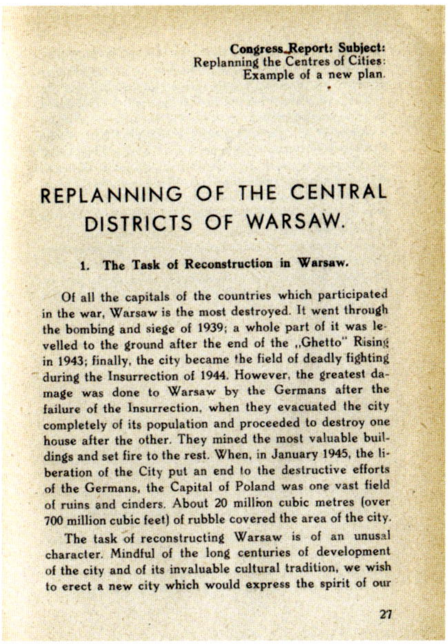

Congress Report: Subject:
Replanning the Centres of Cities:
Example of a new plan.

REPLANNING OF THE CENTRAL DISTRICTS OF WARSAW.

1. The Task of Reconstruction in Warsaw.

Of all the capitals of the countries which participated in the war, Warsaw is the most destroyed. It went through the bombing and siege of 1939; a whole part of it was levelled to the ground after the end of the „Ghetto" Rising in 1943; finally, the city became the field of deadly fighting during the Insurrection of 1944. However, the greatest damage was done to Warsaw by the Germans after the failure of the Insurrection, when they evacuated the city completely of its population and proceeded to destroy one house after the other. They mined the most valuable buildings and set fire to the rest. When, in January 1945, the liberation of the City put an end to the destructive efforts of the Germans, the Capital of Poland was one vast field of ruins and cinders. About 20 million cubic metres (over 700 million cubic feet) of rubble covered the area of the city.

The task of reconstructing Warsaw is of an unusual character. Mindful of the long centuries of development of the city and of its invaluable cultural tradition, we wish to erect a new city which would express the spirit of our

27

fig. 3 The text *Replanning of the Central Districts of Warsaw* written by the Bureau for Reconstruction of Warsaw, Town Planning Department, in *Physical Planning and Housing in Poland 1946*, ed. Ministry of Reconstruction (Warsaw: Trzaska, Evert & Michalski, Ltd. And E. Kuthan, 1946).

The objective of this chapter is to reveal the specificity of the reconstruction plans as well as of the international committee in the immediate postwar years – in the time before the outbreak of the Cold War, that is to say; and before Polish architecture's shift from modernism to socialist realism. To reach this goal, I will break down two key texts from this period. In the case of the reconstruction plans, the text will be the essay "Replanning of the Central Districts of Warsaw,"[3] which sums up BOS's essential ideas in the first plans. In the case of the international committee, it will be the document "Streszczenie opinii zagranicznych rzeczoznawcow o planie generalnym Warszawy" ["Summary of Foreign Architects Reviews on the Warsaw General Plan"][4] a compilation of excerpts from the full recordings (undiscovered to date) of the architects' reviews. In both cases, I will argue that uniqueness lay in the intention to resurrect Warsaw as a new and truly social(ist) city.

The introduction to "Replanning of the Central Districts of Warsaw," written by the BOS Town Planning Department (figs. 2, 3), familiarizes the reader with the fate of Warsaw during the war, then goes on to describe visions for its reconstruction in the main body of the text. There, it especially discusses the main principals of the first plans, their general structure and key urban-design elements. Between the lines, however, three implicit layers of the plans occur: architectural, social and political. These layers are central for the final understanding of the new Warsaw as a social(ist) city. The section below will introduce the layers in the way they are presented in the "Replanning" text.

First Reconstruction Plans: The Architectural Layer – the Layer of Modernism

The architectural layer in "Replanning" discusses four town-planning concepts: the division of the city into functional zones, neighborhood units, city centers and open spaces. These were all part of the permanent CIAM agenda, especially during the war and postwar eras. In the light of CIAM, thus, "Replanning" argues that "the city is to possess a functional pattern" and will be divided "into the main functional categories (residential, industrial, recreational areas, etc.)."[5] Other elements – the residential units, the city centers and open spaces – were discussed in such a way that they would have been very well received at early postwar CIAM congresses.

The residential units were imagined by the "Replanning" authors to have three different, overlapping scales.[6] The largest was the "residential district" for thirty to sixty thousand inhabitants, providing a "community hall (or halls for boys and girls), a church, a public library, a health center, a sports center with a gymnasium, playgrounds, buildings for state administration and local authorities, a post office, groups of shops and repair workshops, etc." The middle scale unit of about ten thousand inhabitants was the "neighborhood unit." It consisted of "its own community center" and of "two or three public primary schools, one secondary school, and various other schools." It also possessed "a shopping center, and often some small production." The smallest entities were the "estates" of "two thousand inhabitants". They contained many elements of neighborhood life: "provisions for children (crèches, nurseries and preparatory schools), for cultural, educational and recreational purposes (reading rooms, clubs), and for business and trade (distributive stores of essential articles). The residential units could be composed of either single-family houses or collective housing objects called "blocks."

Another key element of resurrected Warsaw was the city center.[7] Though the original city center was largely devastated, the BOS planners decided to locate it in the same place in order to "ensure continuity between the city of the past, the present, and the future." Nevertheless, the planners did not perceive the center as a single whole, as in the prewar period. They now drew a line between three city centers, differentiated by historical and functional value.

The "first" city center would cover historical areas built up from the Middle Ages to the eighteenth century. Though this part of the center was badly damaged, the "solicitude for national culture and for its monuments" induced the planners to preserve "certain buildings," although "from a purely material point of view" it was "unjustifiable." From the functional point of view, "the social and cultural life of the metropolis" was concentrated here as were the "agoras" of people, the "seat of Parliament and National Assembly" and the "National Museum." The second area of the city center was defined as the heavily destroyed nineteenth-century area ("up to Marszałkowska Street"), imagined from a reconstruction point of view as a "passage from historical to modern forms [...] in a harmonious manner." Here "a predominance of administrative buildings" such as government and municipal offices was imagined. The third part ("beyond Marszałkowska Street"), a "faulty nineteenth-century development" that was also all but destroyed, was previewed as a hub of economic institutions such as "managements of industrial undertakings, centers of exchange, cooperative societies, insurance companies and a variety of others," to be grouped in "skyscrapers."

Along with the CIAM-like application of new social functions for the postwar city centers, the similarly CIAM-like treatment of historical monuments as well as historical architecture in the city cores can be recognized in BOS-planning intentions for the new Warsaw. Modernists could only appreciate the value of a historical monument as a historical artifact; eighteenth- and nineteenth-century housing architecture was for them mostly historical capitalist trash.

The last architectural elements were "open spaces."[8] Based on the description in the text, these were mostly public spaces in the midst of built-up areas, or islands of green in the form of gardens, public parks or sport centers.

All elements considered, it is no accident that the planners were so close to CIAM debates. In Warsaw, a Polish CIAM group headed by Helena and Szymon Syrkus was active from virtually the beginning of the organization.[9]

During the war, the Syrkuses led PAU, a semilegal studio[10] where they also prepared underground reconstruction plans for a city that was being systematically destroyed.[11] Those plans, along with employees of the atelier including the Syrkuses, formed the foundations of BOS and of its first plans.[12]

The Social Layer – the Layer of Equality and Communality

As regards the social layer, "Replanning" introduces two key terms closely bound up with these architectural elements: community life and the equalizing of living conditions, occasionally described as the democratization of life. The idea of community life is most tightly interconnected with the element of the residential areas: "Territorial units are a frame favorable to the desired development of community life."[13] The planners of the new Warsaw imagined that community life originated in the smallest units, in the estates. In order to initiate people's interactions, BOS architects proposed common reading rooms and clubs as well as small trades and businesses, possibly imagined as open-air markets or groceries. The neighborhood units provided advanced-education institutions as well as larger shopping centers and small-size producers. Residential districts interconnected community life with leisure-time activities such as sports, public services such as libraries or local government and state administration. Among suitable open spaces for forming communities were especially large "sport facilities," as these could "serve as forums for assemblies on the occasions of national holidays and other festivities."[14] A far better space for the production of "a high-quality form of community life," however, was the historical center, as it was here that "initiatives and ideas find a platform for a versatile exchange of ideas and feelings."[15] These public spaces were compared to "the Agoras of the ancient city." Combining community life with the allegory of ancient agoras seems to point to another ancient term: *demokratia*. That term's combination of two words, *demos* ("people") and *kratos* ("power") then points to another expression: people's democracy.[16] This term was often used for those countries where the so-called popular fronts were in power in the aftermath of the Second World War. In a way, a people's democracy was an interim stage on the way to socialism.

Socialist thinking can also be detected behind the other "social" term: the equalization or democratization of living conditions. The primary idea was to ensure that all inhabitants had the same quality of life regardless of their social class or background. Equality was an important factor in formulating the concept of residential areas: "In choosing the most suitable type of layout for residential districts, the important object seems to be the provision of ample and easily accessible open spaces and community-life facilities for all inhabitants."[17] Equality also played an important role in terms of travel distance between housing and work: "We wish to place the areas of different types of work in such a way, that the representatives of all professions will be able to live in all parts of the city within a short distance of their working places."[18] All social classes should also be equally involved in establishing the new Warsaw: "We feel that to exclude any social group from the composition of the city is equally as harmful as social segregation inside the individual parts of the city or the creation of workmen's quarters separate from those inhabited by social groups having the highest standard of living. We aim at the full democratization of life."[19] Eventually, it is easy to argue that both concepts – the concept of community and the concept of equality – were certainly an expression used for a new society: a social or, more properly speaking, socialist society. The social aspects of the new Warsaw were already present in the PAU concepts and studies.[20]

The Political Layer – the Layer of the Socialist Regime

The new plan could never be realized and the new society would never emerge if there were not a corresponding political regime behind them. The description in the first plans gives us a clue to the character of this power: "The nationalization of a large part of the productive and distributive machines facilitates the control over the localization of industry and population. The communalization of land in Warsaw enables us to designate the land for appropriate purposes."[21] Communalization of land and nationalization of production were undoubtedly highpoints in a left-wing political agenda. In early postwar Poland, the political scene was in the hands of the Provisional Government of National Unity, in which the Communists occupied more seats than any other political party. Furthermore, the head of the State National Council – the parliament – was also a Communist, Bolesław Bierut. This position predisposed Bierut to play an important role in the Chief Council for the Reconstruction of the Capital, the so-called NROW,[22] whose task was to set down "principles for the reconstruction of the capital city and express its opinions on projects or programs that were submitted to it and that are related to the reconstruction."[23] Though the Communists were obviously the most influential power behind the reconstruction plans, they must also have had the support of their coalition partners, the Socialist Party and the People's Party. Furthermore, it is possible that the interconnection of the reconstruction plans and the Communist Party had its roots in wartime when some PAU members entered the Party.[24]

In what way were the first reconstruction plans unique? I would argue that it was in the interconnection of the three layers: architectural, social and political. It was the intention of the new Polish political power to resurrect

Warsaw as a truly social(ist) city by applying key elements of social living: life in communities and equality. These social(ist) ideas were then to be expressed by the principles of modern architecture. The close link between the left-wing political regime and international modernism represents very well the situation in early postwar Central Europe, and not only there. The rejection of modernism by the Communist regime, including these first plans, and the subsequent turn to socialist realism came no earlier than the first half of 1948 in Poland and was done by the same politicians (Bolesław Bierut) and architects (Helena and Szymon Syrkus) who supported the idea to shape postwar socialist Warsaw as a modernist city.

To sum up – in what way did the first reconstruction plans in their three-layered form reflect CIAM – or, more exactly, how might they have reflected CIAM? Generally speaking, CIAM would have perceived the architectural layer of the first reconstruction plans as a dream come true. Almost since its founding, the organization had been yearning for the possibility to build modernist cities virtually from scratch. From this single perspective, the Warsaw plans must have seemed an utter success to every CIAM member. Social ideas had also been an integral part of the organization since the very beginning. In postwar times, these became a special part of a discourse on neighborhood units, regardless of the actual geopolitical situation. The character of the discussion, however, varied from debates on communal services in the units to debates on communal living and equality, as was the case in Warsaw. There, the first reconstruction plans could raise interest from the broad spectrum of CIAM members. The idea of correlating architecture with social issues and left-wing politics was also a hot issue through CIAM's history. There were always those in the organization who believed that CIAM ideas could be realized only by socialist regimes – these members eventually played a minor role in the organization – and those who believed they could be realized under any regime. In the postwar world, therefore, the Warsaw reconstruction plans could be upheld especially by the former, and could be a danger for the latter. The city's reconstruction plans, thus, necessarily had to catch all eyes at CIAM.

The International Review

Once the first plans were introduced to the political representatives and to the public, the international architects came to Warsaw to view the BOS work as well. As noted above, the "committee"[25] was made up of two Soviets (Chernyshev and Baburov), two Swiss (Schmidt and Bernoulli) and two French (Lurçat and Nelson).[26] It is quite significant that, except for the Soviets, the invited reviewers were CIAM members or had close relations to

CIAM.[27] For this reason, they could have a genuine affinity for the architectural layer, though the intensity of their support for the social and political layers could vary. The Soviets, on the other hand, could be expected to go the other way, with the closest affinity for the political layer, and possibly also the social one, while their affections for the architectural aspect could be doubtful. The actual reviews of the architects are recorded in excerpts in the "Summary" (figs. 4, 5, 6) and will be presented in the lines below. Based on the "Summary," the committee members did not explicitly comment on the functional divisions of the city, suggesting that there was agreement on these, including with the Soviets. There were however some serious observations upon, and criticisms of, the remaining elements.

Studying the residential units, the Soviets apparently did not have any significant objections. Actually, they were very much in favor of the model as "the dimension of the unit imagined for 50–100 thousand inhabitants [...] resembles the proportions used in our own country."[28] Baburov (and Chernyshev) could still detect one serious impropriety: a unit composed of single-family houses. They equated this idea with the model of "garden cities" located on the outskirts of large cities, a concept which in their eyes was unacceptable. In their view, the inhabitants of the contemporary city (whether in Moscow or in Paris) preferred to live in collective houses located a short distance from the city center.[29] Their rejection of the single-family house in favor of collective housing can undoubtedly be interpreted as playing the social card.

The same card was also played in respect to the city centers. It was irritating for Eastern European architects that one part of downtown would be composed of skyscrapers hosting commercial and business functions. They immediately recognized the danger of a similarity to the American "capitalist" centers. For this reason they came up with a much more honorable and representative concept resembling true democracy: a parliament or a museum.[30] Subsequently, the Soviets greatly appreciated the intention to create "public spaces,"[31] arguing that this was the element which supported democracy: "In the democratic countries the city must have its 'gathering spaces' located under the open sky, in front of a parliament, in front of a city hall, in front of a theater [...]"[32]

A month after the Soviet visit, the first Swiss delegate, Hans Schmidt, came to Warsaw. With respect to the residential units, Schmidt principally agreed with the model presented – excluding, however, the units made of single-family houses, on which point he concurred with Baburov and Chernyshev. His argument, though, was slightly different than that of the Soviets. In Schmidt's view, families did not necessarily need to live solely in single-family houses, as other types of housing were also available, and the children of these

figs. 4, 5, 6 The original report made of the excerpted reviews of the international committee, fonds of Stanisław Tołwiński at Archiwum PAN in Warsaw, fond III-185, folder 191. First two pages describe the members of the committee; the third page shows the excerpts.

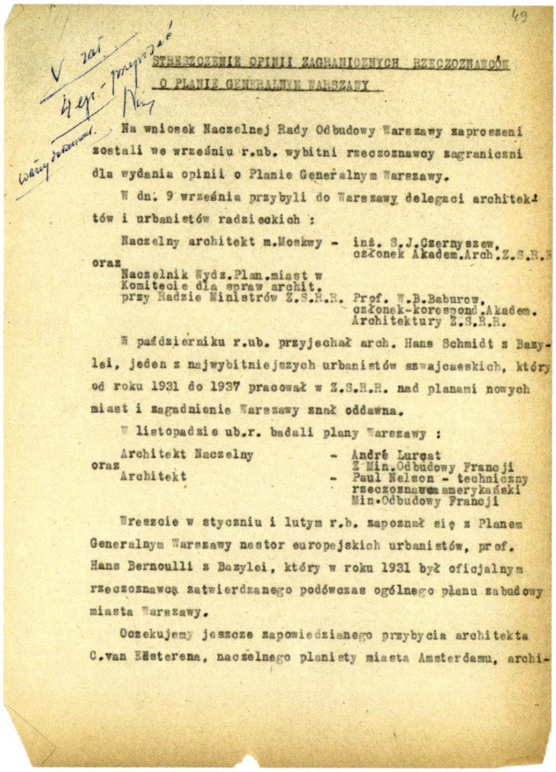

49

STRESZCZENIE OPINII ZAGRANICZNYCH RZECZOZNAWCÓW
O PLANIE GENERALNYM WARSZAWY

Na wniosek Naczelnej Rady Odbudowy Warszawy zaproszeni zostali we wrześniu r.ub. wybitni rzeczoznawcy zagraniczni dla wydania opinii o Planie Generalnym Warszawy.

W dn. 9 września przybyli do Warszawy delegaci architektów i urbanistów radzieckich :

Naczelny architekt m.Moskwy - inż. S.J.Czernyszew, członek Akadem.Arch.Z.S.R.R.
oraz
Naczelnik Wydz.Plan.miast w Komitecie dla spraw archit. przy Radzie Ministrów Z.S.R.R. Prof. W.B.Baburow, członek-korespond.Akadem. Architektury Z.S.R.R.

W październiku r.ub. przyjechał arch. Hans Schmidt z Bazylei, jeden z najwybitniejszych urbanistów szwajcarskich, który od roku 1931 do 1937 pracował w Z.S.R.R. nad planami nowych miast i zagadnienie Warszawy znał oddawna.

W listopadzie ub.r. badali plany Warszawy :

Architekt Naczelny - André Lurçat Z Min.Odbudowy Francji
oraz
Architekt - Paul Nelson - techniczny rzeczoznawca amerykański Min.Odbudowy Francji

Wreszcie w styczniu i lutym r.b. zapoznał się z Planem Generalnym Warszawy nestor europejskich urbanistów, prof. Hans Bernoulli z Bazylei, który w roku 1931 był oficjalnym rzeczoznawcą zatwierdzanego podówczas ogólnego planu zabudowy miasta Warszawy.

Oczekujemy jeszcze zapowiedzianego przybycia architekta C.van Eesterena, naczelnego planisty miasta Amsterdamu, archi-

families did not need to be brought up (individually) in gardens of single-family houses, as they could be better educated (collectively) in the children's centers.[33] Schmidt also commented on the public spaces. He justified their presence mainly on account of their historical predecessors and their socializing effects, without giving any further details. The forms of public spaces should, in Schmidt's opinion, reflect those of contemporary society,[34] which seemed to exclude the use of historical forms.

After the Swiss architect's visit, Warsaw welcomed another team. It was made up of the French architect, André Lurçat, and the American-born architect Paul Nelson – both representing the French Ministry for Reconstruction. Lurçat, in giving his views on either public or open spaces, expressed his distrust of the amount of green space that the planners of Warsaw imagined for their capital. Sadly, he did not offer any arguments clarifying this objection.[35] He also spoke out against the concentration of some functions, especially businesses and cultural activities in the city center and called for their redistribution among the housing areas.[36] The unspoken argument behind this view may have been the strengthening of community life or the improvement

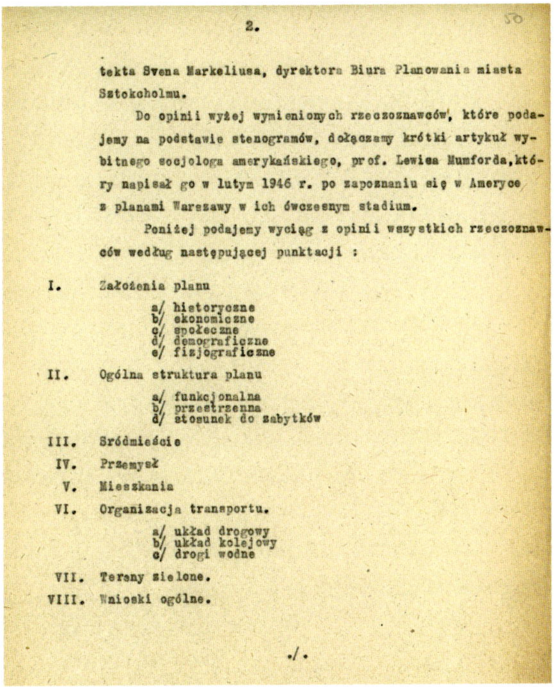

2.

tekta Svena Markeliusa, dyrektora Biura Planowania miasta Sztokholmu.

Do opinii wyżej wymienionych rzeczoznawców, które podajemy na podstawie stenogramów, dołączamy krótki artykuł wybitnego socjologa amerykańskiego, prof. Lewisa Mumforda, który napisał go w lutym 1946 r. po zapoznaniu się w Ameryce z planami Warszawy w ich ówczesnym stadium.

Poniżej podajemy wyciąg z opinii wszystkich rzeczoznawców według następującej punktacji :

I. Założenia planu
   a/ historyczne
   b/ ekonomiczne
   c/ społeczne
   d/ demograficzne
   e/ fizjograficzne
II. Ogólna struktura planu
   a/ funkcjonalna
   b/ przestrzenna
   d/ stosunek do zabytków
III. Śródmieście
IV. Przemysł
V. Mieszkania
VI. Organizacja transportu.
   a/ układ drogowy
   b/ układ kolejowy
   c/ drogi wodne
VII. Tereny zielone.
VIII. Wnioski ogólne.

./.

fig. 5

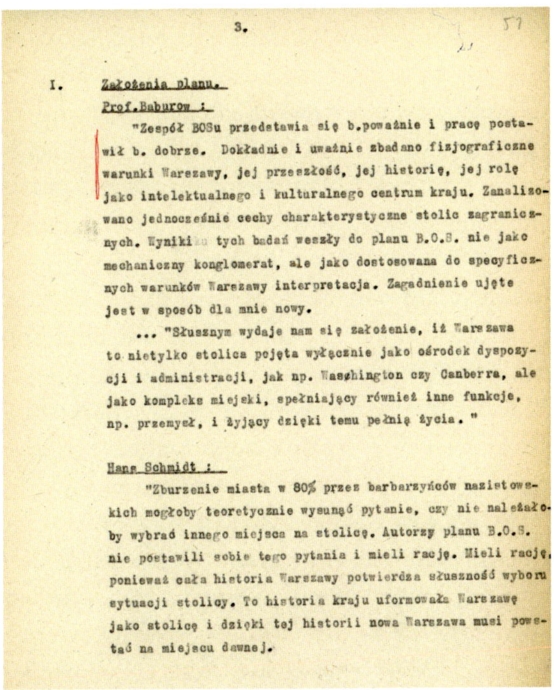

3.

I. Założenia planu.

Prof. Baburow :

"Zespół BOSu przedstawia się b.poważnie i pracę postawił b. dobrze. Dokładnie i uważnie zbadano fizjograficzne warunki Warszawy, jej przeszłość, jej historię, jej rolę jako intelektualnego i kulturalnego centrum kraju. Zanalizowano jednocześnie cechy charakterystyczne stolic zagranicznych. Wyniki tych badań weszły do planu B.O.S. nie jako mechaniczny konglomerat, ale jako dostosowana do specyficznych warunków Warszawy interpretacja. Zagadnienie ujęte jest w sposób dla mnie nowy.

... "Słusznym wydaje nam się założenie, iż Warszawa to nietylko stolica pojęta wyłącznie jako ośrodek dyspozycji i administracji, jak np. Washington czy Canberra, ale jako kompleks miejski, spełniający również inne funkcje, np. przemysł, i żyjący dzięki temu pełnią życia."

Hans Schmidt :

"Zburzenie miasta w 80% przez barbarzyńców hitlerowskich mogłoby teoretycznie wysunąć pytanie, czy nie należałoby wybrać innego miejsca na stolicę. Autorzy planu B.O.S. nie postawili sobie tego pytania i mieli rację. Mieli rację, ponieważ cała historia Warszawy potwierdza słuszność wyboru sytuacji stolicy. To historia kraju uformowała Warszawę jako stolicę i dzięki tej historii nowa Warszawa musi powstać na miejscu dawnej.

fig. 6

of living conditions in the housing areas. As for the residential units composed of single-family houses, he was strongly against this model because people who were assigned to live at the underprivileged periphery would be unable to profit from some functions located at the center.[37]

Unfortunately, Lurçat's companion, Paul Nelson, was not given extensive space in the "transcriptions" of the jury's comments. For this reason, Nelson's observations are not easy to understand. However, it is possible to deduce his views as follows: there should be greater equality of housing within the residential units (equal density, an equal approach to services, equal interactions of people). In the concluding part of this review, Nelson states: "Architecture that wants to be a social architecture must be honest in the message it wants to convey to the people. Only in this way will it teach the people to think and speak honestly."[38] Though this part is similarly difficult to interpret, it seems to put across the following message: the new Warsaw must be planned with regard to the people. Only in this way can we talk about a truly "social architecture" that will also teach people to behave like social beings.

The last member of the committee to travel to Warsaw and oversee the first plans was the other Swiss architect, Hans Bernoulli. As for the city center and the residential units, Bernoulli argued that the centralized functions placed in the city's core should be dissolved into housing units to serve inhabitants in their everyday lives.[39] At the end of his review, he made a very enthusiastic observation: "After a long 150 years we can see an urban plan that could be realized. Your government issued an Act on Land Communalisation. Thanks to this the plan will be put into practice." No wonder he was excited: the nationalization of land was Bernoulli's professional dream and it was finally coming true in Warsaw.

As we have just observed, there are notable differences in the way the first plans were praised or criticized. A good example is the residential unit made of single-family houses. For the Soviets, it was unacceptable for its connotations of bourgeois garden cities; for Schmidt, for its low community factors; and for Lurçat, for its unprivileged absence of communal services. Nevertheless, all the criticisms, recommendations and notes apparently had a single objective: to make the new Warsaw a better social(ist) city. In this city, people would be living in harmonious communities in which each inhabitant, regardless of class, would be provided with the same quality of living, and in which the values of true democracy would be expressed. Besides, we can recognize that some of the architect reviewers wanted to exclude elements that resembled capitalist cities.

These observations show how much the architects (again, excluding the Soviets) had in common, suggesting they might have been selected on ideological grounds. A short overview of their biographies demonstrates remarkable overlap: Schmidt and Lurçat were members of Western "brigades" working in the Soviet Union in the 1930s. They had also joined the Communist Party during the war. Schmidt, Lurçat, Nelson and to a certain extent Bernoulli were CIAM members, representing its progressive left wing. To sum up, we are confronted with a group that might have been expected to feel strong affinities for the first plans. A recently discovered document confirms that these architects had to be approved by Bolesław Bierut – that is to say, by the president of NROW.[40] Though the document does not give any further details, it would have been logical that Bierut favored those reviewers who could closely identify themselves with the first plans. The specificity of the committee thus lies in an intention to form a group that would review the plans from the perspective of creating a truly social(ist) city.

Though it might appear that the international review was a matter of a close community of like-minded people, the contrary is in fact true. The Syrkuses, the Polish architects, also consulted other international members of the profession in their respective countries in the first half of 1946.[41] We know that the Warsaw plans were reviewed by Alfred Forbát (and possibly by Sven Markelius), Martin Wagner, Alvaro Aalto and most importantly also by Walter Gropius and Lewis Mumford.[42] The latter became, according to the Syrkuses, "an enthusiast of social residential units"[43] and mourned "the very short time of social planning in the USA, especially the first five years of Roosevelt's governance."[44] He also supported the idea of "nationalization of Warsaw's land," arguing that as "the city has been destroyed, property lines have become meaningless."[45] The names on this list, however, indicate that the architects could identify themselves with the first, second and possibly also the third layer of the plans. The fact that they did not come to Warsaw can be attributed either to less identification with the plans or to less interest on the part of NROW to invite them.

Besides external reviewing, the ideas connected with the first plans were also present in postwar CIAM. Most aptly, they are expressed in the proposal "Statement by CIAM" written, quite significantly, by the Syrkuses, Schmidt and Mart Stam.[46] In this statement, these left-wing architects expressed their hope that the principles of "social architecture" (the term includes all three layers of the plans) would be fulfilled and that they would have such importance that CIAM would be renamed "INTERNATIONAL CONGRESSES FOR SOCIAL ARCHITECTURE & TOWN PLANNING" (upper-case emphasis in original). Unfortunately, so far we have not succeeded in tracing any direct reaction to the statement. However, the four progressive architects might have had justifiable expectations that their concept of "social architecture" would resonate in CIAM, as social architecture discourse (including on the political level) was already part of the new "Aims of CIAM" presented at the first postwar CIAM congress in Bridgwater, England, in September 1947.[47]

In this chapter, I have tried to argue that the new postwar Warsaw was planned as a social(ist) city. My research has also revealed that Warsaw and its social concept for reconstruction, in the period shortly after the war, became part of a vivid East-West discussion. Thus the first plans are a unique legacy of the time preceding the outbreak of the Cold War, before the division of the world into "socialist" and "capitalist."

Endnotes

1 BOS (Biuro Odbudowy Stolicy), a huge state-run organization, employed some one and a half thousand architects, urban planners, engineers of various professions, economists, lawyers and other staff.

2 Various examples from the literature and from archival sources talk about the general plan. Since this plan was never approved by state authorities due to the swiftly changing political situation and was formally still in elaboration, I use the term "first plans" instead of "first general plan" or "first master plan." For the sequence of various postwar reconstruction plans, see Barbara Klain, "Warsaw 1947: Plan for the Reconstruction," in *Mastering the City: North-European City Planning, 1900–2000*, eds. Koos Bosma and Helma Hellinga (Rotterdam: Netherlands Architecture Institute Publications, 1997), 274–281.

3 See Bureau for the Reconstruction of the Capital, Town Planning Department, "Replanning of the Central Districts of Warsaw," in *Physical Planning and Housing in Poland 1946*, ed. Ministry of Reconstruction (Warsaw: Trzaska, Evert & Michalski, Ltd. and E. Kuthan, 1946), 27–59.

4 "Streszczenie opinii zagranicznych rzeczoznawcow o planie generalnym Warszawy," in the folders on Stanisław Tołwiński at PAN in Warsaw, fond III-185, folder 191. A reprint of this archival document is in "Streszczenie opinii zagranicznych rzeczoznawcow o planie generalnym Warszawy," in *Warszawa stolica Polski ludowej*, 1, ed. Jan Górski (Warsaw: Państwowe Wydawnictwo Naukowe, 1970).

5 Bureau for Reconstruction, "Replanning," 31.

6 For residential-unit description see Ibid., 46–49.

7 Ibid., 38–43.

8 Ibid., 56–59.

9 Izabella Wisłocka, *Awangardowa architektura Polska 1918–1939* (Warsaw: Arkady, 1968).

10 Pracownia Architektoniczno-Urbanistyczna.

11 Helena Syrkus, *Ku idei osiedla społecznego, 1925-1975 (Warsaw: Państwowe Wydawnictwo Naukowe, 1976), 229–280.*

12 Ibid., 280, 333. Syrkus mentions in the first place about Town Planning Department employees.

13 Bureau for Reconstruction, "Replanning," 49.

14 Ibid., 57.
15 Ibid., 40.
16 Interconnections between the ancient agora and Warsaw as well as between ancient and Polish democracy were demonstrated again by Helena Syrkus in her lecture in Prague in April 1948. See Marie Benešová, "Přednáška polské architektky Heleny Syrkusové v Praze," *Architektura ČSR VIII*, 4 (1948), 158.
17 Bureau for Reconstruction, "Replanning," 46.
18 Ibid., 29.
19 Ibid., 29.
20 See Helena Syrkus and Szymon Syrkus, "A Community Development on the Background of District, City and Region" (1942), gta/ETH archives, Zurich, 42-JLS-26-46.
21 Bureau for Reconstruction, "Replanning," 28.
22 NROW: Naczelna Rada Odbudowy Warszawy.
23 "DEKRET z dnia 24 maja 1945 r. o odbudowie m. st. Warszawy," Art. 2 (2), http://www.prawo.pl/dz-u-akt/-/dokument/Dz.U.1945.21.124/16778681/7368.
24 See Syrkus, "Życiorys Heleny Syrkus /zalocznik do ankiety dzalacza Polskiej Partii Robotniczej po wyzwoleniu/," folder 2/A, Wydział Architektury Politechniki Warszawskiej, archival sources of the library.
25 "Committee" members came to Warsaw either individually or in national groups in the second half of 1946.
26 Paul Nelson was originally from the US. However, in the interwar period he worked in the Le Corbusier atelier and in postwar times he was employed by the French Ministry for Reconstruction, as was his colleague André Lurçat.
27 Schmidt, Nelson and Lurçat were CIAM members. Bernoulli had rather close relations with CIAM: his name is recorded in some meetings of the Swiss CIAM group, but he does not seem to have been a full member. Bernoulli had already been involved in reviewing the general plan of Warsaw in the interwar period, perhaps one reason he was invited to Warsaw again.
28 "Streszczenie opinii zagranicznych rzeczoznawcow o planie generalnym Warszawy," in *Warszawa stolica Polski ludowej*, 1, ed. Jan Górski (Warsaw: Państwowe Wydawnictwo Naukowe, 1970), 376.
29 Ibid., 376.
30 Ibid., 373.
31 The Polish text talks about *sale zgromadzeń* (literally "gathering spaces," freely translated as "public spaces").
32 Ibid., 373.
33 Ibid., 376–377.
34 Ibid., 373–374.
35 Ibid., 381.
36 Ibid., 374.
37 Ibid., 378.
38 Ibid., 382.
39 Ibid., 374.
40 A letter addressed "Do Obywatela Podsekretarza Stanu w Ministerstwie Spraw Zagranicznych Z. Modzelewskiego" then forwarded to the Polish Embassy in Washington, D.C. (Warsaw, probably dated January 1946 – the

date is hard to read), Archiwum PAN in Warsaw, documents of Stanislaw Tolwiński III-185, folder 204.

41 The Syrkuses: "Sprawozdanie z podróży zagranicznej Heleny i Szymona Syrkusów dla skontrolowania założeń planu Warszawy i regionu stołecznego" (Washington, D.C., March 28, 1946), Archiwum PAN in Warsaw, documents of Stanislaw Tolwiński, III-185, folder 372.

42 Ibid.

43 Ibid., 6.

44 Syrkus, *Ku idei,* 385.

45 Lewis Mumford, introduction to *Warsaw Lives Again!* exhibition catalog, ed. Stanislaw Albrecht (Place of publication not identified: Committee on Exhibition "Warsaw Lives Again," 1946), 2.

46 The Syrkuses, Hans Schmidt and Mart Stam, "Statement by CIAM" (September 16, 1946), 42-HMS-1-301-302, gta/ETH archives in Zurich.

47 "Reaffirmation of the Aims of CIAM," in CIAM 6 documents, 42-AR-1-1(-29), gta/ETH archives in Zurich, 10–12.

Marijke Martin, Cor Wagenaar

Building a New Community – A Comparison Between the Netherlands and Czechoslovakia

Today, very few politicians, urban planners, architects and housing experts would claim that building a new community is the primary aim of their work. In the reconstruction period after the Second World War, on the other hand, promoting a sense of community was seen as one of the most pressing issues. There was widespread consensus that the fragmentation of society in social, religious, ideological and cultural segments had been the deeper cause of the miseries that had occurred all over Europe in the first half of the twentieth century. It was seen as a sign of weakness. Strengthening the community spirit was a safety device. The conviction that people's living conditions directly impact the quality of the community transformed housing, especially the design of new neighborhoods, into a new frontier where architects and urbanists explored new grounds.[1] The issue became particularly important after 1948, when the Iron Curtain divided Europe in two ideologically distinct parts, forcing planners and politicians to translate opposing political ambitions into spatial structures that not only reflected their views, but actually helped to bring them about. Here, the outlines of a new society were literally built. How does this work? Which models were applied? Obviously, housing estates need to be humane – in this respect, all ideologies agree. But what does that mean? Did the answers in the Soviet empire differ from those in the capitalist world?

This article sketches the outlines of a transnational, comparative analysis of community concepts from the Netherlands – a country that ended up as part of "Western" society – and Czechoslovakia, which was incorporated into the socialist empire led by the Soviet Union. In both countries in the 1960s, the humane qualities of the new neighborhood developed into the main criterion to assess their value as a booster of a new sense of community. The Dutch section is largely based on existing research, the Czechoslovakian on studies the results of which have not been published before. Partly historiographical in nature, one of its aims is to correct the clichéd views that can be attributed to the fact that the political divide not only impacted the everyday realities of the new housing estates, but also determined the views of contemporary critics and architectural historians, resulting in two distinct narratives. Thus, we hope to shed some light on the differences and similarities on both sides of the Iron Curtain, opening windows for further research.

Europe in 1948

The postwar housing estates in the Netherlands and Czechoslovakia were built in a completely new historical context. The Cold War destroyed Europe as a container of shared cultural values and living ideals. Moreover, all Europeans shared the imprint of historical events – the First World War, the Depression of the 1930s, the Second World War, to mention only the most recent and dramatic ones. The views of the intellectual elite had always crossed borders – their world was transnational long before the word was coined. Now their universe was divided in two. For a time, communication across the political divide was quite difficult – and this obviously effected architecture and urbanism.

Long forgotten, moreover, is the immense prestige of the Soviet Union in the first postwar years. One only needs to look at the map and the number of casualties to realize that Nazi Germany was beaten by the Soviet Union – and not by the Western Allies. In Great Britain and the United States especially, the military, political and to some extent possibly even the moral superiority of the Soviet Union in these years was seen as a major challenge, forcing the "West" to create prospects of an alternative social model that appealed to the "man in the street." One of the success factors of socialism was that it catered for deeply felt needs: it promised economic success (which failed to materialize), and improving the fate of the lower classes appeared to be inherent in its doctrine.

Hardly conceivable today, calling upon the arts to help create the attractive imagery needed to build popular support for politically motivated social ideals was almost universally accepted. All political regimes, whether left or right wing, democratic or totalitarian, were willing to use the arts as a billboard for their ideals, and since architecture and urbanism actually built these ideals, they played a particularly prominent role. This echoes cultural ideals deeply rooted in nineteenth-century art history – notably the view that art develops as an evolutionary process that reflects the technical, economic, political and social evolution of society.[2] This view presupposes a very close link between art and society and a strong collective responsibility for art and especially architecture and urbanism. Moreover, it implies that art and architecture can be used as tools for propaganda. Propagated for over half a century by leading scholars in Europe, this approach was seen as totally respectable. Recent research shows that the emergence of a consumer oriented, carefree, worriless, leisurely and happy form of modernism that became known as the International Style was actively supported by leading institutions in the United States as a response to Stalin's socialist realism – which was believed to be successful in strengthening public support for communism.[3]

Finally, as we shall see when discussing the Netherlands, the clichéd view of Western society as a safe haven for individual freedom does not correspond with historical fact. Controlling the "masses" – the body of all citizens – was at least as important as liberating them from the miseries of the past, and building a new community was one of the tools to do so. The political elite deemed spontaneous, individualized (American) forms of culture dangerous and demonstrated a complete lack of confidence in the lower classes – Tony Judt pointed out that until the end of the 1950s, most European intellectuals shared these views.[4]

The Netherlands

In 1945, the Netherlands had to face the consequences of five years of Nazi occupation. It had resulted in a death toll of 301,000. The vast majority of Jews did not survive the holocaust. Industry was in ruins, the infrastructure heavily damaged, Rotterdam and several other cities largely destroyed. In the years following the liberation, Dutch politics were characterized by two overriding motives: emergency measures to deal with the most urgent needs – and fear. Shocked by the perspective that, inspired by the Soviet Union, the radical left might gain the upper hand in parliament, the authorities postponed the election – a decision without parallel in Europe. Leading politicians, mainly from social-democrat and catholic origin, hoped to enhance national unity on the basis of a national ideology that was to be inspired by Christianity and Humanism – communists were excluded. It was termed "personalist socialism" ("*personalistisch socialism*") and was intended to be the glue of the new society.

Personalist socialism deeply impacted the characteristically Dutch variant of the neighborhood unit concept. By far the most influential book propagating this concept, A. Bos' *De stad der toekomst, de toekomst der stad*,[5] is completely saturated with it. What had been unthinkable before the war had now become standard practice: instead of adding expansion plans to the already built-up areas, they were now designed as separate modules that included all facilities needed for everyday life, and separated from similar modules and the older parts by green belts. This resulted in an urban composition that broke away from the compact model urbanists had preferred earlier. What appeared to make the neighborhood unit an ideal vehicle for promoting personalist community ideals was the way it divided the masses into relatively small social groups that promoted family life as the foundation of community life. The new community was built up around the individual home, seat of the family. "Family life is of the utmost importance," Wim van Tijen, before the war one of the Netherlands' more dogmatic modern architects, contended. "Family life is the prelude to all other community life with its own laws, relations, harmonies, and conflicts, and with its own equilibrium of authority and freedom."[6] The next level was the so-called "housing unit" (*wooneenheid*); it comprised homes of all sizes and a mixture of all housing typologies. The typical Dutch neighborhood would accommodate between fifteen and twenty thousand inhabitants, and combine a number of these units and a neighborhood center with small shops, health facilities and buildings that served cultural purposes. Presented at the time as vehicles for liberating people, recent scholars see these neighborhoods as control mechanisms. As David Kuchenbuch pointed out, the conviction that the construction of separate neighborhoods should literally contain its inhabitants is perfectly illustrated by the way the new estates were being represented: by diagrams that show cities made up of circles. In his view, "... such media provide a key to understanding widespread – transnational – anxieties regarding urban mass culture and fragmentation, the risks of democratic participation, if not the contingencies of modernity itself."[7]

If one sees modernism as an ideology driven by the urge to liberate people, the coercive aspects of the postwar neighborhoods are strangely at odds with it. Nevertheless, the housing stock that gave life to them showed many characteristics usually attributed to modernism; a consequence of new industrial building technologies forced upon a building trade that until the mid-1940s was seen as utterly conservative. In public housing, the number of floor plans was severely limited and defined solely by family size – in principle, people's social status, education or preferred lifestyles were not taken into account; an approach that was sometimes justified by the egalitarian qualities of the post-

fig. 1 Slotervaart, Amsterdam. Housing by Piet Zanstra, 1960. Archive of the author.

fig. 2 Housing in Tilburg, 1950s. Archive of the author.

fig. 3 Plan for Pendrecht, Rotterdam, 1947–1953. Designed by a team headed by Lotte Stam-Beese, Pendrecht comprised clearly marked sub-neighborhoods (buurten), which in turn were made-up of separate so-called housing units. Archive of the author.

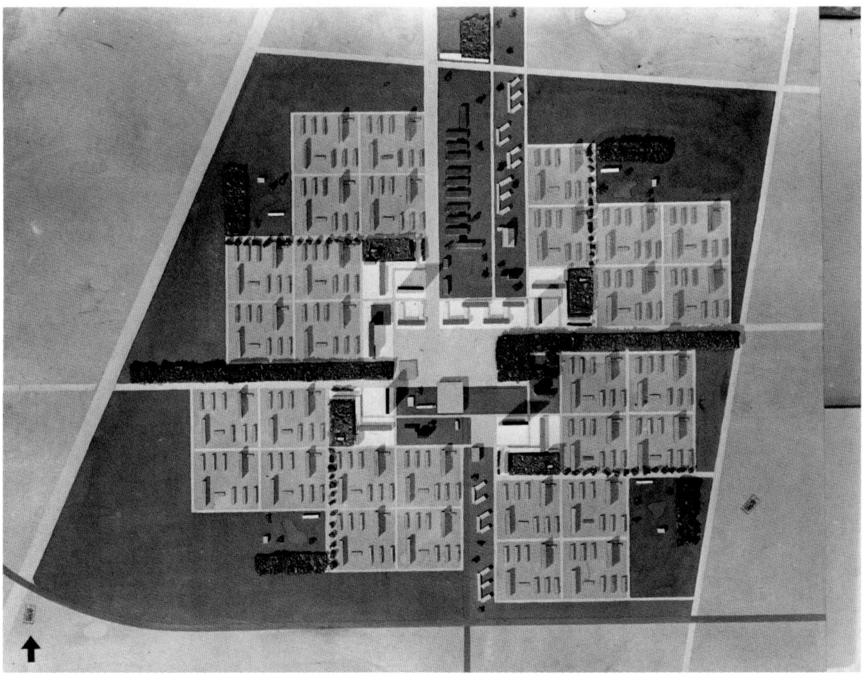

war world (as opposed to the inequalities of prewar and wartime society). The number of building types was also limited. Row houses, high-rise buildings and the so-called portico flats (*portiekwoningen*): a type of long-stretched flats of usually four floors where all homes had front doors that opened directly to a staircase that, in turn, led to the streets. Neighborhoods following these principles were built all over the Netherlands – internationally renowned examples are the Western Garden Cities in Amsterdam, and Pendrecht in Rotterdam (1947–1953) (figs. 1–3).

Obscuring the intentions to be control mechanisms rather than liberation devices, renderings always show these neighborhoods as the epitome of a free, democratic and open society; a quality allegedly enhanced by the modern qualities of their architecture. The first thing that catches the eye is the abundance of empty space. Most renderings – often beautiful, handmade drawings – show landscapes and open skies, and buildings that look as if they have been carved out of infinite space; a suggestion that was enhanced, as Hans Ibelings has pointed out, by the use of specific perspective drawing techniques.[8] Trees and greenery are always there, but they never fill the void. Endless space suggests endless opportunities and freedom of choice and destination. These housing estates were clearly designed as the counter imagine of the densely built up historical cities, places inhabited by the urban poor in overcrowded, unhealthy and slum-like houses, destined to become tomorrow's graveyards during the air raids of the next war. The new estates are distinctly anti-urban, they anticipate the ideal of urban life without urban form that in the 1960s culminated in the concept of the megalopolis.

Re-humanizing Dutch Postwar Housing Estates

Remarkably, the attempts to re-humanize Dutch housing estates partly coincided with an attempt to re-modernize Dutch architecture. After 1945, the Netherlands prided itself on having played a prominent role in the evolution and spread of modernism. In the 1920s, J. J. P. Oud had built his seminal public housing estates in Rotterdam, and in 1934 his colleague C. van Eesteren had presented his famous General Expansion Plan for Amsterdam (figs. 4, 5); moreover, he had been president of the CIAM practically from the start in 1928 (though after the war he had been replaced by Josep Lluís Sert). Nobody mentioned the fact that, as in most European countries, modernism had virtually disappeared in the late 1930s – this is one of the major differences with Czechoslovakia. From the early 1950s, architects joined the ranks of literary and art critics, who also blamed postwar society for its rigorously bourgeois nature. They began to question the basic assumptions of postwar architecture in general, and the new estates in particular. From a hygienic

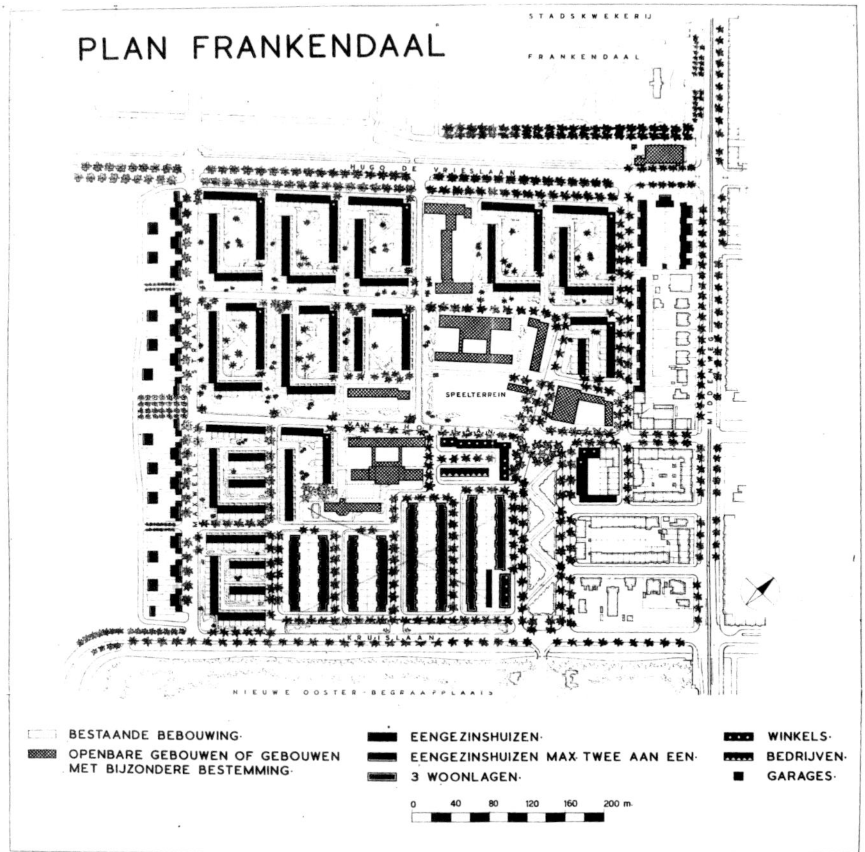

fig. 4 Plan for Frankendaal, Amsterdam, 1952. Part of Cornelis van Eesteren's General Expansion Plan for Amsterdam, it was modified after the Second World War to accommodate the Dutch variant of the neighborhood unit concept. Archive of the author.

and technological point of view, these were far superior to the housing stock from earlier periods. However, sociological research demonstrated that they had failed to boost a sense of community; moreover, numerous conferences of medical doctors proved that they produced much more stress than older neighborhoods. Jaap Bakema and Aldo van Eyck were among the angry young architects. They criticized the new estates because they lacked architectural qualities. They debunked the postwar housing estates for being the product of purely technocratic ways of thinking (not entirely without reason, since the modernization of Dutch housing had been ushered in by building engineers, not by architects). The rigidity of administrative rules, prescribed standard floor plans, and the growing demands of the mechanized building industry frustrated the work of architects – architects were becoming slaves

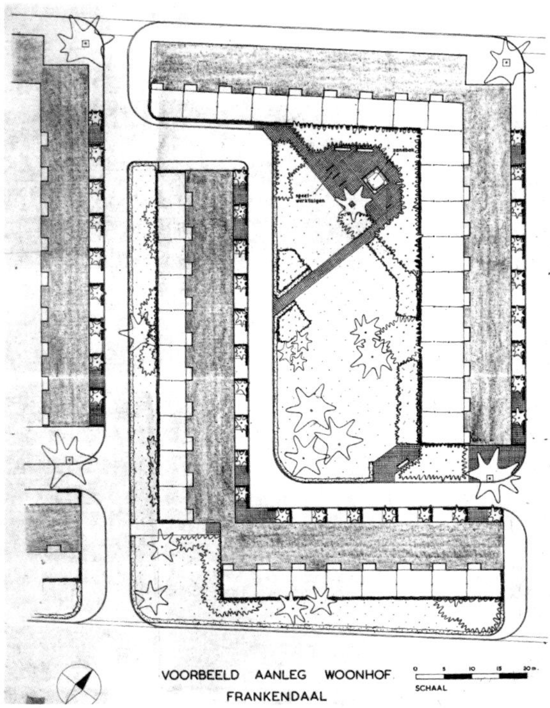

fig. 5 Frankendaal, Amsterdam. Semi-enclosed courtyards were believed to foster a sense of community; in Frankendaal, the urbanists tried to shape these courtyards using two L-shaped high-rise buildings. Archive of the author.

of a massive, collective system and as a consequence had to abandon their artistic ambitions. Architects, however, were not technocrats. Aldo van Eyck asserted that "... the wonderful thing about architecture (is) that it is an art."[9]

What – in the eyes of Bakema, van Eyck and their circles – could be gained if the architects were able to do a proper job? Their critique of the new neighborhoods took inspiration from like-minded colleagues in England (notably Alison and Peter Smithson), Italy, Germany and France. Bakema and van Eyck became active members of the Team 10 movement that in 1959 blew up the flagship of modern architecture that dated back to 1928, the CIAM. One of the qualities that were lost in the abundantly green new estates was, paradoxically, the opportunity for their inhabitants to live their lives in close harmony with nature, the critics argued. Nature had a broader meaning than simply providing people with access to green and ideally unspoiled surroundings. Gardens and landscapes positioned modern man relative to universal nature (sometimes referred to as the "cosmos" – it can hardly be a coincidence that the ubiquitous celebration of space in these years coincided with the first attempts to explore it ...). *Forum*, the platform of the critical generation of architects in the Netherlands, showed numerous scenes from African tribes supposedly living in harmony with nature, suggesting that the

fig. 6 Cover of *Forum*, 1960–1961, third issue. *Forum* developed into the main platform of the Dutch members of Team X, among them Aldo van Eyck, Jaap Bakema and Herman Hertzberger. Archive of the author.

fig. 7 Pages from *Forum*, showing African tribes allegedly not yet corrupted by Western modernism. Archive of the author.

modern city only alienated people from it (figs. 6, 7). Another negative consequence, Bakema and van Eyck maintained, was the destruction of healthy social relations, a consequence of the rigorous spatial separation of "functions." The new estates accommodated housing and facilities for everyday life such as shops, but little else. Allegedly inspired by the Athens Charter, the modern city was made up of mono-functional chunks that reduced the range of social activities people encountered to the bare minimum, making it impossible for them to experience the "wholeness of life," to borrow a typical expression from the early 1960s. Their life, therefore, was incomplete, and the only way to make amends was to mix as many functions as possible. In practice, this implied that the new housing estates should make room for cultural facilities – most Dutch estates were very poor in this respect – and, equally importantly, provided public spaces that acted as a kind of theater that invited people to behave as actors and spectators at the same time. This implies a fundamental expansion of the classical definition of function, which should be enriched with aspects of a psychological rather than material nature – psychology had made spectacular advances in the 1950s and 1960s. These ideas called for a different approach to the construction of new neighborhoods. The first signs were a slightly different way of representing them: the voids of 1950s became filled with images of people who were enjoying the scenery and each other's company (fig. 8). Although very few of the rebellious young architects saw American society as a model, the happiness they projected in their drawings perfectly coincided with the image of a carefree, optimistic consumer society ...

Czechoslovakia: Normalization

While the ideas of the Dutch Forum and similar – Team X related – visions seemed to gain acceptance in the Netherlands as well as in Czechoslovakia, the latter entered the phase of what was called "normalization" in 1968. The term suggests that something extraordinary had come to an end, and it did: before Russian tanks crushed the Prague Spring, cutting short a reform movement that wished to humanize socialism, post-Stalinist political thaw had opened windows of opportunity in every possible domain, including architecture and urbanism. Critical architects and planners addressed the inhumane nature of the *sídlištěs*, as the housing estates were called, and their opinions were remarkably similar to those voiced by their colleagues on the other side of the Iron Curtain. The tragic end of the Prague Spring brutally silenced them. Normalcy was restored – but not quite: as Today in one House (*Dnes v jednom domě*) – a popular television series from 1979 – illustrates, part of the rhetoric of the 1960s found its way to the propaganda for the new neighborhoods built after the Prague Spring. Sadly, for a time that was the only reminder of what, in retrospect, was a brief but exceptionally productive interlude in postwar Czechoslovakian architecture and urbanism.

Today in one House reached Czechoslovakian private households every evening at prime time; it paints a picture of daily life in one specific housing unit in a fictive *sídliště* near Prague.[10] The first episode introduces a natural hillside which the voiceover epically describes as a former kingdom of animals where "bees buzzed and frogs croaked," where amorous couples used to meet, and which has never been affected by any kind of war or cruel event whatsoever. When bulldozers appear on the screen, the voiceover announces the birth of the best *sídliště* ever, consisting of lush greenery, fresh air, spatial apartments, daily comfort; an ideal neighborhood so to speak, for which foreign delegations will queue to visit and jealously appreciate. The following

fig. 8 Regional Plan for Kennemerland, Van den Broek en Bakema, 1957–1959. Archive of the author.

episodes sketch the construction of the estate, the arrival of its first pioneering residents – a medical doctor, a Party official, a teacher, mothers and children – and their everyday lives, united in a collective effort to build Socialist society…

The happy overtones of the television series were just a form of window dressing.[11] Normalcy implied a return to a type of modern planning that envisaged the construction of massive panel housing in large peripheral *sídlištěs* – each meant to house an average of 100,000 people – as part of a mainly quantitative effort to solve decades of housing shortages with extremely limited technical and economic means. During the normalization, planners mostly refrained from attempts to humanize the *sídlištěs* since this might imply criticism of the communist establishment. No matter how hard the makers of *Today in one House* tried to prove the opposite, the psychological needs of the inhabitants were no longer an issue.

Echoes of Prewar Modernism

Like the Netherlands, Czechoslovakia suffered great human losses and massive destruction during the Second World War. Rather than the rebuilding of ruined cities – most escaped severe war damage – solving the housing question would turn out the main issue of the forthcoming forty years of communism. Not only had the short-lived First Republic not been able to tackle it, despite its serious professional and institutional efforts, but the combination of a planned economy, a continuous shortage of materials and the political desire to (re)house all citizens in newly constructed communist housing estates made it a mostly impossible task. Also, after the so-called commu-

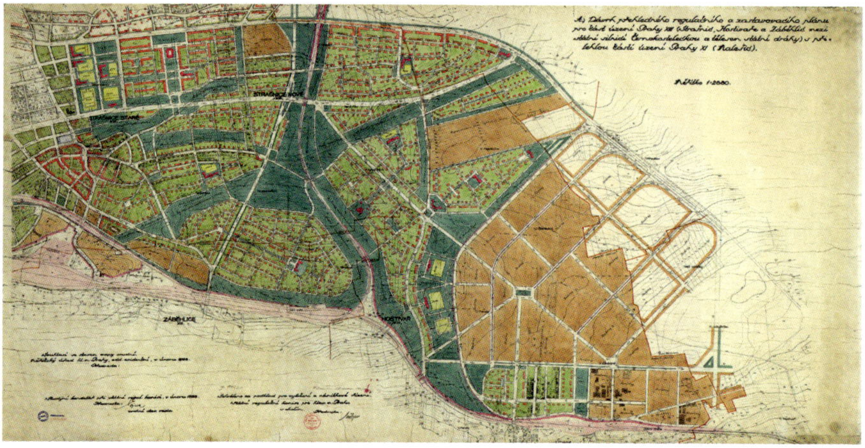

fig. 9 Proposal for a regulation and building plan for Strašnice/Prague, including Solidarita neighborhood at north-western border (prepared by State Regulatory Commission), 1928. © IPR Prague.

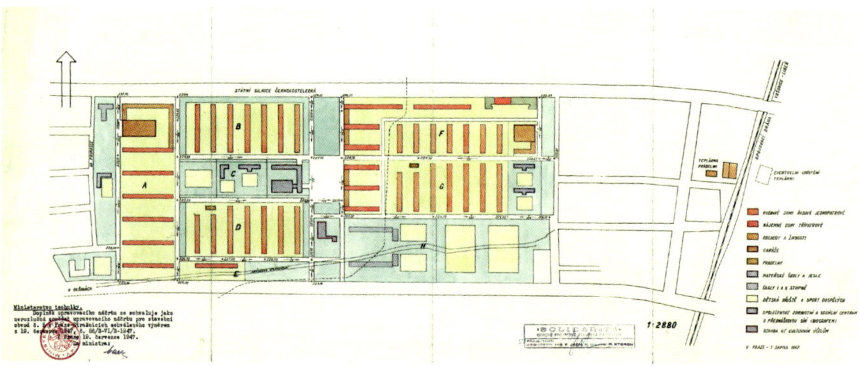

fig. 10 Detailed lay-out Solidarita by František Jech, Hanuš Majer, Karel Storch, 1947. © IPR Prague.

nist coup of February 1948, most investments were channeled towards heavy industries (which, apart from producing industrial products also expanded the class of industrial workers). Housing lagged behind and in the late 1940s and 1950s only a few *sídlištěs* were built (figs. 9, 10).

With Klement Gottwald's rise to power, architects and urbanists were expected to contribute to what should be communist in nature. Remarkably, Czechoslovakia could boast a sizable and influential group of designers who had already committed themselves to this task before the Second World War. A prime example is the neighborhood of Zelená liška (Green Fox), a low-income housing estate situated at Prague's left Vltava river bank, south of the future Pankrás district. Zelená liška's realization was based on Pavel Janák's winning entry for the 1931 competition; it replaced the plan made by the same

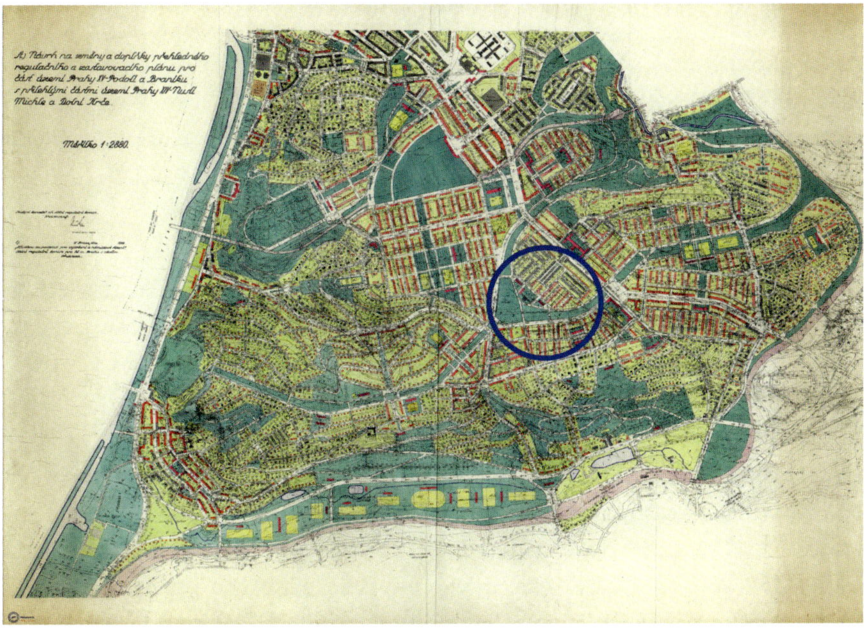

fig. 11 State Regulation Plan for Nusle/Prague with sídliště Zelená liška: its realized parts are in blue, the not-yet-realized parts in red; Pankrás is projected North of Zelená liška, 1938. © IPR Prague.

architect in 1927[12] (fig. 11). Its program and typologies mirror contemporary modern trends: a mathematical rhythm of abstract row buildings combined with the then already assumed collectivization of daily life as exemplified by the provision of collective facilities: a launderette, cooking facilities, a kindergarten and schools, most of them situated along the central axis. Of the collective facilities, only a school and launderette had been built during the first building phase between 1936 and 1938. Individual small dwellings (with an average surface of 34 m^2, a minimum norm that had been defined in the Housing for the Poor Act of 1930) were provided in *pavlačový* (gallery flats), the entrance galleries of which were explicitly meant to promote a collective lifestyle. The architecture was designed by different architects, among them the well-known Antonín Černý, in an international modernist vocabulary of plastered cubical masses. The architecture of Zelená liška illustrates that in Czechoslovakia, modernism had not withered away as it had done in most European countries including the Netherlands. On the contrary: The interwar years up until the late 1930s had been a period of "over boiling" building activity, as the architect Jiři Novotný would later call it, partly the result of an extremely active, leftish, and internationally imbedded generation of architects and ground-breaking juridical reforms.[13] Scientific research into advanced typologies, allotments, typification and standardization, and the optimum urban setting was the basis of Czechoslovakian modernism. Research by individual architects, housing experiments like Bata's model factory town and international exchange activities, lectures and publications provided models and concepts in which these ideals materialized.[14]

Zelená Liška and the Sorela Flirtation

Under Stalinist rule, socialist realism was the officially decreed architectural and urban style. In Czechoslovakia, it was nicknamed Sorela.[15] Most examples of socialist-realist architecture were built outside Prague, the result of those Czechoslovakian economic policies which favored the industrialization of the countryside. In Prague, already existing and sometimes partly realized *sídliště* plans were modified to reflect the aesthetics of Sorela. This trend can be seen in the second phase of Zelená liška (mid-1950s). Behind the decorated, socialist realist facades, however, Zelená liška represents continuities rather than breaks. Janák's prewar layout was respected and the most fundamental change was caused by experiments with so called T40 prefabricated dwelling units (40 houses in a four level high slab) – a characteristically modern approach that contradicts the architectural finishing of the project, such as the stripped classicist roof frames and pilasters mounted on the demarcation lines between prefab modules, hiding and softening their inherent technical character. French balconies with iron fences mark the interior staircases from the outside; pitched roofs and sculptured reliefs above the entrances add to a supposed vernacular, popular style. A later phase (north-east) consists of higher and less detailed apartment buildings (fig. 12). All buildings were equipped with underground shelters that were meant to provide safety in case of an atomic war. Solidarita (1947–1950) is another example of a volatile adaptation of prewar plans to the new stylistic rules. Construction of both housing estates was based on the most advanced prefab methods, illustrating the continuity in the field of industrialized building. Besides, Solidaritá turned out to be the last postwar lower income *sídliště,* in Prague at least, which combined various housing types including single-family terraced houses, under a gabled roof and with front- and backyards. Solidarita was published in *Architektura ČSSR* in 1965 as an example of human scale, greenery and differentiation, although not densely built enough (fig. 13).

Urban design plans for other Prague *sídlištěs* also show the impact of Sorela, proving that convinced modernists didn't hesitate to flirt with Stalinist rules if necessary. In 1954 and 1956, head of Town Planning Jiři Novotný supervised the redesigning of the master plans like the one for Petřín, a housing estate that had already been planned and for which earlier layouts had

fig. 12 The second, Sorela phase of sídliště Zelená liška as built in the mid-1950s. © Voženílek family.

fig. 13 Single family terraced housing in Solidarita sídliště as realized in the late 1940s (the B-marked part of the 1947 plan) as shown in fig. 10. © Voženílek family.

fig. 14 Detailed spatial plan for Petřiny neighborhood in Sorela style, by Josef Kubín, 1954. © IPR Prague.

originally been made during the First Republic.[16] The modified variants by architect Josef Kubin show a classicist pattern of semi-enclosed monumental blocks around nicely detailed green spaces, interspersed with tree-lined avenues, a monumental central boulevard, and endowed with large public squares and manifestation grounds (fig. 14). Contrary to the earlier phases, the Sorela plans were presented in colorful bird's eye perspectives, in this case as part of the Petřín Hill landscape with the river Vltava flowing below.[17]

Back to Modern Roots

In the mid-1950s, socialist realism was abandoned and functionalism returned. This was part of an ethically motivated de-Stalinization (both the Czechoslovakian communist president Klement Gottwald and Stalin passed away in 1953) as well as a purely pragmatic strategy to catch up with functionalist principles that were easier to reconcile with industrialized construction methods. In fact, even during the Sorela intermezzo, experiments with new industrial building technologies and housing prototypes had continued, although "largely out of the public eye and with little acknowledgement in the professional press."[18] *Sídlištěs* were now redesigned to reflect a more modern idiom – again by the same authors. When Petřín was finally built between 1956 and 1959, it was based on the revised plans of Kubin, with Novotný still being head of Prague Town Planning. The result pays tribute to both its prewar and Sorela scenarios, as far as rows of apartment buildings were arranged around huge rectangular green spaces (replacing the earlier semi-enclosed block structures) at both sides of the initially projected central boulevard.

One of the outcomes of the continued research in typologies and innovations in prefab construction was the introduction of the large panel structure building method, which had economic, technological, but allegedly also stylistic (rational) advantages for mass housing.[19] The results of this building method (better known under the German name "Plattenbau") have become exemplary for the sidlistes that followed; the need for large numbers of dwellings was evident after a decade during which most investments had been channeled towards industry. In 1960, the building program of ČSSR was set at 1.2 million houses for the next decade, tripling the volume that had been realized since 1945. Also, Prague was now allowed to participate in the projected national economic expansion; to prepare it for this new task, it planned to annex the neighboring municipalities. Most importantly, de-Stalinization ushered in a period of political thaw. In all fields, liberalization opened new opportunities; urban planning and architecture re-established their international contacts.

Re-establishing Broken Continuities: The Reform Movement of the 1960s

The 1960s marked an exceptional if short period during which planners in the socialist East and the capitalist West simultaneously developed ways to re-humanize architecture and town planning, leading them to explore the exact same themes. In Czechoslovakia, since the late 1950s, a group of architects, planners and human scientists had been eagerly fighting for a "de-vulgarization" of the built environment. The group's transdisciplinary character mirrored international, Western tendencies in which urban sociology, ecology and biology were seen as natural counterparts of the technical domains such as mechanics and statistics. Architects and planners saw it as their task to balance these fields and integrate them in their designs.[20] Articles and (international) lectures of its members were saturated with notions like human being, child, natural landscape, biological diversity, care for historical monuments and ecological awareness; they radiated the internationally popular existentialist discourse of the period, of which urban sociologist Jiří Musil – like most members of his group – was a fervent supporter[21](figs. 15a, b, c). At least part of the reform group considered their activities as the final step towards the fulfillment of Czechoslovakia's interwar promises to build a socialist society, returning to an honest (not perverted) form of modernism. Earlier attempts were seen to have sadly failed, as the consequence of a failing planning economy and the repressive Stalinist era.

Especially architects who started their careers during the First Republic and held prominent positions in the 1960s were convinced that the time had come to realize the goals of the prewar period. Among them, Jiří Voženílek (1909–1986) and Jiří Novotný (1911–2000), played crucial roles during the humanizing sixties in Prague's urban planning and design. Both had participated in prewar avant-garde activities; they had been members of Levá Fronta (Left Front), graduated from Prague Technical University in 1933 and 1935, and then started remarkable careers at the very end of the First Republic. As a student, Voženílek had co-founded the radical Progressive Architects Group (PAS) in 1930, believing in a natural alliance between a socialist society and functionalist, industrialized architecture. Novotný, who was slightly younger, was a fervent supporter, though not a member of this group. One year after his graduation, Voženílek was hired at the urban design office of Bata Shoe factory, working on the model factory town that was built near Zlín since the 1910s. The office investigated standardized building methods in order to export its model town to countries abroad, including the Netherlands. Some of the architects working at Zlín would play leading roles in the design and application of panel building methods during the early 1950s. After the

figs. 15a, b, c Jiří Musil, "Děti v městě" (Children in the City) in Architektura ČSSR 1963/1, 37–42.

DĚTI VE MĚSTĚ

JIŘÍ MUSIL • Snímky ZDENĚK VOŽENÍLEK

Druhá část článků: „Lidé ve městě", jejichž zahájení bylo uveřejněno v Architektuře ČSSR č. 8, r. 1962.

Město je svět dospělých

Dalo by se říci ještě přesněji, že dnešní město je projevem mentality a zájmů dospělých a zaměstnaných lidí. Je složitým a velkým mechanismem, kterému jsou cizí nejen dětské rozměry — což je nutné — nýbrž i základní dětské potřeby — což je neprozřetelné. Nám tu však nejde pouze o teoretickou a akademickou úvahu. Chceme ukázat současnou situaci městského dítěte tak, aby vyvolala zájem u těch, kteří mají v rukou tvorbu jejich životního prostředí.

Svědectvím o poměru dospělých k dětem nejsou pouze spory o plochu pro garáže a dětská hřiště, nýbrž i výsledky průzkumů našeho způsobu bydlení. Víme například, že rodiny se dvěma dětmi, bydlící ve dvoupokojových bytech, mají v naprosté většině obytné místnosti zařízeny tak, že jedna z nich je ložnicí dospělých — kde jsou někdy i postele dětí — a druhá je obývacím pokojem určeným rovněž pro dospělé. Velmi často však v tomto pokoji spí děti. Anebo jiný důkaz našeho poměru k dětem; na pražské výstavě „Nové bydlení" r. 1961 byly vystaveny 4 různé makety bytů pro 4 osoby. Při stejné ploše bylo možno byty řešit tak, že měly buď 3 ložnice — což umožňovalo oddělené spaní dětí rozdílného pohlaví — nebo 2 ložnice a jídelní kout bezprostředně napojený na kuchyni. Valná většina návštěvníků výstavy dala přednost bytům s jídelními kouty, jejichž přednosti jsou nepopiratelné, avšak jsou výhodou opět především pro dospělé.

Několik nezbytných údajů o městských dětech

O tom, že je město skutečně prostředím zařízeným pro život dospělých, svědčí opakovaná pozorování, která ukázala, že čím jsou města

147

37

41

liberation, Voženílek continued to work for Bata for three years as head of the design office.[22] He was asked to organize Czechoslovakia's socialist design sector based on his experiences and was appointed director of the massive, state-run architectural offices of Stavoprojekt right after its creation in 1948. When the Party, loyal to the course dictated from Moscow, enforced the principles of socialist realism, he left and founded the Research Institute for the Development of Architecture in Prague. In the mid-1950s, when Sorela was officially abandoned, Voženílek became State Secretary at the Ministry of Building. In 1961 he was the first to be appointed City Architect of Prague, a position he combined with a professorship at the Technical University; this position allowed him to chair most of the juries for Prague architecture and town planning competitions in the 1960s, the heydays of the reform movement that wanted to re-humanize architecture and urbanism.

Jiří Novotný also represented the continuities between prewar modernism and the reform movement. For a short time during the 1930s he had been member of the State Regulatory Commission in charge of Prague's extension plans, and then joined its German successor in 1939. Being married to a Jewish woman, he was forced to resign. After the liberation he joined the Stavoprojekt national design office – at that time directed by Voženílek – and in 1951 he was appointed director of the newly installed Office for the Urban Plan of Prague. During the reform years of the 1960s, he became vice chief architect of Prague working directly under his friend Jiří Voženílek on the design of housing estates that perfectly illustrate the humanizing intermezzo of the 1960s.[23] We could mention several other architects and planners who, likewise, represent strong links between pre-war modernism and the reform movement of the 1960s, among them Karel Janů (1910–1995), who, with Voženílek, had co-founded PAS and was to become one of the godfathers of Czechoslovak socialist prefab building.[24]

While continuing in the Czechoslovakian tradition of a politically motivated modernism, with its strong emphasis on the rationalization of building methods, typologies and floor plans, these architects wanted to humanize the design of the new housing estates. The two ambitions – boosting production and humanizing the results can best be traced in *Architektura ČSSR*, a journal which, since its creation in 1949, survived all ideological changes – as did some of its authors. Thanks to their prominent institutional positions, Novotný and Voženílek – among others – were allowed to travel abroad, re-establishing contacts with the international scene by visiting conferences and World Exhibitions such as the ones in Brussels (1958) and Montreal (1967). The Czechoslovakian humanizing discourse was imbued with an existentialist flavor, matching the growing role of human sciences within habitat-related issues. Jiří Musil was a regular contributor. As a sociologist, he worked for the Research Institute for Building and Architecture (VÚVA, created 1954). Originally meant to provide the theoretical framework for technical experiments, VÚVA changed course in the late 1950s when it wanted to make mass housing less technocratic, prioritizing dwellers' perspectives.[25] *Architektura ČSSR* regularly published the work of VÚVA members on the benefits of social research, and the results of neighborhood surveys in Western countries.[26] A renewed interest in collective lifestyles and typologies is also noticeable; with the paradoxical intention of strengthening individual consciousness about collective needs. Musil also wrote on health-related issues, comparing city and country life in terms of air pollution, the quality of drinking water, interaction with nature, life expectancy and even scales of happiness. Besides, he studied the so-called childlike size, insisting on better playground facilities to compensate for the small indoor spaces averaging only 12 square meters per person, illustrating his article with photographs of Aldo van Eyck's Amsterdam children playgrounds (fig. 15c).[27] Karel Honzik, a prewar avant-garde functionalist who became a well-known critic during these years, digressed on the alleged negative effects of dogmatic modern architecture on people's minds, long before this topic would become familiar among archi-

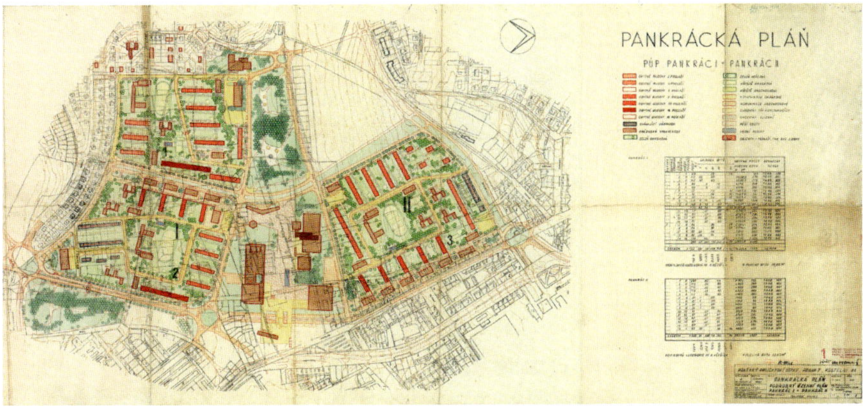

fig. 16 Urban lay-out plan for Pankrás district Prague, 1962. © IPR Prague.

tects. He referred to Western debates on the need to humanize the built environment for the sake of people's mental and physical health.[28] In the same issue, another author warned about the alienating effects of an over-rationalized built environment that didn't respect individual needs or emotional ties, instead being characterized by a hygienic sterility of glass and concrete open spaces; provoking defensive feelings, and lacking the intimacy of historical cities. The author referred to the work of Team 10 that was presented at the CIAM conference in Dubrovnik, for instance Georges Candilis' Toulouse Le Mirail project, and quoted Bakema saying that "the crisis of contemporary urbanism [was] caused by the fact that most people feel completely indifferent towards the concept of their own built environment."[29] Detailed drawings of the period, some of which were published in *Architektura ČSSR*, show newly planned *sídlištěs*, satellite towns and communal centers that perfectly reflect the Team 10 discourse. Sometimes they replicate Bakema's designs: they have trees, artificial ponds, pergolas, shopping arcades and nicely paved pedestrian squares, while children play and adults stroll around, lean over balconies or sit in their hanging gardens. Publications in *Architektura ČSSR* on exemplary foreign housing projects were complemented with good practices in Czechoslovakia, for instance the *sídliště* Lesná in Brno.[30] It combined an organic integration into the natural, terraced landscape with varied housing typologies of different heights; even so, construction was based on the usual, limited series of standardized panels.[31] Schools and shopping areas containing a library, a restaurant and a cultural center were realized as efficiently as possible, and so were the brutalist play gardens. The public part of Lesná was actually finished before house building construction even started – something that would never be repeated. The architect, Viktor Rudiš

fig. 17 Impression of future Krč housing estate, 1962. © IPR Prague.

(1927–) claimed to be inspired by examples like Tapiola suburb near Helsinki in Finland, a country where he had worked for some time.[32] Lesná also broke with the standard procedure of eradicating nature in order to build a new neighborhood, providing excellent conditions for the integration of men and nature instead.

Another example is the redesign of a 1938 masterplan for the Prague Pankrác district. The 1962 proposal reflects an international canon of habitat models, consisting of a large neighborhood, subdivided into three smaller units around a community center, each with its own sub-center and designed as a differentiated composition of row layouts (fig. 16). Green wedges separate the housing units and accentuate their shared inner core. Some beautifully detailed, colored drawings for Krč housing estate can be dated to the same year, a little further south and next to Zelená liška; the community center is depicted by the architects in the way Bakema would have done, with playing children, sand pits, small ponds and high-rising adult trees[33] (fig. 17). Realized Krč is similar to these drawings, but the communal facilities, including the abundant greenery and designed playing fields were not built at the time, as was usually the case.

One year before Prague Spring, *Architektura ČSSR* published a project for a theoretical city: "Etarea – A study of Environment." Meant to house 135,000 inhabitants and projected at the southern border of Prague's left bank, its program and design were prepared in close collaboration between a design collective and a wide range of disciplines including architecture, planning, psychology, criminology, geology and sociology; the latter in the person of Jiří Musil.[34] Novotný acted as consultant. The authors claimed that the study had been elaborated with "hitherto unheard-of profoundness, beginning with sociology and the considerations of the structure of the settlement, urban hygiene, the problem of architectural concepts and the gradual construction of the whole city with particular respect to the entirety of environment in all phases of construction."[35] The models and drawings show metabolist

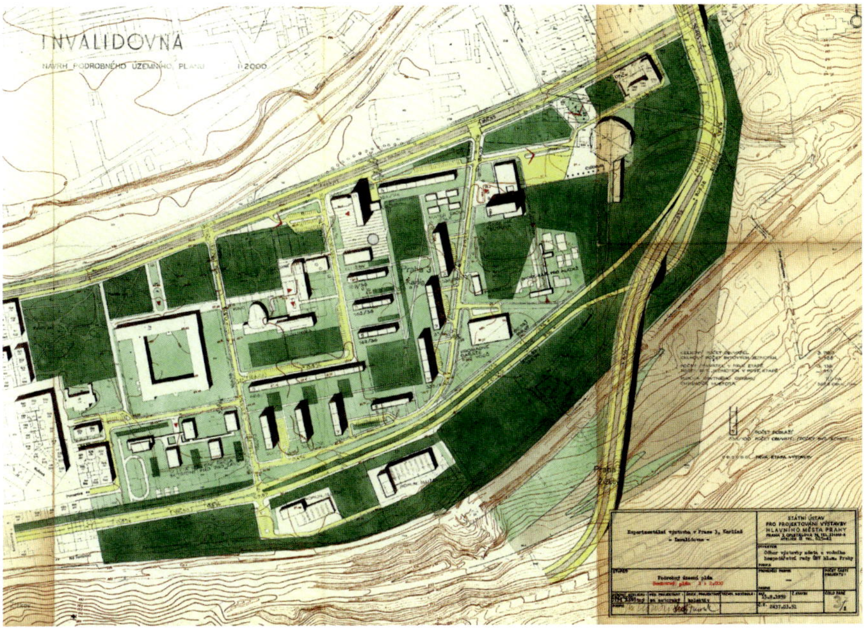

fig. 18 Revised lay-out for Invalidovna, by Novotný's collective team, 1959 © IPR Prague.

buildings of different heights and widths, arranged around a monumental community center, whereas traffic is separated into at least two superimposed, interacting ground levels.

Invalidovna, a Potemkin *Sídlište*

The same 1967/7 issue of *Architektura ČSSR* contains an analysis of the recently finished Invalidovna housing estate which, until today, stands out as one of few built *sídlištěs* that were able to absorb the humanizing discourse of the time.[36] Its initial master plan had been the result of a competition in 1931.[37] Jiři Novotný's collective team prepared a new masterplan in 1959[38], which was then detailed and realized under supervision of Josef Polák, an architect who had already been practicing before the war and a colleague of Novotný (fig. 18). Polák closely cooperated with the VÚVA Research Institute, with exceptional results in the panels used for the hotel-house. It explains why Invalidovna was propagated as a prototype for decent industrialized panel house building and as a model sidlište for a radiant socialist future. The neighborhood's main entrance at Sokolovská street was indicated by filigreed fence-like screens, leading to an atrium-like area around an artificial pond that served as the symbolic heart of a community center (fig. 19). The latter was monumentalized by brutalist sculptures, and would later also accom-

fig. 19 Main entrance to Invalidovna, as seen from Sololovská street, with Hotel House in the background. © Voženílek family.

modate the subway entrance. Spaces in between the buildings were designed to foster social reciprocity, inviting celebrations, picnics, children's playing, and elderly community life. Model houses showed modern kitchens and furniture (fig. 20). An iconic high-rise hotel-house (clad with aluminum relief panels and partly lifted on stilts) combined collective free time facilities on the ground floor and around the building, with the persisting ideal of less family-bound lifestyles. Invalidovna proved that in the end is was possible to attain both complexity and unity within one single neighborhood.[39] It was loved and praised unanimously; on the cover of its booklet from 1964, Novotný placed a picture of the *sídliště* under construction against the background of Vitus cathedral.[40]

Back to Normal ...

The end of the Prague Spring marks the end of the reform movement. All that was left was propaganda – *Today in one House*, the television series we mentioned above representing one of the finest examples.[41] What life was really like in the new *sídlištěs* hardly ever made it to the television screen or the movies. Vera Chitylová's *Panelstory* (Prefab Story, 1979) is an exception to the rule. Escaping state censorship, it perfectly illustrates her interest in everyday banality, stripped of all references to a paradisiacal state. The movie is about daily life in a just-completed Prague prefab housing estate, hilariously sketching its residents struggling and finding their ways through monotonous housing blocks, muddy public spaces, unfinished sidewalks, untraceable everywhere-the-same addresses, stuck elevators, noise disturbance, lack of privacy, and the absence of communal facilities, greenery and public transportation. More or less at the same time, scientists also ventilated critical notes on urban planning and housing policies, foremost among them Jiří Musil in his studies on Prague. Later, Musil would define *sídlištěs* as vulgarized icons of the

fig. 20 Model interior, Invalidovna, 1961. © IPR Prague.

Athens Charter, stating that due to the self-destructive delay mechanisms at work within socialism, the latter was never seriously criticized nor modified. Musil used the term "perversion" to describe the way the socialist regime re-interpreted prewar modernism in its postwar *sídlištěs* – especially in those built in the period of normalization.[42]

Conclusion

This article focuses on the Netherlands and Czechoslovakia, exploring similarities and dissimilarities, continuities and breaks between the attempts of architects and urbanists to create a human living environment in the housing estates built after the Second World War. Community building was top priority in both nations. The urban models were very similar (although this doesn't mean a thing for the actual living qualities found in them, nor for the design and construction processes: life in communist Czechoslovakia was very different from what it was in the Netherlands). Whereas in the Netherlands the concept of an unbroken evolution of modernism was a myth, it was reality in Czechoslovakia even in the personal biographies of some of the protagonists. Moreover, in as far as research into rational building methods, typologies and floor plans was the heart of Czechoslovakian modernism, not even the socialist-realist intermezzo marked a break. In Czechoslovakia, the continuous references to pre-war modernism underlined real continuities; in the Netherlands they were a rhetorical tool for criticizing the first postwar housing estates. In the 1960s, during the heydays of the humanization efforts, international contacts were re-established as were some of the alternative models and even the way these were represented. The same themes played a role: nature, psychology, spontaneity, the participation of the inhabitants. The crushing of the Prague Spring ended the humanizing phase in Czechoslovakian architecture and urbanism, ushering in a return to a hard, production-oriented, quantitative form of modernism that had little use for the playful side of life …

Endnotes

1 See "The art of living", in Cor Wagenaar, *Town Planning in the Netherlands since 1800. Responses to Enlightenment Ideas and Geopolitical Realities* (Rotterdam: NAi010, 2015), 408–432.

2 See "Towards an evolutionary theory of art," in Cor Wagenaar, *Town Planning in the Netherlands since 1800: Responses to Enlightenment Ideas and Geopolitical Realities* (Rotterdam: NAi010, 2015), 185–187.

3 Noor Mens, Cor Wagenaar, "Amerika: het nieuwe Duitsland? Of Duitsland: het nieuwe Amerika?" in *Stadsperspectieven. Europese tradities in de stedenbouw* (Nijmegen: Vantilt, 2015), 160–183.

4 Tony Judt, *Postwar. A History of Europe since 1945* (New York: Penguin Press, 2005). Chapter VII: Culture Wars, 197ff.

5 A. Bos, *De stad der toekomst, de toekomst der stad* (Rotterdam: Voorhoeve 1946).

6 Willem van Tijen, *Gronden en achtergronden van woning en wijk: een bijdrage tot het "herstel" van de "vernieuwing" op het gebied van het wonen* (Amsterdam 1955), 58. Cited in Stefan Couperus, "The Invisible Reconstruction. Displacing People, Emergency Housing and Promoting Decent Family Life in Rotterdam, Hamburg and Coventry," in Jörn Düwel, Niels Gutschow (eds.), *A Blessing in Disguise. War and Town Planning in Europe 1940–1945* (Berlin: Dom publishers 2013), 68.

7 David Kuchenbuch, "Circles within Circles. Visions and Visualizations of the City of Tomorrow," in *A Blessing in Disguise*, eds. Düwel, Gutschow, 55.

8 H. Ibelings. *De moderne jaren vijftig en zestig. De verspreiding van een eigentijdse architectuur over Nederland* (Rotterdam: NAI publishers, 1996).

9 Cited in: Oskar Newman, *CIAM '59 in Otterlo. Arbeitsgruppe für die Gestaltung soziologischer und visueller Zusammenhänge* (Stuttgart: Karl Krämer Verlag, 1961), 216.

10 *Dnes v jednom domě*, 1979 (https://www.youtube.com/watch?v=sbkQaABDpCo*)*.

11 Pauline Bren, "Envisioning a 'Socialist Way of Life': Ideology and Contradiction in Czechoslovakia, 1969–1989" in *A Decade of Transformation*, IWM Junior Visiting Fellows Conferences, Vol. 8 (Vienna 1999).

12 Pavel Janák (1881–1956) was head of the State Regulatory Commission in charge of Prague's Interwar extension plans, and of which Jiri Novotný would be a member in the late 1930s. See: Vendula Hnidková (ed.), *Pavel Janák: Obrys doby* (Praha: Arbor Vitae, 2009). The history of Prague regulation plans can be traced via www.uppraha.cz and http://mpp.praha.eu/SRK/ and in: Jaroslav C. Novák, *Klícové tendence ve vývoji prazských územních plánu* (pdf via: *www.ekoporadnypraha.cz/…planovani/klicove_tendence_ve_vyvo.)*

13 Jiři Novotný, *Prahou Posedlý*, (Praha: ed.Univerzita Karlova v Praze, 2002), 20.

14 Alena Kubova, *l'Avant-garde architecturale en Tchécoslovaque 1918–1939*, Pierre Mardaga, Liège 1992; Jaroslav Andel, *The new vision for the new*

architecture. Czechoslovakia 1918–1938, First English Edition, (Slovart Publishing, 2005); Katrin Klingan (ed), *A Utopia of Modernity: Zlín. Revising Bata's Functional City*, (Berlin: Jovis Publishers, 2009).

15 SoReLa is an acronym for the words Socialist Realism and the name of one of is most fervent advocates, architect Zdeněk Lakomý (–2014). After working at Bata's building division in Zlín during the war, Lakomý would join and become head of the VÚVA research institute in the 1950s, and later fulfill various politically loaded cultural, and important educational, functions. See: http://www.archiweb.cz/zdenek-lakomy.

16 For 1956 plans see: *Útvar rozvoje hlavního město Prahy, Praha v plánech a projecktech* (Katalog výstavy, Praha 1999), 86–87.

17 Described plans and drawings are from the collection of the Prague Institute of Planning and Development, for which consultation we are grateful to Martina Flekačová, archivist and historian of modern architecture.

18 Kimberley Elman Zarecor, "The Local History of an International Type: the Structural Panel Building in Czechoslovakia" in *Home Cultures* 7:2 (Spring 2010), 217–236, (p. 220).

19 It made Czechoslovakia the first country where this technology would become dominant so quickly. See Kimberly E. Zarecor, "The Rainbow Edges: The Legacy of Communist Mass Housing and the Colourful Future of Czech Cities" (2008). Architecture Conference Proceedings and Presentations. Paper 26. http:/lib.dr.iastate.edu/arch_conf/26. Issues relating the technical construction developments in CS housing are based on Zarecor's articles, and on her *Manufacturing a Socialist Modernity. Housing in Czechoslovakia 1945–1960* (Pittsburgh: University of Pittsburgh Press, 2011).

20 Oldřich Ševčík/Ondřej Beneš (eds), *Architektura 60.let. "Zlatá sedesátá léta" u ceské architecture 20. Století*, (Praha: Grada Publishing, 2009) is one of the rare Czech publications describing art and architecture during the "golden sixties."

21 Besides his articles in *Architektura ČSSR*, also see: *Jiří Musil*, "The development of Prague's ecological structure," in *Readings in urban sociology*, ed. R.E. Pahl, (Oxford: Pergamon Press, 1968) 232–259.

22 The office produced some iconic buildings, the most prominent being the Collective House in Zlín (1948–1951).

23 His publications showed a growing interest in the relation between natural environment and architecture, for instance: Jiří Novotný, "Přírodní Prostředí a Architektura Prahy" (The Natural Environment and The Architecture of Prague) in *Architektura ČSSR* 1965/1, 40–44.

24 Zarecor for instance, focusses on the former PAS members, including Vozinilek and Janu, in her detailed analysis of local continuities in Czechoslovak building industry, for instance: *Manufacturing a Socialist Modernity. Housing in Czechoslovakia 1945–1960* (Pittsburgh: University of Pittsburgh Press, 2011), 77.

25 Markéta Žáčková, "'Byl sice jistý plan…' Výzkummný ústav výstavby a architektury (VÚVA) a experimentální bytová výstavba přelomu padesátých a šedesátých let dvacátého století'/ 'Although There Was a Plan…' The Research Institute for Building and Architecture and the Experimental Housing Construction in the Late Fifties and Early Sixties" in *Sešit pro umění, teorii a příbuzné zóny/Notebook for Art, Theory and Related Zones* ed. VVP editions, 2014/17, 20–49, (p. 37). Also see: Lucie

Zadrazilová, *Když se utopie stane skutečností 1953–89*, (Praha: ed. U(P)M Arbor Vitae, 2013), 88.

26 For instance: Eva Librová, Karel Brix, Dr. Jaroslav Klofác, "Průzkumy soudobé výstavby v ČSSR z hlediska vytvaření příznivého prostředí v hromadné bytové výstavbě" (Surveys of contemporary construction in the ČSSR with the aim of creating a favorable environment for mass housing)" in *Architektura ČSSR* 1961/2, 141–147.

27 For instance: Jiří Musil, Karel Simon, "Město jako životní prostředí" (The City as Life Environment) in *Architektura ČSSR* 1961/9, 648–650; Jiri Musil, "Lidé v městě" (People in the City) in: *Architektura ČSSR* 1962/8, 542–547; Jiri Musil, "Děti v městě" (Children in the City) in *Architektura ČSSR* 1963/1, 37–42.

28 Karel Honzik, "Prostředí celého člověka" (The environment of the man in full) in *Architektura ČSSR*, 1966/2, 98.

29 Jaromír Stván, "Urbanismus a Odcizení" (Urbanism and Alienation) in *Architektura ČSSR* 1966/2, 94–96, (p. 94).

30 F. Zounek, V. Rudiš, I. Veselý, "Nová obytná čtvrť v Brně" (A new housing estate in Brno) in *Architektura ČSSR* 1961/6, 459–461. Another good practice that is regularly referred to is Sídliště Sítná in Kladno by Václav Hilský, Otokar Jurenka and Jiří Náhlík.

31 Interview with Ivan Oberstein by the author, Prague, Spring 2014.

32 Interview with Victor *Rudiš* in *Proměny města Brna, 14.díl – Sídliště, hromadná bytová výstavba* (documentary film, Aidem & Museum of Brno 2008) via http:/www.youtube.com/watch?v=Dqu91R_zKVk.

33 The architects were Josef Kalous, Josef Polák and Jaroslav Vlašánek.

34 G. Čelechovský, J. Stehlík, L. Sýkora, "Studie životního prostředí Města" (study of an environmental town) in *Architektura ČSSR* 1967/7, 399–408.

35 As stated in the English summary of the main article, in *Architektura ČSSR* 1967/7, 456.

36 Josef Polák, "Ukončení výstavby na experimentálním sídlišti Invalidovna" (The end of the construction of experimental sídlište Invalidovna) in *Architektura ČSSR* 1967/7, 409–415.

37 It was won by avant-garde architect and theorist Emanuel *Hruška* (1906–1988). The typological solution was a response to the regulation-policies of the time: comb-like blocks along the main streets and four-story rows of flats perpendicular thereto and surrounded by green loans.

38 The other masterplan designers involved were František Šmolik and Stanislav Horák.

39 Ladislav Zikmund-Lender, "Úvod aneb hledání experiment," in Ladislav Zikmund-Lender (ed.), *Experimentální Sídlište Invalidovna*, Praha 2014, 9–13, (p. 12).

40 Jiří Novotný, *Nové bydlení v Praze*, (Praha: Pražská informační služba orbis, 1964).

41 Paulina Bren, *The Greengrocer and his TV: The Culture of Communism after the 1968 Prague Spring* (Cornell University Press 2010); Blanka Soukupová, "Father Frost Welcomes You or the Myth of New Prague as a Beautiful City in a Socialist Way" in Blanka Soukupová, Hedvika Novotná, Zuzana Jurková (eds), *Myths and "Reality" of Central European Cities*, Urban People/Lidé Města, 11, 2009/2, 263–291.

42 Pavla Horská, Eduard Maur, Jiří Musil, Zrod Velkoměsta. *Urbanizace českých zemí a Evropa* (Praha: Paseka, 2002), 276–284.

Dana Vais

"Social Efficiency" and "Humanistic Specificity": A Double Discourse in Romanian Architecture in the 1960s

The period from the late 1950s to the early 1970s was the time of modernism in postwar Romanian architecture. This was also the most "humane" phase of Romanian communism, at the time of the Khrushchev Thaw. Here lies an initial ambiguity when we address the question of the postwar re-humanizing of architecture: although this re-humanizing could be understood to be against the modernistic machine, in Romania it is precisely modernism that is associated with a time of humanization.

Another ambiguity lies in the fact that postwar modernism came after an interlude of socialist realism, which legitimated itself through a humanist rhetoric. Architects may have been using the required wooden language, in early 1950s publications, when they presented "the Stalinist care for the human" as the leading idea in Romanian architecture.[1] But the humanistic argument was even used on less formal occasions. In his memoirs, architect Ion Mircea Enescu describes how a colleague, engaged in the socialist-realist style at the time, tried to persuade Enescu that modernism must be avoided, not only for its exaggerated functionalism, technicality and cosmopolitanism, but for "its lack of any humanistic message."[2]

This apparent regress in humanist claims in 1960s Romanian architecture was not far from the situation in British postwar architecture, described by Reyner Banham in an article on Brutalism[3] – a movement quite well known to Romanian architects, given the relative openness to the West during the 1960s. Architect Nicolae Porumbescu (1919–1999), for example, confessed that he "care[d] very much about the Brutalists."[4] Brutalism followed the tendency of New Humanism, a turn that – interestingly enough – Banham puts in the context of the "Communists versus the Rest" dispute. It was "Communists" (i.e., British Marxists) who preferred the "picturesque" architecture of New Humanism; their polemic had actually been "taken the guts out" of when Nikita Khrushchev reversed the Party's architectural line[5] – that is, by the return to modernism in the communist world.

Banham also stressed the impact that Rudolf Wittkower's book *Architectural Principles in the Age of Humanism* (1949) had on the postwar generation, fostering "Neo-Palladianism."[6] Andrea Palladio's *I quatro libri* was published in Romania in 1957,[7] edited and translated by a reputable architectural history professor, Richard Bordenache. The fact that this work was issued at a time when socialist realism had been abandoned – no longer serving as a prescriptive method of design, but just as a reminder of a larger humanistic sense in architecture – reveals the ambiguity of its "humanist" legacy. As Banham remarked in his article, the real question at this turning point (from "Routine Palladianists" to Brutalism in his case, from socialist realism to modernism in ours) would be: "Humanist principles to be followed? Or humanist principles as an example of the kind of principles to look for?"[8] Even if non-explicit, humanism remained an issue for modernists too.

In Romanian architecture, the humanist claim remained explicit, even emphatically stated, throughout all those years. Hence the problem of the humanist discourse – both the official discourse of the regime and architects' discourse – becomes the distance between discourse and reality. As theorist Hilde Heynen remarked in the larger context of modernity critique, the concept of humanism can be "the ideal camouflage for the actual inhumanity of the system."[9] This rupture between discourse and reality was indeed the case with communist modernity.

But does this mean that the discourse was irrelevant just because it was controlled and manipulated? On the contrary: anthropologist Katherine Verdery remarked that "struggles in the realm of discourse" even gained "special significance" in communist societies and that "discourse ha[d] a disproportionately productive role."[10] Verdery here is referring to Romania's written culture, but architectural discourse – both as architects' words accompanying architecture and the rhetorical dimension of architecture itself – could also be seen in this "productive" sense.

fig. 1 Aerial view of Balta Albă district in Bucharest, 1961–1964. Source: *Arhitectura* 4/1967, p. 31

fig. 2 Blocks of flats in Balta Albă district in Bucharest. Source: *Arhitectura* RPR 4/1963, p. 34

Verdery argues that, in Romania, a stronger Party control "made the discursive field more unified than most."[11] It is this unified discursive field that explains the contamination between political and architectural discourse. We will address here a series of particular subjective discourses; but the chorus of individual voices was inscribed in this objective discursive field, which determined the sense of the notion of humanism in Romanian architecture at the time.

Scientificity

From the late 1950s through the first half of the 1960s, the central issue in Romanian architecture was the return to modernism – although architects didn't call it by that name. It was not just a question of aesthetics, but concerned the essential modernistic interest in serial dwelling, efficient industrialized technologies and the functionalist city. Far from humanizing architecture, this was a time of reinstating the modernistic machine (figs. 1, 2).

The architectural simplicity of the first large housing ensembles in Romania was the direct result of the still-simple industrialized methods of construction, which were just being introduced. Industry, however, was not just a means to the end of modernizing constructions; it was the means for modernizing the entire society, a key to urbanization. Architects were widely involved: 30 percent of them worked for the industrial sector.[12] The large scale of the process of urbanization through industrialization was controlled by the integrative concept of "systematization." This gave a "scientific base" to the "rational distribution of population within the territory" and the "appropriate organization of all human settlements."[13] The entire territory of the country was organized as a systemic machine of scientific spatial control.

The communist regime strongly believed in scientific methods. As historian Lucian Boia has shown, scientificity was part of the basic communist mythology.[14] Architects at the time pleaded for "the great development of scientific research in the field of architecture."[15] It was this belief that shaped the concept of the human in 1960s Romanian architecture.

Science was part of modernist discourse in the West too. In a visit to Romania in 1963 – which was truly influential[16] – Richard Neutra advised local architects to make experiments on human habitat using science research models, like those of social psychology and, most of all, biology. Architects should learn from veterinarians who study the behavior of animals in zoo cages; methods tested on them should work for humans too, he claimed. Man can be educated to live in small capsules and can be instructed on how to behave in them, Neutra wrote in his *Arhitectura* article.[17]

This concept of the human as a product of biosocial engineering was one addressed by Romanian architects too. They argued that architectural space should be the "optimal environment for the most favorable organization of biological and social processes."[18] When man proves unwilling to adapt to this concept, it was not seen as architecture's fault but as man's. It is the lack of the "science of inhabiting" that prevents inhabitants from appreciating their apartments, architects believed.[19] But the science of inhabiting could be taught; and they pleaded for the necessity of educating the inhabitants in order to dwell correctly.[20] Architecture should consider "man as a totally social product."[21]

In order to deal with this matter scientifically, architects resorted to sociology. *Arhitectura* published sociological studies and dedicated a special issue (2/1969) to the "sociology of housing." Sociology as an academic field had been abolished with the education reform of 1948; it would be reestablished in 1965, at the peak of the Thaw.[22] During the period in which their discipline was banned from universities, sociologists continued to be active in other areas. Project institutes, especially the IPCT (Project Institute for Type Constructions), used sociological studies in order to inform the process of typification.[23] Now that architects did not directly communicate with the individual user – as sociologist Max Lupan has said – they had to work with well-defined "social types," and this was precisely "what housing sociology provided."[24] Lupan also wrote that the dwelling was not a "machine," but it pertained to the human-science system.[25] Sociologists brought about a humanistic approach in housing projects, without betraying their scientific ethos.

fig. 3 Blocks of flats on Giurgiului Road in Bucharest. Source: *Arhitectura* 6/1969, p. 19

fig. 4 Blocks of flats in the industrial town of Gheorghe Gheorghiu Dej (today Onești). Source: *Arhitectura* 6/1969, p. 33

Sociologists' methods of research inspired architects through the 1960s and 1970s – for example, Mihail Caffé, who came up with the notion of "statistic variety." In a debate on how to diversify housing projects, Caffé remarked that, unlike experiments in physics and chemistry, "the final objective of the architectural experiment is man." But architects cannot work with the "infinite variety of family types, with all their social and psychological characteristics"; therefore they should address a "variety in statistical sense."[26] Architect Gheorghe Sebestyen tried to inform the notion of economic efficiency with the social perspective; he defined the "social efficiency" of housing developments as "the totality of social effects" of an investment and the rate at which it generated the socialist lifestyle.[27]

Concepts like "statistic variety" and "social efficiency" show that not only were housing estates designed for their inhabitants, but vice versa too. One might argue that this resulted in a reversal of means and ends. Should housing be scientifically adjusted to man? Or was it man who had to be transformed by housing? Both seem to hold a certain truth. So when architect Octav Doicescu spoke about the "large humanist horizon" of architecture as being "the right relation between man, society and its material means,"[28] that ambiguity was assumed in the meaning behind the "right relation" (figs. 3, 4).

However, the architects' discourse soon became critical. The social homogeneity they accepted in theory translated itself into homogeneous buildings. They intended to build "intimate, humane housing estates"[29]; then produced monotonous ones instead. Cezar Lăzărescu remarked that spatial organization – the indefinite open spaces around the isolated rectangular "matchboxes"[30] – was itself to blame for the failure to create social cohesion, inter-human contacts, and community life in these ensembles.[31] His argument was produced only later, in order to promote the (not so humanizing) densification and reduction of green space during the 1970s. However, Lăzărescu was right; community life was absent in the modernistic social-architectural machines of the 1960s. Even if a "softer notion of collectivity"[32] was provided by the notion of *microraion* – the neighborhood unit of the new housing estates – this was still predetermined and generic. Gheorghe Sebestyen criticized the discrepancy between the neighborhood-unit theory and its actual materialization and remarked on these neighborhoods as being "totally deprived of humanizing elements, of scale and intimacy."[33]

Indeed, 1960s Romanian housing estates lacked "the true complexity of human association", which historian Alan Colquhoun for example found in Brutalist housing by the Smithsons.[34] The word "community" was all but absent in Romanian architects' discourses. As Colquhoun remarked, the Smithsons considered community relations as being created in the very habitat; the key to community lay in housing, not in a core of representative buildings.[35] In Romania, it was the other way around; the lack of any sense of community at the housing level would lead to a need for representative buildings.

Specificity

A shift would occur in Romanian architecture by the mid-1960s in order to satisfy this need. This was bolstered by the fact that the state – the sole commissioner – decided to raise a relatively large number of cultural and administrative buildings in just a few years. Architects turned their interest from the anti-rhetoric of housing estates to the expressive language of these programs. "It is time for housing to leave the place to buildings with more representative functions," Horia Hudiță wrote.[36]

However, state housing developments were not abandoned; they would carry on, with heavy prefabrication no less, till the end of the regime. It was not their humanism that was in question: they sheltered people at a time of housing shortages; they provided generous green spaces and all necessary urban facilities; apartments were well equipped and hygienic; they meant real material and social progress for the people who moved into them. What was in question was the "specificity" of their architecture.

The notion was not politically neutral; the head of the Party, Gheorghe Gheorghiu-Dej, had asked architects to embody "certain particularities specific to the city" in new housing estates.[37] But neither was it something imposed. Like the return to modernism, it was a true belief. For Octav Doicescu, it was architecture's very definition: "architecture was born as the specificity of a given human environment."[38]

Arhitectura had tackled the subject on occasion; now it dedicated two special issues (2, 3/1967) to "problems of contemporary architectural aesthetics" in Romania, more precisely to the "particular hallmark, variety and local specificity of our architecture."[39] However, the notion was vaguely used and widely controversial. It stirred up a true debate. What was specificity? What could be considered as particular urban design? Or peculiar architectural detailing? Was it the expression of the designer's personality? The use of original art objects? The relation to local natural landscape? To folklore? Inspiration from historical monuments or, more generally, historical culture? Reference to a place, a city, a region, or reference to a national identity?

Architect Pompiliu Macovei, vice president of the UAR (Union of Architects in Romania), presented it as a political imperative: the leaders of the Party required "an architecture that is specific to the country, the region and our cities."[40] But between country, region and city, the level closest to the human scale prevailed in architects' discourses during the 1960s. A specific environment for the working people, architect Ernst Szigeti wrote, was not produced by some archaic language but by new plastic expressions, using works of visual art, landscaping and green space, and a variable combination of type-projects.[41] For Gustav Gusti, "local specificity" involved the use of "the laws of composition" and "the science of controlled perspectives, succession and the hierarchy of architectural moments."[42] Specificity went along perfectly with scientificity and meant rigorous aestheticization.

Aestheticization had been one of the main topics in Western postwar architecture too. In *Architektur und Gemeinschaft* (1956), Sigfried Giedion pleaded for aesthetic values in architecture. Giedion, however, contrasted them with methods imported from science; we have had enough, he wrote, of approaches from biology, sociology and economics.[43] Most importantly, he related "humanizing of the city" to a "new regionalism."[44]

It was this regionalist impulse that fed the new kind of architecture in Romania too. The profession had been extremely centralized in the first decade of the communist regime – confined to state institutes in 1948,[45] with more than 90 percent of these concentrated in Bucharest and only 4 percent of architects working outside the capital.[46] In 1957, sixteen regional design institutes were created.[47] Another administrative reform in 1968 multiplied

fig. 5 Exterior detail of the Unions Culture House in Suceava, arch. Nicolae Porumbescu, 1966–1969. Source: *Arhitectura* 4/1969, p. 43

fig. 6 Interior of the Unions Culture House in Suceava, arch. Nicolae Porumbescu, 1966–1969. Source: *Arhitectura* 4/1969, p. 46

territorial units to thirty-nine counties, creating new county capitals, which needed representative buildings. This official decentralization gave a regional sense to the notion of "specificity" (figs. 5, 6).

Unlike rather anonymously designed housing estates, these new buildings would have architects' names on them – for instance, that of Nicolae Porumbescu, the newly assigned director of the regional project-institute in Suceava. His Houses of Culture in Suceava (1966–1969) and Baia Mare (1967–1969) and the Political and Administrative Center in Botoșani (1968–1970) would prove seminal. Porumbescu looked for inspiration in local peasant art, which he translated into a modern sculptural expression. He took Constantin Brâncuși – whose atelier he visited in Paris in 1967[48] – as a model. Porumbescu defined "specificity" as the "lyricism" that "humanizes" architecture, making it "an art of human will."[49] He did not forget his belief in science either. In order to properly define specificity, "a comprehensive scientific research of Romanian folklore art is necessary," he declared.[50]

The places to start such a research were precisely the regions Porumbescu worked for. In Bucovina and Maramureș (where Suceava, Botoșani and Baia

fig. 7 The Political-administrative Centre of Botoșani County in Botoșani, arch. Nicolae Porumbescu, 1968–1970. Source: *Arhitectura* 1/1973, p. 22

fig. 8 Interior of the Political-administrative Centre of Botoșani County in Botoșani, arch. Nicolae Porumbescu, 1968–1970. Source: *Arhitectura* 1/1973, p. 27

Mare are located), peasant culture was still alive. However, his regionalist approach was also accompanied by an essentialist discourse, which pertained to Romanian architecture on the whole – "peasant architecture" was "the true source of our architecture,"[51] providing "our own architectural mother tongue"[52] – a discourse that would eventually relate the notion of specificity to national identity (figs. 7, 8).

As several other remarkable buildings with programmatic "specificity" emerged (including Mircea Alifanti's Political and Administrative Center of Maramureș County in Baia Mare, 1968–1970; Horia Maicu and Romeo Belea's National Theater in Bucharest, 1964–1973; Constantin Săvescu's National Theater in Tîrgu Mureș, 1969–1974, etc.), theorist Mircea Lupu was able to raise the issue of a "national school" by the mid-1970s. Architecture epitomized the "spiritual profile of a collectivity," Lupu wrote; a "national architecture" reflected the "methodical quest for the fundaments of the spiritual structure of a people."[53] "Lyrical functionalism" was the "humanistic specificity" of Romanian architecture, he concluded.[54]

The timing of the shift in how architects defined specificity from local to national closely followed a similar one in the corresponding political discourse. The general secretary of the Party, Nicolae Ceaușescu, asked for "greater attention toward local specificity" in architecture in 1965;[55] his UAR speech in 1971 demanded representation of "our national specificity."[56] This is precisely the interval in which the proper architectural debate was engulfed by nationalistic political discourse. From the early 1970s on, specificity would become a generic instrument of aesthetic representation in the service of the national-communist state.

This mutation occurred across Romanian culture at the time. Verdery also observed "the post-1965 flood of writings on the Nation and its essence" and its "purposeful instrumentalization by the Party."[57] It was the "utilization in argument, this discourse and counterdiscourse, definition and counterdefinition, that made national ideology so salient in Romania. Few other ideas [...] managed to enter into such a dialogue."[58] If nationalism prevailed, it was not because the Party imposed it, but because "all intellectuals, even those who considered themselves to be opposing the Party, were serving it [...]."[59]

Opposition and Interference

The 1960s was a decade of genuine architectural debate in Romania. Two distinct discourses emerged: the first related to the "social efficiency" of large-scale housing estates in the early 1960s, and the second to the "human specificity" embodied by the new administrative and cultural centers of the late 1960s. Two shifts occurred between and within them: from the scientificity of housing developments to the specificity of symbolic buildings by the mid-1960s, and from local to national in understanding specificity by the early 1970s.

The difference between the two discourses seems evident: on the one hand, the technicality and efficiency of mass standardized architecture for the new man of serial production; on the other, the creative lyricism of an expressive architecture for a localized man – a generic spatial system versus a multiplicity of distinctive rhetoric objects, the machine versus the human.

Nevertheless, this seemingly clear opposition was blurred. The two discourses seemed to succeed and oppose one another, but they overlapped and interfered as well. Scientificity – a basic communist myth – never left the scene. Specificity mutated from local particularism into national generality. Eventually, both discourses endorsed a politically instrumentalized architecture at the service of the state, addressing the same human being: the newly urbanized man of communist modernity.

Endnotes

1 Pompiliu Macovei, ed., *Arhitectura în Republica Populară Română* (Bucharest: ESLA, 1952), n.p.
2 Ion Mircea Enescu, *Arhitect sub comunism* (Bucharest: Paideia, 2007), 221.
3 Reyner Banham, "The New Brutalism," *The Architectural Review* (December 1955), 354–361.
4 Nicolae Porumbescu, "Interview with Ileana Murgescu," *Arhitectura*, 2–3 (1981), 60–62.
5 Banham, "The New Brutalism," 356.
6 Banham, "The New Brutalism," 358.
7 Andrea Palladio, *Patru cărți de arhitectură*, trans. R. Bordenache (Bucharest: Ed. Tehnică, 1957).
8 Banham, "The New Brutalism," 361.
9 Hilde Heynen, *Architecture and Modernity: A Critique* (Cambridge, Mass.: MIT Press, 1999), 221.
10 Katherine Verdery, *National Ideology Under Socialism. Identity and Cultural Politics in Ceaușescu's Romania* (Berkeley: University of California Press, 1991), 305, 91.
11 Verdery, *National Ideology*, 11.
12 Ladislau Adler, et al., *Arhitectura industrială în RPR* (Bucharest: Ed. Tehnică, 1964), 274.
13 Gustav Gusti, "Două decenii de sistematizare complexă și construcție socialistă a teritoriului," *Arhitectura RPR*, 4 (1964), 26–39 (p. 30).
14 Lucian Boia, *Mitologia științifică a comunismului* (Bucharest: Humanitas, 2011).
15 "A doua Conferință pe țară a Uniunii Arhitecților din RPR. Discuții," *Arhitectura RPR*, 3 (1965), 22–43 (p. 34).
16 Enescu, *Arhitect*, 245.
17 Richard Neutra, "Arhitectura ca activitate umană," *Arhitectura RPR*, 3 (1964), 36–45.
18 Pompiliu Macovei, "Darea de seamă a Comitetului de conducere al uniunii arhitecților din RPR," *Arhitectura*, 3 (1965), 11–21.
19 Dorian Hardt, "Noi tipuri de locuințe de masă," *Arhitectura*, 5 (1968), 25–31.
20 Ignace Șerban, "Unele considerații asupra rezultatelor «anchetei cu privire la condițiile de folosire a clădirilor locuit,» *Arhitectura*, 3 (1967), 32–37.
21 "A doua Conferință," p.31.
22 Maria Larionescu, *Istoria sociologiei românești* (Bucharest: Ed. Universității București, 2007), 195.
23 Mihail Caffé, "Aspecte de aplicare în proiectare a cercetării sociologice de arhitectură," *Arhitectura*, 2 (1969), 7.
24 Max Lupan, "O anchetă privind condițiile de folosire a locuinței urbane," *Arhitectura*, 3 (1967), 20–31.
25 Max Lupan, "Condiții pentru dezvoltarea sociologiei locuinței și un mod sociologic de abordare a problemei specificului," *Arhitectura* 2 (1969), 3–4.
26 "A doua Conferință," 30–31.
27 Gheorghe Sebestyen, *Eficiența economică și socială a ansamblurilor de locuit* (Bucharest: Ed. Tehnică, 1975), 55, 74.
28 Octav Doicescu, "Probleme actuale ale esteticii arhitecturale contemporane românești," *Arhitectura*, 2 (1967), 2–17.

29 Ernst Szigeti, "Dezvoltarea proiectării de arhitectură în Regiunea Brașov," *Arhitectura RPR* 6 (1962), 4–5.
30 Cezar Lăzărescu, et al., *Urbanismul în România* (Bucharest: Ed. Tehnică, 1977), 69.
31 Lăzărescu. *Urbanismul în România*, 50.
32 Juliana Maxim, "Mass Housing and Collective Experience: On the Notion of Microraion in Romania in the 1950s and 1960s," *The Journal of Architecture*, 14:1 (2009), 7–26.
33 Sebestyen, *Eficiența*, 63, 70.
34 Alan Colquhoun, *Modern Architecture* (Oxford: Oxford University Press, 2002), 219.
35 Colquhoun, *Modern Architecture.*
36 Horia Hudiță, "Construcția și reconstrucția orașelor și noile ansambluri de locuit," *Arhitectura*, 1 (1966), 21.
37 Ernst Szigeti, "Cu privire la particularitățile specifice ale orașelor," *Arhitectura RPR*, 4 (1963), 56.
38 Doicescu, "Probleme actuale," 6.
39 [Editorial] *Arhitectura*, 2 (1967), 2.
40 Macovei, "Darea de seamă," 13.
41 Szigeti, "Cu privire," 57.
42 Gusti, "Două decenii," 36.
43 Sigfried Giedion, *Architecture et vie collective. Redonner la ville aux hommes*, trans. Georges Pauline (Paris: Denöel/Gonthier, 1980), 9.
44 Giedion, *Architecture et vie collective*, 119, 139.
45 Alexandru Panaitescu, *De la Casa Scânteii la Casa Poporului* (Bucharest: Simetria, 2012), 32.
46 Grigore Ionescu, *Arhitectura în România 1944–1969* (Bucharest: Ed. Academiei, 1969), 61–64.
47 Gusti, "Două decenii," 30.
48 Virgiliu Onofrei and Tudor Grădinaru, *Nicolae Porumbescu. O viață în arhitectură* (Iași: Soc. Acad. M. Botez, 2003), 39.
49 Nicolae Porumbescu and Maria Vaida-Porumbescu, "Specificul în arhitectură," *Arhitectura*, 2 (1967), 12–17 (p.12).
50 Porumbescu and Vaida-Porumbescu, "Specificul," 16.
51 "A doua Conferință," 36.
52 Porumbescu and Vaida-Porumbescu, "Specificul," 16.
53 Mircea Lupu, Școli naționale în arhitectură (Bucharest, Ed. Tehnică, 1977), 34–35.
54 Lupu, Școli naționale în arhitectură, 154–155.
55 Discourse in 1965, cited by Mihai Florescu, "Funcția socială a arhitecturii și urbanismului," *Arhitectura*, 6 (1969), 2–12.
56 "Cuvîntarea Tovarășului Nicolae Ceaușescu, a III-a conferință a UA din RSR, 4–5 martie 1971," *Arhitectura*, 2 (1971), 3–8.
57 Verdery, *National Ideology*, 121–122.
58 Ibid., 126.
59 Ibid., 309.

Karin Hallas-Murula

Sociological and Environmental-Psychology Research in Estonia during the 1960s and 1970s: A Critique of Soviet Mass-Housing

In the context of industrial production of mass-housing in the Soviet Union, which accelerated in the late 1950s, architecture and planning research concentrated in large part on quantity, mathematical modeling and on statistical and technical matters. During the 1960s and 1970s, the focus widened remarkably with side disciplines: sociology re-emerged and new sciences appeared, including environmental psychology. This article highlights the importance of sociology in developing a critical attitude towards the Soviet living environment and lifestyle. The sociological research at the University of Tartu played a decisive role in the formation of new human-centered disciplines: urban sociology and environmental psychology, which in the 1970s started qualitative research on the Soviet living environment, aiming at the improvement of architectural practice.

The poor quality of Khrushchev-era industrial mass building quickly discredited the highly humanistic rhetoric of Soviet building policy. In the mass production of homes, quantity was preferred over quality and abstract ideals of Soviet humanist society overruled the needs of individuals. Monotonous new housing districts were not able to satisfy the social and psychological needs of the people. In the state economy system ruled by the Communist

Party there were few possibilities to change the situation. Criticism was allowed, but strictly limited. It was acceptable to criticize "some shortages" of Soviet life – or construction companies for their slow work, or architects for leaking plumbing pipes; but not the system itself, let alone Soviet ideology. Despite the fact that architects had started to improve prototype plans since their appearance in the 1950s, they had few opportunities to struggle against the industrial system in general. Architects and planners were also much inclined toward implementing mathematical methods and structural modeling into planning and design, which would emphasize people as units of the system. It was sociologists who became most active and effective in criticizing mass housing and stood for a humanization of architecture and the living environment. In the 1970s, new sciences – including environmental psychology, urban ecology and behavioral sciences – joined in the criticism of Soviet building practice. Sociological research in Soviet Estonia from the 1960s, and environmental psychology research there in the 1970s, contributed considerably to the architectural theory of the period. I will also discuss the characteristic parallel existence of official ideological rhetoric, scientific knowledge and hidden criticism recognized by those who were able to read "between the lines." The ability to encode and decode published texts was a widespread and appreciated skill during the Soviet era.[1] When rereading texts from those years, these skills need to be applied again. The majority of Soviet-era documents, records and articles consist of several layers of information, direct and indirect, open and hidden. The use of additional resources (written and unwritten memoirs) is also vital.

Soviet Mass Building of the Late 1950s and the 1960s in Estonia

As elsewhere in the Soviet Union, the industrial mass-dwelling in Estonia was propelled by Khrushchev. In the early 1960s, the Tallinn Dwelling Construction Factory (1961) was established and the first satellite town, Mustamäe, was founded according to the theory of micro-districts adapted from the West. The majority of dwellings were built; while public centers, shops and services, which existed in the plans, usually remained unbuilt. As a result, new districts quickly turned into mono-functional bedroom communities.

The standard projects of dwellings were worked out in Moscow project institutes; because of the standardized structure, there were few possibilities to change them according to local needs, though it was clear from the start that unified housing prototypes could not satisfy the different needs in the many regions of the Soviet Union. It was a lengthy process to increase the minimum number of square meters per person: from 7.7 m^2 per person in

1956 to as much as 15.8 m^2 in 1989. Paradoxically, criticism regarding living conditions rose steadily along with the increase in square meters per person.

In Estonia, the plan was to build 1.6 million square meters of new flats within seven years starting from 1957.[2] The most popular versions of the *khrushchovka*-type dwellings were projects Nos. 1-317 and 1-464. The 1958 all-union building regulations replaced the previous corridor-type of communal flats with single-family flats where the living room became a walk-through room. Despite the inconvenience in terms of privacy, this remained the Soviet standard for a long time.

It was a time when many scientific-research institutions were founded, and it was characteristic that all decisions had to be scientifically proven. The emergence of demographic research in the Soviet Union was an important undertaking. It soon revealed that in some parts of the Soviet Union the building types did not correspond to the real demographic situation at all. Thus, in Leningrad it occurred that 45 percent of households had only one or two members, which constituted 84 percent of the demand for new apartments. At the same time, only 24 percent of new flats were built for this group.[3] From 1956 to 1958, a statistical survey was compiled by the Scientific Institute of Construction and Building Materials in Estonia, led by Leonid Volkov. The survey discovered that on average there was 7 m^2 of living space per person in Estonia at that time. In very critical cases, it was as low as 3 m^2 only. It was also noted that in reality as much as 46 percent of one- and two-room flats were overcrowded. In some cases, six or seven people were living in one single-room flat.[4] The recognized norm for this kind of flat was officially three people; for a two-room flat, the norm was a family of four. The greatest number of flats built were two-room flats. One-room flats (on average 19 m^2) were soon abandoned because it was difficult to accommodate three people sleeping in one room, even in the Soviet era.

Estonian architectural research also dealt with the aims and uses of different rooms. Serious discussion was held about the necessity of cellars in Soviet housing. It was thought that the Soviet way of life, with its wide use of communal eating places, reduced the need for cellars, and kitchens were scaled back accordingly. In reality, the quantity and quality of public eating places as well as other services remained low. Cellars were used for storing products (potatoes, vegetables, jam jars, etc.) because there was not enough cold space in the flats. Cellars were also places to keep bicycles, skis, sleighs, prams, car tires, car fuel, etc.[5] Balconies were another controversial issue. Architects thought these were not much needed, but the research cited above revealed that people liked them very much – if only in the cases when the balcony faced the sunny side and not a noisy street. Thus the architectural research included questions about the usage of rooms but qualitative questions were not yet posed about the satisfaction of dwellers and their essential needs.

From 1964 onward, the comfort and quality of standardized dwellings were more accentuated in Soviet building regulations. Walk-through rooms were excluded, additional storage space and loggias were added, etc. Still, bad construction quality, the dependence on industrial production and the small number of prototypes remained the main obstacles for meeting people's needs better. Free planning resulted in large areas between buildings, which turned into no-man's-land. In Estonia, additional problems arose from Soviet immigration policy: the majority of inhabitants of new homes were people from all over the Soviet Union; of different nationality, culture and language. On that basis, social and national conflicts were inevitable.

Official criticism was widely practiced at Communist Party plenums during Stalin's rule as well as under Khrushchev. There were always institutions and people to blame for the slow speed of achieving Communism, which never arrived. Criticism for the mass-produced architecture and environment had already started in the late 1950s, Leningrad architects being first.[6] In Estonia, criticism of monotonous architecture could already be found in the early 1960s. In 1961, architect Mart Port published an article about the limits of industrial methods in architecture, suggesting differentiation between the types of flats and increasing the flexibility of their planning with the help of removable walls.[7] As head of the Estonian Architects Union (since 1955) and having served in the Soviet Army during the war, Port could afford to be far more critical than many others at that time. In 1962, he stated: "Sometimes one can hear about literature: there are lines of text but no poetics. In contemporary architecture one could say: there are buildings but no architecture."[8] Not all industrially produced houses should look similar and the demands of individual families ought to be considered, Port wrote this in the same year that the building of Mustamäe, the first panel-housing area, had started in Tallinn.

The Rebirth of Soviet Sociology, and the Kääriku Seminars in Estonia

The Soviet system has often been seen by foreign researchers in black-and-white terms. In reality, one should be careful using the totalitarian paradigm equally for the entire Soviet Union or each of its regions. There were relatively liberal periods; the 1960s being one (the Khrushchev Thaw), as well as regions with relatively more freedom, including the Baltic States. The Iron Curtain was not so "iron" at all times and places. When Khrushchev started his reforms in the late 1950s, contacts with the West were even encouraged for a short period. Departments of libraries which had been closed under Stalin were reopened (in Estonia in 1957), and a great deal of foreign literature became available again. Naturally, information sources were controlled by the KGB and some topics remained prohibited for ideological reasons. As a countertactic, there was the practice of "smuggling books" using personal contacts, and making handwritten copies of them.

After Stalin's death, the rebirth of sociology in the Soviet Union had become possible. In 1956, for the first time, Soviet scientists participated in the Third World Sociological Congress in Amsterdam, organized by the International Sociological Association (ISA). Remarkably, the document on the participation of the Soviets in the ISA conference was issued at the highest political level – as a Decree by the Presidium of the Communist Party of the USSR.[9] In 1957, the international conference of sociologists on the question of peaceful coexistence was held in Moscow, in which some of the world's most eminent sociologists participated, such as Raymond Aron, Georges Friedman, A. N. J. den Hollander, Everett C. Hughes, Helmut Schelsky and Tom Bottomore.[10] In 1958, the Soviet Sociological Association was founded, then in 1960 the first sociological unit was created as part of the Institute of Philosophy of the Academy of Sciences, Moscow.[11] In the same year, the Soviet Union's first sociology laboratory was created at Leningrad State University.[12] That institution invited Western scientists, for example Talcott Parsons and Robert Merton, to give lectures in Leningrad.[13]

Leningrad sociologists started with studies of the social typology of Soviet society and socialization, the value structure and value orientations of the individual, social activity and other issues, which to a different extent were also related to the physical environment.[14] In the 1970s, questionnaires about the Soviet way of life in big cities were more in the focus. Officially, Soviet researchers had to oppose Western "bourgeois" sociology and had to fight it ideologically. Alas, objective statistical results of demographic research at the time, and later those of questionnaires, were not so easy to oppose with ideological slogans.

The University of Tartu became one of the important centers of liberal thought in the Soviet Union. In the 1950s, the scientists who were repressed in Leningrad for their Jewish nationality could continue their work in Tartu. Among them were Yuri Lotman, Mikhail Bronstein, Rem Blum and other remarkable scientists who, for understandable reasons, were far from applauding the achievements of Soviet ideology.

Already in the late 1950s, a students' sociology group was formed in Tartu. The Sociology Laboratory was officially opened in 1967, with Ylo Vooglaid as its head. It focused first on mass communication, mass media and value orientations but soon expanded into research on the quality of working space, the Soviet lifestyle, home and environment, as well as technical aesthetics.[15]

Thus officially controlled science and more liberal science coexisted in the Soviet Union. From 1966 to 1969, during the relatively liberal years, sociology seminars were organized near Tartu in Kääriku which attracted liberal-thinking scientists from all over the Soviet Union (Moscow, Sverdlovsk, Novosibirsk, Vilnius, Riga, Tbilisi, etc.). Among them were Vladimir Yadov, Yuri Levada, Boris Firsov, Igor Kon and other leading specialists in sociology, philosophy, psychology, architecture and planning in the Soviet Union. Kääriku seminars have been described as "an oasis in the desert sand of Soviet normative socialism" where "sociologists from all over the Soviet Union aspired for the breath of freedom of expression."[16]

The proceedings of the seminars were published in cheap rota-print bulletins in a small number of copies (five to seven hundred), which remain an important source for studying the alternative research of the time. It was possible to hold very open scientific discussions there. In those rota-printed proceedings, one found no quotations from Lenin or references to resolutions of the Communist Party congresses, which were absolutely obligatory in all other Soviet scientific publications. Abstracts and articles were published in Russian with summaries in English, which was also uncommon in the Soviet era.

Officially, the Western concept of humanism was confronted with the concept of "Soviet humanism" in the Soviet Union. Still, it seemed to be necessary to also deal with the "essentially Western" social problems caused by the new mass-produced living environment in the Soviet Union, such as rising crime rates, especially in new dwelling areas, divorces, and above all, "alienation." The Western proliferation of the concept of alienation in the 1950s and 1960s also entered the Soviet Union. In controlled publications, Western researchers were accused of falsifying the Marxist theory of alienation.[17] In more scientific and less ideological publications, the problem was addressed with more serious discussion. In Estonia, an article by Rem Blum cleared the topic of alienation for the Estonian cultural audience in 1969.[18]

It became difficult for Soviet authorities to oppose scientific research with ideological argumentation, and soon sociology was acknowledged as a danger to the Soviet regime. The reaction started across the Soviet Union after the Prague invasion in August 1968. Already in 1969, Yuri Levada, the first Russian professor ever to lecture on sociology, was accused of jeopardizing Marxism-Leninism and his statements were classified as "ideologically erroneous." In 1972, Levada's institute – the Russian Institute of Concrete Social Research – was closed down. During the second half of the Leonid Brezhnev era (1964–1982), around two hundred sociologists were purged from research institutes and universities. Estonian scientists were accused of blindly and uncritically following Western scientists.[19] Kääriku seminars were forbidden (the final one was held in 1969), and the last proceedings were never published. In 1975, the sociology laboratory in Tartu was closed too, and its head, Ylo Vooglaid, was expelled from the university and the party. The KGB searched sociologists' offices and homes.[20]

This harsh reaction of the Soviet system is the best proof of the oppositional character of Tartu sociology research. (Not surprisingly, it was Tartu sociologists of the 1960s – Vooglaid, Marju Lauristin and others – who would then stand at the forefront of the Estonian liberation movement and became parliament members in independent Estonia.) Despite the reaction, criticism of the Soviet living environment with its mass building became prevalent in the 1970s. The famous Soviet film *The Irony of the Fate or Enjoy Your Bath!* (1975), included sharp irony towards Soviet panel districts for being confusingly similar all over the Soviet Union. The first Estonian novels to include criticism of the living environment in panel districts date from 1978 – *Autumn Ball* by Mati Unt and *Love in Mustamäe* by Arvo Valton – both reflect on the alienation caused by an anonymous living environment. The novelists were openly accused of copying the problem of alienation from the West, but actually their novels rose to the top of oppositional texts loved by the Estonian audience who read "between the lines."

New Disciplines in the 1970s

On the basis of sociology and psychology from the early 1960s, new interdisciplinary sciences dealt with the realities of the living environment, such as environmental and architectural psychology, urban sociology, urban ecology and others. These emphasized human qualities in interaction with spatial environment, and brought focus to the individual human being. In developing new theories concerning human need for space, these were very close to the fields of architecture and planning.

New environmental-psychology research was initiated in Tallinn by disciples of the University of Tartu sociologists, as a reaction against the closing of the sociology laboratory. They started with research themes at Tallinn Pedagogical Institute[21] in the early 1970s. In 1979, the Environmental Psychology Research Group (EPRG) was established, the first of the kind in the Soviet Union. This took place after the US and England had opened the first postgraduate university programs for environmental-psychology studies. The first major book, *Environmental Psychology*, was published in 1970 and also became the main important study resource in Estonia.[22]

Personalization of environment as man's "environmental self," "environmental settings," ergonomics and other new concepts were introduced in the debates of the 1970s in Estonia. Phenomenological and psycho-geographical urban research was conducted in papers at environmentalist conferences. Focusing on individual perception, environmental research followed sociology research in being critical, perhaps in a more veiled way. The high density of dwelling areas, their anonymity, lack of sociability and similar problems were obvious in the Soviet urban environment. As has been alluded to, in Estonia these were sharpened by the political situation of Soviet occupation.

In 1981, the first environmental-psychology conference in the Soviet Union was organized in Lohusalu, Estonia, under the title "Man and Environment: Psychological Aspects." Again, the site of the conference was not Tallinn or a major town, but a small secluded resort, similar to Kääriku. The Lohusalu conference attracted as many as ninety papers from all over the Soviet Union, thus growing into a representational forum broadly reflecting the state of new environmental and urban research. The next conferences were entitled "Psychology and Architecture" (1983) and "The Socio-psychological Basis of Environmental Design" (1985).

EPRG, the Tallinn group, concentrated on personal interaction with spatial and architectural surroundings, housing issues, neighborhoods, public and private places, administrative and recreational facilities, etc. "Spatial Regulating of Human Interaction," "Man in Socio-physical Environment," "Density and Crowding" – these and many other topics were discussed at the Estonian conferences. The EPRG group also studied urban density and its influence on psychology, as well as the impact of other aspects of mass residential areas on the human psyche.

Among Western theoretical concepts of social and physical environmental behaviorism and cognitive research, behavioral geography, the concepts of congruence, proxemics, ergonomics, density, "environmental settings" and numerous others were introduced in conference debates in Estonia. Literature overviews in articles by Mati Heidmets, Toomas Niit, Jaan Kruusvall, Maie Raudsepp and others indicate extensive use of Western scientific literature.[23] Works including those of William H. Ittelson, Edward T. Hall, Harold M. Proshansky, Robert Sommer, Irwin Altman and Daniel Stokols were quoted in Estonian conference publications. New journals were founded including *Environment and Behavior* (1969), *Man–Environment Systems* (1971), *Human Ecology* (1972), *Environmental Psychology and Nonverbal Behavior* (1976), and were also available in the Soviet Union. The list of literature on urban density and overcrowding includes nearly two hundred Western books and scientific articles on that subject alone.[24]

Realistic data on the living conditions in Soviet micro-districts, people's opinions, statistics, etc., obviously could not have been published anywhere but in limited-edition university bulletins. The influence of residential density on family relations and the rise in divorces, as well as the growth of social passivity were put in focus while analyzing the theme of "social pathology."[25] Serious issues such as the rise in criminality, increases in deaths and suicides, drug addiction, diagnosed psychoses, etc., were described as negative indicators of living conditions. Officially, these problems did not exist in the Soviet Union. The statistics of suicides, psychoses as well as criminal cases were strictly classified and not available publicly.

It was also stated in the late 1970s that standard homes in the Soviet Union still did not meet the needs of families: one third of families in new residential areas lived in densities above the norm and another third below the norm.[26] Even when apartment size corresponded to family size, only 40 percent of the families used the apartments in the way intended by the architect, which clearly showed a further need to improve the layout of the flats.[27]

During the 1980s, the Tallinn EPRG group carried out more than twenty research projects dealing with a person's interaction with the built environment and architecture. The Estonian initiative helped substantially in starting environmentally oriented social and psychological studies in Russia, Ukraine, Georgia and Kazakhstan.[28]

Conclusions

The sociological and environmental-psychology research of the 1960s and 1970s opened the scientific practice of dealing with problems in Soviet society. Tackling the living conditions of people and the actual needs of inhabitants, sociological research was far from being a "pure science" only. Revealing problems connected with the "import" of Soviet lifestyle into Estonia, it quickly became politically oppositional. Demographic and sociological studies were the first to state the need for changing Soviet mass-building policy, despite the fact that not all research directions were directly connected to urban planning and architectural issues. Arising on the basis of sociology and psychology, the new discipline of environmental psychology continued to emphasize the need for humanizing the urban environment and replaced "the average person" in architectural planning with human beings of different psychological needs. Estonia was at the forefront of developing environmental psychology in the Soviet Union.

A series of seminars and conferences, which started in the 1960s in Estonia, united open-minded sociologists, philosophers, psychologists, architects and planners from all over the Soviet Union. They shared common ground by criticizing existing Soviet reality and were enthusiastic in their aims toward improvement. Creating scientific arguments against the prevailing ideology was one of the few ways of expressing essential criticism of the Soviet way of life. The most important achievement was the synergy created by different disciplines as a remarkable contribution to architectural and planning theories. The interdisciplinarity of the progressive research of the 1960s and 1970s is worthy of further study. It could also be instructive and inspiring for architecture and planning today, recognizing the need for a wide variety of living conditions and environments and acknowledging the importance of greater participation in the decision-making processes.

Endnotes

1 Marju Lauristin, *Punane ja sinine. Peatükke kirjutamata elulooraamatust: valik artikleid ja intervjuusid 1970–2009* (Tallinn: Eesti Ajalehed, 2010), 100; Olaf Kuuli, *Sula ja hallad Eesti NSV–s. Kultuuripoliitikast aastail 1953–1969.* (Tallinn: s.n., 2002), 152.

2 *Elamuehituse küsimusi Eesti NSV-s* (Tallinn: ENSV MN Riiklik Ehituse ja Arhitektuuri Komitee, 1960), 3.

3 Blair A. Ruble, "From Khrushcheby to Korobki," in *Russian Housing in the Modern Age: Design and Social History*, ed. William Craft Brumfield, Ruble (Woodrow Wilson Center Press, Cambridge University Press, 1993), 232–270 (p. 253).

4 Leonid Volkov, "Elanikud elamust," in *Elamuehituse küsimusi* (Tallinn: ENSV MN Riiklik Ehituse ja Arhitektuuri Komitee, 1963), 22–41 (p. 27).

5 Ibid.,39.

6 Ruble, "From Khrushcheby to Korobki," 252.

7 Mart Port, "Mõtteid masinatega toodetud arhitektuurist," *Sirp ja Vasar*, Jan. 28, 1961 and Feb. 3, 1961. The idea of removable walls probably was taken from Leningrad architects.

8 Port, "Pärlid ja konnakarbid," *Rahva Hääl*, May 23, 1962.

9 Gennadi Osipov, "The Rebirth of Sociology in Russia," *Sociological Research*, 5:48 (2009), 16–44 (p. 20).

10 Ibid., 20.

11 The New Forms of Labor and Everyday Life sector, headed by Gennady Osipov.

12 Osipov, "The Rebirth of Sociology in Russia," 20.

13 Asalkhan Boronoev, "Sociological Research in Leningrad–St. Petersburg (1960s–1990s)," in *Sociological Research*, 5:48 (2009), 45–54 (p. 46).

14 Ibid., 47.

15 Lauristin, *Punane ja sinine,* 93.

16 Leonid Stolovitsch, *Kohtumised eluradadel* (Tallinn: Ilo, 2006), 146.

17 E.J. Sitnikov, *Problema "otsuzhdenija" v burzhuaznoi filosofii i falsifikatsija markzisma* (Moscow: Izdatel'stvo pri Tsentral'nom Komitete Kommunistitsheskoi Partij Sovetskogo Sojuza, 1962).

18 Rem Blum, "Mis see võõrandumine siis on?", *Sirp ja Vasar*, Jan. 31, 1969.

19 Kuuli, *Sula ja hallad Eesti NSV–s*, 140.

20 Stolovitsh, *Kohtumised eluradadel*, 148.
21 Later Tallinn Pedagogical University, now Tallinn University.
22 H.M. Proshansky, W.H. Ittelson, L.G. Rivlin, *Environmental Psychology: Man and His Physical Setting* (New York: Holt, Rinehart & Winston, 1970).
23 Toomas Niit, "The Density of Environment and 'Social Pathology': What Kind of Pathology Are We Talking About?", in *Man and Environment: Psychological Aspects* from the conference in Lohusalu Jan. 20–22, 1981, eds. Niit, M. Heidmets, J. Kruusvall (Tallinn: Tallinn Pedagogic Institute, 1981), 127; Mati Heidmets, "Subject and Environment," in *Man and Environment: Psychological Aspects.*
24 Niit, "Density and Crowding: Theories and Hypotheses," in *Man in Sociophysical Environment*, eds. H. Liimets, Niit and M. Heidmets (Tallinn: Tallinn Pedagogic Institute, 1983), 128–141.
25 Niit, "The Density of Environment and 'Social Pathology.'"
26 P. Orlov, "Obespechenie zhilym prostranstvom na etapah razvitija semeinyi struktury naselenija bolshih gorodov," in *Man and Environment*, 135–138.
27 V. Ovsjannikov, "Kolitchsestvennye i katschestvennye parametry vo vzaimosvjazi 'semja – kvartira,'" in *Man and Environment*, 139–142.
28 Niit, Heidmets, "Estonian Environmental Psychology: A Die-hard?", *Trames* 5:55/50 (2001), 195–197.

III
The Urban Context

Vladimir Kulić

Bogdan Bogdanović and the Search for a Meaningful City

The Serbian-Yugoslav architect, writer, and politician Bogdan Bogdanović (1922–2010) is internationally known for his exuberant memorials to the Second World War. Around twenty of his monuments, cemeteries, mausoleums, memorial parks, necropolises, cenotaphs and other commemorative sites, designed between the early 1950s and early 1980s, have been widely exhibited and published in the region and abroad.[1] What is less known today is that Bogdanović was also a prolific writer on the city.[2] Certainly, his interests in the questions of urbanism and commemoration were intimately connected; but one might argue that the former aimed at an even more far-reaching goal than his memorials: to turn the tide against the dominance of modernist urban planning and to recuperate the dimensions of urbanity neglected by the overt rationalism of postwar urbanization. In Bogdanović's view, the very survival of the city was in question: as the processes of uncontrolled urban growth blurred its definition, the exclusive attention given to rational, quantitative methods of planning further undermined the very essence of urban life, ultimately stripping the citizens of their deep intellectual and affective bonds and leading to social anomie. During his most creative period, parallel to his practice in the field of commemoration, Bogdanović thus engaged in writing on the city, its origins, history, and meanings, as a way of sensitizing the profession to the intangible qualities holding the city and its citizens together.

For a brief moment in the mid-1980s, it seemed as if his advocacy was finally producing results: in 1982, Bogdanović was elected Mayor of Belgrade, he had cultish following among students, and he emerged as a figure of increasingly international stature. It was under his mayorship that the city of Belgrade in 1986 organized an international competition to reimagine New Belgrade, the flagship modernist project of postwar Yugoslavia, thus officially consecrating the postmodern turn in urban planning. Semantics and phenomenology entered the mainstream of the professional discourse. But the moment of influence was not to last long; by 1987, Bogdanović got into a bitter political conflict with the newly-elected Slobodan Milošević and his nationalist policies; by the early 1990s, he was forced into exile as the war ravaged the defunct Yugoslavia. In his subsequent writings, it was the death of the city, rather than its survival, that became his dominant theme. Translated into multiple languages and internationally circulated, these texts overshadowed his earlier, intellectually more challenging and creative texts, at the same time obscuring their historical significance.[3]

This essay contends that Bogdanović's early writings constitute an important and highly erudite contribution to the postwar discourse on the city. They paralleled and incorporated the main intellectual currents of the period, but they also offered confident and highly original arguments and methods, which are irreducible to mere cultural transfer from abroad. Bogdanović shared many of his concerns with his European and American peers, such as those who came to be associated with postmodernism, like Aldo Rossi and Denise Scott Brown. He explicitly drew from some of those peers, for example, Konstantinos Doxiadis or a generation older Lewis Mumford, but he also engaged in polemics with their writings. Three texts are key in this respect: the collection of essays titled *Small Urbanism* (1958),[4] a celebration of urban experience and the pleasures of the small scale, and two books of Bogdanović's mature "anthropological" phase, arguing in favor of mythical and symbolic roots of cities: *Urbanistic Mythologems* (1966),[5] and *Urbs & Logos* (1976).[6] Bogdanović's pedagogical experiments were a natural extension of these writings: he engaged students in rather unconventional practices at his summer school in Mali Popović outside of Belgrade in order to teach them about the anthropological roots of cities and to sensitize them to the social construction of urban meaning, a precondition of urban life.

The Pleasures of Urban Life

Bogdanović's intellectual erudition was rooted in his formative experiences with surrealism, setting him onto a rather unconventional path for an architect and urban thinker. Born in Belgrade in 1922 to the family of Milan Bogdanović, a well-known literary critic, young Bogdan was surrounded by the left-leaning intellectual elite of interwar Yugoslavia from an early age. Especially significant was the influence of the circle of Belgrade surrealists, whose leader, poet and theorist Marko Ristić, became Bogdanović's mentor, role-model, and the source of inspiration for his dreams of surrealist architecture.[7] For surrealists, of course, the city was the prime site of fascination:

fig. 1 Bogdan Bogdanović (1922–2010). Courtesy of Ksenija Bogdanović

suffice it to recall that the movement's canonical texts, such as Louis Aragon's *Le Paysan de Paris* (1926) and André Breton's *Nadja* (1928) were written from the perspective of a Baudelairean urban flâneur. Bogdanović wrote much of *Small Urbanism* from a similar perspective, albeit with a far more didactic goal of drawing the attention of the public and of his fellow professionals to the neglected pleasures of urban life. The shift to anthropological literature in his subsequent writings can also be explained, at least in part, through his early contacts with the surrealists, who maintained a consistent interest in the "primitive." It should thus be less of a surprise that Bogdanović – as an architect known primarily for his work in the field of commemoration – would spend most of his career at the Department of Urbanism at Belgrade's Faculty of Architecture, where he established and taught a popular course on the History of the City.

Small Urbanism was Bogdanović's first book, a collection of essays written for various Yugoslav periodicals. A paean to *architettura minore*, the picturesque, and the irrational – more in the tradition of Camillo Sitte than of Otto Wagner's *Großstadt* – the book revolted against the dominant rationalism of Yugoslavia's ongoing urbanization.[8] It thus celebrated the "fantastic," "literary," "uncontrolled," and "emotional" potentials of the city, as opposed to the "scientific," "schematic," "sterile" and "lifeless" "big urbanism" responsible for large-scale new developments such as New Belgrade and New Zagreb.

About forty essays – most of them only a couple of pages long – cover a range of themes, from practical issues of the day to broad poetic celebrations of the urban experience. The book's goal is didactic; one may describe it as a manifesto of urbophilia, a manual on how to love the city in all of its quirky, contradictory, surreal beauty, written at a time when these qualities became endangered by rapid urbanization and rationalist planning. Bogdanović's voice is that of a guide through the pleasures of urban life, a flâneur who delights in the city's complexity and gladly shares his enthusiasm in order to construct the city as a meaningful place for civic life.

On the most practical level, the book reacts to the specific problems of the day, focusing on certain urban sites or proposing solutions to their problems: it discusses the placement of a fountain in downtown Belgrade, or the unsightly walls surrounding the houses on the periphery. On a more general level, it also promotes role models for "small urbanism," such as Gordon Cullen, a British architect, graphic artist and prominent figure of the Townscape Movement, or the Slovenian architect Jože Plečnik, whose interventions at Hradčany Castle in Prague and in Ljubljana were seen by Bogdanović as quintessential examples.[9] Another positive example is the postwar reconstruction of Rotterdam, with its intertwined scales of broad urban planning gestures and small, pedestrian-friendly spaces.[10] The essay singles out Rotterdam's new commercial center as especially successful, but omits any specific reference to its architects; nevertheless, it is hard not to recognize in the description the Lijnbaan by Jo van den Broek and Jaap Bakema, one of the most influential European urban projects of the 1950s. Comments like these reveal Bogdanović as partly aligned with the concerns of Team 10, of which he must have been well aware, not least through his university peer Aljoša Josić of Candilis-Josic-Woods.

Another parallel with the activities of Team 10 was Bogdanović's interest in the urban experience. Although similarly fascinated with the liveliness of the street, his goals were less instrumental, aimed not at distilling abstract principles applicable to urban design, but at detecting the meanings of urban space in the broadest sense. His most poetic essays celebrate the transitory experiences of the city and the ways it changes as the sun sets, or as the night falls, or as the neon signs light it up, producing unexpected, often surreal effects and – consequently – the potential for affective identification. Urban humor in its different manifestations is another important topic Bogdanović was fond of detecting in the various urban rituals and witty signage he had encountered in his travels around Yugoslavia and Western Europe.

Considering its pronounced emphasis on the way the city is experienced, *Small Urbanism* could be seen as an anticipation of architectural phenomenology. Indeed, the book was first published in 1958, the same year as Gaston Bachelard's *Poetics of Space*, one of the foundational texts of phenomenological theory. Terms like genius loci and the "character of the place" appear in several instances in *Small Urbanism*, evoking the later discourse of writers like Christian Norberg-Schulz. But unlike Norberg-Schulz and the circle around him, Bogdanović never went in the direction of antimodern Heideggerian pathos, nor did he ever make the theoretical shortcut of trying to deduce the meaning of architectural and urban forms merely from their unmediated appearance. For Bogdanović, meaning was neither fixed nor inherent to urban space, but ultimately socially constructed, and it is that conviction that would decisively characterize his subsequent writings on the city.

Urbanism as Applied Anthropology

Bogdanović's next book on urban themes titled *Urbanistic Mythologems* appeared in 1966, shifting the genre and the tone of his writings away from lighthearted journalism toward a more erudite scholarly study. The book was based on an impressive range of references and a methodology informed by contemporary humanities, especially anthropology and archaeology. Bogdanović once defined architecture as "applied anthropology", but that definition seems even more relevant for his understanding of city-building, already revealed in the title of the book.[11] The key word "mythologem" comes from Carl Gustav Jung and the Hungarian classical scholar Károly Kerényi in their 1949 book *Essays on a Science of Mythology: The Myth of the Divine Child and the Mysteries of Eleusis*.[12] Kerényi and Jung's mythologem denotes the elemental motifs and images that comprise different mythologies, often common to several of them. Another important conceptual source, very much related to Jung, was the influential French philosopher and armchair anthropologist Lucien Lévy-Bruhl.[13] Bogdanović repeatedly acknowledged him as formative to his own thought, which is consistent with the fact that Lévy-Bruhl's theories were significant in the formulation of surrealism.[14] Lévy-Bruhl claimed that the "primitive mind" operates on the basis of what he called "prelogical thinking," which allows for the coexistence of contradictory concepts and principles, but he also argued that much of this prelogical thinking survived in the various niches of the modern world, thus maintaining its relevance until today.[15] Following Lévy-Bruhl, Bogdanović set out to identify the "prelogical abstractions" or "collective representations" – or, in Kerényi and Jung's terms, mythologems –that organized the first cities in human history, from Mesopotamia to China. He thus delved into a study of ancient history, archaeology, and mythology, to find several key mythologems common to many ancient cities: the circular plan as a source of magical pro-

fig. 2 Bogdanović at his studio in Mali Popović, with the student work from his summer school in the background. Courtesy of Ksenija Bogdanović

tection, the "constructed mountain" as a physical link to the supernatural, and the water as the primordial source out of which the city emerges and into which it periodically disappears.

With its plunge into ancient history, the book *Urbanistic Mythologems* appears as a true creation of 1960s culture and its peculiar obsession with temporality that art historian Pamela Lee has termed "chronophobia."[16] As such, it displays an affiliation with other influential, similarly themed texts of the decade, such as Lewis Mumford's *City in History* (1961), Sigfried Giedion's *The Eternal Present* (1962), George Kubler's *The Shape of Time* (1962), or Sybil Moholy-Nagy's *Matrix of Man* (1968). Indeed, Bogdanović opens *Urbanistic Mythologems* with a polemic against Mumford's "biologism," i.e., the famous American writer's view of city-making as an extension of the animalistic instinct to build, as is found in bees and ants. Bogdanović critiques such a view as "scientific myth-making," arguing that the emergence of the city cannot be divorced from the evolution of human thought. In other words, the evolution of the city is intrinsically bound to meaning, which in turn belongs to the social sphere rather than to biology. It is thus the meaning of mythologems such as sacred mountains or circular settlements he tries to recover while digging through dozens of volumes of archaeological and anthropological studies.

A precise focus on socially constructed meaning is also what set Bogdanović apart from another group of his contemporaries, those that would come to be identified with postmodernism. Some of them, of course, gave considerable currency to Jung's ideas; consider, for example, Peter Eisenman's famous interpretation of Aldo Rossi's work through the lens of the Jungian archetype.[17] Bogdanović's interest in Jung, however, produced rather different results. Unlike Rossi, he never sought to distil an immutable, abstract formal "essence" of archetypes in order to vindicate architecture's autonomy; instead, he always stressed a vital interdependence between urban and social fabric as the precondition for a successful city. As a good surrealist, he remained interested in exploring and exploiting the fundamentally ambiguous relationship between form and its content and in undermining, rather than buttressing, disciplinary boundaries.

If *Urbanistic Mythologems* maintained such motivations as implicit vis-à-vis the contemporary city, Bogdanović's next book, *Urbs & Logos* (1976), stated them explicitly. The volume is driven by profound anxiety. "What is the city today," Bogdanović asks, "what is it that is still the city around us? Or, what is it that is no longer the city, but remains covered by that beautiful traditional designation?"[18] In order to answer those questions, he again turns toward the ancient past, always with an eye on the present. The ghost that haunts him is the threat of total dissolution through uncontrolled urban growth beyond any scale previously known in history, threatening to completely obliterate nature and transform it into mere commodity. The emergence of super-cities was a recurrent theme of the 1970s, giving rise to such popular portmanteau names as "BosWash" for the urban continuum between Boston and Washington, D.C., or "Chipitts" for the stretch from Chicago to Pittsburgh; Bogdanović must have been amply aware of these discussions, not least due to his yearlong stay in the United States in 1970. The same problem was certainly also of relevance in Belgrade, which had more than doubled in population since the end of the Second World War, engulfing a range of surrounding small towns and spreading toward the neighboring city of Pančevo.[19] Doxiadis saw such development in an optimistic light, forecasting the emergence of a harmonious "Ecumenopolis," a single global city that would cover most of the earth's surface. Two of the four essays from *Urbs & Logos* were originally partially published in Doxiadis' journal *Ekistics*, but Bogdanović saw the prospect of the Ecumenopolis in decidedly pessimistic terms, as a "thin sickly spider web" stretched across the earth; even the term reminded him of the name of a disease, "for example, something like elephantiasis."[20]

For Bogdanović, the chief problem of uncontrolled urban growth was the loss of "*logos*," or the city's foundational meaning, its social identity, and its historicity. Far more than merely a pragmatic instrument for inhabiting physical space, he saw the city as an instrument of intellection, a lens through which the world is viewed and conceived, a model of the cosmos. Despite its ups and downs, the relationship between *urbs* and *logos* survived in a more or less tenuous balance until modern times. Echoing Ernst Cassirer's understanding of symbolization as a uniquely and indispensably human trait, Bogdanović suggests that even new cities start acquiring the beginnings of their own symbolism and mythology as soon as the first generation of children grows up in them. But when a city loses its boundaries and pure instrumentality begins to motivate its construction, the loss of meaning becomes inevitable. With its logos lost, the city replaces symbolism with literal signification akin to mass media. Information is everywhere, but there is no enigma: "The modern city is a 'Sphinx without a secret.'"[21]

The tendency toward the loss of logos is not new. In the longest essay eponymous with the book, Bogdanović traces the split between the city and its organic meaning to as far back as ancient Rome and its simplified, instrumentally understood symbolism, taken over from the Etruscan civilization as pure ritual devoid of meaning. Similarly problematic for him were the various Renaissance utopias; ostensibly futuristic, in their claims to ancient origins they were in fact driven by archaic thought, proposing simplified and petrified visions frozen in time. Although Bogdanović is never exactly explicit in this regard, it appears that for him a healthy urban *logos* establishes a complex "organic" relationship toward nature and the entire cosmos:

> If urbs and logos eventually found themselves in irreconcilable opposition, then the factors of disturbance should not be sought far from that area within man and his surroundings that we call noosphere […] If man manages to keep the city within the fragile membrane of his noosphere, … everything is in its place. But if the city escapes man, if the abstraction becomes a fact, […] the city exceeds the boundaries of man's knowledge, and everything becomes a matter of coincidence. Between man and the cosmic drama there is no longer any protective structure of meaning[…] urbs and logos have divorced.[22]

Here we encounter another moment of divergence between Bogdanović and his contemporaries, as he appears to oppose not only modernist abstraction, but also the emerging postmodernist interest in semiotics and the resulting focus on explicit signification. *Learning from Las Vegas* comes to mind as the most obvious point of comparison; even though Bogdanović was probably sympathetic with the book's populist nod towards a modern vernacular, Scott Brown and Venturi's open celebration of denotative communication went against his understanding of urban symbolization as something much more complex, more ambiguous, and more deeply embedded in the collective (sub) conscious.[23] Despite numerous shared concerns, the meaningful city that Bogdanović had in mind was very different from the "meaningful city" of Denise Scott Brown's eponymous 1965 essay, which posited urban fabric as a system of signs to be decoded.[24] In contrast to much of the American theory of the period, from Kevin Lynch onward, Bogdanović was largely uninterested in parsing the mechanics of urban signification; what interested him instead were the foundational metaphors constitutive of the organic, living bonds between the city and the community inhabiting it. Irreducible to explicit signification, it is these metaphors that he perceived as terminally endangered and no amount of analysis was sufficient to bring them back to life.

What, then, was to be done? Bogdanović was skeptical about the future of the city because the very image of cosmos escapes our comprehension: "To put cosmos back into a single whole and to subject it to some supreme meaning – who are today's priests who could do that? Which of today's religions could achieve that? Which science today would even dare tackle such a task? In some monstrous way, the old analogy is still valid, but now in a terrifying sense: there is, no doubt, some simultaneity between cosmos that in our consciousness escapes into unintelligible images outside of the power of comprehension, and the cities that disappear in front of our eyes, exploding in every direction like cosmic nebulae."[25] But perhaps there is also a way out; reaching back to his surrealist upbringing, Bogdanović found hope in the *homo ludens,* whose resurgence he apparently recognized in the contemporaneous interest in studying play and games.[26] Most essays in the book cryptically mention various "simulation games," some of them played in "futile planning endeavors," some by game theorists, others in psychotherapy, hinting that they could provide a solution to the contemporary urban woes, yet without explaining how exactly. Indeed, the bibliography at the end of the book is peppered with titles from game theory, standing out from the prevalent entries on history, anthropology, and archaeology.[27] But what was the point of such a turn?

At precisely the same time as he published *Urbs & Logos*, Bogdanović started his summer school in the village of Mali Popović outside of Belgrade, offering an annual elective course for ten to fifteen students of the Faculty of Architecture. It was there that he and his students started testing the applicability of games and simulation in urban planning. In an unlikely combination of performance art, group therapy, and design workshop, the students would design a city for an imaginary civilization of their own invention. But before starting to develop the shape of the physical structure, they had to devise as much as they could about the civilization itself: the landscape it inhabited, the structure of social relations, its history, economy, mythology, religion, etc., – sometimes even an alphabet. Anthropological literature – such as the writings of Lévy-Bruhl or Claude Levi-Strauss – provided support, although Bogdanović stopped inviting anthropologists for consultation because he felt they constrained the students' imaginations. Despite its playful character, the project was taken very seriously and required the full attention of its participants. The success of the experiment was such that in 1980 the summer school was included in BITEF, the annual international festival of experimental theatre, which that year coincided with the UNESCO congress taking place in Belgrade, thus attracting a large audience of prominent cultural figures.[28]

It is easy to imagine Bogdanović's pedagogical experiment in Mali Popović being designed as a way to make an oblique impact on urban planning by sensitizing future planners about the importance of the meaning of urban space and its origins in the structure of society. Indeed, the experiment profoundly influenced several generations of Belgrade architects, but practical effects ultimately were almost non-existent. In 1987, Bogdanović retired from teaching at the University of Belgrade and his opposition to the nationalist policies of Slobodan Milošević's regime soon transformed him into a pariah in the official media. Within a few years, war broke out. As Yugoslavia collapsed, some of its most beautiful cities came under attack. Bogdanović published widely against such "urbicide," which eventually forced him into exile in Vienna. The young architects who had learned his lessons on the meaning of the city would have had hardly any chance to make an impact in real life, where every notion of planning was eclipsed by physical destruction, a grey economy, and urban speculation. After the fall of Milošević in 2000, Bogdanović returned to Belgrade only for a few short visits. He died in Vienna in 2010, his relationship with his native city still strained.

Conclusion

Bogdan Bogdanović's writings on the city paralleled other reactions to postwar reconstruction in Europe through his attention to human scale, experience, and the meaning attached to urban space. Just a glance at the bibliographic sections of his books reveals him to have been well-informed of the broader discourses of the period, even if he often preferred to present himself as a unique figure uninterested in the work of others. But such self-confidence was not unjustified. While drawing from a wide range of sources in anthropology, psychology, the studies of classical mythology, and other fields, Bogdanović's attempt at rehumanizing urbanism offered a rather original vision that stressed the significance of the socially-constructed meanings of urban space. In his view, the modern city required symbolic identification as much as technical rationality in order to sustain itself as a social space. Without it, the city becomes formless and meaningless, it undermines the bonds of the community, which ultimately leads to its own downfall. Less systematic, but with a broader perspective in comparison to other writers with interest in semiotics, Bogdanović was patently aware that meaning in the built environment is fragile, transitory, and multivalent, requiring it to be constantly reinvented. It is such openness that secures the continuing relevance of his writings for the globalized cities of the twenty-first century.

Endnotes

1 Bogdanović's retrospective was shown at the Architekturzentrum Wien in Vienna in 2009; for catalogue, see: Ivan Ristić, ed., *Bogdan Bogdanović. Memoria und Utopie in Tito-Jugoslawien* (Vienna: Architekturzentrum Wien and Wieser, 2009).

2 For an overview of Bogdanović's literary output, see Vladimir Vuković, *Bogdan Bogdanović: Das literarische Werk* (Vienna: Anton Pustet Verlag, 2009).

3 For the most consistent collection of these texts, see: Bogdan Bogdanović, *Die Stadt und der Tod,* (Klagenfurt and Salzburg: Wieser Verlag, 1993).

4 Bogdan Bogdanović, *Mali urbanizam* (Sarajevo: Narodna prosvjeta, 1958).

5 Bogdan Bogdanović, *Urbanističke mitologeme* (Belgrade: Vuk Karadžić, 1964).

6 Bogdan Bogdanović, *Urbs & logos* (Niš, Serbia: Gradina, 1976).

7 Belgrade had one of the strongest Surrealist groups outside of Paris, in direct contact with Breton's circle from the very beginning, but it remains omitted from the international map of Surrealism. For recent accounts of the group's activities, see: Sanja Bahun-Radunović, "When the Margin Cries: Surrealism in Yugoslavia," in: *RiLUnE-Revue des Littératures de l'Union Européenne,* n. 3 (2005), 37–52; and Henri Béhar and Jelena Novaković, eds., "Surréalistes Serbes," special edition of *Mélusine: Cahiers du Centre de Recherche sur le Surréalisme,* n. XXX (2010).

8 Bogdanović makes a reference to *architettura minore* at the very beginning of the book, thus proclaiming his interest in vernacular architecture, as well as demonstrating his acquaintance with the broader international discourse of the period; see: Bogdanović, *Mali urbanizam,* 5.

9 See the essays titled "Gordon Kalen" and "Veliki majstor malog urbanizma," both in Bogdanović, *Mali urbanizam,* 16–20.

10 See: "Dve razmere," ibid., 134–138.

11 The reference to "applied anthropology" appeared on multiple occasions; see, for instance, his interview with Zoran Milović, "Razgovor s autorom 'Mrtvouzica,'" *Start* (Zagreb), no. 518 (November 28, 1988), 12–19.

12 Carl Gustav Jung and Károly Kerényi, *Einführung in das Wesen der Mythologie* (Amsterdam: Pantheon, 1941).

13 For Levy-Bruhl's influence on Jung, see: Robert A. Segal, "Jung and Lévy-Bruhl," in: *Journal of Analytical Psychology,* no. 52 (2007), 635–658.

14 Bogdanović strongly emphasized his indebtedness to Lévy-Bruhl in an interview I conducted with him in May 2005. For Lévy-Bruhl's influence

on surrealism, see: Patricia Morton, *Hybrid Modernities: Architecture and Representation at the 1931 Colonial Exposition, Paris* (Cambridge, MA: The MIT Press, 2000), 106–110.

15 See, among other sources: Lucien Levy-Bruhl, *Primitive Mentality,* trans. Lilian A. Clare (Boston: Beacon, 1966).

16 See: Pamela Lee, *Chronophobia: On Time in the Art of the 1960s* (Cambridge, MA: The MIT Press, 2006).

17 See: Peter Eisenman, "Introduction," in *Aldo Rossi in America: 1976 to 1979*, ed. Kenneth Frampton, exhibition catalog (New York: Institute for Architecture and Urban Studies, 1979), 6. Rossi himself briefly referred to Kerényi and Jung's work in *The Architecture of the City*; see: Aldo Rossi, *Architecture of the City,* trans. Diane Ghirardo and Joan Ockman (Cambridge, Mass.: The MIT Press, 1984), 192.

18 Bogdanović, *Urbs & logos,* 9.

19 For a discussion of Belgrade's postwar development and the anxieties about its uncontrolled growth through "rogue construction," see: Brigitte Le Normand, *Designing Tito's Capital: Urban Planning, Modernism, and Socialism in Belgrade* (Pittsburgh: University of Pittsburgh Press, 2014), esp. Chapter 5.

20 See: Bogdanović, *Urbs & logos,* 74. For English translations of two of the essays, see: Bogdan Bogdanović, "Town and Town Mythology," in: *Ekistics* 35:209 (April 1973), 240–242; and Bogdan Bogdanović, "Symbols in the City and the City as a Symbol," in: *Ekistics* 39:232 (March 1975), 140–146.

21 Bogdanović, *Urbs & logos,* 52.

22 Ibid., 122.

23 See: Robert Venturi, Denise Scott Brown, and Steven Izenour, *Learning from Las Vegas* (Cambridge, MA: The MIT Press, 1972).

24 See: Denise Scott Brown, "The Meaningful City," in: *AIA Journal* 43:1 (January 1965), 27–32.

25 Ibid., 75.

26 "Homo ludens" is the term coined by the Dutch historian and cultural theorist Johan Huizinga in his eponymous 1938 book. Bogdanović does not cite Huizinga, but he likely knew his book, not least through its Serbo-Croatian translation published in 1970. Another prominent cultural theorist of play and games, Roger Caillois, also features in the bibliographical section of *Urbs & Logos,* although not his influential book *Les jeux et les hommes* (1958), but his earlier writings on myths.

27 Some of the titles include Clark Abt's *Serious Games* (1970), Louis Martin's *Utopique: Jeux d'espace* (1973), and J.L. Taylor's *Instructional Planning Systems. A Gaming-Simulation Approach to Urban Problems* (1971).

28 For a brief description of the context and the concept of the Summer School in Mali Popović, see my article "New School and Summer School," in "Radical Pedagogies Insert," edited by Beatriz Colomina and Evangelos Kotsioris, in *Volume* (Amsterdam), no. 45 (2015), 10–11.

Elke Beyer

From "New Units of Settlement" to the Old Arbat: The Soviet NĖR Group's Search for Spaces of Community

To address the urbanistically rather gloomy outlook of the Soviet construction industry juggernaut that was getting into gear during the 1960s, several research institutes and architect collectives in Moscow embarked on research and design projects in order to define the parameters of an ideal urbanism on the road to Communism. One of the most prominent and internationally noted among them was the NĖR group around the architects and urban planners Aleksei Gutnov, Zoia Kharitonova, Il'ia Lezhava et al. and the sociologist Georgii Diumenton – an informal group whose members were otherwise pursuing professional careers well-embedded in Soviet academic and planning institutions. This paper traces their pathway from 1960s proposals of "New Units of Settlement"[1] – starting off as moderately rebellious poster children of late Soviet Modernism – to projects for the preservation and reactivation of the historic streets of Moscow, like Stoleshnikov Lane or the Old Arbat, worked out in the 1970s by a team around Gutnov and Kharitonova at the Institute for the General Plan of Moscow. A closer look shall be taken at the group members' thoughts and research on spaces of community and "free association,"[2] upon which their urbanist concepts were based: Their considerations on the placing and spacing of voluntary social and cultural activities in urban contexts led them to argue for a comprehensive urbanization project based on human scale, privacy and individual freedom as prerequisites for the collective and comfortable lifestyle of a future Communist society. In conclusion, I would like to argue that the persistent focus of the group on the human scale in relation to urbanization at large constitutes a distinct continuity of thought linking the apparently diametrically opposed urban design approaches of the 1960s "New Units of Settlement" and the 1970s proposals for the rehabilitation of historic districts.

"Golden Children" in an Era of Momentous Changes

The work of the NĖR group began with a collective diploma project for a New Town in Siberia at the Department of Town Planning at the Moscow Architecture Institute (MARKhI) in 1959/60. It was the first group diploma project ever in the history of MARKhI, and this approach – as well as its agenda to come up with a complete concept for a "town for the future," based on sociological assumptions about Communist urbanity – resonated strongly with the renewal of architectural education at that point in time. As Daria Bocharnikova has perceptively pointed out in her research on the group, its members should be seen as poster children ("zolotye rebiata," as long-term member Lezhava put it), having been promoted as the fresh faces of a new departure in Soviet urbanist debates at the turn of the 1960s, notably by their supervisor, Ivan Nikolaev, who was of a Constructivist background and recently appointed director of MARKhI.[3] Their project's genesis ought to be read against the backdrop of the momentous changes triggered by Khrushchev's new urbanist policies in the Soviet architectural world.[4]

Architecture students of the mid-1950s in Moscow remember their education at MARKhI as much for being a period of tangible uncertainty and painful restructuring as for being one of new departures.[5] In the wake of the 1955 decree "On the liquidation of excesses in design and building," departments and study plans were re-organized with an emphasis on functionalist, cost-efficient approaches in industrialized construction and town planning. New diploma topics were established and (some) new teachers hired to bring architectural education closer to the practical demands of the mass housing campaign. The production of new teaching materials and books was immediately taken up, but was turned into a long-drawn process as the instructors (or censors) at the Ministry of Higher Education were also just in the process of developing a sense of the permissible[6] – in short, nobody could really be sure about the final outcome of the restructuring processes yet.

On the other hand, several events in the late 1950s marked the sense of an opening towards international architectural debates[7] as well as a tip-toeing re-evaluation of 1920s Soviet architectural and urbanist thought. As Moscow celebrated Khrushchev's new internationalism with open arms during the International Festival of Youth and Students in 1957, MARKhI students were called to design and build temporary structures in the city, while architecture students from 56 countries met for an international seminar at the Institute.[8] Later in the year, in connection with the 40th jubilee of the October Revolution, a conference on the history of architectural education in Moscow since 1917 at MARKhI signaled a re-evaluation of 1920s teaching at the Institute's predecessors, VKhUTEMAS/VKhUTEIN. In the summer of 1958, Moscow hosted the Fifth Congress of the International Union of Architects (UIA). Its numerous international participants were also given the opportunity to explore student work at MARKhI, which some evaluated as the most interesting and exciting part of the entire congress.[9] In summer 1959, the students flocked to the US-American National exhibition in Moscow, featuring not only free Pepsi Cola and glossy Chrysler brochures, but a geodesic dome by Buckminster Fuller – "the first high-tech we ever saw without knowing its name yet"[10] –, a stunning multi-screen show developed by the Eames, and a library of utterly desirable architecture books. Beyond such events, travel abroad became a rare but realistic possibility for architecture professionals and students alike.

The NĖR group members thus started their careers in a climate of relative openness, international exposure, and great opportunities for young cadres and experts in science and technology. They recollect that they strongly felt the need to find their own way and to do their own research on past and current international trends. Like many of their generation, they had formed an informal student circle in order to discuss the urbanist problems of the time and come up with their own solutions, as no reliable precedents or guidelines seemed to be given. In acquainting themselves with the heritage of Soviet architectural and urbanist thought, they could also not fail to become aware of their teachers' momentary disorientation[11], and the stylistic turnabouts and/or biographical ruptures marking the careers of the previous generations – especially those with an architectural family background. This created a sharp awareness of the potential limits in growing up as professionals within the late Soviet system – promising the chance to participate in building up a better life under the banner of Communism, yet bound up by bureaucratic controls, ideological restrictions, and vertical power structures.

A Collective Design of Future Communist Urbanity Based on Privacy and Human Scale

The initial NĖR group diploma project addressed a specific location – the New Town Kritovo near Krasnoiarsk in Siberia – in order to fulfill diploma requirements, but it was explicitly meant to be an ideal and universal model of urban development founded on Communist principles. The concept primarily sought to express the relation between individual or private habitats and collective spaces of association, culture and leisure in a future Communist society, defining the main requirements of the entire population as follows: "1. Organization of intense social life; 2. Creation of the conditions for a normal private life for the individual."[12]

Within a larger economic region, the "New Unit of Settlement" was envisioned as an urban nucleus, structured as a ring of residential groups around a civic center embedded in a park, connected by green "rays" doubling as pedestrian communication channels, zones of encounter, and even as obligatory demonstration routes. A tiered system of services, cultural and civic facilities – most importantly clubs for cultural and scientific projects, reading, and sports – created focal points for voluntary activities and free association, i.e. the formation of individually chosen, interest-based social relationships. The NĖR itself contained no industrial zones. The "primary housing unit" within the NĖR provided individual family apartments for 1500 inhabitants in an area of 250 × 250 m, built up by 40 percent low-rise and 60 percent high-rise structures (the latter quite closely resembling Le Corbusier's Marseille Unité), clustered around a green central courtyard with a canteen, service and childcare facilities connected by covered passageways (fig. 1). The integration of private dwelling space with facilities providing an equal level of comfort and access to services for all inhabitants was seen by the group as an essential prerequisite of living in a collective way, and as the principally new quality of this concept of habitat.[13] At the next levels of grouping, the small housing "kvadrat" provided schools and sports facilities at a short walking distance, whereas the large housing "kvadrat" of 25,000 inhabitants focused on a compact multifunctional district center containing administrative organs, assembly halls, gastronomy, shops, a cinema, and a car-sharing station.[14]

By wrapping a belt of such well-serviced housing groups and green space around the town center, the group meant to combine the advantages of a linear city scheme with that of a compact city, assuring easy and equal pedestrian access to services, culture and leisure facilities (fig. 2).[15] The functions of the NĖR center itself were described as follows: "1. To provide the necessary range of civic complexes … (civic services of the highest level); 2. To unite in one architectural space a large quantity of people (nearly all the population

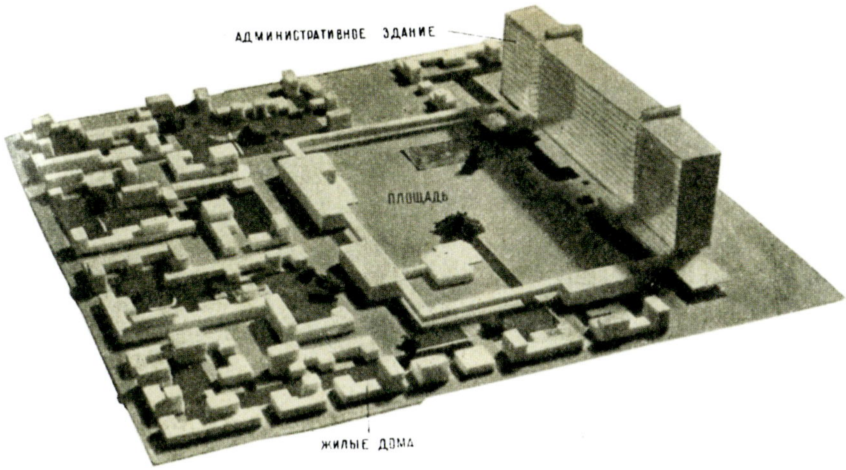

fig. 1 NĖR Diploma project at MARKhI, 1960: Primary housing unit, model photograph published in a youth magazine. Source: A. Baburov et al., "S listov diplomnogo proekta – na kartu Siberii," Tekhnika-molodëzhi (1960, 7), 6.

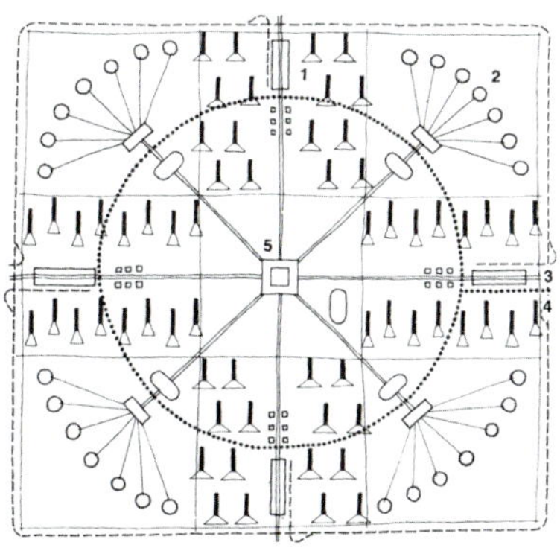

fig. 2 Diagram of a New Unit of Settlement, 1966. Source: A. Gutnov et al., The Ideal Communist City (New York: Braziller, 1970), 118.

of the NĖR) in such a manner that they feel as members of one Communist collective."[16] In order to keep this scale and the balance of collective space and facilities, urban population growth beyond the limit of 200,000 inhabitants would lead to the formation of the next NĖR.

Within this common conceptual framework, each diploma student was responsible for a specific part of the project.[17] MARKhI director Nikolaev actively pushed the presentation to a wider audience, sponsoring new display techniques like large scale model photographs and a 16 mm film shot by the students. Even before graduation, the project was presented and discussed in evening lectures at the MARKhI, at the Moscow Branch of the Architects' Union, and featured in the daily newspaper *Komsomolskaia Pravda*.[18] In July 1960, its authors were given a spread in the popular youth magazine *Tekhnika-molodëzhi* to explain their ideas – with special emphasis on their practical feasibility – to their peers across the USSR, flanked by benevolent comments from the heights of the Academy of Architecture and the Union of Architects.[19] In her PhD thesis, Daria Bocharnikova gives an incisive account of how the project created an occasion within the Soviet architectural professional scene to discuss (or remain conspicuously silent about) different brands and genealogies of modern urbanism since the 1920s, pointing out that its basic premises did not conflict with the dogmas of Soviet urban planning theory, but "shuffled [them] in an original way and spiced [them] with largely forgotten Soviet and Western modernist ideas."[20] But beyond the indisputable significance of the NĖR project as a breach in the history of Soviet architecture, its genesis and early public exposure more generally epitomize the coming of age of a post-Stalin generation of young experts with a critical, informed professional perspective, ready to work out what the shape of Soviet modernity could be in the decades to come, and to recruit and inspire their peers and students to do likewise.

Scaling Up: Exposure and Development of the NĖR Concept in the 1960s

After the NĖR "diplomniki" had individually defended, several members of the group stuck together as an informal circle and continued to develop the NĖR concept, in collaboration with some of their first students. Their work continued to receive considerable professional attention as a path-breaking contribution to the research and debates about the "city of the future" unfolding in the Soviet Union over the course of the 1960s,[21] and gained remarkable visibility within the USSR and beyond: In 1966, the state publishing house Stroiizdat published the group's book-length manifesto for a new approach to urbanization (figs. 3–6).[22] Having caught the attention and enthusiasm of Giancarlo De Carlo, the NĖR book was translated into Italian, and later into English. The group was invited to the XIV. Triennale in Milan in 1968, as an authors' project in the section devoted to the problem of the "great number," next to contributions by Archigram, the Smithsons, and György Kepes.[23] Major international journals published the NĖR proposals and reviews by trendsetters like Archigram's Peter Cook, who was intrigued by "the degree to which they fit in with the familiar scene," or French futurologist Michel Ragon.[24] Last but not least, NĖR became part of the official Soviet exposition at the Expo '70 in Osaka, Japan. International acclaim was not unequivocal, however: Kenneth Frampton, in a truly scathing 1972 review, dismissed the book as "pathetic as propaganda," a concoction of "utterly banal Utopian aspirations" and "pseudo-science," "plagiarized, in a rather stupid fashion, from the technocratic fantasies of the West."[25] But in his ardent call for a more

fig. 3 A manifesto for urbanization at human scale: The NĖR book, Moscow 1966. Source: A. Baburov et al., Novyi ėlement rasseleniia – Na puti k novomu gorodu (Moscow: Stroiizdat, 1966).

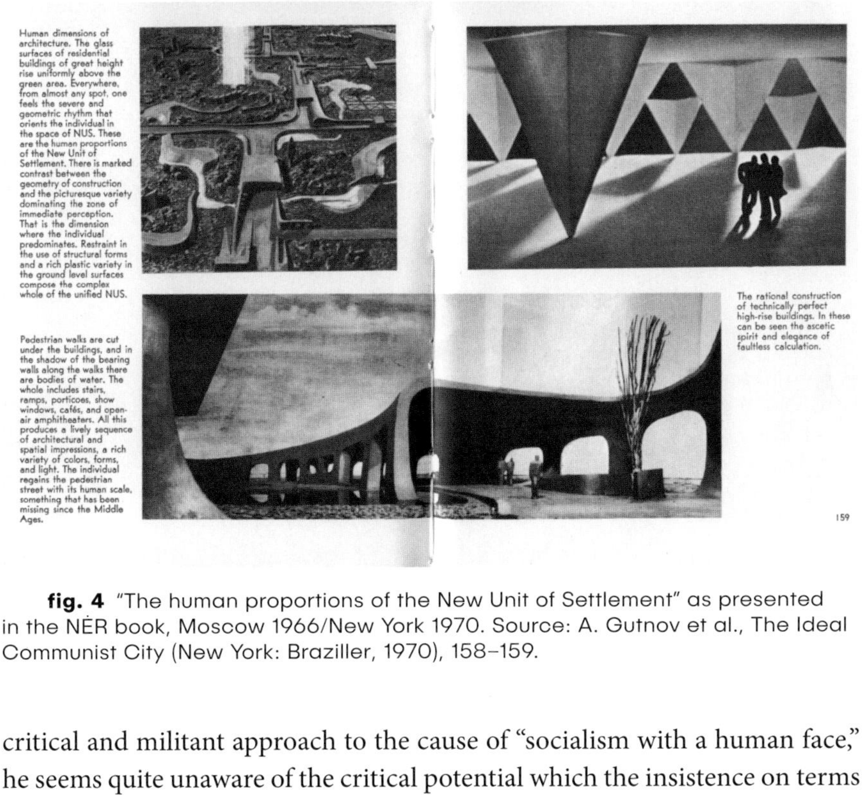

fig. 4 "The human proportions of the New Unit of Settlement" as presented in the NĖR book, Moscow 1966/New York 1970. Source: A. Gutnov et al., The Ideal Communist City (New York: Braziller, 1970), 158–159.

critical and militant approach to the cause of "socialism with a human face," he seems quite unaware of the critical potential which the insistence on terms and concepts like "privacy" and "individual freedom of choice" could acquire in the Soviet context, and of the precarious situation of an informal research group in Brezhnevian USSR.

In the course of its remarkable career, the initial NĖR concept was extended to a scheme for a "total urban environment" on a continental scale, based on three subsystems of social interaction, namely the scientific complex, the residential complex and the industrial complex. Urbanization was

fig. 5 Model of the community center presented in the NĖR: "Here is the place for free relationships among free individuals to develop." Source: A. Gutnov et al., The Ideal Communist City (New York: Braziller, 1970), 162–163.

fig. 6 Isometric drawing of NĖR community center, 1966. Source: A. Baburov et al., Novyi ėlement rasseleniia – Na puti k novomu gorodu (Moscow: Stroiizdat, 1966), 91.

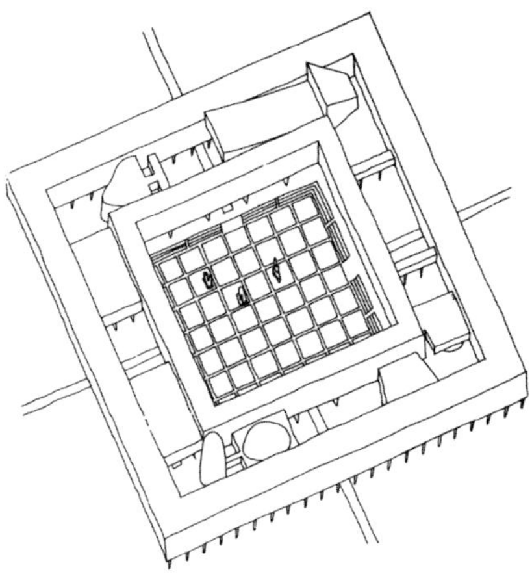

to follow two distinct types of space production: In contrast to the highly dynamic development of science and industry on a large scale ("the world of the machine"), along so-called "riverbeds" of high-speed transport (fig. 7), the NĖR residential nuclei were to provide a stable human-scale environment for everyday social life and leisure, comprising housing and the social and cultural facilities making up the base of a Communist society ("the world of man").[26] The structure of these NĖR nuclei remained the same in essence – residential groups of pedestrian scale, structured around social and cultural

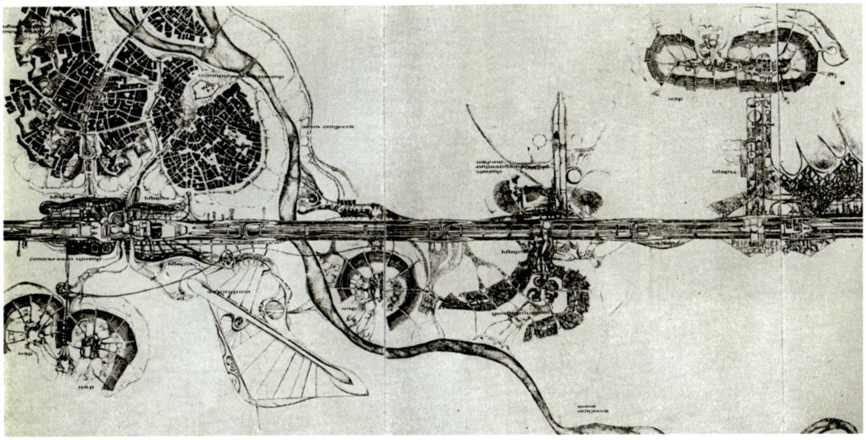

fig. 7 Continental urbanization along "riverbeds" of high speed transport connecting New Units of Settlement, industrial and scientific development, and historically evolved urban areas. Source: A. Gutnov, I. Lezhava, "Gruppa NĖR. Chetyre problemy arkhitektury budushchego," Sovremennaia arkhitektura (1970, 1), 81.

centers, assuring privacy, and universal access to services – even if in architectural terms they had moved on from the Marseille Unité to Plug-In City, so to speak, proclaiming maximum freedom of dwelling choice from caravan or living capsule to urban detached houses.[27]

Also in its more elaborate versions, the NĖR concept remained founded on the assumption that free association, i.e. freely chosen relationships, was the most important aspect of human and social development. According to the group: "Free relationships can easily develop anywhere that privacy is provided in the context of community life, whether the place be attached to a residential unit, an educational center, a research center, or a place of work."[28] Correspondingly, the task of the architect and planner was to create socio-spatial structures allowing for and fostering free association. The group envisioned large clubs for cultural and scientific projects as "the best form of organization for a voluntary group," assigning great importance to their location, as "[t]he masses will spend as much of their time here as at home or at work."[29] They underscored: "A combination of permanence and fluidity in organization is absolutely necessary to preserve genuinely free relationships and to assure the individual both full choice of his pursuit and control of the way it develops."[30] The insistence on mutability and freedom of choice corresponds to the fact that it remained rather open to the imagination how the future spaces of community and association should look like. While the diploma had required the design of actual buildings, the later publications of the group emphasized the conceptual nature of their proposals, illustrated

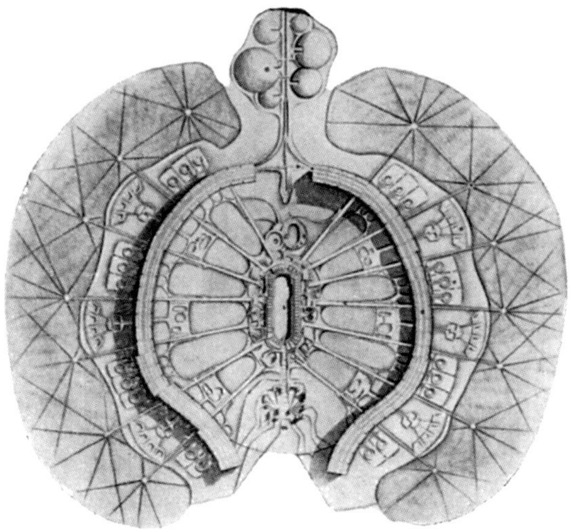

fig. 8 Variant of a New Unit of Settlement, 1967. Source: A. Gutnov, I. Lezhava, G. Diumenton, "Novyi ėlement rasseleniia," Dekorativnoe Iskusstvo (1967, 9), 20.

fig. 9 Section of the NĖR housing structure, 1967. Source: A. Gutnov, I. Lezhava, G. Diumenton, "Novyi ėlement rasseleniia," Dekorativnoe Iskusstvo (1967, 9), 20.

mainly by diagrams and conceptual models. The architectural visions on offer range from an extra-dry grid-based high modernism to some indulgence in high-tech structures on a par with Metabolist fare, to large-scale organic urban shapes professedly inspired by Paolo Soleri (figs. 8–11).

As the group formulated a full-blown urbanization theory, articulated mainly in the writings of Gutnov, Lezhava and Diumenton, they also devoted growing attention to temporality and diversity in urban and architectural development processes, or "life-cycles" and the "behavior" of "spatial systems," made up of "nuclei," "tissue" and "plasma," as they put it in characteristic 1960s jargon borrowed from natural sciences. In this context, the group also began to address issues of reconstruction and the preservation of historically evolved structures, whether on an architectural or urban scale. Conservation, or transformation into a monument, was boldly declared the death of any system.[31] But depending on an evaluation of the resilience and

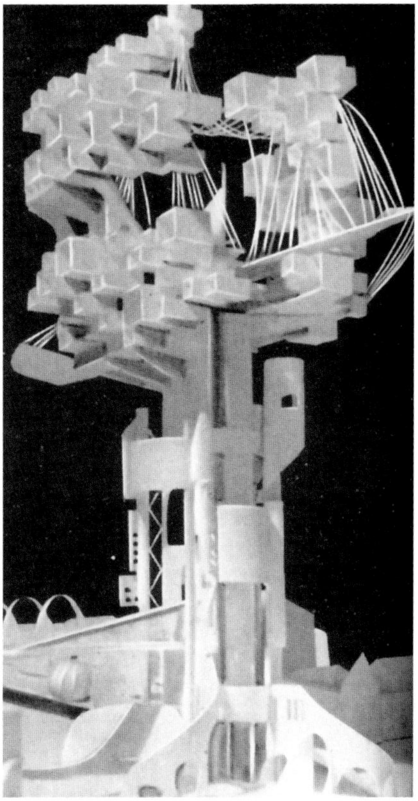

fig. 10 Variant of a NĖR community center, model, 1970. Source: A. Gutnov, I. Lezhava, "Formirovanie strukturnoi edinitsy v sisteme rasseleniia," Arkhitektura SSSR (1970, 11), 44.

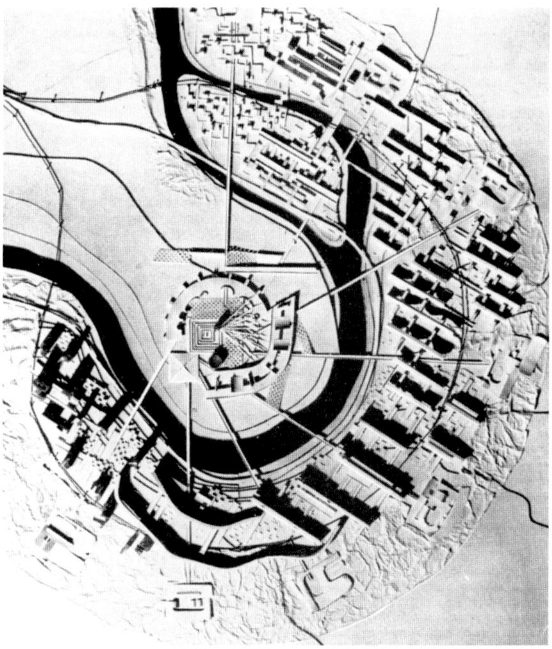

fig. 11 Variant of NĖR, model, 1970. Source: A. Gutnov, I. Lezhava, "Formirovanie strukturnoi edinitsy v sisteme rasseleniia," Arkhitektura SSSR (1970, 11), 42.

potential for reactivation of historical structures within the urban "metasystem," a variety of approaches from physical preservation and "imitation" to complete renewal was recommended to transform them – strategies we shall encounter again in the 1970s urban designs realized in Moscow's historic core.

Career Trajectories and Urban Research of NĖR Group Members

After graduation, the NĖR group members embarked on careers in urban research, teaching and design in different institutional contexts. After a brief spell at the Department for the Design of the Palace of Soviets (before the project was called off in 1962), some, like Lezhava or Kostrikin, began to teach at MARKhI and spent most of their professional life as invigorating forces in this academic environment, while others, like Gutnov and Kharitonova, settled for more practical planning work at Mosproekt-1, and ultimately at the Institute for the General Plan of Moscow. During the 1960s, their professional activity ranged from teaching and urbanist research with the purpose of climbing the academic ladder, through writing on contemporary international architectural and urbanist thought, to participation in major urban planning competitions like the 1965 idea competition for the reconstruction of the center of Moscow,[32] the reconstruction of Novokirovskii prospekt, or Pushkin Square.[33]

In their academic urbanist research during the 1960s, the core group members pursued questions closely linked to the problems addressed theoretically and conceptually by the NĖR project. Lezhava, for instance, devoted his PhD dissertation to the formation and spatial organization of centers of leisure.[34] He analyzed historical architectural and urban forms fostering "free association" (from public squares and main streets through leisure and cultural establishments like bath houses, theaters, or coffee houses, to edifices for political, professional, or religious association), as well as contemporary architectural-spatial systems designed for free association in socialist and capitalist cities (from Leonidov's 1920s workers' clubs to Aalto's 1950s culture centers in Helsinki and Wolfsburg). In conclusion, he formulated proposals for the functional organization of a "complex system of free association," a new type of civic and cultural center for the "great number," and variants for its application in diverse urban situations, based on sociological findings on the development of cultural interests and the spatial organization requirements of different kinds of leisure activities. In parallel, Gutnov defended his PhD dissertation on "The influence of the mutability of the urban environment on design principles,"[35] addressing another NĖR core issue.

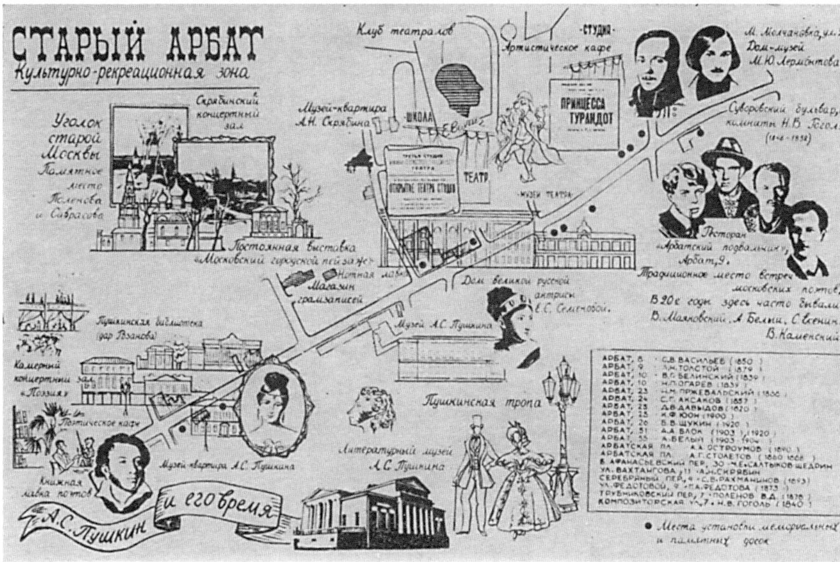

fig. 12 The Old Arbat culture and leisure zone: Historical traditions. Sourca: Z. Kharitonova, "Novoe na starom Arbate," Znanie (Seriia Stroitel'stvo i arkhitektura, 1984, 4).

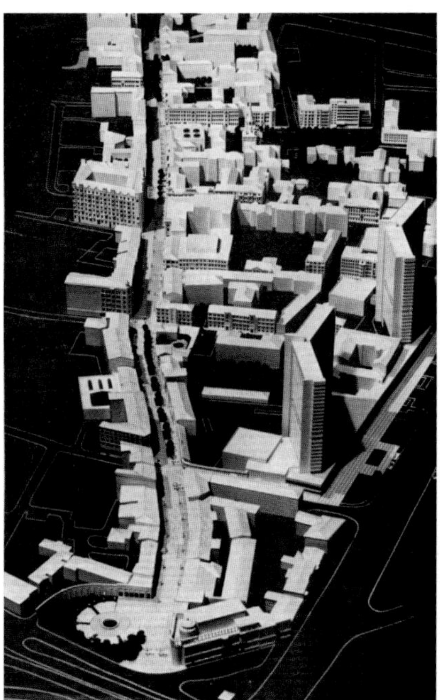

fig. 13 The Old Arbat viz. the New Arbat. Model photograph, 1986. Source: "Arbat. 16 rakursov odnoi ulitsy," Arkhitektura SSSR (1986, 4), 32.

fig. 14 The Old Arbat pedestrian zone in 1986, urban design by A. Gutnov, Z. Charitonova et al. Source: "Arbat. 16 rakursov odnoi ulitsy," Arkhitektura SSSR (1986, 4), 47.

Historic District Rehabilitation Projects of the 1970s

Shortly after the NĖR project's renown had reached its peak, in the early 1970s, Gutnov and Kharitonova took up work at the Research and Design Institute for the General Plan of Moscow. Here, they began to design projects for the preservation and reactivation of historic districts and streets, e.g., Stoleshnikov Lane or the Old Arbat Street quarter in the historic center of Moscow, envisioning a rehabilitation of existing structures and a transformation of streets into pedestrian areas. In this context, they undertook intensive historical research on physical and cultural urban heritage (fig. 12).[36] The Old Arbat rehabilitation project was realized as Moscow was preparing itself to welcome the many international visitors expected for the 1980 Olympics, giving occasion to intense debate on issues of preservation and refurbishment. At first sight, this direction of work seems to be diametrically opposed to the "high modernist" design approach of "New Units of Settlement," and the Old Arbat project constitutes a rather explicit counter-proposal to the neighboring 1960s Soviet modernist flagship Prospekt Kalinina ("New Arbat") (figs. 13, 14). But a closer look at the 1970s projects reveals that Gutnov and Kharitonova did not simply change their professional agenda to conserve the beauty of the past, but aspired to design complex urban environments by introducing new cultural programs and other spaces of free association like covered pedestrian passages, large cafés, or auditoria into existing urban structures – conceptually quite in line with NĖR ideas (fig. 15). In the words of Kharitonova: "We did not create houses, but a space between houses, not a street, but an environment, not an ensemble, but an urban interior."[37] By cre-

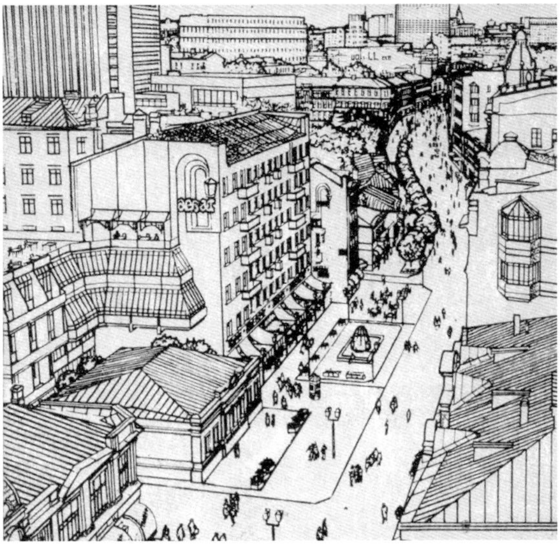

fig. 15 The Old Arbat pedestrian zone: Re-activation of historical urban structures by urban design and selective architectural interventions. Source: Z. Kharitonova, "Novoe na starom Arbate," Znanie (Seriia Stroitel'stvo i arkhitektura, 1984, 4).

ating a complex urban interface of links to the Prospekt Kalinina megastructure and transport infrastructures, the historical Arbat Street was plugged into an urban system of much larger scale – keeping its historically evolved spatial proportions intact and at human scale. Thus, within the framework of the historically evolved city, Gutnov and Kharitonova attempted to achieve a balance between a large-scale, quickly mutable urbanized territorial system – organized by high-speed transport – and a stable, human-scale environment for everyday social life and leisure, comparable in functionality to the NĖR nuclei yet grounded in urban cultural heritage.

Therefore, I would like to argue that a direct conceptual link can be discerned between the NĖR group members' theoretical concerns and urbanist research from its very beginnings in the "high modernist" diploma project of 1960, through its elaboration in later stages flanked by intensified academic research over the course of the 1960s, to their 1970s and 1980s proposals for the rehabilitation of historic centers. This link is constituted by the continuous concern of the group members with the placing and spacing of social activities in multiscalar and mutable urban contexts; allowing for large-scale urbanization processes, development and permanent change at different rhythms, yet simultaneously putting the creation and equipment of human-scale urban and architectural spaces for the everyday social life of individuals and the free association of communities at the very heart of the architects' concerns.

Endnotes

1 Russian: Novyi Ėlement Rasseleniia (NĖR), trans. Renee Neu Watkins, see Alexei Gutnov et al., *The Ideal Communist City* (New York: Braziller, 1970).

2 Russian: svobodnoe obshchenie, see Il'ia Lezhava, "Problemy formirovaniia i prostranstvennoi organizatsii tsentrov dosuga v sovremennom gorode" (PhD diss., MARKhI, 1970), Avtoreferat, 5; Aleksei Gutnov, "Chelovek i zhiznennaia sreda – problemy razvitiia v budushchem. Tekst doklada o kontseptsii ėksperimental'noi tvorcheskoi gruppy NĖR" (1970), in Gutnov, *Goroda i liudi* (Moscow: MP Lad'ia, 1993), 67–96, 84.

3 Daria Bocharnikova, "Inventing Socialist Modern. A History of the Architectural Profession in the USSR, 1932–1971" (PhD diss., EUI, Florence 2014), 181–185, 191–196.

4 Stephen V. Bittner, *The Many Lives of Khrushchev's Thaw. Experience and Memory in Moscow's Arbat*, (Ithaca: Cornell UP, 2008), 105–140; Richard Anderson, *Russia. Modern Architectures in History*, (London: Reaktion, 2015), 215–219.

5 Author's interviews with Il'ia Lezhava (October 30, 2010, June 21, 2011), Zoia Kharitonova (July 28, 2011), Viacheslav Loktev (October 30, 2010), Andrei Gozak (July 28, 2011). See also the memoirs in *MARKhI XX vek*, vol. 3: 1955–1958, eds. Andrei Nekrasov and Andrei Shcheglov, (Moscow: Salon-Press, 2006); I. Nikolaev, "Moskovskaia arkhitekturnaia shkola i eë zadachi na sovremennom ėtape razvitiia," *Arkhitektura SSSR* (1959, 3): 10–12; N. Poliakov, "Uchebnoe proektirovanie na fakul'tete gradostroi-tel'stva," *Arkhitektura SSSR* (1959, 3): 34–44; Bocharnikova, "Inventing Socialist Modern," 166–171.

6 Iakov Kazhdan, "Moskovskii Arkhitekturnyi Institut 1955–1958 gg.," in *MARKhI XX vek*, vol. 3, 15–20.

7 See Catherine Cooke, Susan Reid, "Modernity and Realism. Architectural Relations in the Cold War," in *Russian Art and the West*, eds. Rosalind Blakesley and Susan Reid (DeKalb: Northern Illinois UP, 2007), 172–194; Anna Bronovitskaia, "Dreams of something distant: Soviet Architecture and the West from Thaw to Perestroika," *Project Russia* 34 (2004, 4), 89–104.

8 "Mezhdunarodnyi seminar studentov," *Arkhitektura SSSR* (1957, 7) and (1957, 10), 63.

9 Werner Hebebrand, "Neue Wege der sowjetischen Architektur. Eindrücke von einer Moskaureise 1958," *neue heimat* (1958, 12), 21–34; A. G. Heaume, "Compte rendu du congrès," *L'Architecture d'Aujourd'hui* 79 (1958), VII–XI, here XI; Nikolaev, "Moskovskaia arkhitekturnaia shkola," 12.

10 Il'ia Lezhava, "Istoriia gruppy NĖR," in *MARKhI XX vek*, vol. 3, 72–129, (p. 87–89).

11 Ibid., 81.

12 MARKhI Archive, "NĖR" (Project Presentation, 1959/60), Table 3.

13 Ibid., Table 10.

14 Ibid., Tables 18–21.

15 Ibid., Table 3.

16 Ibid., Table 24.

17 Il'ia Lezhava and Andrei Baburov designed buildings of the civic center;

Aleksei Gutnov, Slava Sadovskii and Andrei Zvezdin different variants of housing districts; and "the girls," Zoia Kharitonova, Elena Sukhanova and Natal'ia Gladkova, district centers, schools and childcare facilities. Nikolai Kostrikin adapted the planning scheme to the actual topography, after three members of the group had traveled to the site in Siberia. Lezhava, "Istoriia gruppy NĖR," 97–100 and 102–103.

18 Lezhava, "Istoriia gruppy NĖR," 91–92; MARKhI Archive, Novyj Ėlement Rasseleniia "Gorod budushchego" (Invitation cards MARKhI, February 18, 1960, and MOSA, March 22, 1960); Iurii Zyrchaninov, "Gorod nashego zavtra," *Komsomolskaia Pravda* (February 28, 1960).

19 Andrei Baburov et al., "S listov diplomnogo proekta – na kartu Siberii," *Tekhnika-molodëzhi* (1960, 7), 6–7.

20 Bocharnikova, "Inventing Socialist Modern," 186 (quote), 191–196.

21 In the late 1960s, a research department devoted to "futurology" was set up at the Scientific Institute for History, Theory and Perspective Problems of Soviet Architecture (NIITI) in Moscow, headed by Andrei Ikonnikov. The exhibitions, conferences and publications produced here show the broader Soviet context of urban research, theory and experimental design, e.g. by Viacheslav Loktev or Konstantin Pchel'nikov. To situate the pioneering work of the NĖR group more precisely within this context remains a task for further research. See "Sotsial'nye predposylki formirovaniia goroda budushchego," vol. 1–2, ed. Gosgrazhdanstroi, *Seriia Gradostroitel'stvo* 30 (1967); Andrei Ikonnikov [et al.], "Budet ili ne budet?," *Dekorativnoe Iskusstvo* (1967, 9), 18–27; Zinaida N. Iargina, "Gorod budushchego," *Znanie* (Seriia Stroitel'stvo i arkhitektura, 1968, 11); Michel Ragon, "Recherches actuelles en U.R.S.S.," *Urbanisme* 127/128 (1972), 36–40; Jean-Louis Cohen, "Les années soixante: De nouvelles utopies," in *L'espace urbain en URSS: 1917–1978*, exhib. cat. (Paris, Centre Pompidou, 1978), 26–27; Andrei Ikonnikov, "Utopias in the Sixties," *L'Arca* (May 1989), 80–87.

22 A. Baburov et al., *Novyi ėlement rasseleniia – Na puti k novomu gorodu* (Moscow: Stroiizdat, 1966); Italian: A. Gutnov et al., *Idee per la cittá comunista*, trans. Alberto Pescetto, (Milano: Il Saggiatore, 1968), in the series "Struttura e forma urbana" directed by De Carlo, in a remarkable line-up with Le Corbusier's *Urbanisme* and Christopher Alexander's *Notes on the Synthesis of Forms*; English: A. Gutnov et al., *The Ideal Communist City*, trans. Renee Neu Watkins (New York: Braziller, 1971), re-edited by MIT Press in 1978.

23 S. Frigerio, "XIVe Triennale de Milan, 1968," *L'Architecture d'Aujourd'hui* 139 (1968), IX; Anty Pansera, *Storia e cronaca della triennale* (Milano: Longanesi, 1978), 105–16 and 531–71.

24 Peter Cook, "The NER Group," *Architectural Design* 38 (Oct 1968), 481–82; "The Ideal Communist City: Excerpts From a Forthcoming Book," *Architectural Design* 40 (Nov 1970), 579–581; Albert Frants, "The Ideal Communist City: Excerpts From a Forthcoming Book," *Architectural Record* (Oct 1971), 111; Ragon, "Recherches actuelles." On Cook's perception of NĖR and a comparison to Archigram etc., see Bocharnikova, "Inventing Socialist Modern," 243–253.

25 Kenneth Frampton, "The Ideal Communist City, by Alexi Gutnov [sic, et al.]. Book Review," *Architectural Forum* 136 (Mar 1972), 13.

26 Aleksei Gutnov, Il'ia Lezhava, Georgii Diumenton, "Novyi ėlement rasseleniia," *Dekorativnoe Iskusstvo* (1967, 9), 20–21; A. Gutnov, I. Lezhava,

"Formirovanie strukturnoi edinitsy v sisteme rasseleniia," *Arkhitektura SSSR* (1970, 11), 42–48; A. Gutnov, I. Lezhava, "Gruppa NĖR. Chetyre problemy arkhitektury budushchego," *Sovremennaia arkhitektura* (1970,1), 78–83, (French: "NER. 4 problèmes de l'architecture de demain," *L'Architecture d'Aujourd'hui* 153 (1970), 78–83); Gutnov, "Chelovek i zhiznennaia sreda," 96. Translation by the author.

27 Gutnov, Lezhava, "Gruppa NĖR," 82; Gutnov et al., *The Ideal Communist City*, 117–118.

28 Gutnov et al., *The Ideal Communist City*, 88.

29 Ibid., 90, 93.

30 Ibid., 92.

31 Gutnov, Lezhava, "Gruppa NĖR," 79, 83.

32 Lezhava and Kostrikin with a MARKhI collective, see *Stroitel'stvo i arkhitektury Moskvy* (1967, 3), 8–37.

33 Gutnov and Kharitonova with Mosproekt-1, see Gutnov, *Goroda i liudi*, 317; Interview with Z. Kharitonova (July 28, 2011).

34 Lezhava, "Problemy formirovaniia."

35 A. Gutnov, "Vliianie izmeniaemosti gorodskoi sredy na printsipy ego proektirovaniia," (PhD diss., Moscow 1970).

36 Z. Kharitonova, "Novoe na starom Arbate," *Znanie* (Seriia Stroitel'stvo i arkhitektura, 1984, 4); A. Gutnov, "Tsentr goroda – muzei ili aktivnaia zhizn?," *Nauka i zhizn* (1978, 4); "Arbat. 16 rakursov odnoi ulitsy," *Arkhitektura SSSR* (1986, 4), 32–47; Z. Kharitonova, "Peshekhodnye ulitsy v istoricheski slozhivsheisia srede krupnogo goroda," (PhD diss., Moscow 1988).

37 Round table statement by Z. Kharitonova, "Arbat. 16 rakursov," 40.

Luca Molinari

Theories and Practices of Re-Humanizing Postwar Italian Architecture: Ernesto Nathan Rogers and Giancarlo De Carlo

> A house is no house if it is not warm in winter, cool in summer, serene in every season, receiving the family in harmonious spaces. A house is not a house if it does not contain a corner for reading poetry, an alcove, a bathtub, a kitchen. This is the house of the man. [...] I want to have a house that may look like me (in better aspects): a house that may look like my humanity.[1]

When Ernesto Nathan Rogers, appointed new editor of the journal *Domus* in 1946, added the subtitle *La casa dell'uomo* (*The House of Man*), he tried to introduce the necessity of humanizing modern architecture, opposing the dogmatic vision of the *machine à habiter*. The nearly three years of his occupation represented a fragile attempt to redefine a vision of modern architecture considered as a discipline open to real life and to dialogue with other forms of modern creativity such as music, cinema, art and design.[2] When Rogers took over *Domus* in January 1946, he had two major issues to contend with: the urgent need to reconstruct Italy and the cultural and ethical redefinition of Italian society. *Domus* reflected the moderate, ambiguous transition to modernism made by the middle classes. It was a fashionable journal which would try to cultivate the radicalism of the architectural avant-garde by embracing the conformist tendencies of the international style in the 1950s.

One of the young Milanese architects invited by Rogers to collaborate with Domus was Giancarlo De Carlo, who immediately after the war curated the first important collection of writings of Le Corbusier published in Italy[3]. This event can be considered the first step in a long and intense collaboration between two of the most interesting characters of two different generations of postwar Italian architecture culture. The collaboration and intellectual exchanges between Rogers and De Carlo influenced the national context, bringing the role of the human being as a prior argument in the re-definition of modern architecture. The process of the humanization of Modern Architecture through a better comprehension of the historical context and of the rooted tradition of the human environment soon became one of the elements of originality and identity of postwar Italian architecture, and the direction of Domus and Casabella-Continuità by Rogers as well as the projects for Urbino of De Carlo became a fundamental reference point in the European context.

From the outset, Rogers understood the ideological strength of a periodical like *Domus*, and considered it an important connection between postwar modern culture and the most prevalent, as well as influential, social class in Italy. The journal became the tool for a radical revision of the dominant values and tastes in Italian society. By adding the subtitle *The House of Man*, Rogers managed to express his terms and the strong ideological value of the operation in a poetic yet immediate manner.[4] That phrase, applied heavily by the architect Giuseppe Pagano, was utilized to specify the nature of the journal and its philosophy of action. It had been used first for the journal *Casabella Costruzioni* in the late 1930s, then was taken over for *Domus,* where Pagano had already changed the subtitle from *The Arts of the Home* to *The Arts in the Home*. "*La casa dell'uomo*" became a new metaphor for the creation of a different, modern way of living and thinking in Italian society.[5] As Rogers wrote in his first essay as editor: "A magazine can act as a tool, a filter for establishing the reasons for a particular choice. […] It is a matter of forming a style, a technique and morality around a single function. It is a matter of building a society. There is no time to waste."[6]

Rogers and his editorial staff published twelve issues of the magazine in 1946. The multidisciplinary contributions continued as they had under Pagano, and were complemented by essays and articles by CIAM members such as Alfred Roth,[7] Max Bill[8] and Sigfried Giedion.[9] At the same time, Lionello Venturi[10] and Gillo Dorfles contributed articles on the state of the arts in Italy, and on the debate between realism and abstraction. During this period, a group of young architects including Giorgio Crespi,[11] Giancarlo De Carlo[12] and Ettore Sottsass Jr.[13] published a series of essays analyzing the evolution of works by modern masters such as Le Corbusier, Frank Lloyd Wright, Richard Neutra and William Morris. At this time, the editorial staff also published articles dedicated to traditional English and Japanese houses,[14] as well as articles about new housing projects by Albert Frey and John Porter Clark,[15] Neutra[16] and Roth,[17] which viewed prefabrication – and with it norming – as highly important.

The apparent heterogeneity and complexity of the contents published in *Domus* during 1946 were part of a broad ideological program exemplified by Rogers's lead articles. The sequence of these articles showed simultaneously the coherence of their agenda, the severity of cultural polemics and the evolution of the political situation in Italy. It was evident from the outset which themes Rogers would focus on: his essays followed a virtual path leading to his main areas of theoretical development. "The house of Man" immediately appeared on the main cultural horizon as a metaphor for the humanistic utopia of modern culture. As Rogers wrote in his first lead article:

> I want a house that is like me (but better): a house that looks like my humanity. If taken to extremes, our argument can lead either to utopia or become a cliché, because if we ask too much, we are asking for the unattainable, but if we only look at what is immediately around us, we risk being content with too little. The house is an issue of limits, but the definition of these limits is an issue of culture; and this is precisely what the house ultimately is.[18]

Postwar Italian modern "humanism" in an international context

At this time, Rogers was facing a cultural battle to enforce the role of modern architecture and its traditions in the debate for reconstruction in Italy. He fought this battle using two weapons: CIAM's cultural and international relevance and the growing significance of modern Italian culture. Rogers was perfectly aware of his divisive cultural position and ideological association with CIAM. He had created a "periodical of tendencies,"[19] and this attempt to promote modern architecture met with strong provincialism and accusations of being overly abstract.

The call for the "humanity" of architecture in the laboratory of *Domus* provides a strong psychological background in the dramatic experience of the Second World War, which played a relevant role in the process of revision in principles of modern architecture in the late 1940s. The use of terms such as "humanity," "warm home" and "house of man" in the early postwar theorization of Rogers and of other modernist intellectuals reflects the linguistic reaction to the rhetoric of the recent fascist regime, which apparently denied any form of "fragility" in the Italian character. At the same time, the search for humanity in modern architecture in Rogers's theoretical work could be linked with another Italian phenomenon represented by the relevance afforded to tradition and history within the process of comprehending reality, which had been fully developed during the 1930s by the Italian modern architecture culture and which would be definitively condensed in the topic of "continuity" in 1953 when Rogers became editor of *Casabella*.[20] But the emergence of the term "humanity" in relation to modern architecture has yet to be fully focused upon. On one hand, we could consider it a cultural contraposition to Roman neorealism, and on the other as a rhetorical definition of a necessity for transformation in modern architecture after the war (fig. 1).

The relationship between humanity – or humanization – and the idea of the city mainly enters modern architectural culture with the eighth CIAM congress, in Hoddesdon, with the selection of the "Core of the City" as the key theme. The CIAM discussion, as can be seen in the 1954 publication of *The Heart of the City* edited by Rogers, José Luis Sert and Jaqueline Tyrwhitt,[21] moved between two different visions represented by the Dutch group: considering the form of the core a representation of a different, emerging social reality on one hand, and on the other some older members whose position was to still refer to the model of the "Italian" piazza as the best reference. In the publication of the CIAM congress, Rogers's essay was confronted with Jaap Bakema's contribution reflecting on the necessity for a humanistic vision of the contemporary city. Both essays were supported by the idea that modern architecture should be seen as a real tool for social improvement in postwar society and as a positive instrument for democracy. Each moved from a critical vision of modern architecture seen as a movement that should recognize its own history as an instrument for deep transformation (fig. 2).

Giancarlo De Carlo: Urbino as a laboratory for modern architecture

In September 1955, Rogers brought Giancarlo De Carlo[22] to La Sarraz, Switzerland, and in few years he become one of the young protagonists of emerging postwar European architecture, and one of the key actors in the process of realizing the emerging idea of humanization in postwar modern architecture. De Carlo[23] had been involved as a collaborator of *Domus* from 1945 to 1947, and then as part of the board of *Casabella Continuità* in 1953. In 1955, De Carlo curated a section on urbanism at the Triennale of Milan, presenting an idea of architecture necessarily related to the design and form of the city

fig. 1 Ernesto Nathan Rogers, Vittorio Gregotti, Giotto Stoppino: *Architettura misura dell' Uomo*, Triennale of Milan, 1951, Entrance of the exhibition. Source: Archivio della Triennale di Milano.

fig. 2 G. E. Kidder Smith: *Italy builds*, 1953; cover of the first edition.

and, at the same time, asserting that the "aim of urban planning is to improve the condition of the anonymous forces of society, the real protagonist of the human events; and it is an aim that cannot be realized without their consensus and participation."[24]

De Carlo's cultural and political background influenced his theoretical work and design methodology. From the mid-1940s, he had frequented anarchist circles in Milan and had upheld relations with intellectuals including Elio Vittorini, Vittorio Sereni and Italo Calvino[25] that helped him focus on the idea of the city as a dense, contradictory context, to be fully felt and analyzed as a dramatic representation of the human environment and symbolism. The originality of his cultural background was fully engaged at *Casabella Continuità* from 1953 until 1956 when De Carlo resigned. Since the first issue of *Casabella* edited by Rogers, in late spring 1953, when he appended the title with the term *continuità* (continuity), we can recognize the conscious design of the journal as an ideological tool able to critically define the position of modern architecture in the postwar Western panorama through a problematic balance between traditions, history and modernity. This cultural position, which we could consider as a form of "ideology of continuity," supported the conceptual design of the journal and the criteria of choice of every single argument that was then published.

In an editorial, "Responsibility of the Tradition," Rogers clearly defined his interpretation of the word "tradition." On one side, he contrasts what he defined as "the modern formalism" and every form of stylistic approach in architecture; on the other side, he affirmed the necessity for a dynamic and open vision of tradition seen as a product of "continuity in the permanent exchange of relationships, and without any form of crystallization." Tradition is seen as the result of two forces: a vertical force related to the resistant and permanent character of the place, and a horizontal one due to the fluid and dynamic intellectual relationship between people.

Fully ensconced in this cultural environment in the early 1950s, De Carlo began one of the most relevant experiences in postwar Italian architecture culture: his work in Urbino. It was 1951, and De Carlo would continue to work at Urbino and in its region until his death, in 2005, giving birth to one of the most continuative architectural accomplishments in postwar European architecture. De Carlo emotionally recalls his first visit to the place, together with Carlo Bo, then newly elected Rector of the University of Urbino, and known to De Carlo since the *Resistenza*:

> On his first visit, Bo met me at Pesaro station on the Adriatic coast and we slowly drove up to the hills of Urbino. With three miles still to go, suddenly Bo had the car stopped, we got out and there was the Urbino

fig. 3 Urbino and Giancarlo De Carlo: The built works. Source: Studio Giancarlo De Carlo

skyline in front of us, with its typical fifteenth-century landscape. "Here is Urbino," he said. "This is the real Italy." I will never forget his comment.[26]

Over four decades, De Carlo conceived two different master plans for Urbino, and worked for the University of Urbino as chief architect, designing the different seats of the faculties of law, pedagogy and economy in the town's historic center, and the university campus on the outskirts of the city (fig. 3). Regarding his work at Urbino, De Carlo once stated: "We proposed to replace the traditional urban-centric perspective with a more current environmental perspective, eliminating all the mechanical relationships and the zoning approach, replacing that with a system of organic relationships,"[27] while considering the urban history of the city and the Ducal Palace of the Montefeltro family as key references in his design approach.[28]

Urbino and its history, landscape, community and the way people meet, live and move in the urban environment became crucial characters in the work of De Carlo. For the design of the campus, these same elements were introduced. "Carlo Bo and I thought that if we expected them to study in a different way, students deserved a renewed respect. They should no longer be treated as a crowd, but as individual people given a chance to develop their individuality,"[29] he recalled. The centrality of the students and of community life drove the design process in the different colleges De Carlo designed from 1962, when he started the Collegio del Colle student housing, a seminal project in his career where the experience of *Casabella Continuità* met with the strong influence of Team 10, which he had been part of since 1958.

De Carlo presented his project for Collegio del Colle in Urbino at the 1965 Team 10 meeting in Berlin. The axonometric schemes effectively interpreted the idea of connective spaces as the new, communitarian places for students as well as fundamental elements of visual connection between the modern architecture and the pre-existing context (figs. 4 and 5). The voids connecting different student units suddenly became the new, original actor of the project, and the system of pedestrian connections, seats and open windows onto the landscape represented a different way of imagining public space for the student community. In this project, De Carlo definitively merged the cultural experience of the *continuità* with the incentive of Team 10's discussion on urban mega-structures and infrastructures.[30]

Rather than exchanging any ostensible stylistic features, De Carlo's attraction to Team 10 rested in a shared cultural interest and the urge to explore new ways of implementing architectural and urban projects with regard to their social effects on people and communities. Aldo van Eyck formulated this in 1966:

> What makes this building so house- and city-like (hence successful)? […] It is at once both places; a way of access and communication; both open and closed; both inside and outside; both large and small; and has, above all, both individual and collective meaning. It belongs to the "building" as much as it belongs to the "site," in fact through it the building is the site, the site is the building.[31]

Van Eyck is echoed a few years later by a statement De Carlo made about Urbino:

> My study sought to decipher the system of relationships, present and potential, between the built and the natural, treating them as a single whole, which is what they in fact are: because the natural is also entirely constructed and repeats the forms and rhythms characteristic of the fabric of the city.[32]

The student residences are conceived as a sophisticated complex of relationships between the spaces and their inhabitants, between the new buildings and the landscape, between the inhabitants and their experience of the environment. Perhaps this principle is the concept that brings us closest to experiments being conducted at the same time by other members of Team 10, in which the rigidity of the Grille CIAM is molded and folded under the weight of concern with the social and environmental community, its psychology,

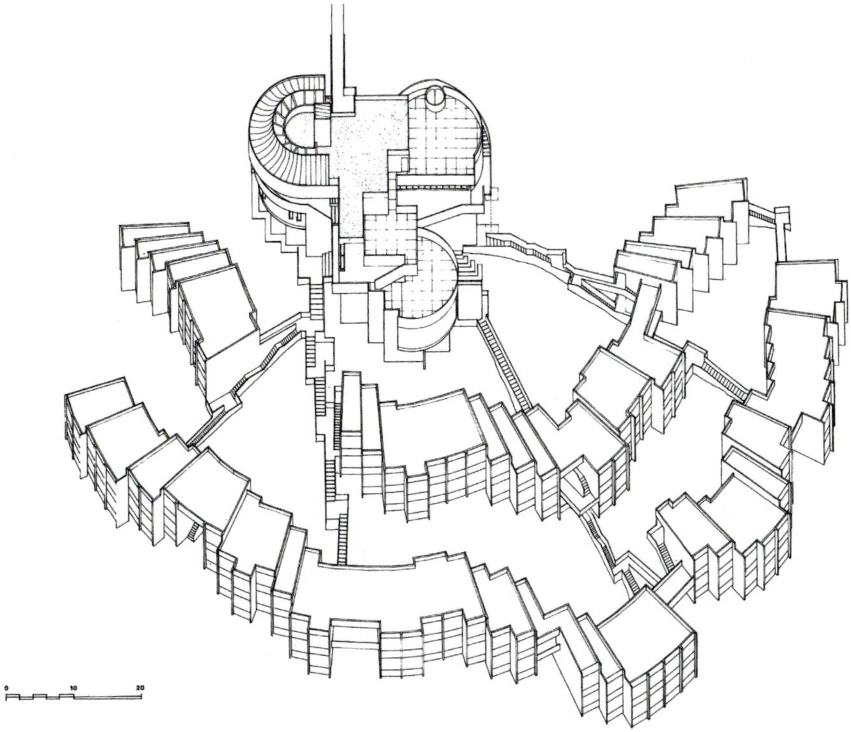

fig. 4 Giancarlo De Carlo, Collegio del Colle: Urbino, 1965, axonometry. Source: Archivio Giancarlo De Carlo, IUAV.

fig. 5 Giancarlo De Carlo, Collegio del Colle: Urbino. Source: Photo by Luca Molinari

fig. 6 Giancarlo De Carlo, Collegio Aquilone: Urbino, Detail of the communal spaces. Source: Photo by Luca Molinari

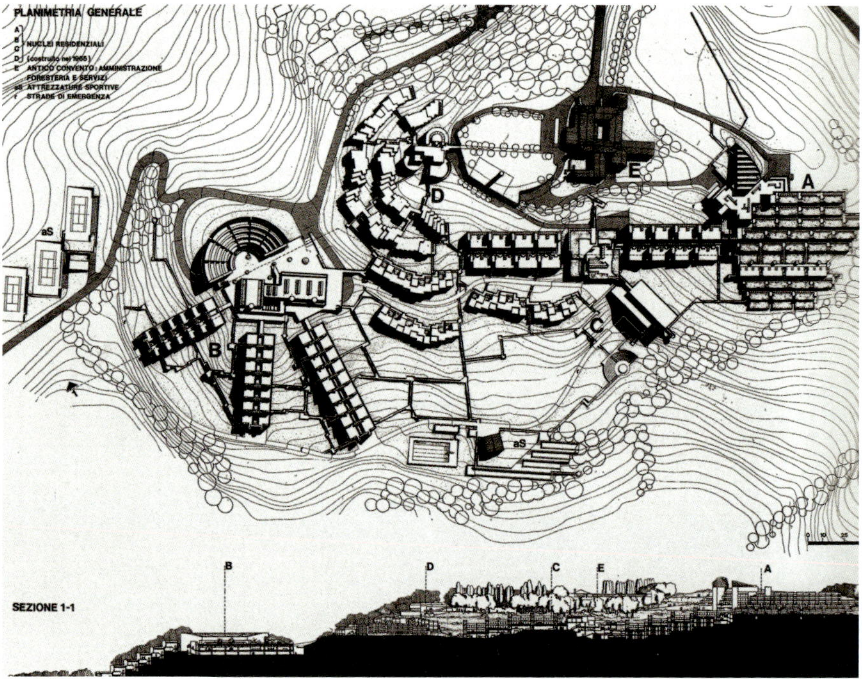

fig. 7 Giancarlo De Carlo: Masterplan of the Collegio del Colle, Urbino, Archivio Giancarlo De Carlo, IUAV

symbolism and profound relationship with space. In this respect there is a striking similarity between the axonometric representations of the spaces of transit and connection developed by De Carlo to represent the residences with similar drawings for the Freie Universität in Berlin, for the universities of Zurich, Bochum and Toulouse by Candilis, Woods and Josic, and with reflections on the use of public and connective spaces on Golden Lane Road by Alison and Peter Smithson; and above all in van Eyck's Nagele (1954) and

fig. 8 Giancarlo De Carlo: Collegio La Vela, detail of the communal spaces. Source: Photo by Luca Molinari

fig. 9 Giancarlo De Carlo: Collegio La Vela and Collegio Aquilone, Urbino. Source: Photo by Luca Molinari

Orphanage (1956), in which the concept of "architecture in the form of a city" (and vice versa) attained an important maturity.

From 1973 to 1983, De Carlo designed three new colleges in Urbino (Il Tridente, La Vela, L'Aquilone) where the relationship between the single-student unit and the diffused system of public spaces became the core of the project. The sequence of colleges, built below the Collegio del Colle, was designed as new elements of the town and of the landscape; the community's life is considered as the warm core of the design and functional program, defining the physical and visual sequences of public and half-private spaces. The idea of the campus as an open, living organism transformed the project from a functional mechanism to a place able to enhance the humanity in students' daily lives and create a section of a new town connected to the local community (figs. 6–9).

Several years later, De Carlo tried to develop the idea of a "humanist" and open architecture in the project for a new housing settlement for workers in Terni.[33] The idea of a population's profound participation in the design process evolved from the vague idealization of an architecture able to fulfill human needs. But the Terni experiment didn't work because of the impossibility of managing a realistic discussion between inhabitants, clients and designers. The theoretical contribution of De Carlo to the role of the community as center of the urban-design process remains one of the most interesting elements of cultural identity in Italian postwar architecture, nevertheless, giving to the project the fundamental role of mediating between human scale, political participation and the form of the living city.

Endnotes

This article is part of a PhD research project co-financed by the European Social Fund through the POPH (Programa Operacional Potencial Humano) and by national funds from FCT (Fundação para a Ciência e a Tecnologia) under the PhD Grant with reference SFRH/BD/87825/2012.

1 Ernesto Nathan Rogers, "Program: Domus, the House of Man," in ed. Joan Ockman, *Architecture Culture 1943–1968* (New York: Rizzoli, 1993), 79.

2 Luca Molinari, *Continuità: A Response to Identity Crises: Ernesto Nathan Rogers and Italian Architectural Culture after 1945* (Delft: TU Delft, 2008), 127–168.

3 (ed.) Giancarlo De Carlo, *Le Corbusier* (Milano: Rosa e Ballo ed., 1945)

4 "He added the subtitle 'la casa dell'uomo', echoing the title of the book published by Le Corbusier and Francoise de Pierrefeu in 1942." Rogers, "Program: Domus," 77.

5 Giuseppe Pagano was the editor-in-chief of *Domus* with Massimo Bontempelli and Melchiorre Bega between July 1941 and October 1942.

6 Rogers, "Program: Domus," 79.

7 Alfred Roth, "La casa di Mme Mandrot," *Domus*, 206 (1946); "Tendenza dell'architettura scolastica svizzera," *Domus*, 220 (1947).

8 Max Bill, "Pittura Concreta," *Domus*, 206 (1946); "La costruzione concreta ed il dominio dello spazio," *Domus*, 210 (1946).

9 Sigfried Giedion, "L'età della meccanizzazione totale," *Domus*, 216 (1946); "Il progresso della comodità," *Domus*, 217 (1947).
10 Lionello Venturi, "Considerazioni sull'arte astratta," *Domus*, 205 (1946).
11 Giorgio Crespi, "La casa geometrica e la casa umana," *Domus*, 205 (1946); "Le Corbusier vecchio e nuovo," *Domus*, 206 (1946); "Destino degli oggetti," *Domus*, 207 (1946).
12 Giancarlo De Carlo, "L'insegnamento di F.L.Wright," *Domus*, 207 (1946); "William Morris, pioniere dell'arte sociale," *Domus*, 211 (1946).
13 Ettore Sottsass Jr., "Coerenza di Neutra," *Domus*, 215 (1946).
14 Eugenio Gentili, "La casa inglese," *Domus*, 208 (1946); Vittorio Gandolfi, "Esperienze giapponesi," *Domus*, 209 (1946).
15 John Porter Clark and Albert Frey, "Casa in California," *Domus*, 213 (1946).
16 Ettore Sottsass, "Coerenza di Neutra," *Domus*, 215 (1946).
17 Alfred Roth, "La casa di M.me de Mandrot," *Domus*, 206 (1946).
18 Rogers, "Programma: Domus, la casa dell'uomo," *Domus*, 205 (1946)
19 Rogers, "Saluto," *Domus*, 223/224/225 (1947).
20 Molinari, *Continuità*, 170–203.
21 Rogers, José Luis Sert, Jaqueline Tyrwhitt, eds., *Il Cuore della città*, (Milano: Hoepli, 1954).
22 Max Risselada, Dirk van den Heuvel, eds., *Team 10: In Search of a Utopia of the Present (1953–1981)*, (Rotterdam: NAi, 2005).
23 For detailed biographies of Giancarlo De Carlo: Angela Mioni, Connie Occhialini Etra, eds., *Giancarlo De Carlo. Immagini e frammenti* (Milan: Electa, 1995); John McKean, *Layered Places: Giancarlo De Carlo* (Stuttgart, London: Edition Axel Menges, 2004); Margherita Guccione, Vittorini Alessandra, eds., *Giancarlo De Carlo. Le ragioni dell'architettura* (Rome: Electa-DARC, 2005).
24 McKean, *Layered Places*, 52.
25 Franco Buncuga, *Conversazioni con Giancarlo De Carlo. Architettura e libertà*, (Milan: Eléuthera, 2000), 94–100.
26 Ibid., 128–129.
27 McKean, *Layered Places*, 55.
28 De Carlo, *Urbino: The History of a City and Plans for Its Development* (Cambridge, Mass.: MIT Press, 1966), 76–80; *Gli spiriti dell'architettura* (Roma: Editori Riuniti, 1992), 331–346.
29 McKean, *Layered Places*, 58.
30 Molinari, "Constructing New Continuities in a Post-War World: The Relationship between Jaap Bakema and Ernesto Nathan Rogers," in ed. Carlo Togliani, *Un palazzo in forma di parole. Scritti in onore di Paolo Carpeggiani* (Milano: Franco Angeli, 2016), 487–494.
31 Aldo van Eyck, "University College in Urbino by Giancarlo De Carlo," in *Zodiac*, 16 (1966), 17. Also his reflections and studies on the Dogon developments in the same period.
32 Livio Schirollo, *Giancarlo De Carlo. Gli spiriti dell'architettura* (Rome: Editori Riuniti, 1992), 268.
33 Molinari, "Matteotti Village and Gallaratese": Design Criticism of the Italian Welfare State," in *Architecture and the Welfare State*, eds. Mark Swenarton, Tom Avermaete and Dirk van den Heuvel (London: Routledge, 2015), 259–276.

Sven Sterken, Eva Weyns

Urban Planning and Christian Humanism: The Institut Supérieur d'Urbanisme Appliqué in Brussels under Gaston Bardet

In the historiography of twentieth-century urban planning, there is little room for those actors who challenged the universalistic aspirations of the Modern Movement by trying instead to safeguard tradition and cultural differences. One such figure is the prominent French urban theoretician Gaston Bardet (1907–1989).[1] Striking against the technocratic and ahistorical character of the modernist doctrine as developed by the *Congrès Internationaux d'Architecture Moderne* (CIAM), which he denounced as reductionist functionalism, Bardet sought to establish forms of spatial and community planning in the service of a general moral and spiritual regeneration of postwar society. To this effect, he developed an extensive theoretical framework based on graphical survey techniques and a Christianized interpretation of the neighborhood-unit principle.

This chapter investigates a specific period in Bardet's career, namely his directorship of the Institut Supérieur d'Urbanisme Appliqué (ISUA) in Brussels between 1947 and 1973. The political and cultural climate in Belgium at that time was characterized by a strong ideological polarization between Socialists and Christian Democrats. Whereas the first group promoted collective housing in the urban outskirts, the latter advocated a decentralized, rural model based on the single-family dwelling. This sociopolitical dividing line became institutionalized with the founding of several planning institutes after the war; the ISUA, for instance, clearly put forward its Catholic inspiration.

In providing an understanding of how the discipline of urban planning was supposed to revitalize Christian values within contemporary society, this chapter aims at contributing to a more nuanced account of Belgian planning history in the postwar era, beyond the selective focus on modernist planners and their principles.

The Founding of ISUA

After the Second World War, municipal authorities in Belgium could only claim public funds for reconstruction upon approval of a town-planning scheme by the Ministry of Public Works. In order to meet the anticipated wave of assignments, almost all architecture institutes in Belgium developed curricula in urban planning. In Brussels, for example, no less than three post-graduate institutions existed: one at the Free University of Brussels (1936), another at La Cambre (1942) and finally the Institut Supérieur d'Urbanisme Appliqué at the Ecole d'Architecture Saint-Luc in Brussels-Schaerbeek (1947).[2] The latter was founded by Frère Raymond (Henri Gillis, hereafter Brother Raymond) at the instigation of the Christian Democrat Minister of Public Works, Oscar Behogne.[3] Typically for the so-called pillarization of Belgian society in the postwar era, it was meant as a Catholic counterpart to the planning institute at La Cambre, perceived as a bastion of modernist and socialist thought.[4]

To direct his new institution, Brother Raymond called upon the French urban theoretician Gaston Bardet. Forgotten nowadays but a well-known personality in his day, Bardet can be regarded as the spiritual and intellectual heir to the urban historian Marcel Poëte (1866–1950), the "godfather" of the French tradition of *urbanisme*: an approach to urban planning as a social science, along with geography, economics, sociology and history, based on precise knowledge with regards to the interaction between man and his environment.[5] Poëte's contribution may be compared to the role of Patrick Geddes in Britain – both shared the conviction that the city was a complex organism that developed through evolutionary processes. In this view, the city was not so much the inert product of this process but a "being" that reflected the collective and changing identity of its population. Bardet endeavored to put these ideas into practice. In particular, he wondered how they might assist the postwar problems of expanding and reshaping cities and towns in France.

Bardet's attachment to the historical, biological and communal aspects of planning made him the evident opponent of modernist urban-planning doctrines as developed by CIAM and progressively adopted by the French ministry

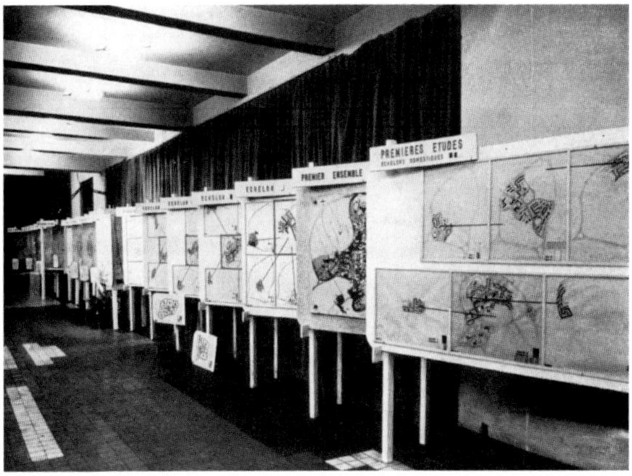

fig. 1 *Cité de l'air*, view of the project as displayed at the *Journées internationals de l'urbanisme appliqué* at the Palais des Beaux-Arts in Brussels, 1949. Source: ISUA course prospectus, 1954, p. 9.

of reconstruction after the war.[6] As a consequence, when reconstruction effectively began, Bardet found himself struggling to find opportunities to put his ideas to the test. This sense of isolation might explain why he accepted the collaboration with Brother Raymond in setting up a new urban-planning institute in Brussels. For Bardet, it offered an opportunity to continue the research and teaching he had carried out in the framework of the Atelier Supérieur d'Urbanisme Appliqué in Paris, while Brother Raymond speculated that Bardet's reputation would attract students both nationally and internationally.[7]

The *Cité de l'Air*

Effective as of October 25, 1947, the ISUA's three-year program covered a large variety of subjects in various fields (history, economics, sociology, geography and psychology), taught by a range of specialists from the academic, professional and political worlds. Bardet taught a seminar on the spiritual, intellectual and cultural dimension of urban and monumental ensembles called "Evolution du grand art dans les civilisations," while his wife, Françoise Poëte (daughter of Marcel Poëte), introduced the students to the method of "social topography."[8] This surveying technique was developed by Bardet and enabled mapping not only the built environment of a specific community but also its sociological profile and evolution over time.[9] The pinnacle of the ISUA curriculum was the diploma thesis. Due to lack of real commissions, Bardet used it as a testing ground for his planning concepts and pedagogical principles. This was perhaps best exemplified by the very first thesis, the *Cité de l'Air*, the blueprint for a (fictional) new town near Paris to house the personnel of the newly created Orly Airport (fig. 1). In particular, the *Cité de l'Air* project was a demonstration of two of Bardet's key concepts: the theory of échelons and the *organisation polyphonique*.

According to Bardet, the social structure of a town consisted of a federation of communities, small and large, as expressed by the town's great variety in parishes, neighborhoods, residential units and streets. As he stated, his technique of social topography had allowed the empirical verification of the existence of three types of social groupings (échelons) in the city: the échelon *patriarcal*, the échelon *domestique* and the échelon *paroissial*.[10] Scales of community rather than spatial categories, the échelons reflected Bardet's understanding of the urban environment as a social rather than a physical construct. According to his theory, the échelon *patriarcal* was the most elementary degree of urban life: it formed "the elementary group in which neighbors co-operate with and help one another. It may be a small isolated hamlet or village of five to ten families who happen to have a feeling of community because of their proximity and constant contact in daily life."[11] In Bardet's view, this was the organic cell of social life, reflected in the care of each other's children, sharing tools or spending leisure time together. Next, the domestic echelon comprised a number of streets and squares characterized by their own particular way of life. Composed of fifty to a hundred and fifty households, this was the first properly urban level where exchange and intercourse exceeded family bounds. Bardet described it as "a number of streets and squares which have their own particular way of life, their own characteristics, even their own customs. Housewives meeting in their shopping several times a day create links among various households. [...] This is no longer an elementary group of families; it now consists of from 50 to 150 households depending upon a local group of shops."[12] Then the parish degree consisted of a federation of several domestic degrees, totaling five hundred to fifteen hundred families. It usually possessed a certain autonomy in spiritual and administrative matters, spatially expressed by the centrally located church, a particular commemorative monument or a public building. At this level, it became possible to distinguish real neighborhood life. Bardet called it the parish degree "as a reminder of the community role played by the parish many centuries ago."[13] Finally, each of the three echelons had its proper role to play in the *Cité humaine*, comprising between five thousand and fifteen thousand families – the natural size of an urban settlement for Bardet, as he believed that beyond this number, biological equilibrium was lost. Whereas the échelon *patriarcal* formed the biological unit of the *Cité humaine*, the échelon *domestique* functioned as its economical backbone; the échelon *paroissial* structured the spiritual and political dimension of urban life. Although the échelon theory bears much resemblance to contemporary ideas about the neighborhood unit, it differed from the latter, according to Bardet, in that it was empirically verified and provided a way to design new towns as a feder-

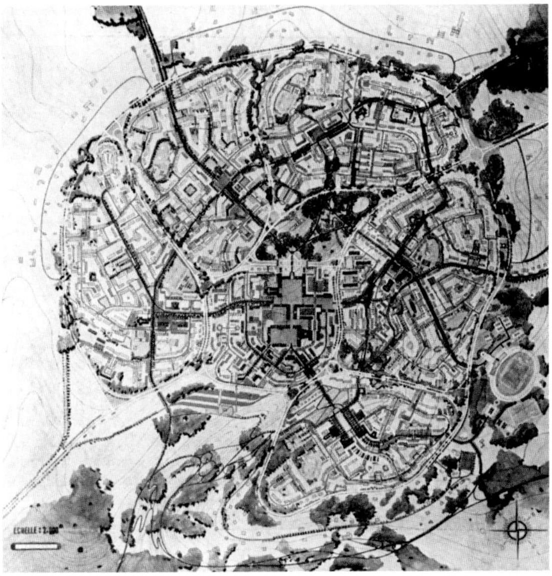

fig. 2 *Cité de l'air*, general layout of the project. Source: ISUA course prospectus, 1954, p. 15.

ation of structured communities shaped to the scale of man. *Cité de l'Air*, for example, was divided into six "parishes," each equipped with its own sports infrastructure, cinema and church (fig. 2). These quarters were physically and visually delineated by roads for motor traffic, their cores interlinked by independent pedestrian routes. At the level of the échelon *domestique*, each of the six parishes was further partitioned into eight to ten neighborhoods and further subdivided at the patriarchal scale.

The hierarchical scheme thus obtained formed the blueprint for all further steps in the project, including the repartition of tasks within the design team. Here, Bardet's principle of *organisation polyphonique* was called upon. Refuting excessive specialization and repetition of the Taylorist division of labor, Bardet proposed that, instead, each team member alternately coordinate the design process of a particular echelon or collaborate in elaborating a specific aspect of it.[14] A team member could, for example, determine circulation patterns within one parish and simultaneously work on the domestic echelon in another. Balancing team spirit and individual expression, planning thus became a group affair that benefited from a wide spectrum of competencies (fig. 3). The result was perhaps less a plan in the modernist sense of the word (a fixed, functionalist blueprint) than "human geography created by man"[15] (fig. 4).

Planning and Spiritual Reform

In 1944, Bardet wrote: "If the profession of urban planner formerly seemed to me one of the best jobs in the world, one of the richest in terms of living complexity, I realize now its true social significance and its spiritual mission."[16] The underlying idea, namely that planning ought to transcend the material dimension of the built environment and address more fundamental social and spiritual needs of society derived from the conviction – which Bardet shared with many Catholic intellectuals at the time – that Western society was undergoing severe moral impoverishment. Many held that the unbridled growth of cities was responsible for the degeneration of communal life and the rise of individualism. Similarly, the decline of spirituality in favor of growing materialism was perceived as a symptom of general ethical and intellectual decline. As an antidote, Bardet propagated a Christian humanism based on personalist ideas as developed by Catholic philosophers such as Jacques Maritain and Emmanuel Mounier. In opposition to the notion of the liberated "individual" (having freed himself from tradition and family ties), they defined the "person" as a spiritual being who derives their identity from being embedded within a community of like-minded fellows.[17] At the basis of this identification lay the typically Christian concept of charity or unconditional love for the other.

This led Bardet to the idea of *urbanisme chrétien* [Christian urbanism], in reference to Maritain. In his famous treatise *Art et Scholastique*, the latter had defined the essence of the "Christian" in art: "The work will be Christian to the exact degree in which love is vibrant."[18] Maritain meant that the Christian aspect of art did not reside in the use of a particular style or form but in its capacity to express (and also encourage) charity through artistic means. Applying this idea to town planning (which he considered as both an art and a science), Bardet stated that "love can be alive only if this translation expresses an organization enabling the customary practice of charity, or love between men."[19] In other words, he believed that it was the duty of the planner to arrange the form of a town in such a way as to promote and nurture love for our fellow man. In the context of the disruption caused by the war, the planner thus occupied a crucial position; his task consisted not only in reconstructing cities and towns but also re-establishing a sense of community and strengthening its spirituality.

In its first years, ISUA was very successful: by 1954, a hundred eighty-seven students had enrolled and thirty-four diplomas had been awarded. It quickly became evident that Bardet's vision of a decentralized rural society, nevertheless, was untenable in the rapidly changing cultural and economic climate of Belgium in the late 1950s. The clearest instance of this can be found

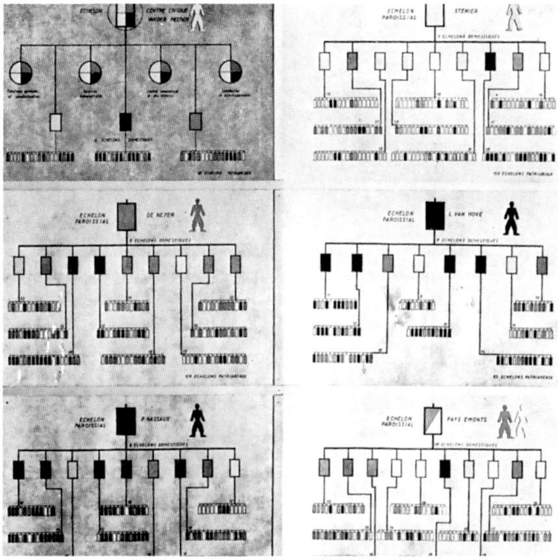

fig. 3 *Cité de l'air*, charts showing the distribution of the various echelons amongst the designers. Source: ISUA course prospectus, 1954, p. 10.

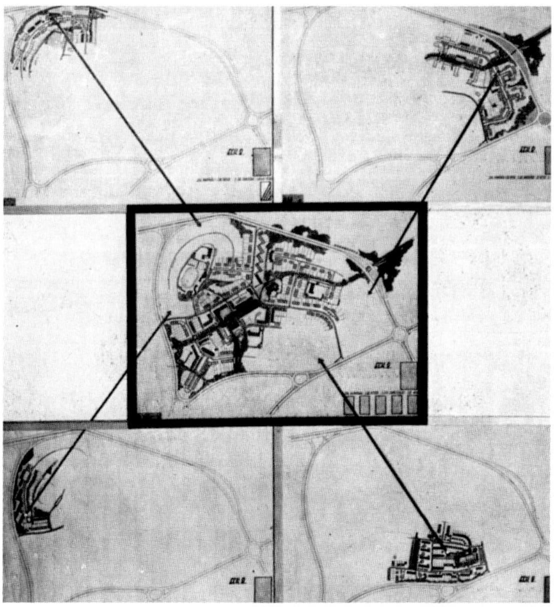

fig. 4 *Cité de l'air*, detail of one parish as designed by one particular team member (center) and the contributions made by the four other team members. Source: ISUA course prospectus, 1954, p. 12.

in the work of Groupe Structures, the architecture firm founded by the student authors of the *Cité de l'Air* project, upon their graduation. The firm's first commission was the master plan for Wezembeek-Oppem, a municipality west of Brussels that underwent rapid demographical transformation due to the influx of inhabitants from the capital. Resulting from the administrative fusion of two existing villages, the municipality's decentralized nature was further reinforced by the layout to the east of a new, purely residential allot-

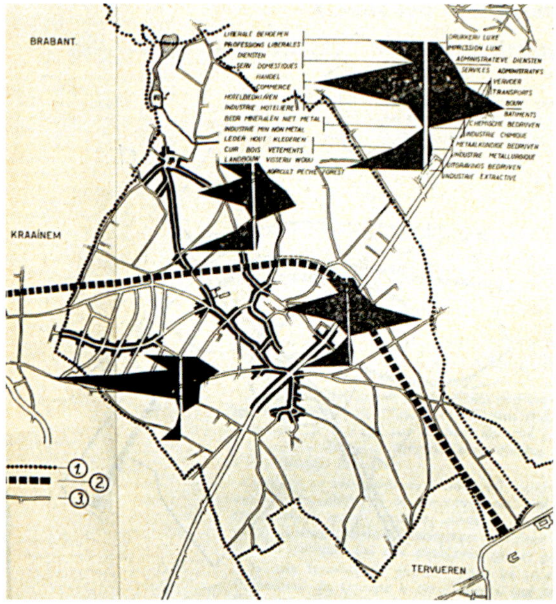

fig. 5 Wezembeek-Oppem, sociological profiles of the various quarters. Source: *Le Mouvement communal*, No. 253, 1949, p. 230.

ment for commuters (called Bel Air). A detailed sociological profile of the town, classifying its four thousand inhabitants according to profession, origin and precise place of residence, revealed that the various quarters were not only spatially separated but also very distinct socially[20] (fig. 5). It was therefore decided to consider these quarters as three separate parish echelons, grouped around a central core. To this effect, Bel Air was equipped with its own parish church and a preparatory school while the intersecting area between the three residential quarters was to become the administrative and commercial center for the entire town. Unlike the church and school, this urban infrastructure was not realized, depriving Wezembeek-Oppem of a real town center until the present day (figs. 6, 7). Apart from its urban-planning projects, Groupe Structures later entered the public eye with a number of well-planned housing estates, acclaimed for their systematic use of prefabricated building components. However, pressed by the rapidly rising costs of building materials, land and labor, the firm gradually lessened its humanist aspirations and rapidly became the ultimate embodiment of the merciless planner at the service of the political and financial establishment.[21]

The increasingly religious dimension of Bardet's thinking also affected his teaching at ISUA, which in his mind became a center for the dissemination of Christian thought. At the Catholic artists' congress in Bologna in 1955, for example, Bardet stated: "Our institute […] is primarily a center of Catholic thought; it aims to educate men […] who are Catholics and children of God in the first place, and only then according to their specialty: architects,

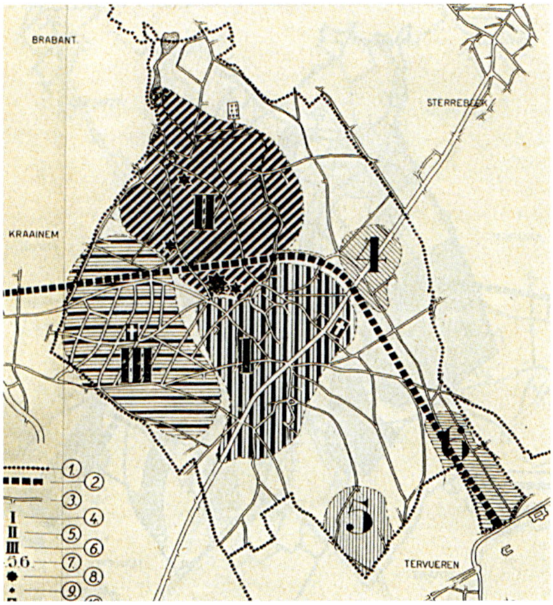

fig. 6 Wezembeek-Oppem, distribution of the various échelons. Source: *Le Mouvement communal*, No. 253, 1949, p. 234.

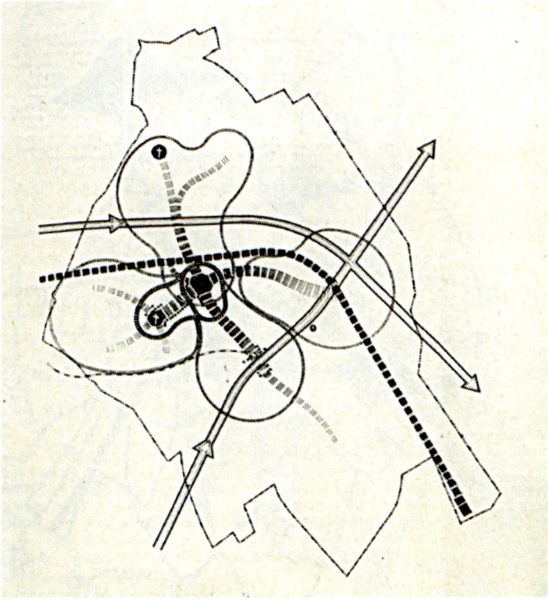

fig. 7 Wezembeek-Oppem, concept of the master plan Source: *Le Mouvement communal*, No. 253, 1949, p. 229.

engineers, sociologists, etc."[22] Bardet's drift into mysticism also increasingly infected his academic integrity and his relations with students and colleagues alike. The titles of some of his lectures ("Le Feu qui purifie," "Les Fausses Profondeurs de la psychanalyse") left no doubt about their dogmatic content, while his public statements on Catholicism and criticism of the church hierarchy led to conflicts with episcopal authorities and with the directorship of the Ecole d'Architecture Saint-Luc. After a major ISUA reform, Bardet was dismissed in 1973.

Despite the fact that he was among the most well-known urban theoreticians writing mid-century (eleven reissues of his *Urbanisme* volume in the popular series *Que sais-je?* were released between 1945 and 1990), Bardet is almost completely forgotten today. With his hopes for a spiritual revival, his rejection of the large city, his favoring of a decentralized pattern of small communities and his sensitivity to the history of the city and local traditions of building, it is easy to dismiss Bardet as an exponent of a bygone era. His conservatism and the increasingly religious tint of his ideas only reinforce this perception. Typically, Françoise Choay had already reduced Bardet in 1965 to no more than a footnote in her canonical *L'Urbanisme, utopies et réalités.*[23] As Jean-Louis Cohen has pointed out, the doctrinal character of Bardet's thinking may partially explain his absence in the historiography of urban planning.[24]

Indeed, much of his writing consists of impulsive, often overlapping statements based on empirical findings and intuitions. But can't the same be said about Le Corbusier? Bardet's fate therefore also informs us about the selective mechanisms of architectural historiography. In Anthony Vidler's book *Histories of the Immediate Present*, in which Vidler deals with precisely this one-sided nature of recent historiography, he states that a true understanding of the Modern Movement requires a continuous review of its ideas and protagonists.[25] This means that we have to deal with the heroes but also have to take into account those figures who undermine the idea of modernity as a homogeneous construct. Only then will we be able to gain nuanced insight into what was essentially a very disparate phenomenon. Gaston Bardet was precisely such a figure: despite his peripheral position, he exerted a major influence in his day. An understanding of the impact of his work and thinking therefore constitutes an essential ingredient in grasping the essence of the ideologically polarized debate on urban planning in postwar Belgium and beyond.

Endnotes

1 The research for this article was carried out on the basis of the archives of the St. Lucas architecture institute kept at KADOC KU Leuven; the archives of ISUA, Brussels; Gaston Bardet's personal archives at the Institut français d'architecture, Paris; the personal archives of Jacques Boseret-Mali, ISUA secretary and founding partner of Groupe Structures, kept by the author. Conversations with Judith Le Maire and Irene Lund (La Cambre/ Université Libre de Bruxelles) have been instrumental in the authors'

understanding of the intellectual context in which Bardet was operating. For an introduction to Bardet, see Nicholas Bullock, "Gaston Bardet: Post-War Champion of the Mainstream Tradition of French *urbanisme*," *Planning Perspectives*, 25:3 (2010), 347–363; Luigi Manzione, "Economie du lien et biopolitique. Gaston Bardet et l'urbanisme comme science sociale," *Espaces et sociétés*, 140–141 (2010), 193–213; Jean-Pierre Frey, "Gaston Bardet" in *Les faiseurs de villes*, ed. Thierry Paquot (Cholion: Infolio, 2011), 101–113.

2 The Ecole d'Architecture Saint-Luc was founded in 1862 in Ghent by the Frères des Ecoles chrétiennes (Brothers of the Christian Schools). It quickly developed (autonomous) branches in other cities such as Tournai (1877), Liège (1880) and Brussels (Schaerbeek, 1887; Saint-Gilles, 1904), Mons (1904) and Namur (1913). Set up as a joint venture of the two Brussels branches, the Institut Supérieur d'Urbanisme Appliqué's administration was taken care of by the branch at Saint-Gilles, while the courses took place at 74, rue des Palais in Schaerbeek. The only ones to be situated in Flanders, the schools in Ghent and Schaerbeek merged in 1995 and became the Faculty of Architecture of the KU Leuven in 2014. The Institut Supérieur d'Urbanisme Appliqué was renamed as ISURU (Institut Supérieur d' Urbanisme et de Rénovation Urbaine) in 1973 and operates (autonomously) under this name today.

3 On Brother Raymond, see Wilfried Wouters, *Van Tekenklas tot kunst-academie. De Sint-Lucasscholen in België, 1866–1966* (Brussels: UGA, 2013), 378–379.

4 "Pillarization" refers to the politico-denominational segregation of society into several sections ("pillars") according to religious and ideological beliefs. Where planning is concerned, Belgian Catholicism traditionally favored single-family houses in a rural setting while the Socialist block generally encouraged collective dwelling in apartment blocks.

5 On Poëte, see Donatella Calabi, "Marcel Poëte: Pioneer of 'l'Urbanisme' and Defender of 'l'Histoire des villes'," *Planning Perspectives*, 11:4 (1996), 413–436.

6 Bullock, "Gaston Bardet: Post-War Champion," 349.

7 Bardet was well known in Belgium at the time; his articles were published in architecture periodicals such as *La Maison*, *Architecture-Urbanisme-Habitation*, *Reconstruction* and *Schets*. His public appearances rarely went unnoticed. One lecture by Bardet in 1946, for example, spurred a polemical response from Renaat Braem, the self-proclaimed spokesman of modernist ideology in Belgium. The latter criticized Bardet's conservative views and his demonization of the industrial complex as the alleged cause of social disruption. Braem's response was published as "Op zoek naar een basis voor het nieuwe urbanisme. Beschouwingen bij een voordracht gegeven door Gaston Bardet," *Bouwen*, 3 (1946), 45–49.

8 Institut Supérieur d'Urbanisme Appliqué, course prospectus, 1954, 23–56.

9 Gaston Bardet, "Social Topography: An Analytico-Synthetic Understanding of the Urban Texture," *The Town Planning Review*, 22:3 (1951), 237–260.

10 Bardet presented his échelons theory for the first time in Bardet, "Les Échelons communautaires dans les agglomérations urbaines," *Économie et Humanisme*, 2:8 (1943), 501–521. This article was reprinted under the same title in Bardet, *Pierre sur pierre* (Paris: Editions LCB, 1945), 233–249.

11 Bardet, "Social Topography," 248.
12 Ibid., 248
13 Ibid., 249.
14 Bardet, "L'organisation humaine est polyphonique," *La vie franciscaine sacerdotale*, 4 (1951), 62–69; Frère Raymond (Henri Gillis), "De Polyfonische organisatie. Een nieuwe methode voor het stedenbouwkundig ontwerpen," *Schets*, 4 (1950), 113–119.
15 Bardet, *L'Urbanisme* (Paris: PUF, 1945), 66. Bardet seems to have been particularly pleased with the *Cité de l'air* project, as he prominently displayed it at the Journées Internationales d'étude d'urbanisme appliqué in 1949 in Brussels (organized by ISUA) as a demonstration of the colloquium's theme, "Comment créer un tissue urbain réellement vivant?" The project was discussed by Bardet in "Une nouvelle démonstration: l'organisation polyphonique," *Architecture–Urbanisme–Habitation*, 2 (1950), 29–36; "L'organisation polyphonique appliquée à la composition des grands ensembles," *L'Architecture française*, 101–102 (1950), 3–15; "De Polyfonische organisatie. Een nieuwe methode voor het stedenbouwkundig ontwerpen," *Schets*, 4 (1950), 113–119.
16 Translation by the authors. Original text: "*Si le métier d'urbaniste m'apparaissait autrefois comme l'un des plus beaux métiers du monde, l'un des plus riches de complexité vivante, je me rends compte aujourd'hui de sa véritable portée sociale et de sa mission spirituelle,*" in Bardet, "L'Urbanisme chrétien. La Structure communautaire," *Pierre sur pierre*, 271–276.
17 Bullock, "Gaston Bardet: Post-War Champion," 354.
18 Translation by the authors. Original text: "*L'œuvre sera chrétienne dans l'exacte mesure où l'amour sera vivant,*" in Jacques Maritain, *Art et Scolastique* (Paris: Librarie de l'art catholique, 1920), 96.
19 Translation by the authors. Original text: "*L'amour ne peut être vivant que si cette traduction exprime une organisation rendant possible l'exercice coutumier de la charité, de l'amour entre les hommes,*" in Bardet, *Pierre sur pierre*, 273.
20 Groupe Structures, "Essai de diagnostic sur une commune de l'agglomération bruxelloise," *Le Mouvement communal*, 253 (1949), 228–234.
21 On Groupe Structures, see Sven Sterken, "Architecture and the Ideology of Productivity: Four Public Housing Projects by Groupe Structures in Brussels (1950–1965)," *Footprint*, 5:2 (2012), 25–40.
22 Translation by the authors. Original text: "*Notre institut* [...] *est avant tout un centre de pensée catholique; il vise à former des hommes* [...] *qui soient d'abord catholiques, enfants de Dieu, puis selon leur spécialité: architectes, urbanistes, ingénieurs, sociologues, etc.*" Source: "Adresse du professeur Gaston Bardet," *Schets*, 6 (1955), 175–176 (p. 175).
23 Françoise Choay, *L'Urbanisme: utopies et réalités* (Paris: Seuil, 1965), 63.
24 Jean-Louis Cohen, "Gaston Bardet. Un Humanisme à visage urbain," *Architecture, Mouvement, Continuité*, 44 (1978), 74–77 (p. 76).
25 Anthony Vidler, *Histories of the Immediate Present* (Cambridge, Mass.: MIT Press, 2008).

Stanislaus von Moos

The Monumentality of the Matchbox: On "Slabs" and Politics in the Cold War[1]

"Crisis" Rhetoric

In the 1950s the matchbox was still a universal household item and a passenger in every smoker's pocket. Thus when Edmund Goldzamt described the recently completed UN Secretariat in New York as "stretched like a sky-high matchbox on extended foundations" and when Hans Schmidt insisted, "that a high-rise building could be more than a matchbox put up with *n* number of office floors," everybody knew what they meant.[2] Note that east of the Iron Curtain, such comments reflect an official consensus regarding architecture in the West. In its January 1954 issue, the Soviet magazine *Arkhitektura SSSR* found "contemporary architecture in the capitalist countries" to be obsessed with a new American fashion, the "slab block." The UN Building and the Lever House in New York, the US Embassy in Havana, and the Ministry of Education in Rio were the buildings listed (among others) as models for this "functionalism for the rich" (figs. 1a, b): All were seen as synonymous with American cultural decline, due not least to that country's fixation on business and military supremacy on the world stage. For those who might not have gotten the point, the author added: "At the time when contemporary architecture of the Western Countries has no aesthetic forms of its own and resorts to the repetition of the uniform template of European and American functionalism, Soviet architecture is enriching itself with new forms (… based on the task) of maximally satisfying the growing requirements of the entire population."[3]

What debunked this postwar "crisis" of capitalism was the alleged "cheapness" of its products, resulting from the imperatives of the military build-up. Cost-efficiency and expediency – indeed the "militarization" imposed on con-

figs. 1a, b New York, UN Secretariat (1947–52). Wallace K. Harrison, architect. Photos by Alfred Roth, 1949 (1a) and 1952 (1b). (Source: Alfred Roth Files, gta-archive, ETH-Z)

struction – appeared about to ruin architecture altogether. To these Eastern Bloc critics, slabs – that is, the stacking of a maximum number of identical floors, one on top of the other – appeared as the ideal building form for a society under "strain," mainly for being time-saving in design and relatively cheap to build, and for promising fast returns with a minimum of capital investment. Therefore (following this logic): if the UN Secretariat was built in the form of a slab, it was because cost efficiency was the supreme imperative in the center of New York, where land property is most expensive – even under the conditions of the proverbial Rockefeller check by which the site had become available in the first place.

Norman Mailer's "empty television screen" …

By the mid-1960s, however, not long after the slab-formula had been successfully exported to Brazil (fig. 2) – and, by the way, to the Soviet bloc, thus significantly changing the conditions of its reception behind the Iron Curtain – economic expediency re-surfaced as an argument in the war against "slabs"; except that, by that time, the criticism was mostly American. It started with Norman Mailer. Such "mere boxes" are "dead as an empty television screen," Mailer stated. Rationalization is revealed here as having but one goal: to make up for the exorbitant costs involved in the purchase of a site, in taxes, in mar-

fig. 2 Brasilia, Senate Chamber and the towers of the Secretariat Building (1957–60). Oscar Niemeyer, architect. Photo: René Burri (Source: Magnum)

keting, in publicity, not to mention what Mailer calls the "dollar-anemia" caused by the arms-race and by taxation. "In this context the formulas of modern architecture have triumphed," Mailer writes, "and her bastards – those new office skyscrapers – have triumphed everywhere."[4] The best reason is, so he goes on, "that modern architecture offers a pretext to a large real-estate operator to stick up a skyscraper at a fraction of the money it should cost, so helps him to conceal the criminal fact that we are given a stricken building, a denuded, aseptic, unfinished work, stripped of ornament, origins, prejudices, not even a peaked roof or spire to engage the heavens (…etc.)."[5] And he continues in view of what he refers to as the "prison phantasies of urban renewal" and more specifically of Lyndon B. Johnson's vision of the "Great Society" and his call to use the next forty years in order "to re-build from scratch the City in the United States:" "The mind recoils from the thought of an America rebuilt completely in the shape of those blank skyscrapers forty stories high, their walls dead as an empty television screen, their form as interesting as a box of cleansing tissue propped on end."[6]

… and Vincent Scully's "American Nightmare"

Modern architecture has often been described as an evolutionary process that parallels an implied progressive dynamic of modern society at large. By the mid-1960s however, and in the light of discussions like those just referred to, some historian-critics began to re-conceptualize the legacy of modernism according to a rather melodramatic, if not frankly apocalyptic register, castigating the uniformity and "monotony" of corporate architecture either as the tragic degeneration of a design ethos that was no longer adequate to the needs of business, or, depending on the viewpoint, as the fatal result of modernism's pact with business. Vincent Scully was no doubt the most authoritative voice among the latter group. In 1963, he vigorously challenged Mailers's unqualified dismissal of modernism; a few months later he turned to ranting ever more forcefully at today's "Motorized Megalopolis" that he saw proliferating all over America – as nothing short of "America's Architectural Nightmare."[7] Soon after, and with the help of an ominous reversal of what one would expect to be the normal cycle of "Life" and "Death," Jane Jacobs set the tone even more clearly with her famous *Death and Life of Great American Cities* (1966). In *American Architecture and Urbanism*, Scully later re-calibrated Mailer's blow against modern architecture in somewhat more serene terms by describing Lever House – most likely the trigger for Mailer's harangue – as a "typical Bauhaus object: freestanding, shiny, weightless, asymmetrical, and fundamentally non-urban. It both cut a serious hole in Park Avenue as a street and created an unusable Plaza of its own."[8] (fig. 3)

As the writings of Mailer and Scully seem to indicate, the maladies of modernism, be they real or merely alleged: bigness, formal blandness, semantic silence, expressive nullity, boredom (or any other quality suggestive of metaphysical disgust) are most impressively invoked and anathemized when they occur in slabs. Even though its underlying design philosophy tends to drain traditional notions of representation and symbolism, "the slab" thus turned out to become a projection surface for multifarious shared notions regarding form, space, progress, or power, thereby generating a tension field of semantic expectation that could easily compete with the communicative potential of any inherited form of architectural "symbolism." Seen in such a perspective, Mailer's notion of the slab as "empty television screen" may turn out to be more poignant than Mailer himself suspected.

"Less Is a Bore"

As to the notion of "boredom:" "It's all very well to say we admire Mies [...], but what if one is bored ...?" – Note that this was said in 1961; not by Venturi, but by Philip Johnson, the architect who basically built the Seagram Building.[9] Though Johnson was sufficiently familiar with Andy Warhol as to be aware of the latter's fascination with the phenomenon ("I like boring things [...] but that doesn't mean I'm not bored by them")[10], boredom was

fig. 3 New York, Lever House (1950–52). Skidmore, Owings and Merrill, architects (Gordon Bunshaft. Designer. Advertisement for "General Bronze Corporation" (Progressive Architecture; 1952). (Source: Author's collection)

anathema in the sentimental universe of postmodernism then championed by Johnson. Five years later, Venturi had gone one step further by parodying Mies' "Less Is More" by his rather wanton "Less is a Bore" – though interestingly in his text it is not Mies directly that Venturi takes issue with, but indeed Johnson.[11] And by the 1970s, it is arguably Manfredo Tafuri and Francesco Dal Co who offer the most emphatic reading of Mies' Seagram Building in terms of its absoluteness, its alleged semantic and expressive silence (fig. 4): There is "[n]o longer a plurality of signs, but only the entire building as a neutral sign," they claim. "The absoluteness of the object is total: the maximum of formal structurality corresponds with the maximum absence of images."[12] It is Mailer's empty television screen again. A "language of absence" that is both reflected and brought to its climax in the "*piazzetta*" in front of the building: "the overturning [*ribaltamento*] of everything that a skyscraper can signify: what we have is two "voids," one responding to the other, both speaking the hallucinated language of nothingness, of the "silence" that – by ways of Kafkaesque paradox – assaults the noise of the metropolis. [...] The relinquishment, the classical *Entsagung*, is definitive. In order to proclaim it, Mies steps one step back and remains silent."[13] Interestingly, Robert Venturi and Denise Scott Brown in *Learning from Las Vegas* (1972) take an alternative stand when they point at the system of tectonic signs that make up the after all rather Vitruvian grammar Mies had chosen for the Seagrams Building, reminding the reader that the added window mullions are not to be seen as structure but as an anticipation of the "Decorated Shed:" "Less may have been more," they write, rather apologetically: "… but the I-section on Mies van der Rohe's fire-resistant column, for instance, is as completely ornamental as the applied pilaster on a Renaissance pier or the incised shaft in the Gothic column."[14]

Smoke Signals in the Cold War

There is hardly a more hilarious rebuttal of Mailer's and many more serious critics' prejudice on the "cheapness" and the semantic "silence," the conceptual "blandness" of the slab than Charles Luckman's account of the story of Lever House in New York. At first sight, the slab may have appeared to be the self-evident solution in terms of structural economy or the provision of elegant, maximum-lit office space. In terms of rent yields, however, it must have looked like an absurdity in one of the most expensive locations worldwide, especially so since it came in combination with an open plaza, as the board members didn't fail to remark (see fig. 3).

Lever House and the "Humanation of Cities"

In the world of consumer goods, "symbolic value" is most aggressively marketed when the price is high. Similarly, in architecture, "meaning" and "symbolism" tend to become an issue when there is a contradiction that needs to be bridged between the planned structure and the costs involved. In these circumstances, there is a special need to convince. Lever House is a good example in this context. To assuage the understandable skepticism of his board members, Charles Luckman, the President of Lever and himself an architect, argued that open space at the foot of the building that would result from the sacrificed office space would make people feel "part of Lever."[15] The plaza would contribute a "very human feeling" on the level of the street to the transparent and polished surface of the curtain-wall facade, the purity of which symbolized the soap company. Luckman "wanted the entire ground floor at Park Avenue left open so that people could walk in and feel part of Lever; so that there might be a very human feeling at the ground level to contrast with the kind of slick and gleaming tower which I felt would properly reflect a soap company." Apart from the positive effects on Lever's "image," Luckmann argued, all this would promote what he called the "humanation of cities."[16] For people need "freedom of space" to dedicate themselves to the "pursuit of happiness" in a life of freedom, Luckman pursued.[17]

Luckman was clever enough not to submit a project himself, but to assign the task to one of the promising younger architectural firms in New York, Skidmore, Owings and Merrill. In order to define the best position for the slab, SOM used a model that allowed the examining of its visual effect in various positions along Park Avenue. In such a way, the elementary stereometrics

fig. 4 New York, Seagram Building (1956–1958). Ludwig Mies van der Rohe und Philip Johnson, architects. (Photo: Ezra Stoller)

of the box form promised to make the building a unique sculptural presence in the city. The visibility studies appear ultimately to have convinced Lever to massively invest in the symbolic function of its headquarters.[18] As Luckman's diatribes suggest, the neuroses of McCarthyism didn't stop at architecture's doorstep. Not content to provide a striking trademark for the company, the chairman even wanted the building to be seen as a symbol of "American values" in the face of the malignancies of socialism and communism.[19]

Power and Ambivalence

Luckman's Cold War fantasies about "American values" in the face of the "malignancies of socialism" would be a mere curiosity if they were not so directly related to events in Europe, and more specifically in Berlin. In 1949, the year of the West German currency reform and of the creation of the German Democratic Republic (GDR) as an autonomous state – not least in response to NATO's massive nuclear armament – the Cold War was about to become a primary fact of life in that city, and an inevitable and permanent subject of conversation – including also of conversation about architecture.[20] Slabs and ruins turn out to have been a highly suggestive constellation in this context.

For decades, the ruin of Berlin's Gedächtnis-Kirche (Kaiser Wilhelm Memorial Church) alongside its crystalline substitute by Egon Eiermann has played its ambivalent role as tourist logo and mysterious symbol of the city's perseverance in the Cold War (fig. 5). That nobody knows for sure what the combination of old and new exactly represents is part of the magic:

the phoenix-like rise of the new from the debris of the old? Mourning and soul-searching regarding German responsibility in the war? Or merely nostalgia for former national glory, romanticized in terms of ruin aesthetics? Considering the endless complications involved in the project's realization, the complex should perhaps rather be seen as emblematic of the difficulties of reaching a compromise when it comes to public representation in democracy.[21] Seen in this way, it is precisely the diffuse nature of its messages, combined with the power of the sign as such – for Alexander Calder, the church ruin was "perhaps the greatest abstract sculpture in the world"[22] – that make the Memorial Church the built paragon of the "New Monumentality."[23]

In its simplicity, Eiermann's new church encapsulates the mystery of the complex: it gives it a poetic, even spiritual dimension. Yet the slab-shaped office building and hotel behind the church, though banal in comparison, is certainly more of a marker than the elegant church could ever be. Like thesis and antithesis, the ruin and the slab characterize the physiognomy of the place while also, in fact, marking out two extremes within the range of possibilities in architectural signification at hand in the early postwar years. The one form seems to refer dialectically to the other: Towering over and framing the church ruin at the same time, the office building forms a paradoxical alter ego to the Gedächtniskirche, even recreating its toppled tower cross in the form of a colossal Mercedes-Benz star.[24]

While the slab-shaped Hotel building was thus seen in Berlin as an "exclamation point of free enterprise," the complex as a whole was described as "the most important commercial project of the postwar period *on our continent*" – in fact, the "first response to New York's famous Rockefeller-Center," as *Der Tagesspiegel* reported on the opening day.[25] So as to fit the convention of postwar International Style, and unlike the UN Secretariat in New York with its walled-up short ends (see fig. 1), the slab is here fully glazed like Lever House, a building that Helmut Hentrich, the leading architect of the Center, studied closely during his 1954 trip to New York.[26] Note that Gordon Bunshaft, the designer of Lever House, later played a key role in consulting for the glamorous "three-slab" Thyssen Building in Düsseldorf (designed by Hentrich, Petschnigg & Partner, HPP). When Karl-Heinz Pepper looked out for an architect for his Berlin project, Hentrich, Petschnigg & Partner were thus the obvious choice.

As to the small open-air rink attached to the air-conditioned "ladies' shopping paradise,"[27] it was presented at the time as the European counterpart to the skating rink at Rockefeller Center, whereas the shopping center – whose small open court could not really compete with both the Rockefeller Center's and the Lever House's main attraction, its open plaza – was subsequently marketed as an adaptation of the shopping arcades of Bern.[28] While

fig. 5 Berlin, Breitscheidplatz with Kaiser Wilhelm Memorial Church and Europa Center. Postcard, c. 1975 (Source: Author's collection)

the comparison with such "models" makes the Europa Center look rather paltry, it also reminds us that, in order to acquire its "civic" aura, the office slab as a type needs to be combined with a "plaza."

Excursus: Re-Discovering Rockefeller Center

The slab had been a "blind passenger" of the functional city ever since the 1920s, as virtually any project from that period can demonstrate. More often than not, Hilberseimer and Mies actually envisioned such solutions for Berlin. In Europe, innovative research in that field was paralyzed since the mid-1930s, so it was indeed via the United States and Brazil that the combination of "slab" and "plaza" reappeared on the European horizon. This happened even before 1945. Whereas Europe began to be confronted with the challenges of reconstruction, America struggled with its slums and its increasingly depopulated city centers. In this situation, the combination of slab and plaza appeared as one way of restoring "urbanity" to the inner cities.[29]

Rockefeller Center was the emblematic reference point in that context. Note that by 1951, when CIAM caught on to this subject (the proceedings of CIAM 8 appeared in print one year after the respective Congress in book form, as *The Heart of the City: The Humanization of Urban Life*),[30] architects like Edmund Bacon, Kahn and Stonorov in Philadelphia, Sert and Wiener in South America, but also Edward Durrell-Stone in New York had already shown the way (figs. 6, 7). Not to mention the Ministry of Education and Health in Rio de Janeiro by Lucio Costa, Oscar Niemeyer and others (including Le Corbusier), the "most beautiful government building in the Western world" (Philip Goodwin).[31] It is in this context that Giedion's invocations of the Agora of Priene, the Forum of Pompeji, or finally the Campidoglio in Rome – as models towards the "Humanization of the City" in the name of the "rights of the pedestrian" – began to influence the way a younger gener-

fig. 6 Louis I. Kahn, "'Business Neighbourhood' in 194X." Advertisment for "Barrett Specification Roofs" (Source: Architectural Forum, June 1945). (In: Andrew Michael Shanken, *194X: Architecture, Planning and Consumer Culture on the American Home Front*, 2009

ation of architects conceptualized the "Humanization of Urban Life."[32] That these humanistic invocations ended up mystifying the processes by which inner cities after 1945 were opened up to shopping (often at the expense of the inhabitants that were displaced is another story.

Giedion, the Slab, and other "Constituent Facts" of Modern Architecture

Sigfried Giedion's famous textbook *Space, Time and Architecture* first appeared in 1941. While the short chapter on Rockefeller Center in New York no longer qualifies as the last word on the complex, it is all the more interesting as a gauge for modernism's fascination with the dynamics of visual perception and the power of abstract form.[33] One can't help stumbling over "slabs," "slab-like blocks," "slablike units" and "planes" as one browses through the book. That the concepts belong to the "constituent facts" of modernity that form the book's backbone becomes clear in the section entitled "Construction and Aesthetics: Slab and Plane."[34] But the genealogy of the term is given only towards the end, in the short chapter "The Civic Center: Rockefeller Center, 1934–39," where Giedion quotes the 1939 New York City Guide's description of

fig. 7 New York, Rockefeller Plaza; Corbett, Harrison & McMurray, Hood & Fouilhoux, architects (1928–35). Photo 1944. (after J. Tyrwhitt, E. N. Rogers and J. L. Sert, *The Heart of the City*, 1952)

Raymond Hood's Daily Mail Building: "Its huge, broad, flat north and south fronts, its almost unbroken mass and thinness," features that according to this Guide impelled observers to nickname that building "The Slab."[35] In fact, we know better now: it was as early as March 6, 1931, that the *New York Times* referred to the R.C.A. building as a "slab," even though at that time it only existed in model form.[36] "This slab stands on its site like an immense upturned rectangle, a form impossible to realize in any other period," Giedion continues, now referring to the R.C.A. Building as built. He quotes Hood's "functionalist" derivation of the form as a simple result of the determination to offer "adequate light and air to all parts of the building." And he writes: "The result – an immense slab born out of mathematical calculations for utilizing ground and space to the best advantage – is a form proper to our age. Employing the same basic element as that used by the cubist painter in his hovering planes or by an engineer like Maillart in building bridges out of concrete slabs, the skyscraper slab form is as significant and expressive of its period as the monolithic obelisk of Egypt and the Gothic cathedral tower for their periods," Giedion writes.[37]

Then follows a rather surprising section on the optical effects of "bigness:" "The walls of the R.C.A. Building rise up unbroken eight hundred sixty feet. In such a dimension the architectural form, when it is not spoiled by details inappropriate to the large scale, is not of decisive importance," he states. "Its strength and power are expressed in curtain walls, whose windows are reduced to mere grooves like ribbing in the texture of a fabric."[38] The

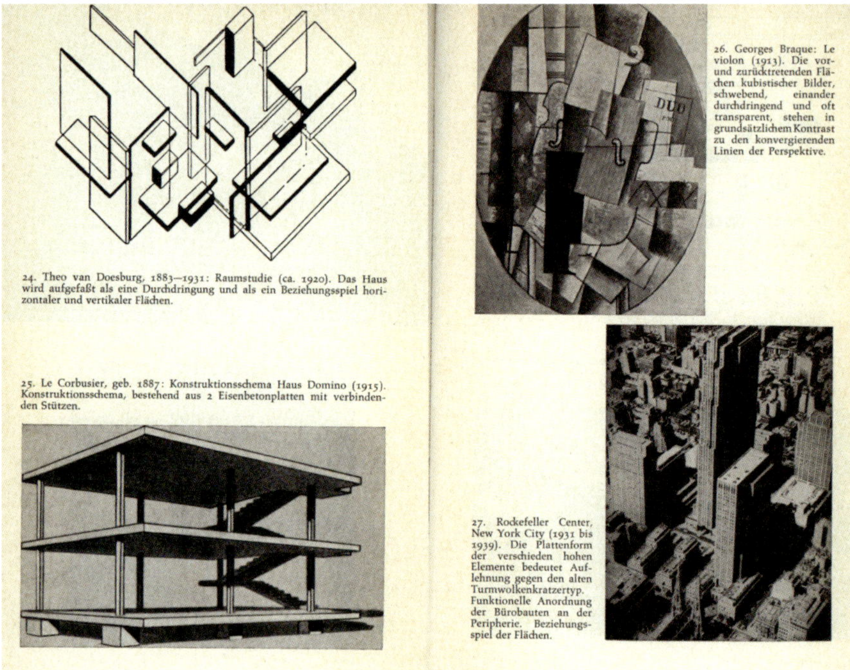
24. Theo van Doesburg, 1883–1931: Raumstudie (ca. 1920). Das Haus wird aufgefaßt als eine Durchdringung und als ein Beziehungsspiel horizontaler und vertikaler Flächen.

25. Le Corbusier, geb. 1887: Konstruktionsschema Haus Domino (1915). Konstruktionsschema, bestehend aus 2 Eisenbetonplatten mit verbindenden Stützen.

26. Georges Braque: Le violon (1913). Die vor- und zurücktretenden Flächen kubistischer Bilder, schwebend, einander durchdringend und oft transparent, stehen in grundsätzlichem Kontrast zu den konvergierenden Linien der Perspektive.

27. Rockefeller Center, New York City (1931 bis 1939). Die Plattenform der verschieden hohen Elemente bedeutet Auflehnung gegen den alten Turmwolkenkratzertyp. Funktionelle Anordnung der Bürobauten an der Peripherie. Beziehungsspiel der Flächen.

fig. 8 Theo van Doesburg, Le Corbusier, Georges Braque and the formal premises of the "slab"-shaped office building. Spread from Sigfried Giedion, *Architektur und Gemeinschaft*, 1956.

description appears to anticipate the transformation of the massive piers of the R.C.A.Building into, indeed, the "curtain wall" of Lever House or even the Seagram Building, except that at the time of writing, neither of the two existed.

Approaching Rockefeller Center from Fifth Avenue, one enters a narrow symmetrical enclosure framed by two massive six-story blocks on the left and the right and confronts the edge of the central R.C.A. Building as a steeply rising, adventurously slender tower – reminding one of a cathedral (see fig. 8).[39] Perhaps not surprisingly, the classicist overall concept of the complex as a whole interested Giedion no more than the "Gothicism" of Hood's stepped tower that dominates the plaza. There was no way a complex like Rockefeller Center could be grasped from "a single viewpoint," he argues, rationalizing the way the passerby will experience the space by walking through it. A collage made of views seen in temporal sequence illustrates the idea, and the "speed photograph of a golf strike" by William Edgerton places the operation into the context of cubo-futuristic visuality.[40] As if by chance, the bird's-eye view that reveals the "open" composition of the windmill-like grouping of the buildings appears to echo this scenario of subjective perceptions. It is due to the non-hierarchical "openness" thus revealed that the contemporary city found a “new order,” based on “the radically new form” developed in response to the unusual height of contemporary office buildings and its effects on the inner organization, i.e.: the “slab.”[41] Theo van Doesburg’s famous study of interrelated vertical and horizontal surfaces, made c. 1920 – an anticipated stenogram of the modernist city made of slabs – is only one step away (fig. 8).

More East-Western Smoke Signals

The decision to build the Europa-Center was taken “a few days after the Wall was built.” The project, realized in the extremely short time between 1961 and 1963, was thus charged with politics from its very inception.[42] For years to come, it played a “key role in the press” as a beacon of the West in the face of the Wall.[43] Eighty meters high, making it the highest office building in Berlin – two meters higher than the somewhat older Springer tower to which I will return below –, the Center unmistakably laid claim to centrality within the city, contrasting sharply in that respect with the earlier buildings on Breitscheidplatz.[44]

Matchboxes can be used to send smoke signals or even result in a dangerous fire. When the publisher Axel Springer decided to move his company headquarters from Hamburg to Berlin and build an office tower in the old newspaper district of Kochstraße, right on the sector border, his intention to use architecture to send a political signal was instantly clear to everybody.[45] It is not worth building “high rises for newspapers without an idea that is greater than ourselves. An idea that means: freedom for all Germans in one fatherland with the legal capital of Berlin in the midst of a Europe at peace.”[46] The Springer building, seventy-eight meters high, built 1959–1962 at a right angle to Kochstrasse, shimmering festively with its golden aluminum coating, was to be understood as a “scream against the wind,” indeed a “powerful architectural exclamation point […] of the belief that Berlin and Germany would soon […] be reunited.”[47] The location directly on the sector border provided the necessary visibility to this program and Müller and Sobotka’s architecture even gave it a somewhat sleazy appearance of luxury.

Just two years after construction, the sector border was sealed off by the Wall. Countless photographs document the situation, among them a picture taken by Rem Koolhaas in 1971 that shows the Springer Building towering in the evening twilight over the wall.[48] In the mid-1960s, Oskar Kokoschka had captured the desolation of East Berlin from the commanding perspective of Axel Springer’s penthouse in a painting.[49] In the area just beyond the wall, reconstruction had in fact hardly begun. As a result, the Springer building, with its neon sign installed on the roof in 1963, could be seen from a great distance day and night. Even from Berlin-Mitte! At about the same time, yet another neon sign blinking towards the east was installed on the nearby GSW Tower (built in 1958); this one being directly fuelled by propaganda from the West Berlin Senate. In the Ministry for State Security of the GDR, this caused considerable nervousness: at any event, Albert Norden, the secretary of the Central Committee for Agitation and Propaganda, had a report prepared on how to limit the effect of this double enemy act. The proposals made included blocking the view of the writing with the help of screens or making the signs illegible by shining light on them.[50]

To put an end to the problem East Berlin seemed to have no other choice than to block the devil of capitalist office buildings with the Beelzebub of socialist housing, which, due to central planning in the East also succeeded.[51] Soon enough – in the 1980s – both the office buildings at Kochstrasse and the nearby housing blocks at Leipziger Strasse were caught up by the then fashionable critique of functionalism – but by the year 2000, a younger generation of architects finally began to view the buildings that marked the "high rise war" in the 1950s and those that tried to neutralize it after 1970 as part of a coherent urban landscape (fig. 9).[52]

DDR: "Overtaking without Catching Up"

In the 1950s, the inner-German border was still passable, at least for large parts of the population. Interestingly, that condition appears to have forced the two systems into a dramatic logic of paragone. That was the time when the contrast between the systems reached its climax, with East Berlin's Stalinallee and West Berlin's new Hansaviertel marking the span between the "extremes."[53] By 1961, however, the situation was about to change in unexpected ways: as, due to the Wall, the overwhelming majority of Berlin residents were no longer in the position of experiencing "live" the contrast between "here" and "there", the architectural and planning cultures in both states were about to move considerably closer – except, of course, as far as the fundamentals of land ownership in the center are concerned. By the standards of 1920s "Fordism", the DDR itself became "Americanized" – and much more thoroughly than ever occurred in the West (or in America, for that matter); moreover, since socialist land reform made implementing modern planning goals in the city centers possible to an extent that was unthinkable under capitalism, this "Americanization" infiltrated the inner cities to an unprecedented degree.

"Socialist" Re-cyclings of Rockefeller Center

This turned out to be Hermann Henselmann's moment. After pleasing the regime with the triumphalist *mise-en-scène* at the service of the "national tradition" at Strausberger Platz and Frankfurter Tor, he now returned to architec-

fig. 9 Sauerbruch & Hutton, architects, Berlin, "Dialogue across the Wall" (1991). Looking along Kochstrasse towards the proposed GSW-administration tower addition, right and the Leipziger Strasse housing blocks, left; Springer-Hochhaus at center. (Courtesy: Sauerbruch & Hutton, architects, Berlin)

tural modernism, of which he had so emphatically declared himself a proponent in the first months and years after 1945.[54] It comes as no surprise that the West's lead in this realm suffered from significant structural lack in his eyes. Writing about the rebuilding of the Zoo area in the 1950s, everything was going wrong and could "easily turn into a tragedy," he insisted: high rises are placed randomly and without adequate space along existing streets, while banks, insurance companies, and business headquarters "that should be located in the city center" were placed in the realm of Breitscheidplatz, etc.[55] – At least, it was clear what kind of sins needed to be avoided in planning Berlin-Mitte!

The slab-shaped office building began conquering the East at about the same time it conquered the West. Since when it came to "overtaking without catching up,"[56] it was the U.S. that provided the criteria, the process can be understood as a kind of parallel recycling of international high-rise modernism under different premises – granted that, when Gerhard Kosel, president of the Deutsche Bauakademie, proposed his "central building" in Berlin Mitte (with 150 meters, it would have been almost twice the size of Europa-Center), he surely had in mind one of the projects for the never-realized Soviet Palace in Moscow (fig. 10).[57] In East Berlin as well as in the West, Rockefeller Center is an obvious reference, though, as the present example suggests, the reception follows slightly different codes on either side of the Iron Curtain: Where the "International Style" is in command, it is primarily the "Slab" of the RCA Building that fascinates, tendentially transfigured into more or less purified prisms and grouped in "free," asymmetrical arrangements, whereas in Kosel's project, it is the way the slab (or rather: the tower) emerges from the symmetrical, "Beaux-Arts" layout of the Plaza.[58] While the arrangement of a rhomboid forecourt lined by colonnades at the foot of the office tower facing Lustgarten resonates with the recently dethroned imperatives of the "national tradition" (or, however successfully, with Schinkel's "Altes Museum" nearby), it owes its conceptual key to Rockefeller Center (see fig. 8).[59]

Meanwhile, American architects had developed their own updates of the mythic model from Midtown New York, e.g., in the once-famous project for the Back Bay Center in Boston, Massachusetts (1953). An elegant, lentil-shaped slab resting on high stilts forms the core of the project by Walter Gropius and TAC (The Architects Collaborative; in collaboration with Pietro Belluschi, Hugh Stubbins, and other architects from the Harvard/MIT circle). A large hall covered by a flat-vaulted roof is linked to the slab by way of a system of asymmetrically grouped, rather narrow squares and promenades.[60] The project was commissioned in 1952/53 by the investor Roger Stevens and was later frequently referred to as a summary of sorts of the ideas discussed at the CIAM congress on *The Heart of the City* (Hoddesdon, 1951).[61] But when Prudential, the giant among American insurance companies, decided to move to Boston in 1957 and establish its headquarters on the location of the proposed Backbay Center, the company had no use for the project. Luckman, who had become the company's architect, subjected the large superblock to a much simpler overall plan, with a high tower based on a square plan as the central element that has left its stamp on the Boston Back Bay area since the early 1960s (Prudential Center was built from 1957–1965). Gropius' and TAC's system of loosely meandering promenades was replaced by a palatial, two-winged freestanding stairway connecting the wide open plaza to street level, all perfectly symmetrical. Thus "humanization" here once again followed the lead of absolutist representation. The cost-benefit analysis seemed to justify the choice.[62]

Gerhard Kosel's similarly organized project for the "*Zentrales Gebäude*" remained unbuilt. Berlin's head architect at the time, Hermann Henselmann, rejected the plan as a "leveling of the art of building." To propose an office building as a monument to socialism is a "serious mistake," he argued. Such might be possible for a "capitalist downtown," but not for a "socialist city center."[63] Is it a coincidence that Henselmann's counter proposal in the form of a "German Pantheon" ["Pantheon der Deutschen"] on Alexanderplatz recalls the Congress Rotunda in Gropius and Belluschi's Back Bay Center project? In a somewhat later revision of his project,[64] Kosel himself not only simplified the volumetrics of his tower but also added two lower side-wings that form a forecourt closed off by a colonnade reflected in a *plateau d'eau* at its base. And finally he, too, added a rotunda at the rear (1959).

Hermann Henselmann and Artistic Autonomy

"The very fact that West German companies were erecting high rises in West Berlin" is enough to refute the idea that "representative buildings of our

fig. 10 Gerhard Kosel, Project for the "Zentrales Gebäude" on Marx-Engels-Forum, Berlin (1959). (Photo: Berlinische Galerie, Berlin)

worker and peasant state cannot be made visible from afar in the skyline of the city." Such was State Council Chairman Walter Ulbricht's rather contorted verdict in 1960. Subsequently, even Henselmann began to entertain the idea of a "Stadtkrone" in the form of an office skyscraper. He did so all the more seriously, as the just completed and widely publicized government center complex in Brasilia, designed by Oscar Niemeyer 1957–1960 (see fig. 2), seemed to offer a particularly promising model in that context.[65] Long before Brasilia, Niemeyer – the Communist star architect – had already played a decisive part in the planning of the UN Secretariat Building. It is no wonder that he soon became a living myth in the GDR. What better model could there be for any attempt to finally checkmate West Berlin's uncoordinated efforts to control the cityscape by way of slabs than the twin towers of Brasilia's Capitol Complex? – Alas, the Brazilian temptation and Henselmann's dream of an East Berlin city crown remained just a brief flash in the pan.

Instead, the Brazilian spark spread to his most important project for the city center: the Haus des Lehrers [Building of the Teacher] on Alexanderplatz (1961–1964) (fig. 11). Ten years before, Henselmann had used an architectural idiom based on the Baroque and on the historicism of the Wilhelminian era in order to satisfy the national leadership's desire for magnificence. The result was Frankfurter Tor in the East of Stalinallee and Strausberger Platz as its preliminary western end. This time the ambition was to connect the recently completed western end of the grand boulevard and Alexanderplatz to international modernism.[66] Gendarmenmarkt with its two majestic domes from the era of Friedrich the Great, the classicism of the Schinkel era, and the architecture of the new Moscow had been the points of reference for Henselmann's earlier projects. Now the models were Brasilia's National Congress and New York's Seagram Building. For GDR architecture, an age of

fig. 11 Berlin, "Haus des Lehrers" on Alexanderplatz (1961–64). Hermann Henselmann, architect. Mosaic entitled "Our Life" by Walter Womacka. (Photo: archive author)

frenetic internationalization had begun, as it had in other Eastern Bloc countries, too. Typically, the attention was often emphatically directed beyond the Federal Republic – including the Netherlands and Switzerland in particular.[67]

In comparison to Brasilia, Henselmann's elegant coupling of an office slab-cum-library with a domed hall remains a miniature, however. The nearby muscular buildings by Peter Behrens that frame the entrance to Alexanderplatz from the West make Haus des Lehrers appear almost delicate. At the height of the library floors, the slab is decorated with a mural of socialist-heroic content – an idea borrowed from Mexico City's University Campus (fig. 12). Inspired by the Byzantine mosaics of Basilica Sant'Apollinare in Classe (and perhaps also by Léger), Walter Womacka created a rather schoolbook-like didactic broadsheet covering part of the lower third of the slab.[68] Henselmann went along with the idea, thus accepting that the pathos of the Miesian curtain wall was now reduced to the role of a mere backdrop for "art."

Naturally, there were and are other ways in architecture and urban design to achieve, as Abbé Laugier famously put it, "du tumulte dans l'ensemble, de l'uniformité dans le detail" [tumult in the overall impact, uniformity in detail] than those used in 1960s residential construction in the GDR. It is enough to think of Le Havre by Auguste Perret. A small 1959 sketch by Hans

fig. 12 Mexico-City, Universidad Nacional Autonoma de Mexico, Central Library Building (1952–54). Juan O'Gorman, architect and painter. (Photo: archive author)

Schmidt, then director of the *Institut für Theorie und Geschichte* at Berlin's *Bauakademie*, may stand for Schmidt's fascination with Perret. At a point in time when he could not even know Henselmann's project, Schmidt experimented with alternative formal possibilities for that building.[69] We do not know what might have resulted if these ideas had been further developed. As it was built, the Haus des Lehrers remained unique in East Berlin. Slightly out of scale considering the context and idiosyncratic with its curious illustrated body-belt, not to mention the playfully ornamental interior of the plenary hall, it points to a symptomatic break in the architectural culture of the GDR. Fighting for the right to artistic autonomy could mean questioning the rationalization of construction and vice-versa. "We have to build better, faster, and more cheaply than capitalism can," Bruno Flierl, speaking more or less on behalf of the Deutsche Bauakademie, summed up the tasks of GDR architecture in 1960.[70] In the terms of the period, this could only be achieved by typification. Meanwhile, the "star architects," a breed known not only in the West, tried to call in a certain degree of autonomy with respect to the administration's logic of "merciless norming and typification" (Henselmann) in the realm of residential construction. The "social buildings" ["Gesellschaftsbauten"] in the urban centers at least offered some promising escapes in this context. Scharoun, Mies, Le Corbusier – or indeed Niemeyer – had shown the way. In any case, once Kosel's proposals for a "central building" were given up, the leadership turned to Henselmann: his Haus des Lehrers is, besides Television Tower, the outstanding example in this context. Although itself based on a strict logic of modular seriality, it wants to be seen as a critique of the frenzy of universal typification that Henselmann considered "distressing enough."[71] Not surprisingly, the *Bauakademie* complained that the building should not have been realized as an individualized design, but should rather have been based on one of the customarily used systems of prefabrication so as to reduce costs. Henselmann later responded with the tautological yet objectively plausible argument that prefabrication was not worthwhile for individual projects.[72]

P.S. "Absolute" and "Relative"

As the skylines of virtually any of today's metropolises reveals – London, Singapore, Shanghai, and even a city like Berlin – the office slab is no longer a dominant feature in skyscraper building. Marginalized in the universe of corporate architecture, it has occasionally re-surfaced as a motive in nostalgically miniaturized form in such projects as the The Hague City Hall by O.M.A. (1986),[73] before the logic of Capitalist diversification, not to mention the misfortunes of mass housing, caused its fatal demise and ultimate dissolution as a type. In the meantime, however, the modernist "slab" appears to have given birth to fresh recyclings in the universe of architectural utopia: thus one finds not only Hilberseimer's and Mies' archetypal housing and office slabs recycled as markers towards the "possibility of an absolute architecture,"[74] but more recently, in the work of the Italian group Dogma, "the absoluteness of the object" claimed for Seagram by Tafuri and Dal Co long ago (see above), appears to be re-configured into quintessential images that make the eerie visualizations in Enrico Gras' movie *La ciudad frente al Rio* of 1949 look almost bucolic. It may be noted that Berlin triggered this "renaissance" at an early moment.[75]

The discussion proposed in this paper suggests that the will towards semantic silence or radical formal abstraction does not prevent its built results from being experienced, communicated, suffered or marketed – let alone conceived – in terms of figurative associations, conventional formal tropes or contextual and controversial political agendas. If all this is part of what constitutes the "history" of architecture, then "slabs" indeed continue to be an extremely promising subject.[76] Granted that this building form has typically been promoted as the most economic and expedient way of organizing domestic or work space (the one who wants to build fast, and at minimum cost, better uses a steel frame in the form of a slab, so it has been understood for decades): Are sacrifice and ascetism in the art of building simply the price to be paid for "beauty as the blaze of truth" (Mies, after Thomas of Aquino)? Or are they to be understood as techniques of representation, similar to the application of the classical orders by ways of marble, columns, pediments and ornaments? Is structural economy the mystified form of capitalism?

There is probably no answer to that kind of question. Nor is there a return to Giedion's catalogue of "constituent facts" – except if one chooses to invoke the "Zeitgeist." Yet the rectangular upright "slab" is nevertheless sufficiently present as a motive in the production and the reception of architec-

fig. 13 Le Corbusier standing in front of the UN Secretariat in New York (1948–52; Harrison and Abramovitz, architects) and comparing it to a model photograph showing his preliminary study for the building. (Photo Courtesy Fondation Le Corbusier, Paris).

ture between 1950 and 1980 to offer food for thought. The random illustration from the *Berliner Morgenpost* of May 25, 1963 – showing the investor Karl Pepper with the model of his work, the Europa-Center in Berlin – is neither a good photograph nor what one would call a unique document in the history of office slabs. But at the same time it highlights an aspect of the slab that qualifies it as an undeniable paradigm of post-World War II visual culture: its unique iconic power, combined with an equally unique capacity towards personalizing corporate identity and even authorship in ways that are probably deeply anchored in the Vitruvian tradition, and in the topos of the building as an analog of human form.[77]

More than any other form, the vertical rectangle of the office slab invites this personalization by its very shape and proportion; in other words: by the frame of the portrait (in most cases the *empty* frame, the frame that is awaiting its host) even though, as creator of the artifact, the host remains external to the work: such as Gary Cooper as Howard Roarke in the movie "The Fountainhead;" such as Mies van der Rohe together with Philip Johnson as the architect of Seagram in Richard Avedon's famous photograph – or as Le Corbusier, standing in front of Harrison's UN Building and comparing it with an old model photograph of his own famous project nr. 23A in an ultimate act of authentication (fig. 13). That the vertical rectangle also happens to be the format of the book page and the form of the tombstone may be noted in passing.

Endnotes

1 An early version of this paper, more specifically focused on Berlin, has been published in Thomas Köhler and Ursula Müller, eds., *Radically Modern. Urban Planning and Architecture in 1960s Berlin* (Berlin: Berlinische Galerie, Wasmuth, 2015), 28–43. I am grateful to Ákos Moravánsky and to José Manuel Pozo for having offered me opportunities to elaborate on the subject at conferences in Zurich and Pamplona. Thanks also go to Teresa Frankhänel (Kunsthistorisches Institut, Universität Zurich) for her comments on an early draft of the text.

2 Edmund Goldzamt, *Architektura zespolow srodmiejskich, i problemi dziedzictura*, Warsaw (Panstowe wydawnictwo naukowe) 1956, quoted in David Crowley, "Europe Reconstructed, Europe Divided," in *Cold War Modern. Design 1945–1970*, ed. David Crowley and Jane Pavitt (London: V&A Publishing, 2008), 43–71, (p. 49); "[...] dass ein Hochhaus noch etwas anderes sein könnte als eine aufgestellte Zündholzschachtel mit n Bürogechossen," Hans Schmidt, letter to Grete Schütte-Lihotzky, June 17, 1953, quoted in Ursula Suter, *Hans Schmidt 1893–1972. Architekt in Basel, Moskau, Berlin-Ost* (Zurich: gta Verlag 1993), 297.

3 "Sovremennaia arkhitektura kapitalisticheskikh stran," *Arkhitektura SSSR*, 1 (1954), 32–37. A year before, Soviet critics had already begun noticing what they called a "sharpening crisis of architecture and town planning in post-war America," due to an overall "militarization of the economy" and the arms race. See O. Smirnova, "Obostrenie krizisa arkhitektury i gradostoitel'stva v poslevoennoi Amerika," *Sovestskaya arkhitektura* (1953), 111–119. A classic in this context is the East German *Handbuch für Architekten* of 1954, where the "shapeless boxes" of the housing blocks, banks, office buildings, hotels and stores in the West are qualified as "an expression of the profit hunger of monopoly capitalism under American dominance." Quoted in Crowley, "Europe Reconstructed, Europe Divided," 49.

4 Mailer's essay first appeared as "The Big Bite" in *Esquire*, August 1963, 16, 18, 21, 24 and was later republished under "Mailer vs. Scully" in *Architectural Forum*, April 1964, 96–97. It was later partially reprinted together with other essays in Norman Mailer, *Cannibals and Christians* (London: André Deutsch, 1967), 233–240.

5 "Mailer vs. Scully."

6 Ibid., quoted after Norman Mailer, *Cannibals and Christians*, 234.

7 Vincent Scully, "America's Architectural Nightmare: The Motorized Megalopolis," *ZODIAC* (1967), 162–167. For Scully's response to Mailer see "Mailer vs. Scully."

8 Vincent Scully, *American Architecture and Urbanism* (New York: Praeger/Henry Holt & Co., 1969), 186. For an earlier and even more rigorous urbanistic dismissal of Lever House see "The Death of the Street," *Perspecta. The Yale Architectural Journal* (1963), 91–96.

9 Philip Johnson, quoted in Franz Schulze, *Philip Johnson: Life and Work* (Chicago: The University of Chicago Press, 1994), 270.

10 See Andy Warhol and Pat Hacket, *POPism: The Warhol '60s* (New York and London: Harcourt Brace Jovanovich, 1980), 50.

11 In the first chapter of *Complexity and Contradiction*, entitled "Simplification and Picturesqueness," two projects by Johnson are chosen as illustration for the qualities of "simplicity" and "serenity" that an archi-

tecture of "complexity and contradiction" should avoid: the Glass House and the Wiley House. In both cases, "the building becomes a diagram of an oversimplified program for living – an abstract theory of either-or. Where simplicity cannot work, simpleness results. Blatant simplification means bland architecture. Less is a bore." Robert Venturi, *Complexity and Contradiction in Architecture* (New York: The Museum of Modern Art, 1966), 25.

12 Manfredo Tafuri und Francesco Dal Co, *Architettura contemporanea*, Mailand (Electa) 1976, p.346. The most authoritative and complete assessment of the building is by Phyllis Lambert, *Building Seagram*, New Haven (Yale University Press) 2013.

13 Tafuri and Dal Co, *Architettura contemporanea*, 346. One remembers Karl Kraus: "Wer etwas zu sagen hat trete vor, und schweige."

14 Robert Venturi, Denise Scott Brown, and Steven Izenour, *Learning from Las Vegas*, (Cambridge, MA: MIT Press, 1972), 79. In their recent treatise on "architectural quality," Georg and Dorothea Franck take a similar stand when they propose the Seagram Building as the ultimate paragon of architectural quality precisely because of the clarity and concreteness of the grammar that underlies its form giving. See Georg Franck, Dorothea Franck, *Architektonische Qualität* (München: Hanser, 2008), 53–61 and passim.

15 Elihu Rubin, *Insuring the City: The Prudential Center and the Postwar Urban Landscape* (New Haven: Yale University Press, 2012), 181. On Lever House and the birth of the "Office Building of the future" see Nathaniel Alexander Owings, *The Spaces In Between: An Architect's Journey* (Boston: Houghtton Mifflin, 1973), 105–109. On the place of Lever House in American architecture of the 1950s, see Gwendolyn Wright, *USA: Modern Architectures in History* (London: Reaktion Books, 2007), 156–161.

16 Ibid., 180 Luckmann's use of the word "humanation" appears to allude to the CIAM debates on the "Humanization of Urban Life." See Jacqueline Tyrwhitt et al., *The Heart of the City: Towards the Humanization of Urban Life* (New York: Pellegrini and Cudahy, 1952).

17 Rubin, *Insuring the City*, 182.

18 The role of models and model photography in the making of the American office slab around 1950 is analyzed in depth by Teresa Fankhänel in her doctoral dissertation (2016, unpublished). For a first summary regarding Lever House, see Teresa Frankhänel, "Skidmore, Owings & Merrill: Lever House," in *Das Architekturmodell. Werkzeug, Fetisch, kleine Utopie*, ed. Oliver Elser and Peter Cachola Schmal (Frankfurt a. M. and Zurich: (D.A.M./Scheidegger & Spiess, 2012), 106–111.

19 Rubin, *Insuring the City*, 182.

20 Only standard texts are referred to at this point: On architecture see Alan Balfour, *Berlin: The Politics of Order, 1737–1989* (New York: Rizzoli, 1990); Jörn Düwel, "Berlin: Planen im Kalten Krieg," in Jörn Düwel, Werner Durth, Niels Gutschow and Jochem Schneider, eds., *Krieg, Zerstörung, Aufbau* (Berlin: Henschel Verlag, 1995), 195–234; on the politics of architecture and urbanism as reflected in the media see Stephanie Warnke, *Stein gegen Stein: Architektur und Medien im geteilten Berlin 1950–1970* (Frankfurt/New York: Campus Verlag, 2009); and Emily Pugh, *Architecture, Politics, & Identity in Divided Berlin* (Pittsburgh, PA: University of Pittsburgh Press, 2014).

21 On Kaiser-Wilhelm-Gedächtniskirche and the controversy on whether to maintain or demolish the building (they reach back to the 1920s), see Vera Frowein-Ziroff, *Die Kaiser Wilhelm-Gedächtniskirche: Entwicklung und Bedeutung* (Berlin: Gebrüder Mann, 1982), 333–340; also Stephanie Warnke, *Stein gegen Stein*, 220–231.

22 Frowein-Ziroff, *Die Kaiser Wilhelm-Gedächtniskirche*, 340.

23 The key texts on the "New Monumentality" are: Sigfried Giedion, "The Need for a New Monumentality," in *New Architecture and City Planning*, ed. Paul Zucker (New York: Philosophical Library, 1944), 549–568; Sigfried Giedion, Josep Lluís Sert, Fernand Léger, "Nine Points on Monumentality," in *Architecture Culture: A Documentary Anthology*, ed. Joan Ockman (New York: Columbia Books of Architecture/Rizzoli, 1993), 27–30.

24 Karl H. Pepper, the initiator and builder of Europa-Center, has a point when he writes that church and monument only became the center of the square once the skyscraper was complete. See Karl H. Pepper, "Erfüllter Traum," *Der Tagesspiegel*, April 2, 1965.

25 Maria Sack, "Erster Spatenstich im Juni 1963: Zwischen dem ersten Projekt und dem letzten Hammerschlag," *Der Tagesspiegel*, April 2, 1965 (emphasis mine). Felix-Erik Laue even calls it one of the "largest built volumes on the continent." See "Anatomie eines Giganten. Summe konstruktiver Möglichkeiten und Umfang einer Stadt," *Der Tagesspiegel*, April 2, 1965. The most recent assessment of the complex also points at the Rockefeller Center as its key reference. See Adrian von Buttlar, Kerstin Wittmann-Englert, and Gabi Dolff-Bohnekämper, eds., *Baukunst der Nachkriegsmoderne. Architekturführer Berlin 1949–1979* (Berlin: Reimer, 2013), 187–189.

26 Helmut Hentrich, *Bauzeit: Aufzeichnungen aus dem Leben eines Architekten* (Düsseldorf: Droste, 1995), 224.

27 Maria Sack, "Ein Shopping-Paradies der Damen: Kleiner Einkaufsbummel im großen 'Center': Zwischen Eisbahn und Blumen," *Der Tagesspiegel*, April 2, 1965. The skating rink was covered in 1980.

28 Ibid.

29 The best recent discussion of New York's urban transformations after 1940 is by Samuel Zipp, *Manhattan Projects. The Rise and Fall of Urban Renewal in Cold War New York*, New York (Oxford University Press) 2010.

30 Tyrwhitt et al., *The Heart of the City*. For a useful survey see Konstanze Sylvia Domhardt, *The Heart of the City: Die Stadt in den transatlantischen Debatten der CIAM 1933–1951* (Zurich: gta Verlag, 2012). On Philadelphia see Stanislaus von Moos, "Monument? Forum? Fair? Louis Kahn, Edmund Bacon and Philadelphia," in *Louis Kahn: The Power of Architecture*, ed. Mateo Kries, Jochen Eisenbrand and Stanislaus von Moos (Weil am Rhein: Vitra Design Museum, 2012) 29–49.

31 "The capitals of the world in need of rebuilding after the war cannot choose a better model than the modern buildings of the Brazilian capital;" quoted in Zilah Quesado Deckker, *Brazil Built: The Architecture of the Modern Movement in Brazil* (London/New York: Spon Press, 2013), 141. Le Corbusier, who went so far as to claim the work his own, realized his own exemplarily monumental use of the slab in a design for the government center in Bogotà (1949). See Willy Boesiger, ed., *Oeuvre complète, 1946–52*, Zurich, Girsberger, 1953, pp.42-45. On Sert see now Mardges Bacon, "Josep Lluís Sert's Evolving Concept of the Urban Core," in *Josep Lluís Sert. The*

Architect of Urban Design, 1953–1969, ed. Eric Mumford and Hashim Sarkis (New Haven/London: Yale University Press, 2008), 77–114. A slightly different view of the birth of the "Office Building of the future" is offered by Nathaniel Alexander Owings, *The Spaces In Between: An Architect's Journey* (Boston: Houghtton Mifflin, 1973), 105–109.

32 Sigfried Giedion, "Historical Background to the Core," in *The Heart of the City*, 17–25; also Giedion, "The Heart of the City: a summing-up," in *The Heart of the City*, 159–163. Note that it is only in the 1953 edition of *Space, Time and Architecture* that Giedion will include the chapter on "Sixtus V. and the Planning of Baroque Rome."

33 Sigfried Giedion, *Space, Time and Architecture* (Cambridge, MA: Harvard, 1941); 5th rev. (1967), 845–856. The most accurate recent assessment of Rockefeller Center is by Mardges Bacon, "Rockefeller Center: Modernist Paradigm for the Urban Core," in *Modernism and Landscape Architecture 1890*-1940, ed. Therese O'Malley and Joachim Wolschke-Buhlmann (Washington, DC: CASVA, 2015), 281–308.

34 Giedion, *Space, Time and Architecture*, 450 ff.

35 Ibid., 848.

36 "Radio City to Create a New Architecture," *New York Times*, March 6, 1931. In the same year, Harvey Wiley Corbett, one of the designers of the Center, explained that a tall building for a New York City block roughly 200 feet long and 800 feet wide "tends to become a slab." See Mardges Bacon, "Rockefeller Center: Modernist Paradigm for the Urban Core," 286; 304.

37 Giedion, *Space, Time and Architecture*, 848.

38 Ibid., 849.

39 Originally conceived as a site for an opera house and adjoining plaza, the project naturally owes its symmetrical layout to the Beaux-Arts tradition of American civic centers. See Werner Hegemann and Elbert Peets, *The American Vitruvius: An Architect's Handbook of Civic Art* (New York: The American Book Publishing Co., 1922).

40 Giedion, *Space, Time and Architecture*, 850–851.

41 Ibid., 845–856.

42 "Mensch, Pepper," *Der Spiegel*, 39 (1963), 97–100. "The realization of project [...] seeks to demonstrate a faith in the future of the city and the achievements of free enterprise, in particular vis-à-vis the communist system," according to Berlin's *Tagesspiegel* (quoted in "Mensch, Pepper"). For more on the details of how the project was financed, see Egbert Steinke, "Peppers großer Coup im 'Pfefferhaus,'" *Handelsblatt*, March 30, 1965.

43 Warnke, *Stein gegen Stein*, 353.

44 On the history of the reconstruction of Breitscheidplatz, see von Buttlar, Wittmann-Englert, and Dolff-Bonekämper, eds., *Baukunst der Nachkriegsmoderne*, 182–189.

45 See Hans-Peter Schwarz, *Axel Springer: Die Biografie*. (Berlin: Ullstein, 2008); see also Axel Springer, *Von Berlin aus gesehen: Zeugnisse eines engagierten Deutschen* (Stuttgart: Seewald Verlag, 1972).

46 Felix Henseleit, ... *und doch ist dies der alte Schauplatz noch: Das Berliner Zeitungsviertel damals und heute* (Berlin: Ullstein, 1965).

47 Schwarz, *Axel Springer*, 296. (The quotation is slightly shortened here). For more details and references see *Radically Modern: Urban Planning and Architecture in 1960s Berlin*, 42.

48 The photograph was taken during Koolhaas' 1971 "field trip" to Berlin. See

Rem Koolhaas, *Field Trip: [A] A Memoir. The Berlin Wall as Architecture* (1971); later published in Rem Koolhaas and Bruce Mau, *S, M, L, XL.*, (New York: Monacelli, 1995), 212–233.

49 Sven Simon (alias Axel Springer, jun.), *Kokoschka malt Berlin* (Berlin: Springer, 1966).

50 Jochen Staadt, Tobias Voigt, and Stefan Wolle, *Feind-Bild Springer: Ein Verlag und seine Gegner* (Göttingen: Vandenhoeck & Ruprecht, 2009), 8–9.

51 The "Städtebauliche und architektonische Direktive für den Investitionskomplex Leipziger Straße inklusive Spittelmarkt" (Urban Planning and Architectural Directive for the Investment Complex Leipziger Straße including Spittelmarkt) was decreed in January 1969. This was the premise for the four large residential twin-towers rowed up at a right angle to Leipziger Straße; they have formed the southern horizon of Berlin-Mitte since the 1970s. The culmination of the project was to be a "ca. 30-story office tower" at Spittelmarkt. This high rise, according to the directive "dominates the axis Hans-Beimler-Straße-Alexanderplatz-Grunerstraße-Leipziger Straße, and blocks the view of the Springer Building," quoted in Staadt, Voigt, Wolle, *Feind-Bild Springer,* 10. For a summary of these events, see Bruno Flierl, *Hundert Jahre Hochhäuser: Hochhaus und Stadt im 20. Jahrhundert* (Berlin: Verlag für Bauwesen, HUSS Medien GmbH, 2000), 193.

52 See here the documentation of the urban context in *GSW Hauptverwaltung Berlin: Sauerbruch Hutton Architekten* (Baden: Lars Müller Publishers, 2000), 28–35. See also "GSW Hauptverwaltung Berlin – Wettbewerb," in *Sauerbruch Hutton Archive* (Baden: Lars Müller Publishers, 2006).

53 See the excellent overview by Francesca Rogier, "The Monumentality of Rhetoric: The Will to Rebuild in Postwar Berlin," in *Anxious Modernisms: Experimentation in Postwar Architectural Culture*, ed. Sarah Williams Goldhagen and Réjean Légault (Montreal/Cambridge MA: CCA/MIT Press, 2000), 165–189.

54 See Elmar Kossel, *Hermann Henselmann und die Moderne: Eine Studie zur Modernerezeption in der Architektur der DDR* (Königstein im Taunus: Karl Robert Langewiesche, 2013), 54–88. On postwar modernism in the Soviet Zone and later the GDR, see Andreas Butter, *Neues Leben, neues Bauen: Die Moderne in der Architektur der SBZ/DDR 1945–1951* (Berlin: Verlag Hans Schiller, 2006), 11–33.

55 Hermann Henselmann, "Wie wir wohnen wollen," *Neues Deutschland,* June 15–16, 1957; reprinted in Henselmann, *Vom Himmel an das Reißbrett ziehen: Ausgewählte Aufsätze* (Berlin: Verlag der Beeken, 1982), 43–51, 50–51. Henselmann was referring to the Telefunken-Wohnhochhaus and the five-story block of the Bikini-Haus that separates the square from Tiergarten. This simply "chaotic" development has more recently been seen in a much more positive light: See for example "Mohsen Mostafavi in Conversation with Sauerbruch and Hutton," in *What You See Is What You Get: Sauerbruch Hutton Architects* (London: Architectural Association, 1999), 13–14. Bruno Flierl was even more vigorous in his critique of the area around Breitscheidplatz: the "power aims of certain companies, the business interests of shopkeepers as well as restaurant and cinema owners, not least the church's ideological determination to join the others in representing the beautiful, 'free' Western world […] has here resulted in a virtually unique chaos of urban design." Bruno Flierl, "Über unser Verhältnis

zur Architektur und zum Städtebau kapitalistischer Länder," *Deutsche Architektur*, 1961 special supplement, 8ff., quoted in Kossel, *Hermann Henselmann und die Moderne*, 146.

56 The semi-official maxim used in the GDR for the cultural policy introduced by Khrushchev, quoted in Kossel, *Hermann Henselmann und die Moderne*, 147.

57 See for example Selim O. Chan-Magomedow, *Pioniere der sowjetischen Architektur: Der Weg zur neuen sowjetischen Architektur in den zwanziger und zu Beginn der dreißiger Jahre* (Dresden: VEB Verlag der Kunst, 1983), 403–404, 405, 418–423. See also Harald Bodenschatz and Christiane Post, eds., *Städtebau im Schatten Stalins: Die internationale Suche nach der sozialistischen Stadt in der Sowjetunion 1929–1935* (Berlin: Verlagshaus Braun, 2003), 170–175, 212–222.

58 Note that the "neo-classical" re-interpretation of the Rockefeller Center had its proponents in the United States, too. Charles Luckman, the de facto patron of Lever House, chose the "classicizing" (as opposed to a "Space-Time"-)*parti* of Rockefeller Center as a reference when he designed the Boston Prudential Center around 1958; for which Gropius, Belluschi and others had earlier proposed a canonically "modern" (i.e., asymmetrical) scheme. See *Radically Modern*, 37.

59 Kosel's interest in classicism should perhaps come as no surprise, considering his erstwhile career as one of the few German architects in Soviet exile who had turned neoclassical under Stalin. On the discussions about the "central building," see in particular Bruno Flierl, "Der Zentrale Ort in Berlin – zur räumlichen Inszenierung sozialistischer Zentralität," in *Gebaute DDR: Über Stadtplaner, Architekten und die Macht.* (Berlin: Verlag für Bauwesen, 1998), 121–171; See also Kossel, *Hermann Henselmann und die Moderne*, 141–144.

60 See Walter Gropius et al., *The Architects Collaborative* (Teufen, AR: Niggli Verlag, 1966), 78–83; See also Giedion, *Architektur und Gemeinschaft* (Reinbek bei Hamburg: Rohwohlts deutsche Enzyklopädie, 1956), 106–107 (fig. 49). On the history of the project, see Rubin, *Insuring the City*, 167–172.

61 Tyrwhitt et al., eds., *The Heart of the City*.

62 Rubin, *Insuring the City*, 106–204.

63 "I cannot accept that socialism should make this building type the central point of its capital as a monument of its great liberating and universally progressive idea. Comrade Ulbricht, if we do that, we would be making a great mistake," according to Henselmann in a letter to Ulbricht on Gerhard Kosel's proposed "central building." See Kossel, *Hermann Henselmann und die Moderne*, 136.

64 See Flierl, *Der Zentrale Ort in Berlin*, 135ff.

65 Ibid., 143.

66 See Stanislaus von Moos, "'No Fear of Monotony:' On Hans Schmidt and Edmund N. Bacon," in *Radically Modern, ed.* Köhler and Müller, 138–147.

67 See for instance Haus des Reisens [House of Travel] on Alexanderplatz, roughly contemporary to Haus des Lehrers, which was clearly inspired by the Zurich high rise Zur Palme (architects Max Ernst Haefeli, Werner Max Moser, Rudolf Steiger, with André M. Studer; built 1955–1959). See von Buttlar et al., *Baukunst der Nachkriegsmoderne*, 209–210. In subsequent years, GDR architecture became even more "cosmopolitan." Apart from its obvious analogies with the reconstruction plan for Rotterdam, Peter

Sniegon's master plan for Prager Straße in Dresden also adopts elements of William Vetter's project for the city center of Lausanne (1951). See Peter Sniegon, "Die Planung des Gebiets Prager Straße in Dresden," *Deutsche Architektur* (1965), 9–13; on Rotterdam, see Hans Schmidt, "Rotterdam, der Neubau einer Stadt," *Deutsche Architektur* (1961), 572–575, and on Vetter's project, see *The Heart of the City*, 143–145.

68 See André Meier, "Preisen will ich... Oder wie man von Womacka über Malewitsch und Rockefeller nach Byzanz kommt," in *Model Map: Zur Kartographie einer Architektur am Beispiel Haus des Lehrers in Berlin*, ed. Bettina Allamoda et al. (Frankfurt am Main: Revolver/Archiv für moderne Kunst, 2003), 18–32; also Peter Krieger, "El mural sobre la fachada del Haus des Lehrers (Casa del Maestro) en Berlin. Aplicación plástica de una iconografia politica y sus contextos," *Crónicas* (2006), 124–125.

69 The sheet from the sketchbook is dated April 27, 1959: building began in 1961. Hans-Schmidt-Archiv, Institut gta, ETH-Zurich.

70 Quoted in Kossel, *Hermann Henselmann und die Moderne*, 147.

71 On Haus des Lehrers and Henselmann's reference to the "merciless norming and typification" ordered by the Deutsche Bauakademie, that are "deterrent enough in residential construction," in particular, see Kossel, *Hermann Henselmann und die Moderne*, 148–165.

72 Ibid., 155.

73 See Rem Koolhaas and Bruce Mau, "Indeterminate Specificity. The Hague City Hall (...) Competition, 1986," in *S,M,L,XL*, 544–577; for a personal view see Stanislaus von Moos, "Dutch Group Portrait: Notes on OMA's City Hall Project for The Hague," *a+u* (1988), 86–95.

74 Pier Vittorio Aureli, *The Possibility of an Absolute Architecture* (Cambridge, MA: MIT Press, 2011).

75 Andri Gerber, "Radikale Projekte in der Tradition der italienischen Utopisten," *werk, bauen+wohnen* (2016), 25–27. For the Berlin Tiergarten project by Herzog & de Meuron, in collaboration with Rémy Zaugg, an early precedent for the more recent work of Dogma, see Vittorio Magnago Lampugnani und Michael Mönninger, eds., *Berlin morgen: Ideen für das Herz einer Groszstadt* (Stuttgart/Frankfurt am Main: Verlag Gerd Hatje/Deutsches Architekturmuseum, 1991), 122–123.

76 As Michela Rosso, Luis Carranza, Eunice Seng, Teresa Fankhänel and André Bideau have recently demonstrated at a session entitled "Scandalous Slabs" at the annual meeting of the SAH in Pasadena, CA (April 2016).

77 In the end, this potential "humanism" of the office slab is also what distinguishes it from the horizontal, i.e., "bar" – (instead of "slab"-)shaped housing block. For housing as an institution of the Welfare State has to be anonymous in character, whereas the office building, in turn, by its very function, calls for personalization.

Susana Constantino

Between City and University: New Monumentality in the Student Center of the Campus of Coimbra

In 1943, José Luis Sert, Sigfried Giedion and Fernand Léger co-wrote a manifesto in which the debate on the expression of monumentality in modern architecture, for the first time within the orthodox core of the Modern Movement, was revived beyond the focus on functionalism of modernism's early years. "Nine Points on Monumentality" presented monuments as "human landmarks which men have created as symbols for their ideals" and "the expression of man's highest cultural needs,"[1] calling on the need for civic expression as a missing dimension of the urban functions defined by the *Congrès Internationaux d'Architecture Moderne* (CIAM).

The manifesto on what would come to be known as the New Monumentality wanted to challenge what its authors considered "empty shells" that "in no way represent the spirit of the collective feeling of modern times."[2] As an alternative, they suggested the reorganization of community life through the planning and design of civic centers, monumental ensembles and public spectacles as modern architecture's new function in the postwar period. In an ideological climate hostile to any kind of monumentality, the main difficulty in this proposal was, as Joan Ockman contends, to "invent forms of large-scale expression free of association of oppressive ideologies of the past and historical bombast."[3] To be sure, since the aftermath of the First World War, with the rise and consolidation of authoritarian regimes throughout Europe, first and foremost in Germany and Italy but also in Portugal, the architecture of national representation in these countries was fashioned according to an idea of monumentality inspired by classical tradition. Moreover, the affirmation of a certain *ordre monumental*,[4] or the predominance of historicist expressions in a given state's representative buildings was pervasive in many Western countries of that period. Thus, in an attempt to demarcate the New Monumentality as independent of any ideological connotations, Giedion raises an alert to the danger of a "new escape academicism" generalized by the dominant taste in almost all countries, regardless of the political or economic orientation of their governments, "whether the most progressive or the most reactionary."[5]

The request for a New Monumentality aimed at creating a distinctive alternative to what Giedion, in his essay "The Need for a New Monumentality," will call "pseudo-monumentality," or the arbitrary use of forms of the past "without emotional justification," detached from their "inner significance."[6] This distinction was key in being able to distance this form of monumentality from authoritarian associations. Instead, modern monumentality was announced as the "new step that lies ahead" in a conscious historic evolution from the functionalist period to a new one, characterized by the reemergence of monumental expression. As Ockman asserts, the authors of "Nine Points on Monumentality" in doing so argued that "monumentality was not incompatible with democracy. It was, instead, a 'true expression' of the human spirit, capable of being conveyed in a language of modern forms and materials."[7]

Another important contribution to the affirmation of this definition came from Elizabeth Mock, director of the Department of Architecture at the Museum of Modern Art in New York. In the 1944 exhibition catalog *Built in USA since 1932*, Mock suggests that, as opposed to a totalitarian nation that demands buildings which express the omnipresence of the state over the individual, "democracy needs monuments, even though its requirements are not those of a dictatorship. There must be occasional buildings which raise the everyday casualness of living to a higher and more ceremonial plane."[8]

In the urban and social reconstruction process that unfolded after the end of the Second World War, the discourse of the New Monumentality would then be accepted as a primary vehicle in the design of civic centers in democracies. In the context of the new welfare-state policies, new collective facilities related to culture and social infrastructures emerged in European cities, operating as a synthesis between the reorganization of urban communities and spaces related to the idea of a collective representation of the zeitgeist. As Maristella Casciato writes,

> In light of the new social and progressive ideals, the traditional rhetoric and the grandiose scale that were manifest in the monuments built in the interwar period is fundamentally replaced by civic representation. Monumentality became detached from size and committed to the expression of ideal and symbolic values; new buildings assume a sort of democratic monumentality. These new monuments were places for the collective's social and cultural life.[9]

In the same period, in Portugal, the topic of monumental expression was particularly sensitive. The Estado Novo, the regime ruling the country since 1926, kept a neutral position in the Second World War, then preserved its authoritarian and colonial policies until its fall in 1974. At the beginning of the 1940s, the regime had intensified its position in favor of a monumental architectural language, recovering classical references, particularly in the state's representative buildings. This paper aims to examine the circumstances in which, notwithstanding this rhetorical position, at the end of the 1950s the regime commissioned a building devised to foster civic representation and to cater to community life: the Student Center on the campus of the University of Coimbra, designed and built between 1956 and 1961.

To support this investigation, the paper will analyze the building complex by exploring aspects such as the New Monumentality and the celebration of community life, in relation to the monolithic and monumental character of the other buildings built in the same period on the campus of the University of Coimbra.

The Campus of the University of Coimbra and the Rhetoric of Monumentality

In 1937, the then leader of the Portuguese regime, Oliveira Salazar (1889–1970) asserted in a speech what urban approach he aimed to be implemented in the design of the new campus at the University of Coimbra.[10] Salazar made it clear that he wanted a new campus to be designed for the site of the old colleges of the university, on the top of the most prominent hill in Coimbra, the Alta. In his speech, Salazar further declared his intention to undertake a large demolition project in order to emphasize the most notable existing buildings and to restrict that part of the city to a single functional character, exclusively dedicated to "education."

Salazar's programmatic framework was fundamental in defining the political agenda and options regarding the development of the plan for the new campus. In effect, the Administrative Commission for the Works of the University of Coimbra Campus (Comissão Administrativa para as Obras da

Cidade Universitária de Coimbra, CAPOCUC) was created to direct the plan according to that vision, led by chief architect José Angelo Cottinelli Telmo (1897–1948).[11]

Cottinelli Telmo's final design for the campus plan shows the new buildings aligned symmetrically along a wide central boulevard ending at an imposing stairway, eventually known as the *Escadas Monumentais* (Monumental Stairs), connecting the campus with the lower part of the hill (fig. 1). A gigantic portico, which remained unbuilt, was to define the new square on the summit of the stairway, emphasizing the monumentality of the entire composition and revealing references to Rome's University Campus designed by Marcello Piacentini in 1935, which the CAPOCUC members selected as a reference after visiting it during the development of the plan for Coimbra.[12]

Work on the construction of the new campus began in 1943, introducing a monumental architectural scale and language on the territory created after a brutal leveling and demolition process (fig. 2). The plan reveals no concern for topography and especially for the existing urban nucleus, and caused widespread demolition, with only a few significant buildings surviving. The demolition deliberately erased the cadaster of land ownership and the medieval urban fabric, where vibrant everyday life had thrived on streets, alleys and squares where the students once mingled with local residents.[13]

Only in the 1950s, after the building process had ensued and demolition was almost complete, did some open criticism arise on fundamental design decisions for the campus project; first and foremost its location on the Alta.[14]

In 1956, *Arquitectura*, an important journal for spreading the principles of the Modern Movement in Portugal, published a special issue on university campuses. One of the main contributions to this issue, written by architects José Rafael Botelho and Celestino Castro, delivers a critical account on the case in Coimbra. Botelho and Castro argued that,

> The first impression is one of excessive compactness of the whole ensemble. The Alta clearly could not accommodate the University Campus demanded by the circumstances. Despite the extensive expropriations and demolitions carried out, despite having removed the residential sectors and the associations […] despite the massive aspect of the new constructions, subjugating the existing buildings instead of stressing their presence, the shortage of space is already noticeable[15] (fig. 3).

Furthermore, the authors emphasize the obliteration of the site's collective memory, arguing that the design solution for the campus, with its destruction of the existing housing nuclei and lively traditions therein, contributed to erasing the character of the Alta, "just in the name of…Tradition!"

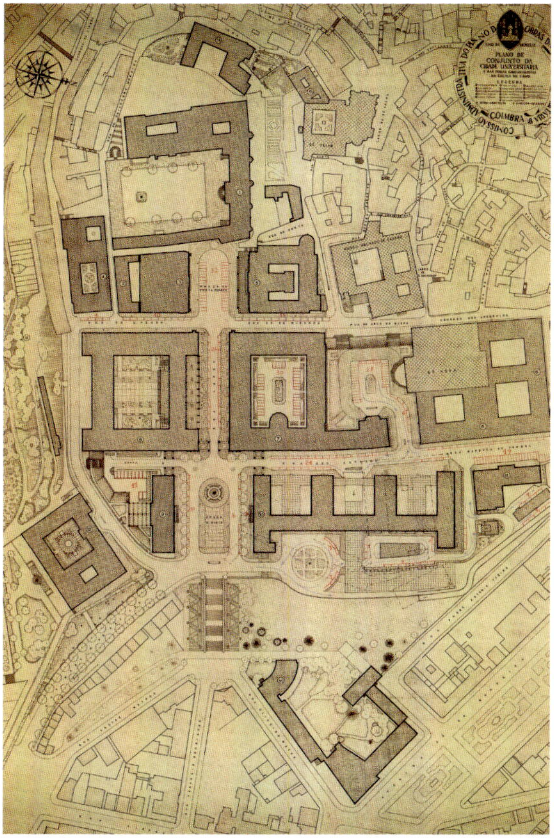

fig. 1 Masterplan for the Campus of the University of Coimbra. 1950s. Source: CAPOCUC, Arquivo da Universidade de Coimbra.

fig. 2 Demolitions during the construction of the Campus of the University of Coimbra. 1943/1944. Source: *A Velha Alta… Desaparecida: Álbum comemorativo das bodas de prata da Associação dos Antigos Estudantes de Coimbra*, (Coimbra: Almedina, 1984), 95.

The second aspect of their criticism addressed "the excessive concern with monumentality." They denounced the choice of that characteristic for a university where "the buildings should entice and deliver a service, and should be extremely flexible to accommodate the adaptations and the extensions suggested by their particular function."[16]

While this sort of criticism was gaining momentum, the building process for a new Student Center for the University of Coimbra was beginning.

fig. 3 Aerial Photo of the Campus of the University of Coimbra with a collage drawing by Cottinelli Telmo for the Monumental Stairs. Exhibition "Os anos 40 na arte portuguesa". Photo by Mário Novais. 1982. Source: CFT003.023783. ic. Colecção Estúdio Mário Novais. Biblioteca de Arte da Fundação Calouste Gulbenkian.

With a multifunctional character, this new complex represented a new type of building designed to accommodate the everyday activities of the students. As the architect Francisco Keil do Amaral noticed in another article in the same issue of *Arquitectura*, these kinds of facilities were already unanimously seen as "elements relatively important in the new university campuses, performing important services for the creation of an atmosphere of collective work in pleasant and efficient conditions".[17]

A Design for Another Idea: Human Scale and the Plan for the Student Center

In 1954, the project for the new Student Center complex was beginning to take shape, determining its definitive relocation from the Alta summit. Luís Cristino da Silva (1896–1976), chief architect of the University of Coimbra campus since 1948, presented a general plan for the project, proposing a location at the base of the monumental stairs descending from the main axis of the campus. With his proposal, Cristino da Silva articulated the program defined by students with a spatial arrangement, and outlined a preliminary scheme for the development of the student center.

The design of the project was commissioned from Alberto José Pessoa (1919–1985)[18]. Working in partnership with architect and painter João Abel Manta (b. 1928), Pessoa developed a preliminary drawing in August 1954 that showed clear affinities with the design strategy advanced in the plan devised by Cristino da Silva.[19] As the proposal developed further, the intention of putting forward an idea opposed to the static design of the campus became clearer. Situated at the lower level of the new campus, the complex demonstrated a new attitude towards the city and towards human scale, in contrast to the classic monumentality that had prevailed in the master plan. Triggered by components of the program, including a canteen, a gymnasium, several

fig. 4 Student Center. Model. Photo by Mário Novais. Source: CFT003.025701.ic. Colecção Estúdio Mário Novais. Biblioteca de Arte da Fundação Calouste Gulbenkian.

fig. 5 Student Center. Courtyard. Photo by Horácio Novais. Source: CFT164.160937.ic. Colecção Estúdio Horácio Novais. Biblioteca de Arte da Fundação Calouste Gulbenkian.

student cultural sections and a theater, the ensemble was organized in three autonomous volumes articulated around a central courtyard according to a hierarchical assessment of their representational value (fig. 4). The final design defines the urban block "through a system of fragmentation – articulating different volumes, with diverse scales, and subtle differences in architectural languages," thus creating in the interior of the block one "big hall" to which "all the volumes are facing."[20] This central courtyard would be designed as a garden by landscape architect Manuel da Costa Cerveira, complementing the connections between the three blocks (fig. 5).

The relation between the volumes and the open space between them, as designed by Pessoa and Manta, resonates with Walter Gropius's idea of human scale, delivered in his CIAM 8 lecture dedicated to the theme "the core of the city." Gropius elaborated on the importance of limits in finding the balance between space and scale, asserting "the invention of the enclosed space is a sort of magic – humanizing a small part of the infinite field."[21] What was necessary, Gropius argued, was "more knowledge about the sizes and proportions of such open spaces in relation to man," for "keeping with the human scale" in the overall composition of built masses and enclosed open spaces. He further asserted that this should be an essential aspect for the construction of the core as the locus of the collective, where new community bonds could be performed.

To illustrate his lecture, Gropius utilized his project for the Harvard Graduate Center, inaugurated in 1950 as a student-facilities complex designed as a modern community center on a traditional university campus. In it, a group of buildings is laid out creating a sequence of open courtyards, reconstructing the proportions and existing spatial theme of Harvard Yard.

Similarly, in the layout of the Student Center complex at the University of Coimbra, the enclosed open space defined by blocks and the topography demonstrates the significance of the core of the student community. As José Luis Sert points out in his speech delivered for the CIAM 8 opening ceremony:

> The social function of the new community centers or Cores is primarily that of uniting the people and facilitating direct contacts and exchange of ideas that will stimulate free discussion.[22]

A Counterimage: New Monumentality and Community Life

As early as 1944, Sert emphasized in "The Human Scale in City Planning" the importance of planning for the community, and of designing cities based on human values.[23] Following this principle, Sert focused the theme of the New Monumentality on civic and cultural centers, going further with his ideas previously presented in "Nine Points on Monumentality." He asserted that this kind of center "constitutes the most important element of a big city, its brain and governing machine." He continues, declaring that these centers should accommodate "the university buildings, the main museums, the central public library, the main concert hall and theaters [...] and areas especially planned for public gatherings, the main monuments constituting land marks in the region, and symbols of popular aspirations."[24]

In this context, to what extent can we recognize the Student Center complex at Coimbra as a paradigm of the idea of a civic and cultural center where New Monumentality was used to the benefit of the community?

Referring to the entire Student Center complex, Portuguese architect and critic Jorge Figueira defines it as a "counterimage [...] operating in opposition to the monolithic character of the university campus" (fig. 6). According to Figueira, "the functionalist methodology by definition refuses the rhetoric of monumentality, searching for a (modern) architecture suitable for each program."[25] With the program organized in autonomous blocks articulated along the perimeter of the plot and around the central courtyard, the global vision of the ensemble is not one of a homogenous object, but of the articulated combi-

fig. 6 Aerial Photo. Photo by Varela Pècurto. Source: Imagoteca da Biblioteca Municipal de Coimbra.

fig. 7 Student Center. Theatre Entrance. Photo by Horácio Novais. Source: CFT164.160943.ic. Colecção Estúdio Horácio Novais. Biblioteca de Arte da Fundação Calouste Gulbenkian.

nation of distinct elements. In this ensemble, the volume of the theater stands out, resonating with its role as the real collective facility, providing culture not only for the academic community but also for the city as a whole. This openness can be symbolically perceived in the way the building is in relation to the

fig. 8 Student protests in the courtyard of the Student Center. May 28, 1969. Source: Espólio Biblioteca Geral da Universidade de Coimbra.

public realm, placed at the corner of the entire complex and oriented towards the square that defines the upper limit of the nineteenth-century boulevard, to which the glazed gallery of the bar, protruding from the building's facade over the main entrance, is oriented (fig. 7).

The location of the Student Center complex also performs an important role in the context of Sert's idea of the Core. The natural core of student activity should be the Alta, the heart of the university campus. However, widespread demolition and the deliberate single-functional character defined by the 1940s plan had destroyed the possibility of creating a sense of community on the campus. The new Student Center complex would thus become a key element in rearticulating the community life of students and their participation in city life. In effect, though the complex is close to the Alta, its main space of affinity is the city's urban fabric, thus bridging the gap between the university and the city.

The urban design and architectural language used to rebuild the campus resonated with a design rationale that the historiography of modern architecture considered "pseudo-monumentality," using forms of the past without "emotional justification." Furthermore, the buildings constructed in the new campus were also not in tune with the values Maristella Casciato refers to of collectivity and civic representation. Instead they had kept "the traditional rhetoric and the grandiose scale that were manifest in the monuments built in the interwar period" that Casciato critiques.

In stark contrast with the static monumentality of the campus, the Student Center complex showed a clear affiliation with the dynamic nature of contemporary cultural and educational buildings built under the auspices of democratic European welfare states. The new multipurpose building, with its enclosed open space, was meant to serve the everyday needs of the academic community, and performed as an alternative space. As an example, the Student Center would play an important role as a symbolic locus in the fight for democratic values. At the apex of the Portuguese students' revolt in 1969, the collective character of the Student Center courtyard as a place where the student community gathered daily gained currency as the main site for protest movements in Coimbra opposing the dictatorial regime[26] (fig. 8).

The Student Center complex of the University of Coimbra symbolizes a "counterimage" to the monumentality of the plan and other buildings of the new campus: Articulation and volumetric hierarchy instead of bulkiness; human scale and a sense of collectivity rather than rhetorical monumentality.

Endnotes

This article is part of PhD research co-financed by the European Social Fund through the POPH (Programa Operacional Potencial Humano) and by national funds by FCT (Fundação para a Ciência e a Tecnologia) under the PhD Grant with reference SFRH/BD/87825/2012.

1 José Luis Sert, Fernand Léger and Sigfried Giedion, "Nine Points on Monumentality," in *Architecture Culture 1943–1968: A Documentary Anthology*, ed. Joan Ockman (New York: Rizzoli, 1993), 29–30. Originally, this text was to be published in 1943 by the American Abstract Artists. However, it was only published fifteen years later in Sigfried Giedion, *Architecture, You and Me: The Diary of a Development* (Cambridge, Mass.: Harvard University Press, 1958).

2 Sert, Léger and Giedion, "Nine Points on Monumentality."

3 Ockman, ed., *Architecture Culture*, 27.

4 As presented by Franco Borsi in *L'Ordre Monumental. Europe 1929–1939* (Paris: Hazan, 1986).

5 Sigfried Giedion, "The Need for a New Monumentality," in *New Architecture and City Planning*, ed. Paul Zucker (New York: Philosophical Library, 1944), 549–568 (pp. 552–553).

6 Ibid., 550.

7 Ockman, *Architecture Culture*, 15.

8 Elizabeth Mock, ed., *Built in USA since 1932* (New York: The Museum of Modern Art, 1945), 25.

9 Maristella Casciato, "Homenagem a um Monumento Vivo," in *Fundação Calouste Gulbenkian: Os Edifícios*, ed. Ana Tostões (Lisboa: Fundação Calouste Gulbenkian, 2006), 242–251 (p. 244).

10 António Oliveira Salazar, *Discursos e Notas Políticas*, II (1935–1937) (Coimbra: Coimbra Editora, 1945), xx–xxi.

11 CAPOCUC was established by Decree–Law 31576, on October 15, 1941.

12 Nuno Rosmaninho, *O Poder da Arte: O Estado Novo e a Cidade Universitária de Coimbra* (Coimbra: Imprensa da Universidade, 2006), 82–86. See also CAPOCUC 46, 271, 361, 471–471C and 514, Arquivo da Universidade de Coimbra. The 1946 trip to Rome was part of an extensive itinerary through Italy and Switzerland; members of the group were Cottinelli Telmo, Manuel de Sá e Mello, engineer and director of

CAPOCUC, and Maximino Correia, rector of the University of Coimbra and de facto president of CAPOCUC.

13 According to Maximino Correia, rector of the university during construction of the new campus, two to three thousand inhabitants were displaced, approximately 5 percent of Coimbra's population at the time. See Maximino Correia, *Ao Serviço da Universidade de Coimbra: 1939–1960* (Coimbra: Por Ordem da Universidade, 1963), 131.

14 For further information on reactions to the plan, see Rosmaninho, *O Poder da Arte*, 61–63.

15 José R. Botelho and Celestino Castro, "Cidades Universitárias. Novas Instalações Universitárias em Portugal," *Arquitectura*, 55–56 (January/February 1956), 30–34 (p. 32).

16 Ibid.

17 Francisco Keil do Amaral, "Cidades Universitárias. Realizações Contemporâneas," *Arquitectura*, 55–56 (January/February 1956), 6–13 (p. 10).

18 Alberto José Pessoa, as the architect hired by CAPOCUC and working under the supervision of Cottinelli Telmo, had been in charge of the architectural design of the first buildings built for the new campus: the University Archive (1948), the Faculty of Arts and Humanities (1951) and the Central Library (1956). According to his own words, those buildings had been designed "to comply with the architectural language envisioned for the new University Campus." In Alberto Pessoa, "Memória Descritiva do Projecto de Arquitectura da Biblioteca Central," June 1944, CUC 2008–97, Arquivo da Universidade de Coimbra.

19 In the initial stage of the project Norberto Correa (b. 1926) was also part of the design team.

20 José António Bandeirinha, "Os Edifícios da Associação Académica e o Teatro de Gil Vicente," *Monumentos*, 8 (March 1998), 82–87 (p. 86).

21 Walter Gropius, "The Human Scale," in *CIAM 8: The Heart of the City*, ed. Jaqueline Tyrwhitt, José Luis Sert and Ernesto N. Rogers, (New York: Pellegrini and Cudahy, 1952), 53–55 (p. 53).

22 José Luis Sert, "Centers of Community Life," in *CIAM 8: The Heart of the City*, 3–16 (p. 6).

23 José Luis Sert, "The Human Scale in City Planning," in *New Architecture and City Planning*, 392–412 (p. 394).

24 Ibid., 403–404.

25 Jorge Figueira, "Para uma Coimbra não sentimental," in *A Noite em Arquitectura* (Lisboa: Relógio d'Água Editores, 2007), 149–154 (p. 151).

26 During the Portuguese academic crisis of 1969, the Student Center courtyard was the stage for meetings, performances and demonstrations, which sometimes drew more than six thousand students. At the *Magna* Assembly of April 22, 1969, held at the gymnasium, academic mourning was declared, which would eventually lead to a general strike against exams.

IV
The Inhabited Nature

Juliana Maxim

Socialist Pastoral: The Role of Folklore in Socialist Architectural Culture, 1950s and 1960s

One recurrent critique leveled against the architectural culture of the Romanian socialist state was that its rush to transform the city was antagonistic to both national building traditions and dwelling customs. One encounters such critique in the recent historiography, as well as in architects' reactions in the immediate postwar period, when the idea of apartment living and mass housing was first introduced to a population used to single family homes. And yet, even a cursory look at the cultural policies of the earliest socialist decades shows sustained support on the part of the governing bodies for tradition – more precisely, for the particular kind of tradition embedded in the folkways and vernacular art of the countryside. Folkloric music and dance festivals, fairs of rural craftwork, or exhibitions of peasant artifacts proliferated during those decades, becoming, for the urban population, as commonplace as the omnipresent construction sites of modernist mass housing estates. This paper is an attempt to account for the interest in the vernacular within a militantly modern architecture culture long seen as openly hostile to tradition, and to recapture the intensely folklorist dimension of the postwar decades.

A look at the debates and practices of the time shows that such interest stemmed less from a concern with the stylistic or formal aspects of building tradition, and instead from a larger and earnest interrogation of the relationship between architecture, maker and inhabitant in a socialist society. In the context of the overarching theme of "re-humanizing architecture," I wish to offer a series of observations about the way the architectural culture of the early socialist decades in Romania pursued at once industrialization and scientific progress and, with equal verve, expressions of "soft" notions such as community, the collective, good life, or self-fulfillment.

The prominent role that ethnographic museums acquired in postwar Romania illustrates some of the ways in which old, even obsolete forms retained their relevance in a socialist world founded on change and novelty. At a time when official architectural culture is believed to have embraced the de-humanizing principles of mass production and efficient, uniform apartment living, the socialist state encouraged and subsidized the opening or significant expansion of more than a dozen ethnographic museums throughout Romania's territory, in a concerted effort to promote the country's rich rural and pastoral architectural tradition (the term used was "monuments of popular architecture," *monumente de arhitectură populară*). The Village Museum in Bucharest, the most prominent among such open-air collections of folk structures and artifacts, demonstrates the cultural currency and popular appeal that small scale, hand-crafted architecture in harmony with nature maintained at a time of rapid socialist modernization and urbanization. How, and why, did the archaic artifacts of the countryside retain their validity at a time when the political conditions that had created them (the peasantry living under a landowning class) were disappearing?

The Village Museum, located close to the center of Bucharest, is organized as a picturesque landscape, with original homesteads arranged along winding pathways, in the midst of greenery, interspersed with churches, windmills, fountains, stables, presses, and roaming flocks of chicken (fig. 1). All artifacts in its vast collection were transported to Bucharest from their village of origin and painstakingly reassembled on the museum's site, often by craftsmen from the same region. Still one of the most beloved spaces of the capital, the Village Museum is today one of the oldest museums in the country, having endured – and thrived – throughout the political upheavals of the twentieth century. The origins of the institution date back to the 1930s, but the crucial transformations and amplification the museum underwent in the 1950s and 1960s under Romania's new communist government make it particularly representative of a socialist cultural agenda.[1]

Throughout the 1950s and 1960s, as the collection expanded and dozens of rural structures made their way to Bucharest, the Village Museum entered in an indirect but unavoidable dialogue with the modernist housing estates under construction at the same time, and often nearby. The romanticized natural order the museum reconstructed for its visitors was part of the same project of spatial and cultural modernization as the reconstruction of the capital. This paper shows how the remnants of the traditional Romanian village

fig. 1 Berbeşti household, Village Museum, Bucharest. Postcard, before 1979.

resonated with the reformist agenda of the new socialist state, and explores the model of architectural creation implied in the museum's exhibitions, the intersections between pastoral and urban, traditional and new, and the role of a visual discourse of the archaic in the architectural culture of socialism.

Un-alienated Labor

The museum's displays presented a peasant's relation to his or her production in terms that came close to the ideal relation of the worker to his or her labor in a socialist society. Far from delivering a stern disquisition on the exploitation of the peasantry by the landowning class (that genre also existed, but was reserved for other mediums), the artifacts projected instead a quiet industriousness, the kind of work that, it was assumed, the peasant undertook freely and willingly and which, as a result, resulted in objects full of human and aesthetic content.

The museum had been originally conceived as a lived-in installation, with peasant families occupying the houses, tending animals or engaging in various daily tasks. (Women were especially encouraged to get on with crafts such as weaving or embroidering in front of the visitors; the building of a cafeteria was considered in order to free them from less visually appealing domestic duties). The last peasants (and their sheep) were sent home in 1948, but the museum continued to represent the households as places of vigorous, continuous, and purposeful activity. In the absence of actual peasants, work was now implied through an extensive repertoire of tools and utilitarian structures. Varied, suggestive, and intriguing, they ranged from a simple carding comb to imposing windmills, and became the peasants' rightful representatives and true inhabitants of the museum (fig. 2). (Cranes, forges, tractors similarly populated socialist narratives and imagery.) The spindle with wool leaning against a wall as if work had only just been interrupted, fishing nets

fig. 2 Windmill and oven, from the collection of the Village Museum, Bucharest. Photo by author, 2013.

drying out in the sun, and the oven in the yard gave the visitor a sense of a world entirely permeated by labor, but a kind of labor that was essential, collective, ingenious, and pregnant with aesthetic feeling all at once – in one word, un-alienated. For the semi-literate new working class visiting the displays (and factories regularly scheduled outings at the museum), the lesson would have been at once powerful and intuitive: work, woven into the fabric of daily life, should be done with fondness for the task at hand rather than simply for material gain.

An un-alienated relationship to labor (on the worksite, in the factory, or at the drafting table) was key to the making of the new socialist man. Marxism had offered a powerful critique of the division of labor between worker and product, and a major goal of socialism was to restore a harmonious, conscious relation of the worker to his or her activity. A dictionary entry under "work" in 1958 put it most succinctly: a socialist society "determined a new, socialist attitude towards work." The new socialist man and woman worked "willingly, without thinking about remuneration."[2]

Unlike the idyllic primitive condition reconstructed in the museum, however, socialism also aimed at liberating labor through the mediation of advanced technology. In fact, at first sight, the contrived romanticism of the primitive wooden huts and the hard economic calculations of the contemporary construction site seem two irreconcilable rather than converging realities. They represent the conventional polarities of the architectural discipline – the hand-made versus the factory production, the unique object versus the series, ancestral custom and intuition versus the standard, the plan, the procedure (figs. 3, 4).

Although exacerbated by the state-imposed tempo of socialist transformations in the capital, the museum had cultivated a contrast between its atmosphere of quiet constancy and craft, and the machine-driven changes

fig. 3 Re-constructing the house from the Straja village, Village Museum, Bucharest, 1961. From G. Focșa, "Etape succesive în elaborarea tematicii Muzeului Satului," *Muzeul Satului. Studii și cercetări*, 1970.

fig. 4 Building with prefabricated panels. Cover of *Arhitectura RPR* 8 (1957).

of the life outside it since its opening in 1936. The first Village Museum had been part initially of a larger open-air exhibition called the "Bucharest Month", described by a visitor in 1936 as "… an extravaganza of lights, wondrous achievements of urbanism, grand constructions, Western civilization, ultra-modern progress. The Village Museum, situated in the same fairy-tale setting, appears modest, arrogantly modest, with a pure-blood Romanian history, with houses at times 150 years old, with all their interior and exterior life and art. The contrast is thought-provoking."[3]

After 1948, the museum maintained such stance of archaism against a background of clamorous modernization, taking on the role of a full-scale archive and demonstration of ancestral handiwork. The museum emphasized in its selection and promotion of artifacts, irregularities and accidents:

crooked timber columns, uneven foundations, sagging roofs were often preserved as examples of the richness introduced by the living interaction with the material. Parts needed for repairs and replacements, such as shingles, for instance, were done by hand, painstakingly, with traditional tools, rather than purchased as generic elements produced on a large scale since – what was being reconstructed was clearly the artisanal touch. By contrast, the narrative about the construction of the socialist city relied on a radical shift in scale in which architecture embraced an ideal of regularity and predictability, standardized solutions, large working crews, and advanced machinery (professional discussions often specified the kind of crane involved in the construction of a building, like an important actor in the plot.)

Romantic primitivism, however, was not simply the inverted image of a modernist socialist ideology, but also shared, clarified, and amplified some of its values concerning work. In a socialist society, it was contended, even physical labor was not alienated labor since its results were not privately appropriated and belonged to the society as a whole. But the end of private ownership of the means of production was not sufficient: to eliminate alienation, the worker's relationship to his or her own activity had to change and become as deliberate and fulfilling as that of the peasant, who, unprompted and uncoerced, artistically enhanced even the most mundane daily objects.

To a Marxist understanding, labor was much more than a means of subsistence, and instead a free, conscious, creative activity.[4] The objects assembled in the museum, although entirely utilitarian, were valued and displayed also for their beauty and decorative qualities. While working, the peasant not only solved practical problems or produced necessary goods, he (and often she) also created, in the process, aesthetic value: "Out of simple objects, of daily use, the people (the folk) produced artworks, by combining with skill and ingenuity the useful and the beautiful." Or: "The objects that satisfy everyday needs have obvious aesthetic qualities: the spinning wheel, the cheese molds, the stag horn flask for the gunpowder, the enameled dish, the bed cover, the pots on the stove."[5] The museum foregrounded the "artistic sense" that permeated both tools and products as evidence of an attitude towards work that found its reward not externally (in wages, for instance), but in the process itself. Far from being an "alien entity" (Marx's expression), the product of pre-industrial peasant labor brought both physical and mental satisfaction.

In the 1950s, "creativity" became a keyword of communist propaganda: the socialist worker was compared to an artist, and work became a "manifestation of the creative activities of the masses freed from exploitation."[6] Discussions on Stakhanovism, the Soviet-inspired movement of hard, selfless work, stressed not only quantifiable gains in productivity, but also the workers' ability to act as innovators and create, for instance, an original work method, thus abolishing the division between material and mental labor.[7]

The prominence of technique

The pre-industrial work illustrated in the museum was less about the objects produced (nowadays, they can be purchased conveniently from the museum shop) and more about tools and processes. The primitive machines scattered in the museum garden, the ingenious constructions and mechanisms, suggested process rather than finished product, such as the sequence of the harvest (threshing, grinding, milling, and baking), and, more generally, the continuous, harmonious choreography of natural work cycles – the exact opposite of commodity production. In emphasizing *how* things were made rather than the things themselves, the museum also de-emphasized the individual maker in favor of his or her technique. Indeed, another characteristic of the architecture displayed in the museum was its authorlessness. Artifacts were put forward not as the accomplishments of a famous craftsman, but as the outcome of customs, collective practices, and shared knowledge.

Without identifiable makers, the architecture illustrated instead the generic aspects of a technique rather than the original individual invention. The structures chosen for display in the museum were presented as exemplars of constructive solutions, such as types of wood joinery or families of timber frames. The museum privileged wood construction, the most widespread material for traditional rural construction in Romania, but also one in which structure and components remained legible both inside and out, with joints, frames, and trusses not only unconcealed but often the principal expressive trait of a construction. The collection of houses gathered in the museum amounted to an open corpus of structures and materials, easy to read and deployed in ways that allowed the viewer to comprehend the building process, recapitulate its steps and decisions, and therefore retrace the relationship between mind, technique, and matter. The examples are numerous: two adjacent constructions from the same Moldovan region of Suceava, the Straja house and the elaborate barn of the Fundu Moldovei household, demonstrate two very different techniques side by side: the walls of the first are built out of massive cylindrical and stark white logs that extend forcefully beyond the corners into elaborate and imposing corbelled projections; the second used for its construction smooth milled planks darkened by age and assembled into regular, delicate dovetail corner joints. Both wooden huts wear their constructive system on their exterior, like in a diagram. In each case, the nature of the material guided the form (fig. 5).

fig. 5 Houses from Straja (right) and Fundu Moldovei (left), Village Museum, Bucharest. Photo by author, 2013.

The concrete technology ardently embraced by the socialist state after 1948 was, of course, radically different from that of wood construction. But here again, the rationality and clarity of timber frames, the easy and quick construction and adaptation to needs, and the humble nature of the material, were traits that translated easily to the architecture of concrete panels and prefabricated components that socialist architects used under the imperative to build efficiently and cheaply. Though seemingly closer to masonry construction, the architecture of concrete pursued the speed, flexibility, and combinatory technique of wood rather than the monumental and lasting (and upper-class-related) character of stone (fig. 6). (Concrete panels and other prefabricated elements, which socialist architects deployed in many sizes and combinations, also shared the limitations of wood construction: the length and thickness of available timber constrained the dimensions of the plan in the same way the industrial component did.) From across their temporal and cultural divide, the architecture of the village and that of the socialist city shared a faith in the role of materials and techniques to deliver rational and economical, as well as meaningful, architectural form.

The pre-industrial architecture exhibited in the museum showed that the most basic timber frame construction techniques could generate endlessly varied and expressive forms. Even a structure as modest as the single-room house from the village of Răpciuni produced its own marked visual effect, for instance in the way in which the corner joints were left exposed (fig. 7). This decision was at once technical (determined by the saddle notching at the corners) and stylistic, as the darkened wood suggestively framed the immaculate white walls, door, and minuscule window, heightening the legibility of the structure's compositional grammar. If the minimal, functional architecture produced by folk culture could induce in the viewer such strong aesthetic

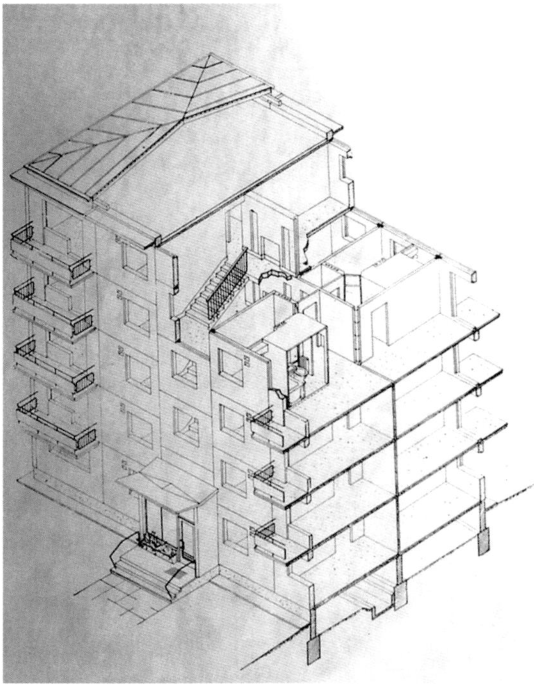

fig. 6 Axonometric diagram of panel construction, Bucharest, 1960. From *Arhitectura RPR* 2 (1960).

feeling, then perhaps socialism could bestow on the products of industry a similar range of meanings.

Advances in the industrialization of construction in the late 1960s intensified architecture's preoccupation with the visibility of technique. The introduction of large prefabricated panels from 1960 onwards forced the architects to consider systematically the building components as a means of expression, and architects spoke of the "sincere expression of the structure on the facade."[8] With the use of large wall panels, facades became a perfect index of building parts and their assemblage, with the seams revealing both the dimensions and position of each panel, and the subdivisions in plan. Although made of an entirely opaque material, the facade functioned as a transparent rendering of the architecture.

Collective forms

A recurrent theme of the postwar years was the need for the socialist designer's work to assume a collective quality, both as an activity and as a product – done by the group for the group, rather than by a single architect for a single patron. Critical writings of the time reminded architects in no uncertain terms that urban and architectural design was meant to serve collective ends: "Architectural activity today is no longer the personal problem of the single creator, but a collective activity within a state organization."[9] Like in most of the Soviet Bloc, the architectural profession in Romania was, after 1952, largely controlled by the state, but the technocratic management of production instituted from the center was constantly intersected by the affective register of "abnegation," "brotherly help," "monolithic unity," "mutual help," which belonged less to the realm of complex managerial and industrial units and more to the kinds of communitarian and harmonious experience of the *Gemeinschaft* staged in the museum.

The museum presented the building techniques of its architectural collection not only as limpidly rational, but also as the shared property of a social group. Before the war, the houses in the museum had retained the name of the family that once inhabited it; but after 1948, the museum designated the structures by their village of origin, and another consequence of their anonymity was to appear as the creations of an abstract collective: the people. The museum organized its collection into families of forms meant to expose the bonds that existed not only between maker and artifact, but also between maker and the culture of the village and the region. The groupings, designated as types, emphasized the ways in which each artifact, albeit unique in its details, was nonetheless representative of a larger reality: "[The museum presents] typical, characteristic elements from the country's main ethnographic areas. … These different types of dwellings reflect evocatively the real life and the material, social, and professional conditions of their inhabitants."[10] Curators, ethnographers, and architectural historians placed considerable value on the artifacts' typical character, or their ability to embody collective values, knowledge, practices and ways of life. This is how Grigore Ionescu, the most important Romanian architectural historian of the twentieth century and a preeminent scholar of Romanian folk architecture, summarized the deeply conventional nature of traditional wood architecture: "Built out of a material that by its nature cannot last centuries when exposed to the elements, folk architecture had to be rebuilt countless times. The rebuilding was, in large part, a restoration: we cannot imagine new churches or houses that are different, or foreign from the model that preceded them."[11]

In socialist architectural culture, type assumed a double function: on the one hand, ethnographers and curators wielded it as a classifying tool that recognized commonalities and norms amidst the vast repertoire of folk architectural forms produced throughout history (the museum, for instance, in addition to regional types, also recognized organizational ones such as dwelling types with one room, two rooms and a porch, etc.). On the other hand, architects practicing under state socialism were also concerned with type, by which they understood the devising of new standards and models meant to guide the creation of contemporary forms. While scholars and ethnographers studied the architectural types of the countryside, architects conceived constructive and spatial norms and efficient and repeatable plans – a design process designated as *tipizare* (typification).

Tipizare and type designs were central to socialist architectural production. The reorganization of the architectural profession in Romania in the 1950s occurred in large part around the conception of type-projects (*proiecte tip*) for a variety of scales, users, and contexts. Designing types required new modes of collaboration between architects, engineers, and other building trades, as well as the formation of large architecture collectives. As early as 1949, the Institute for the Design of Constructions (Institutul pentru Proiectarea Construcțiilor, or IPC) opened an entire department for the investigation of type plans; after 1956, the institute as a whole became the Institute for the Design of Type Constructions (IPCT). In 1955, IPB (Institut Proiect București), the architectural agency for all Bucharest, received a clear mandate to design housing in terms of basic, repeatable and adaptable, plan types. On all levels, architectural design came to mean – with very few exceptions – the conception of types and their adaptation to a variety of conditions.

Here again, the ethnographic type (the classification of existing folk artifacts) and the contemporary type design (the production of new forms) might appear as two distinct endeavors; in both cases, however, the preoccupation with typical solutions revealed a common project to remove design decisions from the realm of individual subjectivity and to relocate them firmly into a collective cultural, social, or political realm. Types, both ancestral and recent, were by definition forms engendered and shared by a community and as a consequence, they provided a method for revealing, or achieving an enriched, organic, and natural relationship between maker, artifact, inhabitant, and society.

The need to maintain or produce a cohesive community in the context of industrializing modernity and migration to the city guided many of the housing projects in the 1950s and early 1960s. Like in the imaginary village life staged in the museum, the new residential environments, often organized around common services and green spaces, were meant to produce small societies of intimates linked by daily life, and to offer a first circle of sociability within the larger, more abstract political collective of the state. Architectural types addressed not only economic imperatives (through the standardization of building components) but also promised to produce familiar, recognizable forms that could foster collective shared experience across all social classes.[12]

An important family of artifacts displayed in the museum was that of the peasant dwelling in its simplest form. Single-room huts (such as the one from

fig. 7 Single-room hut from the village of Răpciuni. Village Museum, Bucharest. Photo by author, 2013.

the village of Răpciuni (fig. 7), represented rudimentary, even threadbare solutions for shelter, but their simplicity and generality allowed them also to stand out as primordial cultural archetypes, like a child's drawing of a house. I propose that the economic, spare forms of socialist architecture aspired to achieve a similar basic and paradigmatic status within contemporary culture. The apartment bloc so characteristic of socialist housing of the 1950s and 1960s, for instance, had a very specific modernist pedigree but was also portrayed as having risen, like the primitive hut, from of the fundamental intersection of need, collective spirit, and constructive logic.

The visibility and strongly-felt cultural relevance of the Village Museum in Bucharest shows that the early socialist decades were far from being under the exclusive spell of a materialist worldview, and instead were colored with concern for human experience. The museum put forth a certain view of architecture and architectural production that was deliberately, even spectacularly archaic but also quite in tune with socialist ideals, allowing unexpected comparisons between rural folk and urban socialist modernity. When taken together, peasant hut and housing bloc represent a daring, even utopian attempt to solve the gulf between city and country, peasant and worker, tradition and upheaval, at a time when the largest part of the Romanian population was still peasant or of peasant origin but was being rapidly propelled into the industrial and urban age.

The chronological and discursive overlaps between the institution of the Village Museum and postwar socialist architectural culture suggest that the formal and spatial motifs of industrialized building were conceived in part as actualized counterparts of folk creation. They also speak of those years' hope of turning the architecture of socialism into a medium of familiarity and collective identity rather than alienation. The task of the socialist architect was to reconstruct and reimagine society through new formal and technical solutions, but also according to a fuller relationship between users and artifacts for which folk culture provided the model.

Endnotes

1 For a history of the Village Museum, see Gheorgeh Focşa, "Etape succesive în elaborarea tematicii Muzeului Satului," *Muzeul Satului. Studii şi cercetări* (1970), 5–39; Ioan Godea, "Ce reprezintă Museul Satului?" in G. Stoica and I. Godea, eds., Muzeul Satului Bucureşti (Bucharest: Editura Museion, 1993), 5–17; Juliana Maxim, "The Village Museum in the first communist decades and the transformation of Gusti's legacy," Special issue on the Bucharest School of Sociology, *Transilvania* 1 (2014), 57–65.

2 B. H. Ponomarev, *Dicţionar politic* (Bucharest: Editura Politică, 1958) and G.A. Kozlov and S.P. Peruşin, *Mic dicţionar economic* (Bucharest: Editura Politică, 1959). Both quotes in Cristina Preutu, "Mişcarea stahanovistă în România: între propaganda şi control social," *Anuarul Institutului de Investigare a Crimelor Comunismului şi Memoria Exilului Românesc* V–VI (2010–2011), 241.

3 Florea Stănculescu, "Muzeul Satului," *Arhitectura* 6 (July 1936), 10.

4 Eastern European writings in the 1950s emphasized the role that the concept of alienation played in Marx's work, shifting the discourse away from official Soviet Marxist emphasis on class and dialectical materialism in favor of more subjective notions such as self-realization. See Murray Yanowitch, "Alienation and the Young Marx in Soviet Thought," *Slavic Review* 26, (March 1, 1967), 29–53.

5 Gheorghe Focşa, *Muzeul satului* (Bucharest: Editura ştiinţifică, 1967): 43.

6 Ecaterina Borilă, "Întrecerea socialistă, metoda comunistă de construire a comunismului," in *Lupta de clasă* 5 (May 1950), 36. Quoted in Cristina Preutu, "Mişcarea stahanovistă în România: între propaganda şi control social," *Anuarul Institutului de Investigare a Crimelor Comunismului şi Memoria Exilului Românesc* V–VI (2010–2011), 242.

7 Cristina Preutu, "Mişcarea stahanovistă în România: între propaganda şi control social," *Anuarul Institutului de Investigare a Crimelor Comunismului şi Memoria Exilului Românesc* V–VI (2010–2011), 239–248.

8 "Locuinţe pe Şoseaua Ştefan Cel Mare," *Arhitectura RPR* 2 (1963), 8.

9 *Arhitectura RPR* 7, 4 (1959), 9. For a similar discussion in the context of East Germany, see Torsten Lange, "Form as/and utopia of collective labor. Typification and collaboration in East German industrialised construction," in K. Lloyd Thomas, T. Amhoff, N. Beech, *Industries of Architecture* (London: Routledge, 2016), 148–159.

10 Gheorghe Focşa, *Muzeul satului* (Bucharest: Editura ştiinţifică, 1967), 5, 7.

11 Grigore Ionescu, "Tiplogii specifice ale clădirilor populare din lemn," *Revista muzeelor şi monumentelor* 2 (1977), 30.

12 A similar discussion about architecture's ability to mitigate social dislocation can be found in Eve Blau, "ISOTYPE and Architecture in Red Vienna: The Modern Projects of Otto Neurath and Josef Frank." *Austrian Studies* 14 (2006), 227–259.

Nelson Mota

Dwelling in the Middle Landscape: Rethinking the Architecture of Rural Communities at CIAM 10

The duality between the pastoral and the counter-pastoral was relentlessly portrayed in nineteenth-century art and literature. It became a token of the mercurial and paradoxical artistic sensibility that had unfolded with rapid transformations sparked by modernity. Several eventful decades later, in the aftermath of the Second World War, this duality emerged once again. This time it was part and parcel of a quest for a more humanistic approach to architecture, geared to the development of new forms of community where art and nature should be reconciled. In this paper, I will discuss this attempt to reconcile art and nature, examining projects presented by four national groups at the tenth *Congrès International d'Architecture Moderne* (CIAM), held in Dubrovnik in 1956. For various reasons, some of these projects became household names while others have been overlooked by architecture historiography and have remained invisible for the last six decades. Notwithstanding these differing fortunes, I will contend that the projects have in common an architectural approach that, following the lead of nineteen-century writers and artists, pursued a reconceptualization of the tenets of architectural modernism in the mid-1950s, blending the experience of modernity with vernacular tradition.

The Dynamo and the Virgin

The intellectual framework for the 1950s debate had been defined a century earlier, and Baudelaire's writings of the mid-eighteenth century masterfully portray the ambivalent character of the experience of modernity in the metropolis. At that time one could enjoy – as Baudelaire did – the experience of "modernity without tears" while concurrently declaring that "modern reality is utterly loathsome, empty not only of beauty but even the potential for beauty."[1] In any case, one side effect of the process of modernization fostered by industrial capitalism and rapid urban growth was the creation of the myth of the countryside as locus of the pure, uncorrupted, virginal Arcadian landscape, as opposed to the contaminated, perverse, pernicious landscape of the industrial city.

Henry Adams (1838–1918) illustrates this dichotomy between metropolis and countryside magnificently with the image of the Dynamo and the Virgin. In his *The Education of Henry Adams*, written in 1905, Adams delivers a Manichean account of the relation between modernity and the vernacular. As Leo Marx points out, this account underlines "a clash between past and present, unity and diversity, love and power." With Adams' binary opposition, Marx goes on, "he marshals all conceivable values. On one side he lines up heaven, beauty, religion, and reproduction; on the other: hell, utility, science, and production."[2] Industrial society is represented by the symbol of the Dynamo that destroys the creative power of the rural world symbolized by the Virgin, which signifies for Adams "the highest energy ever known to man, the creator of four-fifths of his noblest art, exercising vastly more attraction over the human mind than all the steam-engines and dynamos ever dreamed of."[3]

Along with this growing tension between experience of the metropolis and life in the rural world, the Spanish philosopher José Ortega y Gasset (1883–1955) singled out the emergence of mass-culture civilization as a matter of concern. In his *The Revolt of the Masses*, published in 1930, Ortega y Gasset argued that in the last third of the nineteenth century – the time of Baudelaire and Henry Adams – civilization generated by the bourgeois revolutions began to lose historic culture.[4] Ortega y Gasset contended that, beneath the apparent progress, Western civilization had started a process of retrogression. The reason for this, he contended, "is that the type of man dominant today is a primitive one, a *Naturmensch* rising up in the midst of a civilized world." Ortega y Gasset's counter-pastoral vision of the relation between modernity and mass culture was ruthlessly stated: "The world is a civilized one, its inhabitant is not: he does not see the civilization of the world around him, but he uses it as if it were a natural force."[5]

In the early 1950s, this complex intercourse between technology and culture became a central aspect of the intellectual debate. The third postwar CIAM congress, held at Hoddesdon, England in 1951, was dedicated to the theme "The Heart of the City." Curiously enough, while modern architects in Hoddesdon were discussing ways to develop a more humanistic twist to the principles of the functional city, in Germany – which had of course lost the Second World War – German architects, engineers and philosophers gathered in Darmstadt to discuss the relationship between man and space for the 1951 Darmstädter Gespräche conference. Both themes, I would suggest, denote an attempt to re-humanize architecture and urban planning. They testify to the willingness to reassess the position of the individual and the community in the built environment, overcoming the shortcomings of machinist civilization conveyed by the tenets of modernism and the functional city.

Though Ortega y Gasset was one of the delegates at the Darmstadt conference, the most influential contribution was arguably Martin Heidegger's presentation "Bauen Wohnen Denken" ["Building Dwelling Thinking"]. In Heidegger's presentation, and later in his essay with the same title, he discussed the architecture of dwelling – that is, the experience of inhabiting according to memories of ancient tradition – as an opportunity to struggle against and eventually escape the alienation caused by the mechanist tropes of modernity.[6] As with Ortega y Gasset, Heidegger emphasized the growing conflict between the realm of the individual and the territory of collective experiences. In other words, Heidegger stressed the tension between the domus and the megalopolis, as Jean-François Lyotard put it, with an evocation for the *Heimat*, the homeland, where men could be reconciled with nature and tradition.[7]

Reconciling Modernity with the Vernacular at CIAM 10

Neil Leach contends that "Building Dwelling Thinking" brings about the dark side of the domus.[8] He argues that Heidegger's philosophy of the *Heimat* eliminates the possibility of dwelling in the metropolis and upholds a pastoral vision of the countryside as the only place where a sense of homeland may flourish.[9] To be sure, over the first half of the 1950s, the challenges of dwelling in a metropolis became a topic that pervaded many disciplinary fields including architecture, often in tandem with an appraisal of vernacular tradition. For example, at the 1953 CIAM congress held in Aix-en-Provence, the grand vernacular of African tribes was discussed in parallel with the reconstruction of the biggest European metropolises. A year later, a group of young CIAM members gathered in the Dutch city of Doorn and produced a statement on habitat in which they brought up the need to emphasize rela-

fig. 1 MARS-Group (John Voelcker) – Rural Resettlement Grid – Panel 1 (1955). Source: Collection Het Nieuwe Instituut / J.B. Bakema Archive / BAKEf12.

tions between communities, in contrast to the technocratic organization of the built environment supported by mere functional criteria, as in the Athens Charter.[10] The so-called Doorn Manifesto, prompted by the idea of scales of association, encouraged a re-humanization of architecture. The ideologues of this document eventually became responsible for putting together the next CIAM congress. Interestingly, the rural world then emerged in preparation for the tenth CIAM congress as a privileged locus for the development of new forms of community, wherein harmonic relations between modernity and the vernacular could unfold.

In September 1955, at the meeting of CIAM delegates held at La Sarraz, Switzerland, this movement was illustrated by the "Rural Resettlement Project" grid, designed by John Voelcker (1927–1972), a member of the British MARS group and one of the contributors to the Doorn Manifesto. Voelcker's grid shows a project for a small rural community, a hamlet of two to ten houses. In the first panel of the grid, Voelcker asserts his strong commitment to catering for the creation of "vital human associations," one of the claims of the Doorn Manifesto (fig. 1). "The elements signify connections between the inhabitants and the universe beyond," Voelcker claims. He goes on, contending that "in so doing they may provide the means of extension from individual to communal, from man-made to phenomenal."[11] In the second panel, he asserts that this relationship is chiefly inspired by existing dwelling patterns. In effect, the search for new possibilities to create meaningful relations between modernity

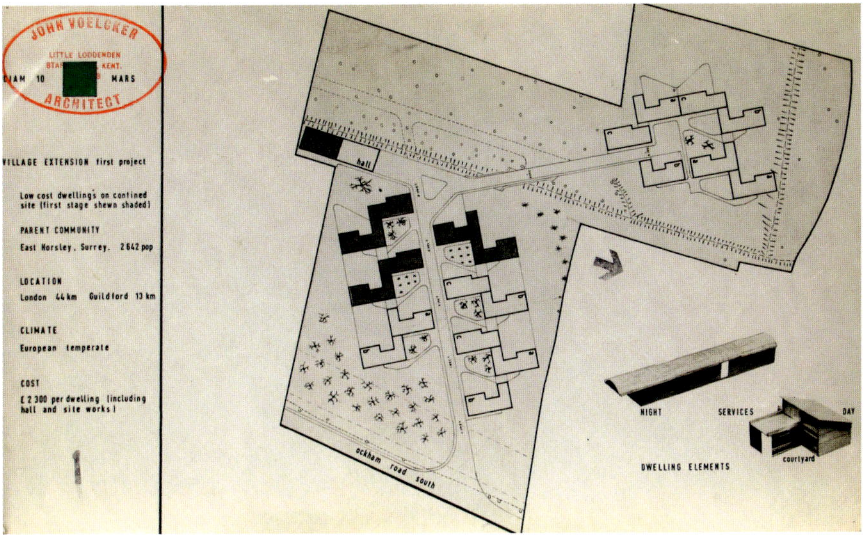

fig. 2 MARS-Group (John Voelcker) – Village Extension Grid – Panel 1 (1956). Source: Collection Het Nieuwe Instituut / J.B. Bakema Archive / BAKEf12.

and the vernacular, suggested by Voelcker's Rural Resettlement grid, would be a central debate topic at the tenth CIAM congress.

That congress was held in Dubrovnik from August 3 to 13, 1956. At the congress, Voelcker presented a revised version of the scheme shown some months earlier in La Sarraz. In this new version, the project had evolved toward a layout defined by a common spine of "night-time" components articulating the unobstructed "day-time" volumes through the service areas (fig. 2). Whereas in the Rural Resettlement grid of 1955 it was still possible to differentiate the realm of the individual from that of the community, in the 1956 project for a village extension, the new pattern of association deliberately mingles both. With this strategy, Voelcker demonstrates his interest in thinking of the community as a total complex.

The same approach would be pursued by Alison and Peter Smithson, also members of the MARS group. The Smithsons, who had been key players in the drafting and dissemination of the Doorn Manifesto, also advocated a "subordination of the four functions to […] more fundamental questions relating to the specific scale and type of human collectivity."[12] In effect, they brought to Dubrovnik no less than five grids, providing several examples to illustrate the four scales of association defined in the Doorn Manifesto on habitat: a) detached buildings, b) villages, c) towns, and d) cities. The scale to which they arguably dedicated the most attention was the village, presenting two grids, "The Galleon Cottages" and the "Fold Houses."

fig. 3 MARS-Group (Alison and Peter Smithson) – Fold Houses Grid – Panel 1 (1956). Source: Collection Het Nieuwe Instituut / J.B. Bakema Archive / BAKEf13.

In the Fold Houses grid, the Smithsons brought about a solution to cope with the problem of inventing a housing type for use in what they called "infill developments" at a village scale. They looked at vernacular settlements on the Scottish island of Tiree and on the Greek island of Poros to exemplify how the use of identical units, articulated with the site's topography, would foster at the scale of the village "an identity of coherence – like red apples on a tree" (fig. 3). In a village, the Smithsons argued, development patterns cannot be pursued since the scale is too small. Instead, they suggested, "infill development is all this type of village can hold." They presented several variants of housing layouts that could be added next to the existing constructions, "placed over the whole of the old alike a new plant growing through old branches."[13]

In the mid-1950s, Aldo van Eyck, a member of the Dutch "de8" CIAM group and another key figure in the drafting of the Doorn Manifesto, was also trying to make sense of possible relationships between modernity and vernacular tradition. Since the early 1950s, van Eyck had been pursuing a very personal survey on the primal elements of architectural language, which would guide him towards an alternative notion of progress. This quest for the primitive and elementary inspired his trips to North Africa in 1951 and 1952. These trips were, according to Francis Strauven, "journeys of discovery through the oases of the Algerian Sahara, where […] the traditional settlements, due to the climate and their physical isolation, had remained, irre-

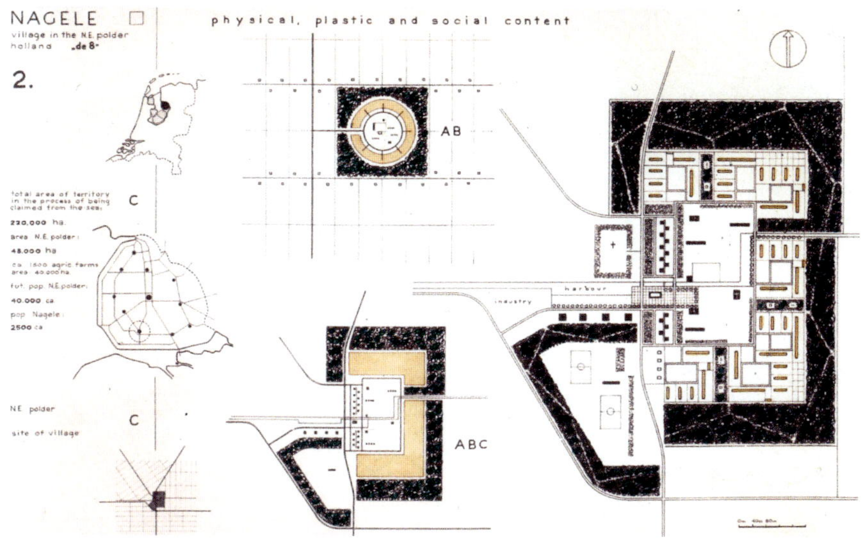

fig. 4 Aldo van Eyck – Nagele Grid – Panel 2 (1956). Source: *Team 10 1953–81*, ed. Max Risselada and Dirk Van den Heuvel, 58.

spective of Western civilization, as constant as the pre-rational world-view that they reflected."[14]

Van Eyck presented in Dubrovnik a grid with the plan for Nagele, a new village in the Dutch municipality of Noordoostpolder[15] (fig. 4). At first glimpse, the Nagele plan shows little resonance with the attributes of Saharan traditional settlements, which van Eyck overtly praised.[16] In fact, the morphological characteristics of the plan more closely resembled a group of Jaap Bakema's rationalist neighborhood units than the vernacular spatial patterns of traditional settlements.[17] On closer inspection, however, the organization of Nagele's neighborhood units reveals design decisions that challenged principles of bourgeois planning and adopted modernist ideals mingled with principles of sub-Saharan vernacular settlements. For example, the egalitarian distribution of the neighborhood units around the open core embodied van Eyck's rejection of the institutionalization of social hierarchies. Indeed, both the thick windswept perimeter of trees surrounding the village and the central core epitomized van Eyck's goal that "the entire village should be the expression of unity."[18]

While van Eyck was chiefly interested in promoting new forms of community, the Norwegian CIAM group Progressive Arkitekters Gruppe Oslo Norge (PAGON) was more focused on exploring new relationships between building and nature. PAGON was represented in Dubrovnik by architects Arne Korsmo and Geir Grung, and the painter G.S. Gundersen. They pre-

fig. 5 PAGON (Oslo-Norway) – CIAM 10 Grid – Panel 4 (1956). Source: Collection Het Nieuwe Instituut / J.B. Bakema Archive / BAKEf17.

sented a proposal at the congress in which they depicted the vernacular (for example, a farm in the countryside or fishermen's homes) as "a simple understanding of living in its relationship to nature as defined through time into a form – expression and milieu of high cultural quality."[19] These references clearly showed an attempt to combine nature and artifact. In fact, they argued, "all these buildings belong to the landscape whether they seem to slip away or lay close to it." In contrast, the group presented examples of standardized housing systems to illustrate the contemporary drive to "shift from tranquility and simplicity to the speed, the typically hurried and economically hazarded impression of our age." In their proposal, PAGON aimed to bring together tempo and quality, essential virtues that influenced the outcome of the work delivered by craftsmen and architects. Thus, they advocated a more personalized society with a more active individual living in it, and they were keen to promote aesthetical quality as a key element in achieving a balance between housing and nature (fig. 5). "The face of each family is to be seen in the facade of each family home." PAGON's project therefore stresses a critical integration in contemporary housing schemes of the qualities of the vernacular, fostering a symbiotic relationship between nature and built artifacts and between the individual and the community.

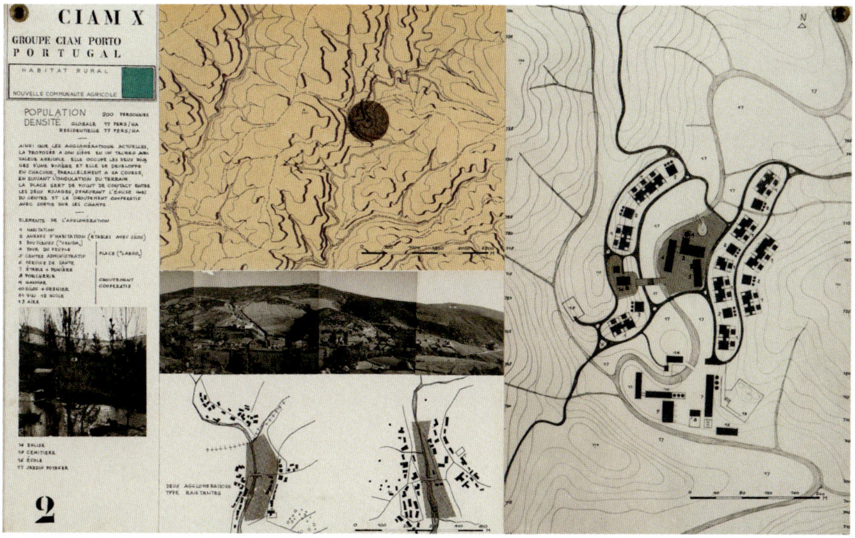

fig. 6 Group CIAM Porto – CIAM X. Rural Habitat. A New Agricultural Community (1956). Panel 2 – General Plan. Source: CEAU-FAUP.

A Vision from the Periphery: The Portuguese CIAM Group's Rural-Habitat Project

The Portuguese contribution to CIAM 10 was a project for an agricultural community, "Habitat Rural. Nouvelle Communauté Agricole." The project was designed by the architects Viana de Lima, Fernando Távora and Octávio Lixa Filgueiras, with the collaboration of students Arnaldo Araújo and Carlos Carvalho Dias.[20] It was located in a rural area in the Bragança region of northeastern Portugal, close to the border with Spain. The project was developed for a community of forty families, a number resonant with the average size of the region's agricultural communities (typically numbering twenty-five to fifty households) (fig. 6). The existing communities also inspired the selection of the project's location in a river valley. The mimicking of extant settlements was deliberate and revealed a noteworthy pastoral belief in the qualities and naturalness of spontaneous agglomerations.

Choosing the design of an agricultural community as the theme for the presentation of the group's project further revealed their commitment to exploring the social and physical qualities of rural settlements as another opportunity to apply the principles of the Modern Movement. In the project description, the group showed the clear intention to reconcile modernity with the domus, as it were. Though inspired by local custom and tradition, the layout of the plan shows notable affinities with principles of the functional city. In any event, they asserted that their proposal was able to contribute to the Charte de l'Habitat by reaffirming "the importance of the rural habitat, which CIAM shouldn't overlook if they want their principles to be truly universal." The group thus pointed out that CIAM principles should look beyond large settlements and the metropolis and also take into account the planning of small communities. Further, they criticized the excessive standardization of modernist planning, highlighting instead "the importance of very intense surveys, mainly in very specific cases, such as this one."[21] Their drive to re-humanize modern architecture was underpinned by a clear intention to engage in a more situated disciplinary approach, which they argued "will gradually eliminate the plans developed without contact with local realities, and [...] will prevent the dangerous tendency towards the centralization that we find everywhere."[22]

The group's engagement with the study of preindustrial settlements, in the "Survey of Portuguese Regional Architecture" (henceforth "the Survey"), deeply influenced the outcome of their project and the formulation of their position.[23] The group's attempt to develop a new form of community was inspired by the re-humanization drive noted above and was clearly expressed in the ambivalent account of vernacular tradition shown in the panels presented in Dubrovnik.

These panels reveal an explicit attempt at translating to the codes and conventions of the architectural discipline and the social and spatial patterns of the community. This can be seen, for example, in the third panel, focusing on the realm of the family (fig. 7). On the left side of the panel, at the bottom of the strip with the textual information, there is a picture depicting the hearth of a vernacular dwelling. This picture, which had been taken during the preliminary works for the Survey, suggests the primitiveness of living conditions in the Portuguese countryside. In the central section of the panel, the plan for new dwelling units is confronted, at the same scale, with the plan of an existing house surveyed in the region. While the compositional quality of the new plan cannot be ignored, the project conveys a more critical approach. It promotes the project as a counter-pastoral alternative to the existing situation. It emphasizes the group's commitment to catering to the improvement of the community's living conditions.

This presentation strategy highlights the group's focus on two fundamental scales: the community (panel 2) and the family (panel 3). Finally, in the fourth panel, the purpose of the project is underlined by a meaningful quotation from the French writer Abel Hermant that seems to synthesize the group's approach: "May our homes and our cities become natural by our wonderful modern methods, and with this beautiful mechanical precision – which is also that of living organisms – but as our ancient rural houses were,

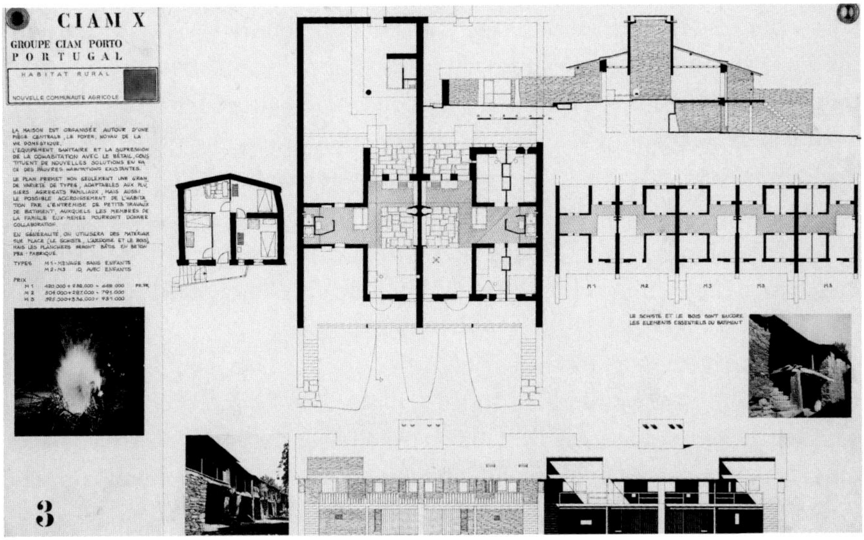

fig. 7 Group CIAM Porto – CIAM X. Rural Habitat. A New Agricultural Community (1956). Panel 3 – Detailed Plan. Source: CEAU-FAUP.

spontaneously generated as plants, from a family and social life in equilibrium with its milieu [...]."

Hermant's quote provides the key to understanding the Portuguese CIAM group's approach to the design of a rural community. The boundaries between the categories of natural and artistic, spontaneous and designed, the organic and the mechanical, are deliberately blended. The pastoral vision of rural houses developed by the people themselves as plants in equilibrium with their milieu was contrasted with a denunciation of the wretched conditions in which the rural population was living. Craftsmanship was balanced with the "beautiful mechanical precision" of modern methods. Hence, the group attempted to demonstrate that architecture could become the vehicle for transporting the experience of modernity to the countryside and thus become a form of emancipation for rural communities.

The Machine in the Garden

The projects presented at CIAM 10 by the four groups discussed above share common tenets suggesting a re-humanization of architecture and the creation of new forms of community in the mid-1950s. In all these projects, one can find a common incentive to challenge binary polarities and to cope with the tensions brought about by a difficult balance between machinist civilization and vernacular tradition. The project developed by the CIAM Portugal group for a rural community explored new possibilities of dwelling in the countryside, negotiating pastoral and counter-pastoral visions of the rural world. The team's approach investigated the qualities of vernacular tradition beyond a mere appraisal of its bucolic qualities. Indeed, with their portrayal of people's dire living conditions, they transcended the imagined qualities of rural communities in the countryside as an idyllic and romanticized habitat. Both the scheme's urban layout and the design of the housing unit reveal a commitment to upgrading the living standards of the community, nevertheless preserving the identifying devices and formal references at both scales.

In similar fashion to the Portuguese group, the projects presented at Dubrovnik in 1956 by the English, Dutch and Norwegian groups proposed a contaminated modernity. These lie between a pastoral vision of vernacular references as a model to foster conciliation between individual and community, and a counter-pastoral motivation to portray challenges faced by people living in the rural world. They underline the ethical role of the architectural discipline in catering for social change and a universal drive to sponsor the betterment of living conditions in the countryside. They attempted to demonstrate, I would argue, the possibility of an architecture of dwelling that challenges the polar opposition between the domus and the megalopolis.

This liminal condition resonates with what Leo Marx calls the middle landscape, a place between art and nature.[24] Marx argues that in Virgil's Arcadia, "Tityrus is spared the deprivations and anxieties associated with both the city and the wilderness." Marx goes further: "Although he is free of the repressions entailed by a complex civilization, he is not prey to the violent uncertainties of nature. [...] Living in an oasis of rural pleasure, he enjoys the best of both worlds – the sophisticated order of art and the simple spontaneity of nature."[25]

CIAM's engagement with the rural world at the 1956 congress in Dubrovnik thus epitomized this search for the middle landscape. It attempted to promote the best of two worlds – the urbanity of universal civilization and the humanism of vernacular tradition – in overcoming the nostalgic appeal for the *Heimat*. In the idea of the middle landscape, the tenets of modernity can be conciliated with local cultures, in contrast to Henry Adams' Manichean image of the Virgin and the Dynamo, where the latter "represents an industrial society that threatens [...] to destroy the creative power embodied in the Virgin."[26] Hence, in the 1950s, to paraphrase the title of Marx's book, the drive to re-humanize architecture and develop new forms of community showed that the machine can be accommodated in the garden.

Endnotes

1 See Marshall Berman, *All That Is Solid Melts into Air: The Experience of Modernity* (New York and London: Verso Books, 2010), 140.

2 Leo Marx, *The Machine in the Garden: Technology and the Pastoral Ideal in America*, 35 Anniversary edition (Oxford: Oxford University Press, 2000), 347.

3 Henry Adams, *The Education of Henry Adams: An Autobiography* (Boston and New York: Houghton Mifflin Harcourt, 2000), 385.

4 José Ortega y Gasset, *The Revolt of the Masses* (New York and London: W.W. Norton & Company, 1964), 92.

5 Ibid., 82.

6 Martin Heidegger, "Building Dwelling Thinking," in *Poetry, Language, Thought*, trans. Albert Hofstadter (New York: Harper & Row, 1971), 145–161.

7 Jean-François Lyotard, *The Inhuman: Reflections on Time* (Cambridge: Polity Press, 1991), 191–204.

8 Neil Leach, "The Dark Side of the Domus," *The Journal of Architecture*, 3:1 (1998), 31.

9 Leach's critical account on potential violence that underscores the domesticated household in Heidegger's idea of dwelling is chiefly inspired by Lyotard's essay "*Domus* and the Megalopolis." See Lyotard, *The Inhuman*, 191–204: the essay was republished in 1996 in Leach's *Rethinking Architecture.*

10 The so-called Doorn Manifesto was republished in Joan Ockman, *Architecture Culture: 1943–1968* (New York: Rizzoli, 1993), 183.

11 MARS Group and John Voelcker, "Rural Resettlement" (La Sarraz, September 1955), BAKEt129, NAI, Bakema Archive.

12 Ockman, *Architecture Culture*, 181.

13 MARS Group (Alison and Peter Smithson), "Fold Houses Grid" – Panel 4 (Dubrovnik, 1956), BAKEf13, NAI, Bakema Archive.

14 Francis Strauven, *Aldo van Eyck: The Shape of Relativity* (Amsterdam: Architectura & Natura, 1998), 144.

15 Aldo van Eyck had been engaged with the plan for Nagele since 1947 as a member of "de8," the Dutch CIAM group. Different versions of this plan were presented at CIAM congresses held at Bergamo (1949) and Hoddesdon (1951). Van Eyck did not attend these two congresses. The project presented at Dubrovnik corresponds to the second phase of the plan's design, which resulted chiefly from van Eyck's ideas.

16 See Aldo van Eyck, "Bouwen in de Zuidelijke Oasen," *Forum*, 1 (January 1953), 28–37.

17 This observation is further validated by the fact that Bakema had been involved with the Nagele plan since 1952.

18 Max Risselada and Dirk van den Heuvel, eds., *Team 10, 1953–1981: In Search of a Utopia of the Present* (Rotterdam: NAi Publishers, 2005), 58–59.

19 Arne Korsmo, Geir Grung and G. S. Gundersen, "CIAM 10 Grid" (Dubrovnik, 1956), BAKEf17, NAI, Bakema Archive.

20 The official delegates of the Portuguese group at CIAM 10 were Viana de Lima and Fernando Távora.

21 The importance of surveys as support for urban planning had already been pointed out in Patrick Geddes' *Cities in Evolution,* published in 1915. See

Patrick Geddes, *Cities in Evolution: An Introduction to the Town Planning Movement and to the Study of Civics* (London: Williams & Norgate, 1915), 329–338.

22 CIAM Porto, "Group Porto, Portugal. Description de la grille" (Dubrovnik, August 7, 1956), 42–JT–13–32/33, gta archive.

23 The "Survey of Portuguese Regional Architecture" was a collective endeavor that became highly influential for the generation of young architects active in Portugal in the 1950s and 1960s. See João Leal, *Arquitectos, Engenheiros, Antropólogos: Estudos Sobre Arquitectura Popular No Século XX Português* (Porto: Fundação Instituto José Marques da Silva, 2009).

24 My use of the notion of "middle landscape" reflects generically Leo Marx's use of the term as a place between art and nature. It does not adhere specifically to Peter G. Rowe's account of "middle landscape" as the suburban metropolitan development of single-family homes, shopping centers, corporate offices and roadway systems as portrayed in Rowe's *Making a Middle Landscape*. See Peter G. Rowe, *Making a Middle Landscape* (Cambridge, Mass.: MIT Press, 1991).

25 Marx, *The Machine in the Garden*, 22.

26 Ibid., 349.

Domonkos Wettstein

A Desire for Innocence? Community and Recreational Architecture around Lake Balaton

"Social origin and positions are left in the changing room with the clothes" – so it was said at Lake Balaton. This especially concerned Lake Balaton in the 1960s, where visitors from a wide range of social levels could relax together in the spirit of consolidation after the suppressed Hungarian revolution of 1956. And it also became a popular meeting point among East and West German tourists, as an even wider gap opened in the Iron Curtain.

Balaton lakeshore development (1957–1968) gave architects opportunities to re-engage with modernism after the post-revolution lessening of socialist-realist pressures, while the country's technology and economic indicators lagged far behind those of Western European countries. This chapter aims to uncover which alternative solutions were drafted by young architects participating in the lakeshore's development, by repositioning modernism within local conditions.

The Balaton district had been a popular holiday resort before the Second World War, but only the upper-middle class was able to afford to take a vacation on the lakeshore at that time. In the 1930s, simple, graceful summer houses were built on newly allocated plots, while owners established bathing associations as grassroots movements. These civic organizations, along with promoting cultural life, actively participated in the development of community areas. Among those striving to develop Balaton architecture, the role of

fig. 1 "You cannot tell apart their children in the water anymore." Source: Vályi, *Balaton*, 65.

young architects deserves highlighting; especially that of Iván Kotsis.[1] Kotsis placed a huge emphasis on elaborating principles for holiday homes that took into consideration regional characteristics.[2] His adaptive way of thinking was greatly influenced by the "haggard and dry regionalism" of German architect Paul Schmitthenner.[3] The Second World War interrupted the process, and during the years after the war, emphasis was placed on the reconstruction of Budapest and on solutions to social problems, which pushed the development of the Balaton region into the background.[4]

Following the unsuccessful 1956 revolution against Communist dictatorship and Soviet occupation, Balaton development became an important tool for social consolidation. The new political system – in order to stabilize its power – intended to make lakeshore holidays available for a wider spectrum of society, primarily for the working class.

These social changes are clearly visible in a photo book published in 1962[5] (fig. 1). The book is narrated by Gyula Illyés, a realist poet highly sensitive to social problems: "You can tell rural grandparents apart from Budapest people walking along the lake. Still. However, you can no longer tell their children in the water apart."[6]

The new government decided to commence large-scale development on the lakeshore in 1957 (fig. 2). It took quite a while for the bureaucracy to re-establish power after the 1956 collapse, however, and this gap in state control left freedom for architects to manage the design processes.

fig. 2 Motel in Tihany planned by Charles Polónyi. Source: Vályi, *Balaton*, 72.

A Change of Perspective: from the Unique Region to Architecture

The key figure in this development was the architect and urban designer Tibor Farkas.[7] At the beginning of 1957, the ministry of construction ordered the state-owned urban design bureau, Városépítési Tervező Vállalat (VÁTERV),[8] to make regional draft plans for the tourist development of the Balaton area and, in addition, the ministry established the position of chief architect as an authority. The young architect Farkas was assigned to compile the Balaton Regional Plan and was the first chief architect, as well. His task was to plan, manage and control the large-scale development within three to five years. In fact, he played a pioneering role. There were no examples to follow in terms of methodical approach.[9]

Farkas conferred with prominent figures in the Academy of Sciences, but they could provide no real advice. However, this also meant that the new chief architect was free to plan as he wished. A year earlier, he had successfully managed the large-scale restoration work following a flood along the Danube, and had proven his practical way of thinking.

Planning then started by thoroughly examining the Balaton region. Initial drafts were often put on paper on site. At the time, no separate positions for regional designers existed, so architects, cooperating with engineers, economists and geographers, jointly discussed all issues and tasks with an interdisciplinary approach. As Farkas recalled: "We were to disregard any artificial borders between regional planning, urban planning and architecture."

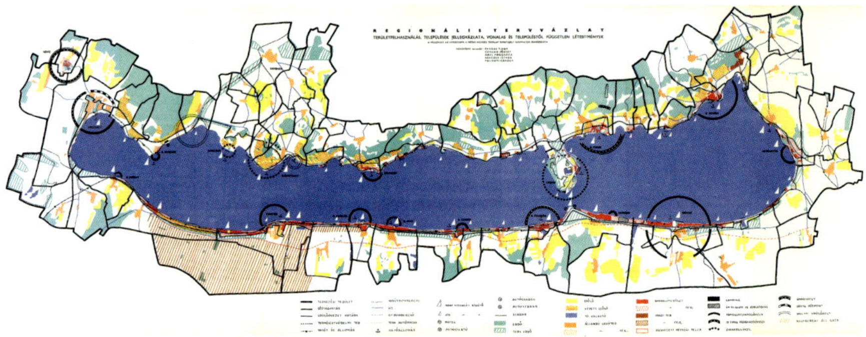

fig. 3 The unique landscape development: Balaton Regional Plan, 1957. Source: *Magyar* Építőművészet 7 (1958/4–5) 145.

The regional plan was built on simple, pragmatic principles such as planning from large to small. The three-scale approach meant a novel structure; it focused on a regional scale that could still handle the entire region as an organic unit (fig. 3). The resulting plan was four meters in length and was presented at the Union Internationale des Architectes (UIA) regional-planning conference at Liège, Belgium, in 1958. Circles showed the different functions of the settlement and the main tourist destinations. Settlement development plans detailed the regional concept, as well as dictating the building of the most relevant community buildings.

For architects, there were "co-ordination plans," drafting locations and architectural characteristics. These unique types of plans meant "a bridge over the gap between urban designers and architects."[10] In many cases, the chief architect and his colleagues were client, authority and designer all in one person, because of the centralized development in the frame of state socialism.

Their special concern for ecological and integrated design is confirmed by the fact that initially they managed to change the government's intention to create separate "Golden Beaches" for Western tourists, as with the Black Sea coast of Romania and Bulgaria.[11] Instead, Farkas and his team saw the entire region as a living organism that they aimed to renew primarily by technical and infrastructural development and that was at the time available for and addressed to inhabitants, vacationers and foreign tourists alike.

The plan gives a detailed description of natural and agricultural areas as well, thereby handling the region as a unique entity. It introduced strict rules protecting against landscape urbanism. This would allow designers, they said, to "have lakeshore towns swim in a large, contiguous green area." Although this approach was sensitive to nature, the large-scale development would transform the region into a "humanized" recreational landscape (fig. 4).

fig. 4 Integrated recreation unit fitted to Tihany Landscape. Source: Tibor Farkas's Archive.

Though Farkas was not allowed to participate for political reasons, the regional plan was greatly appreciated by Western professionals at the UIA congress in Liège. Following this success, Hungary became the leading regional-development expert among the countries of the Council for Mutual Economic Assistance.[12] The development at Lake Balaton enjoyed international attention. Positive reviews appeared in international publications and finally, in 1965, the UIA awarded the plan the Sir Patrick Abercrombie Prize[13].

Modern Architecture on a "Primitive" Path

Buildings representing the main ideas of the regional plan played a major role in its success in international forums. New lakeside buildings were designed by a postwar generation of architects who had been inspired by modern architecture during their university years[14] – however, these designers started their careers in the midst of socialist realism pressures.[15] At the end of the 1950s, as modern architecture legalization took place while the lakeshore planning was in development, their works were characterized by inventive shapes and structures as well as experimental attempts. This chapter will examine specific examples by Charles Polónyi at Siófok and Fonyód.

To cater to the increasing tourist demand, Polónyi, one of the chief engineers, worked out a variable frame structure[16] (fig. 5). The light style of these buildings, unique and outstanding, became a trademark of Lake Balaton and its beaches. Polónyi's motto of a "soft touch to the nature" meant the team

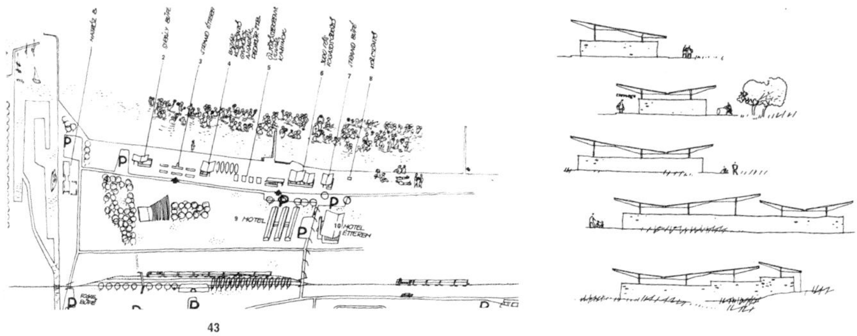

fig. 5 Variable frame structure planned by Charles Polónyi. Source: Newman, *CIAM '59 in Otterlo*, 43.

intended to avoid intruding upon the Balaton landscape by utilizing a modest scale and local building materials. Thermal insulation was achieved without special technical elements: temperature imbalances between sunny and shady sides of a building allowed air to circulate beneath the corrugated slate roof in all weathers. External walls were usually made of local stone, internal partition walls were made from brick, planks or sometimes fishing nets painted in different colors (fig. 6). Over two years, twenty-eight buildings with varied purposes were constructed at key locations: Siófok, Balatonfüred, Tihany and Badacsony.

New plans were introduced by Polónyi at the CIAM conference in Otterlo in 1959.[17] The young architect, who was the chief engineer of Balaton at this time, was attending instead of the Hungarian CIAM member József Fischer,[18] who had had to cancel his appearance at the final CIAM congress for political reasons. Polónyi presented the variable frame structures for the southern shore of Lake Balaton, showing the unified framework of the regional plan. In his presentation, he emphasized regional conditions including limited technical possibilities and low budgets.

His pragmatic planning approach could have reflected the theoretical questions of Team 10, which had an active role at the CIAM congress, and Polónyi later became part of the group. "Reality," the integral unity of creation, and "true expressions" of relationships between forms at various scales from a house to the city, were at the forefront of Team 10 thinking.[19] Their way was the opposite of the functional, analytical thinking of older members of CIAM, and led them back to Patrick Geddes' theory about the planned unity of the "Great Globe" and the "valley sections," which meant the socio-geographic integration of regions."[20] Geddes was the pioneer of regional planning; his works were republished in 1954, on the centennial of his birth.[21]

fig. 6 Prefabricated frame structure using local materials and workforce. Source: Newman, *CIAM '59 in Otterlo*, 42.

Polónyi also mentioned Geddes' influence on Team 10 in his memoirs: "He developed the 'diagnoses before treatment' and proposed 'conservative surgery.'"[22] This planning method may be reflected in the Balaton development, specifically in the complex unity of different scales, the environmental principles of development and the structural relations from regional to building levels.[23] Polónyi's presentation focused on adapting modern architecture to the technological level of underdeveloped regions, maintaining that modern architecture should find its "regional and primitive ways."[24] In this context, the expression "primitive" is free of negative connotations, meaning simply the adaptation to regional conditions.

Due to socioeconomic problems in Hungary, regional adaptation of Western European architectural trends had posed a continuous challenge for architects. Prewar Hungarian architecture witnessed the presence of a "mild" and more regional form of modernism, adapted to low-technological solutions.[25] Representatives of this path included the professors Iván Kotsis and Károly Weichinger, who had a major impact on the postwar generations of architects.[26] As Polónyi wrote: "My avant-gardism often revolted against Weichinger's romanticism, obviously inspired by the Nordic brick, but he taught us to 'humanize' modernism, by introducing some regional and historical elements into the design, which he always did with excellent taste, avoiding the pseudo or pastiche categories."[27] Humanizing architecture in this context meant the regional adaptation of modernism to a local historical and technological context.[28]

Personal Presence as a Way of Humanizing the Profession

Although the purpose of the architects was to integrate a wider segment of society by means of the lakeside facilities, in the wake of developments the increasing demands of tourism led to a differentiation in previously integrated conceptions. In order to cater to international tourism, large hotels were built, while increased areas were assigned to weekend-house construction for citizens.[29]

The central development assured the architectural quality of communal facilities planned by the selected architects from the state design companies, but problems appeared with the private holiday-home constructions of unskilled designers. Although the Balaton Regional Plan tried to have strict control of the cottage planning, the emerging problem was complex. Summer-house characteristics had significantly changed after the war: people traveling to Lake Balaton spent considerably less time there; only about two or three weeks. They spent most of this time in the open air, retreating indoors only when necessary. As the chief architect and his colleagues wrote: "You must accept that a holiday resort is not a wild savannah but a densely populated camping ground. As a result, accommodation to one another is a fundamental requirement here."[30]

The modern holiday house as a building type had no precursors at Lake Balaton; the vernacular architecture couldn't provide an example of this function. Despite the fact that the simplicity of the vernacular architecture in the Balaton Highlands[31] was set forth as a precedent by architecture journals, such copying of vernacular shapes was denied by the chief architect, as a holiday home had "different basic purposes." This lack of existing models resulted in heterogeneous solutions planned without architects.[32] In his memoirs, Polónyi examined the Balaton problem in light of Bernard Rudofsky's *Architecture Without Architects*,[33] and thought the issue was an ever-widening spectrum of building methods: "The house form and the settlement pattern of the spontaneous vernacular architecture is very strongly determined by the climatic conditions, availability of building material, construction skill and the common behavior patterns of people. In our age there is a wider variety of options at hand."[34]

Searching for regional solutions, the chief architect and his colleagues controlled holiday-home plans personally and suggested corrections for clients. In addition, private constructions were supported with building types, prefabricated elements, panels and structures requiring active participation by involved residents. The ministry of construction launched a tender for planning small, modern holiday homes.[35] Based on these plans, the ministry of internal trade had DIY buildings and prefabricated elements made. Plans

fig. 7 On-site meeting with Charles Polónyi. Source: Charles Polónyi's Archive.

used conventional building methods, local building materials and simple tools as well as prefabricated construction elements so that buildings could be easily and rapidly constructed. Plans were available from the ministry for anyone interested, at a reasonable price.

The architects showed solidarity with local communities. As noted above, it took time for bureaucracy to reassert power after the 1956 events, and designers managed to utilize this to their benefit, personally participating in certification processes. They managed presentations, discussions and held on-site meetings for clients, according to their belief that "the best decisions are easiest to make on site." Tibor Farkas and his colleagues not only managed to influence their clients' approaches with empathy and patience but had a major impact on the attitudes of the administrative authorities, as has been discussed (fig. 7).

A voluntary-architect movement also played a key role in the plan's success. The Hungarian Association of Architects initiated a patron movement to support local objectives. Several faculties of the Budapest Technical University participated in this move by involving students in planning preparation and other tasks. Forty architects of the patron movement undertook the supporting of a town each. Architects gave *pro-bono* technical advice or provided detailed plans to local communities when needed.

The leaders of the large state-design bureaus often asked "Why do some architects go lounging to the lake?"[36] Whether or not it was "lounging" to take part in development, Polónyi may provide a final word: "While I could feel as I was the 'viceroy' of the Southern shore of the lake, my way of life was quite sportive. Six out of seven nights of the week I slept in a tent on my little Star-class dinghy boat, which was moored to the pier of the yacht club. When the weather was very stormy, I used to take my sleeping bag into the dressing room of the club."[37]

This anecdote may indicate the enthusiastic attitude of the architects. The humanization of architecture not only meant rethinking shapes and conceptions, but given the position of architects in the community, it also meant emphatic participation in social life. The position between vocation and vacation established experimental territory that was able to provide the opportunity to recreate the practice of architecture.

Architecture Re-Creation

Hungarian architects often mention the Balaton project nostalgically. The expression "architecture of innocence" appears in several recollections. The term "innocence" refers to enthusiastic and playful experimentation[38] while planning small collective facilities and holiday homes. But could this project as a whole be addressed as being innocent?

The development was an ambivalent project on the part of the new Communist government. Lake Balaton, providing an illusion of freedom, served the recreation of society after the revolution had failed, while the planning of small collective facilities made the re-creation of architecture possible for designers then breaking free from ideological pressure. The creative adaptation to local conditions led architects onto a new regional path of modernism.

For a short time, the Balaton lakeshore provided an escape for architects from everyday practice. But after a few years, economic and sociopolitical changes forced an increase in the scale of tourism that led to differentiation of the integrated social concepts and the spread of urbanization. At last, in 1968, the so-called New Economic Mechanism abolished Farkas's authority as chief architect and this process resulted in the even more ambivalent appearance of the scenic framework of leisure at Lake Balaton.

Endnotes

1 Iván Kotsis (1889–1980) was an architect and professor at Budapest Technical University (now Budapest University of Technology and Economics), and a corresponding member of the Academic of Sciences (MTA); see Endre Prakfalvi, *Kotsis Iván: Életrajzom* (Budapest: HAP, Magyar Építészeti Múzeum, 2010).

2 Iván Kotsis, "Művészet a Balatoni építkezésekben," *Tér és Forma*, 4:2–4 (1931), 8–10.
3 András Ferkai, "Architecture Between the Two World Wars," in *The Architecture of Historic Hungary*, eds. József Sisa, Dora Wiebenson (Cambridge, Mass.: MIT Press, 1998), 275–304.
4 István Kisléghi-Nagy, "A Balaton-táj fejlesztése építészeti szempontból; tárgyalási alapul szolgáló javaslat a MÉSZ részére," *Magyar Építőművészet*, 6:1–2 (1957), 51–52.
5 Gábor Vályi, ed., *Balaton* (Budapest: Corvina, 1962).
6 Translation by the author. Original text: "Őket (nagyszülőket) még meg lehet különböztetni a pesti sétálók közt. Gyermekeiket a vízben nem." Source: Vályi, *Balaton*, 75.
7 Tibor Farkas (1922–2015) worked in VÁTERV from 1951; his first regional work was flood-restoration works around the town of Mohács. Between 1957 and 1971, Farkas was a key member of the Balaton Executive Committee and led the regional-planning process. In 1965, his planning group was awarded the UIA Abercrombie Prize in Paris.
8 Városépítési Tervező Vállalat (VÁTERV) was founded in 1950 as a state-owned planning bureau for urban, regional and landscape planning. The name was changed in 1967 to Városépítési Tudományos és Tervező Intézet (VÁTI).
9 Detailed analysis of the regional planning process in Domonkos Wettstein, "Historical Analysis of Regional Planning of Balaton," *Pollack Periodica*, 8:1 (2013), 141–152.
10 György Tőkés, Tibor Farkas, "A területi koordináció gyakorlati kérdései Siófok központjának átépítése kapcsán," *Városépítés*, 4:3 (1967), 31.
11 Michael Zinganel, Elke Beyer, "'Beside the Seaside…' Architectures of a Modern Global Longing," in *Holidays After The Fall: Seaside Architecture and Urbanism in Bulgaria and Croatia*, eds. Zinganel, Beyer, Anke Hagemann (Berlin: Jovis Verlag, 2013), 35–53.
12 Council for Mutual Economic Assistance (COMECON, CMEA) was an economic organization of the Eastern Bloc countries under the leadership of the Soviet Union (1949–1991).
13 The 1965 Abercromibie Prize was shared by Colin Buchanan for the Oxford Street Plan; see "Abercrombie Prize," *UIA Journal*, 34 (1965), 12.
14 Architects in the large state-design companies worked for the Balaton development: Zoltán Farkasdy (KÖZTI), Zoltán Gulyás (IPARTERV), Ferenc Callmeyer (IPARTERV). The two chief engineers on the Balaton project worked part-time for design companies as architects: Charles Polónyi (IPARTERV), István Bérczes (KÖZTI).
15 Endre Prakfalvi, et al., *Modern és szocreál. Építészet és tervezés Magyarországon 1945–1959* (Budapest, Magyar Építészeti Múzeum, 2006).
16 Charles Polónyi (1928–2002) was an architect and town planner, later a member of Team 10. He worked for the Balaton Executive Committee as chief engineer of the southern shore of Lake Balaton (1957–1960). Parallel to the Balaton project, Polónyi worked at the Design Bureau for Industrial Buildings (IPARTERV) in Budapest. Between 1963 and 1969, he worked for the Ghana National Construction Corporation as architect and was a professor in Kumasi. From 1969 to 1980, he worked in Nigeria, Algeria and Ethiopia. After his return to Budapest, he was leader of the Urban Design Bureau of Budapest and professor at the Budapest Technical University.

17 Oscar Newman, *CIAM '59 in Otterlo* (Stuttgart: Karl Krämer Verlag, 1961), 42–47.
18 József Fischer (1901–1995) was an architect and leader of the Hungarian group CIAM. As a politician, Fischer was a member of the Social Democratic Party and a minister during the 1956 revolution.
19 Annie Pedret, *Team 10: An Archival History* (London, New York: Routledge, 2011), 124–165.
20 Pedret, *Team 10: An Archival History*, 127–131.
21 Volker M. Welter, "Post-war CIAM, Team X, and the Influence of Patrick Geddes," accessed October 15, 2015, http://www.team10online.org/research/papers/delft1/welter.pdf.
22 Charles K. Polónyi, *An Architect-Planner on the Peripheries: Case Studies from the Less Developed World. The Retrospective Diary of Charles K. Polonyi.* (Budapest: P&C Kiadó, 1992), 49.
23 For Geddes' influence on regional planning in Hungary, see Domonkos Wettstein, "The Balaton Region as an Experimental Territory: Positions of Architecture in the Emergence of Regional Planning for Recreation in Hungary," Építés-Építészettudomány, 44:1–2 (2016), 129–177.
24 Polónyi's presented material archived in Het Nieuwe Institute (formerly the Netherlands Architecture Institute, NAI), BAKE 0176 (22-0176) Bakema J.B. f22–f33.
25 Pamer Nóra, *Magyarország építészete a két világháború között* (Budapest: Terc Kiadó, 2001), 104–112.
26 Károly Weichinger (1893–1982) was an architect, professor and head of the Department for Public Buildings at Budapest Technical University.
27 Polónyi, *An Architect Planner on the Peripheries*, 41–42.
28 During the war, a required trip to Denmark by architecture students amplified the effects of Nordic modernism, then in the 1950s, classic Scandinavian modernism was used as an example against socialist realism. Alternative modernism using modern local materials and regional samples had an impact on the new generation of architects who designed several structures along the lakeshore. See Mária Palasik, *A Műegyetemisták Odüsszeiája 1944–1946* (Budapest: Műegyetemi Kiadó, 2007).
29 Mariann Simon, "Hungarian Sea Promises a Rich Summer: Collective Good and Economic Interest in Socialist Leisure Architecture," in *Proceedings of the 2nd International Conference of the European Architectural History Network*, eds. Hilde Heynen, Janina Gosseye (Brussels: Koninklijke Vlaamse Academie van Belgie voor Wetenschappen en Kunsten, 2012), 480–484.
30 Translation by the author. Original text: "*Tudomásul kell vennünk, hogy az üdülőterület nem vadon, hanem sűrűn települt táborhely. Tehát az egymáshoz alkalmazkodás térben és formában feltétlen követelmény.*" Source: Farkas, Polónyi, István Bérczes, Károly Kisléghy Nagy, "Beszámoló a Balatonkörnyék fejlesztéséről," *Magyar Építőművészet*, 9:6 (1960), 15–26.
31 Kálmán Tóth, Miklós Nászay, *A Balaton vidék népének építészete* (Budapest: Balatoni Intéző Bizottság, 1936).
32 Farkas, Zoltán Csorba, "A Balaton-környék építési rendje," *Magyar Építőművészet*, 12:5 (1963), 58–59.
33 Bernard Rudofsky, *Architecture Without Architects: A Short Introduction to Non-Pedigreed Architecture* (Albequerque: University of New Mexico Press, 1964).

34 Polónyi, *An Architect-Planner on the Peripheries*, 31.
35 Ferenc Callmeyer, "Hétvégiház pályázat," *Magyar Építőművészet*, 9:1 (1960), 23–29.
36 Farkas, "Ahogy én látom a Balaton-ügy 30 évét I. rész," *Magyar Építőművészet*, 2 (1988), 44–47.
37 Polónyi, *An Architect-Planner on the Peripheries*, 27.
38 That Polónyi benefited from the experience of the Lake Balaton development is evident in his projects in Africa; see Ákos Moravánszky, "Peripheral Modernism: Charles Polónyi and the Lessons of the Village," *Journal of Architecture*, 17:3 (2012), 333–359.

Michael Zinganel

Unexpected Side Effects: Indirect Benefits of International Mass Tourism on Croatia's Adriatic Coast

Tourism in President Tito's Yugoslavia, as in certain other countries like communist Bulgaria and Romania and in Italy, Portugal and Spain, but also in alpine resorts in Western democracies like France, Austria and Switzerland, was welcomed as a motor of modernization: a means to transform what had been a primarily agricultural society. After Yugoslavia's rift with Stalinist USSR in 1948 and its co-founding of the Non-Aligned Movement in 1961, the symbolic role of tourism became of major importance there[1]: tourism operations were therefore conceived as monuments of modernization, combining explicitly modern architecture, design and lifestyle to serve as meeting points of national and transnational reconciliation where the success of Yugoslavia's Third Way policies, along with its distinct cosmopolitanism and unique system of socialist self-management, could be clearly communicated to both domestic and international publics (fig. 1).

The aim of this paper is to inquire first whether or to what extent the socio-spatial solutions for international mass tourism, as developed under these particular conditions – "in-between" East and West – were distinct from those developed elsewhere[2]; and second whether or to what extent the specific political situation in postwar Yugoslavia, the system of self-management, the interconnection of avant-garde art and architecture, and the principles

fig. 1 President Tito looking at the model of the planned conference hotel Adriatic II in Opatija, ca. 1971. Source: Archive of Hrvatski Muzej Turizma Opatija.

of tourist choreography co-contributed to a re-humanization of modernist planning doctrines.

Socialist Self-Management in Tourism and Planning

The widespread belief that land and property belong to all and that everyone should have the right of unlimited access to the seaside was arguably specifically socialist; but the most distinctive feature of Yugoslavia's Third Way policies was represented by the economic system combining "social market economy" and "workers' self-management." This system was first established in the early 1950s, but was only gradually implemented and expanded in different economic sectors, also in large tourism enterprises and the planning and building companies designing and constructing these facilities. Major commercial tourism operations were neither private nor nationalized (those existed in Yugoslavia as well[3]): they were "social property." Coastal municipalities or counties (*općine*) founded "socialized catering and hospitality companies" (*društvena ugostiteljska poduzeća*) and handed them over to the collective administration of the employees, which then democratically elected a workers council and management. Managers had to apply to national banks (and international development programs) for the credit necessary to expand the enterprise and to the regional Party administration for building permits. Socialized tourism companies typically did not build and manage single hotels. In general, they took responsibility for all the major tourist facilities and services of a municipality or county, an island or peninsula: for accommodation from camping sites to hotels, for restaurants, entertainment facilities and means of transport (only supplemented by small-scale private services). And since these companies were also obliged to pursue social objectives, such as full employment and social equality, the local population and the staff strongly identified themselves with the "socialized" tourism companies they perceived themselves as co-owners of.[4]

In Croatia alone, countless bays, peninsulas and islands just offshore amount to 5,835 kilometers of coastline, among the dramatic steep cliffs, gently rolling hills and flat, pebbly beaches of which nestle beautiful historic port towns. Here, the varied topography virtually cried out for a diverse range of architectural typologies, and in general this was in fact realized, often (but not always) with rather high quality, reflecting the late-modernist ideas being discussed in the professions of tourism economy and urban and architectural planning in both East and West.[5]

In federal Yugoslavia and especially Croatia, as distinct from in centralized state-socialist regimes (Bulgaria, for example), commissions for tourism projects were awarded to a broad spectrum of planners: professors at design institutes in the faculties of architecture, urban-planning offices originally founded by the state, planning departments of large industrial companies, big architecture firms under "socialist self-management," and even a few privileged architects and artists operating privately on a smaller scale.[6] Realized projects were often based on pre-existing urban-development plans and design competitions, also published in architecture magazines,[7] but were also repeatedly awarded to architects who had successfully gained the confidence of local managers. The economic success of local tourism enterprises motivated other big firms from around Yugoslavia to found their own coastal-tourism enterprises in the late 1960s, in order to host their employees during holidays (as with many earlier social-tourism projects) but also to gain hard international currency for improving their trade balances.[8]

From "Social Tourism" to a Mass-Market Consumer Paradise

Established tourism infrastructures and architectures had existed on the Croatian Adriatic before Tito's day, however. When the Socialist Federal Republic of Yugoslavia (SFYR) was established in 1945, private hotels, grand restaurants, magnificent villas, transport companies and travel agencies that had been established during the Austro-Hungarian Empire, then the Kingdom of Yugoslavia, were nationalized then merged to form new, large "socialized" enterprises under "workers' self-management."

Clearly, for the new socialist government in Yugoslavia, creating whatever it took to ensure that the domestic population could go to the seaside was more of a priority than opening up the land to foreigners – at least in the rhetoric of its early years in power. First, a system of "social tourism" was established, both at existing sites built during the periods of monarchy and then nationalized, but also in new purpose-built facilities. An extensive network of

fig. 2a Social Tourism Facilities built by the Yugoslav National Army: Children's holiday home in Krvavica near Makarska, currently vacant. Architect: Rikard Marasović, 1961–64. © Photo: Wolfgang Thaler 2009.

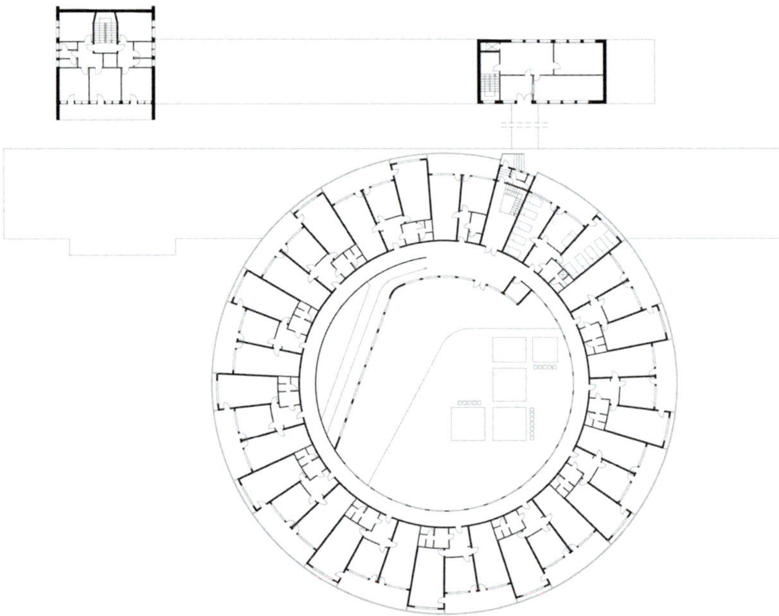

fig. 2b Children's holiday home in Krvavica near Makarska, upper floor. Architect: Rikard Marasović, 1961–64. Drawing by Nikolina Džeko

holiday homes and camps was introduced, each reserved exclusively for staff and/or members of a particular trade union, state administrative unit, youth organization, large "socialized company" or for the Yugoslav National Army (fig. 2). As in postwar France, domestic tourism was considered a tool for nation building and reconciliation – in Yugoslavia, it helped enable the population to know and respect the different cultures of their fellow citizens in the multiethnic federation of republics (many had fought one another in the war years). It was originally planned to establish attractive new destinations

fig. 3a Tourist Village on the island of Sveti Nikola. Source: Archive of Valamar Riviera Poreč. In 1953 Rivijera, the first commercial tourism company during the socialist period, was founded in Poreč: a hotel built during the Austrian-Hungarian monarchy at the very end of the ancient town's peninsula and a small aristocratic castle on the adjacent island of St. Nikola (Sveti Nikola) had been first nationalized and then merged into a self-managed company. Small prefab shelters for modest accommodation had been erected around the park while the old castle and a new pavilion had been used as a public space offering "modern" services and amenities.

fig. 3b Prefab shelters in the pine forest of the resort at Pical. Source: Archive of Valamar Riviera Poreč.

for domestic travelers across the six republics. But from the very start, there was a clear favorite when it came to holiday destinations: the Adriatic coast.[9]

According to architecture critic Maroje Mrduljaš, the first "new" type of tourist resort (*odmarališta*) introduced for social-tourism purposes illustrates the architectural and social vision of "socialist leisure" perfectly: modest one-story pavilions designed as guest-accommodation units, clustered around a social center (*Društveni dom*), a comparably large central building housing a restaurant and other communal facilities for social encounters such as a mul-

fig. 4a Elevation of hotel Ambasador in Opatija. Architect: Zdravko Bregovac, 1966. Source: Hrvatski muzej arhitekture (The Croatian Museum of Architecture), Zagreb.

fig. 4b Source: Archive of Touristkommerc Zagreb © Photo: CCN-images Zagreb

tifunctional hall, a library, pool and chess rooms.[10] Earlier commercial resorts had been similarly designed: as pure camping sites with prefabricated pavilions, which then became increasingly large, more solidly built and more comfortably equipped, while semipublic buildings became more diversified with a range of services and entertainment (shops, restaurants, grills, open-air dance floors, enclosed nightclubs, etc.).[11] Today, smaller facilities like these are the typical elements that co-constitute the Croatian coastal-tourism landscape – still widely acclaimed by many tourists, because they had been placed in an elaborately landscaped setting, with free access to the seaside unconditionally guaranteed for all (figs. 3a, b).

The first newly built motels and hotels had been horizontal low-rise blocks partly elevated on pillars in a sober, modern design language, often consisting of several wings or arranged around courtyards in atrium style, or in clusters discreetly dotted in the pine forests. Individual private rooms remained small and modest, while social meeting spaces were designed in comparably "luxurious" dimensions. But Yugoslavia's cosmopolitanism also called for luxury conference hotels along the coast to show off international celebrities, from international politicians to movie stars hired by Yugoslavia's booming film industry. Therefore, in the mid-1960s, following international trends, a handful of solitary high-rise hotels were built at the edge of the coast and often at

fig. 5a Lobby of Hotel Ambasador, Architect: Zdravko Bregovac, 1966. Source: Archive of Touristkommerc Zagreb © Photo: CCN-images Zagreb

fig. 5b The large scale mural // big abstract-expressionist painting in the sky-bar on the 10th floor of Hotel Ambasador in Opatija by Edo Murtic, illustrates the mundane design of one of the flagship-hotels of the mid-1960s, typically supported by the implementation of modern artworks into the public zones of the hotels. Architect: Zdravko Bregovac, 1966. Source: Archive of Touristkommerc Zagreb © Photo: CCN-images Zagreb

the edge of ancient towns (Neven Šegvić's Hotel Excelsior, Dubrovnik, 1965; Zdravko Bregovac's Hotel Ambasador, Opatija, 1966) (figs. 4a, b). These hotels were no longer modest at all. They offered top standards, mundane interior design and explicitly modern artworks commissioned from the nation's most acknowledged contemporary artists[12] in a policy continued with most new hotels at the Adriatic coast that followed.[13] The style and amenities of these hotels and the curatorial practice had been inspired by Hilton International, the US hotel chain:[14] between communism and the American way of life, international guest were invited to enjoy the fruits of Yugoslavia's Third Way (figs. 5a, b).

When, by the end of the 1960s, demand for much higher capacities had increased, the solitary vertical slab or block was abandoned in favor of architectural types considered more compatible with the landscape. The challenge of designing large-capacity hotels, combining enormous interconnected volumes for public services and backstage zones with a large number of very

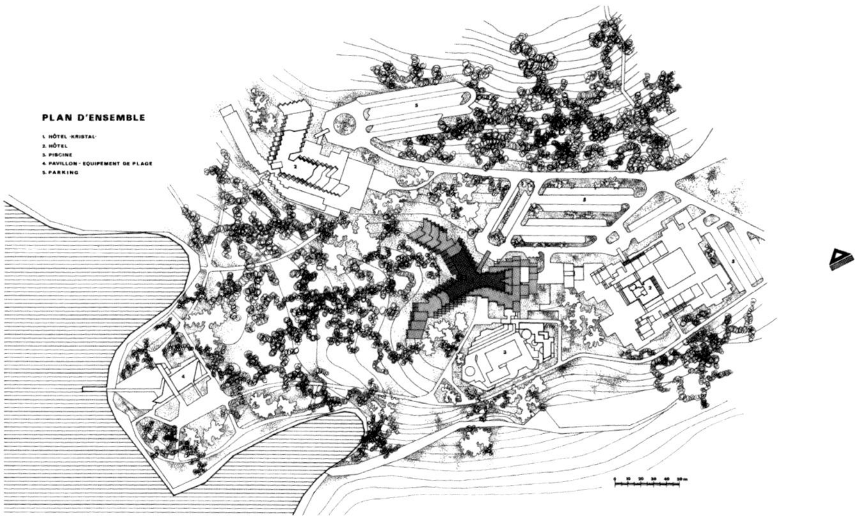

fig. 6a The resort as a structuralist landscape composed of various hotel categories, offering a wide range of amenities: site plan of the Brulo resort in Poreč. Architect: Julije De Luca, 1970. Source: Hrvatski muzej arhitekture (The Croatian Museum of Architecture), Zagreb.

small private-accommodation units, called for more dynamic organization. Large volumes had to be deconstructed and rearranged in new forms: producing clusters of smaller units that reproduced Mediterranean-village imagery (Igor Emili's Hotel Uvala Scott, Kraljevica, 1966–1969), for example, or combining several atrium or courtyard types in a large, seemingly lightweight ensemble (Boris Magaš's Hotel Solaris complex, Šibenik, 1967–1968). On the Croatian Adriatic, Yugoslavian architects and construction companies were compelled to find individual solutions both at gentle coastlines and at awkwardly sloping sites. Outstanding achievements at the Croatian coast included the blend of different building types and remarkable expertise in the use of sliding formworks for concrete cast in situ to realize spectacular structuralist formations in exposed concrete – despite rather limited financial resources. These include staggered complexes expanding as multilayered architectural landscapes in flat slopes of Istrian pine forests (Julije De Luca's Brulo, Poreč, 1970) and the terraced volumes skillfully embedded on rugged rock formations along the Dalmatian coast (Andrija Čičin-Šain and Žarko Vincek's Hotel Libertas, Dubrovnik, 1970) (figs. 6a–c, 7a–c).

The typology developed here was not typically "Yugoslav" or "Croatian." The different types appeared almost simultaneously at wide-ranging seaside destinations with landscapes showing similar characteristics: in socialist Romania and Bulgaria and the USSR's Crimean coast, for example, and in

fig. 6b The Hotel Kristal at the Brulo resort in Poreč, a dramatic orchestration of exposed concrete and natural stone, drawing on the architectural languages of Structuralism and the regional vernacular, 1970. Architect: Julije De Luca, 1970. Source: Hrvatski muzej arhitekture (The Croatian Museum of Architecture), Zagreb.

fig. 6c The terraced lobby of the Hotel Rubin at the Brulo resort in Poreč, and its impressive light and glass ceiling installation, sadly, neither of which has survived. Architect: Julije De Luca, 1970. Source: Hrvatski muzej arhitekture (The Croatian Museum of Architecture), Zagreb.

fascist Spain and Portugal, in redevelopments of Greece, Italy and France supported by the Marshall Plan, and even in Costa Rica, Hawaii and Mexico.[15]

But the call for a "lyrical value" of architecture by means of a new "monumentality" and "plasticity," as well as the call for a "synthesis of art and architecture" as first proclaimed by CIAM architects Sigfried Giedion and Josep Lluís Sert in 1943,[16] had been taken very seriously in Yugoslavia – distinct examples are found in impressive Second World War monuments (*Spomeniks*)[17] and also in some hotel designs of the late 1960s. Biographies of many people involved in planning and building these hotels show strong affiliations to art and even practices in the fields of both art and architecture. They therefore collaborated with each other[18] or at least inspired each other: Vjenceslav Richter, Zdravko Bregovac and Bernardo Bernardi, for example, had been co-founders of the transdisciplinary avant-garde artist group EXAT 51 based

figs. 7a, b A structuralist hotel complex in exposed concrete nestled organically into the rugged cliff face. Hotel Libertas, Dubrovnik. Architects: Andrija Čičin-Šain, Žarko Vincek, 1968–74. Source: Čovjek i prostor 1974, no. 258, 5.

fig. 7c Source: Archive of Touristkommerc Zagreb © Photo: CCN-images Zagreb

in Zagreb. After collaborating on the internationally acclaimed Yugoslavian pavilion at Expo '58 in Brussels,[19] Richter cofounded the artist group Nove Tendencije [New Tendencies][20] in 1961 and increasingly focused on visionary ideas for the synthesis of art and architecture (Sinturbanism, 1964), realized in kinetic sculptures that had been stimulating for many architects. Bernardi became famous for the design of furniture of and for buildings – important for the representation of Yugoslavia's policy – starting with Expo '58, Radničko sveučilište Moša Pijade (the workers' university) in Zagreb in 1961, instructing workers into socialist self-management, new international airports and many hotels. Bregovac devoted his later career exclusively to tourism architecture, translating avant-garde ideas into the practicalities of planning.[21]

Staging the Landscape

For the architects involved, in Croatia as well as in other coastal destinations, the rise of the tourism industry represented a very welcome opportunity for

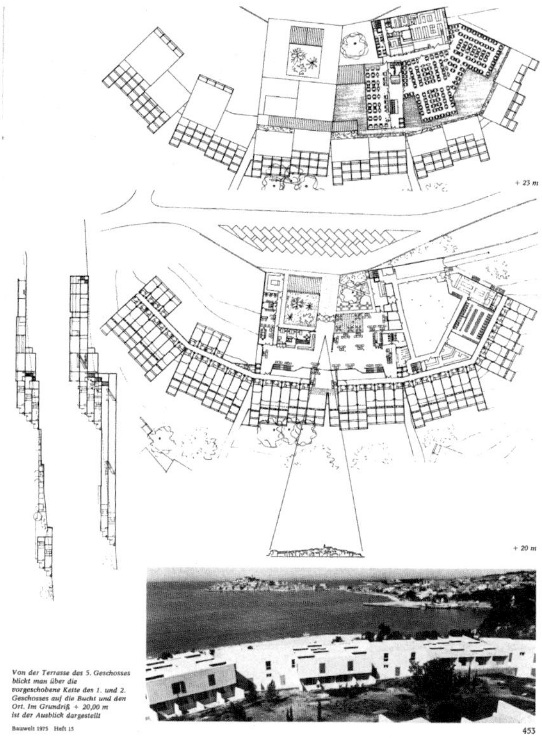

fig. 8a Architecture designed to direct and frame the tourists' gaze: After entering the lobby of hotel Marina Lučica, guests are immediately offered a spectacular view of the old town of Primošten. Architect: Lovro Perković, 1972. Source: *Bauwelt* 1975 Heft 15, 453.

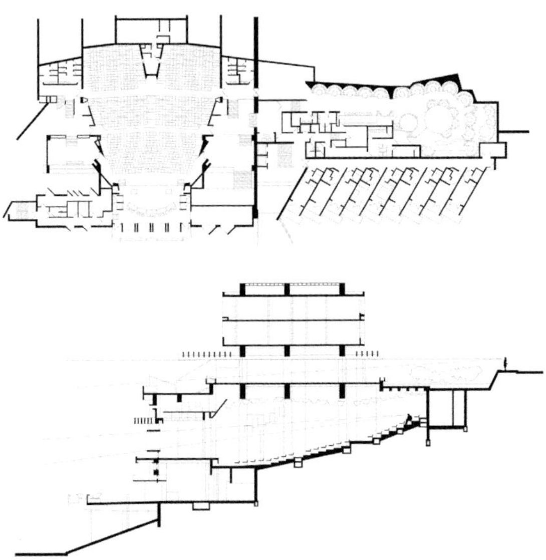

fig. 8b In the Hotel Adriatic II in Opatija even the main congress hall offered a spectacular sea-view. Architect: Branco Žnidarec, 1970–72. Public facilities were distributed throughout all sections of the hotel. Architect: Branko Žnidarec, 1971. Drawing: Kerstin Stramer.

spatial experiments but also for transgressing a modernist self-limitation into purely rational and functional modes.[22] Tourism architecture stages both landscape and people, but also becomes part of the landscape, encountered with all our senses but also endlessly reproduced in catalogs, postcards and

fig. 9a The Resort as a Collage of Different Types: Haludovo Resort in Malinska, Krk Island, Architect: Boris Magaš, 1971 / 72. Site plan of the entire resort in 2012. Drawing: Kerstin Stramer (Source: Arhitektura, Zagreb, 1972, no. 115, p. 34)
1 Reception, Gateman's lodge (vacant, last used as an architects' site office)
2 Hotel Palace, Category A, with both an indoor and outdoor pool (vacant ruin)
3 Hotel Tamaris, Category B (demolished)
4 Beach bar and restaurant (vacant ruin)
5 Bungalows, each with their own atrium (vacant ruins)
6 Terraced 2-storey apartment houses (renovated and in use)
7 Fishing port with restaurant and pier (renovated and in use)

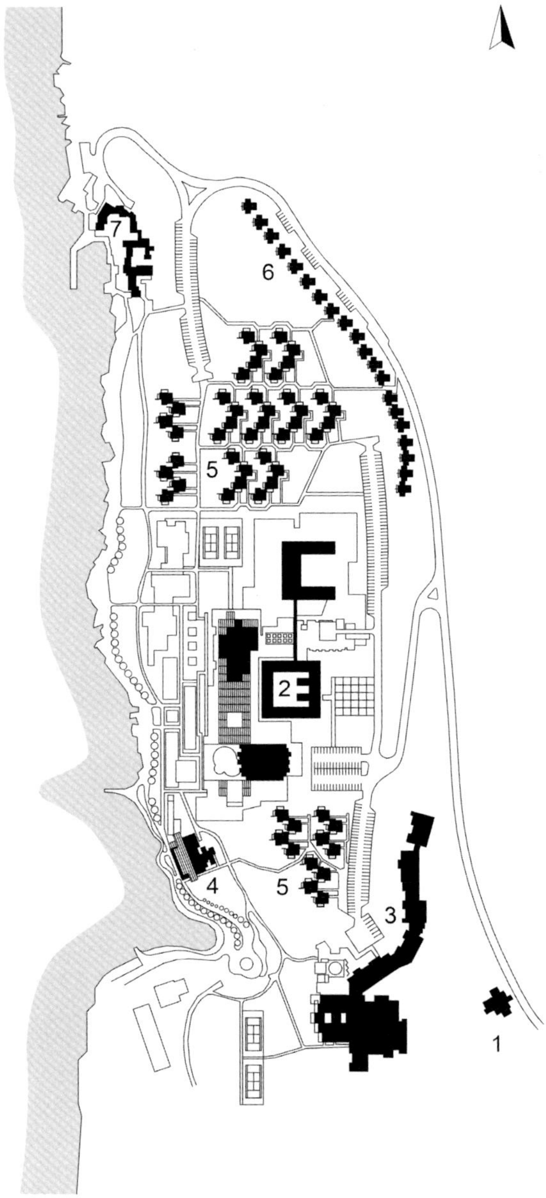

snapshots that trigger and substantiate the experience of tourists abroad and the narratives they recount once home again. At its best, tourism architecture is as modern as the tourist practice and the beach experience, yet conveys a destination's special qualities simultaneously, respecting tourists' longing for exceptional and even romantic experiences. It calls therefore for regional references, for the integration of local building traditions and materials, and

fig. 9b The pool area of Hotel Palace at the heart of the Haludovo resort. Architect: Boris Magaš, 1971/72. Source: Archive of Touristkommerc Zagreb © Photo: CCN-images Zagreb

fig. 9c The lobby of Hotel Palace. Source: Archive of Touristkommerc Zagreb © Photo: CCN-images Zagreb

the implementation of a more expressive and emotional design language. Architecture has to offer a set of stages and backstages, places to hide and places to meet and to perform. Architecture guides tourists' feet as well as their gazes along the most attractive sights and sites of the touristic landscape.

Architects brilliantly understood and supported these longings: plants permeated from the surrounding landscape onto semipublic, often terraced spaces, lobbies, dining rooms, staircases and room balconies. Entering the lobby, guests immediately enjoy a framed image of the seaside horizon, the silhouette of a Venetian village on a peninsula at a decent distance – at best the sun would even set behind the clock tower (figs. 8a, b). Harbor towns and fishing villages were interconnected by seaside promenades passing through pine forests. Dance floors placed near pools used vivid light reflections on the water to enhance the atmosphere.

During the short period of the boom years – between 1968 and 1972 – a number of brilliant new ensembles were built. Interestingly, the same architects simultaneously built both huge structuralist complexes and postmodern Mediterranean-style villages, in some cases next to each other,[23] as exemplified in the design of Haludovo (1971–1972), an entire resort by Boris Magaš on a bay on the island of Krk near the town of Malinska, commissioned by the firm Brodokomerc in Rijeka.

In the words of Magaš, Malinska was neither a Venetian pearl of a peninsula town nor a picturesque fishing port, and there was no guarantee of pleasant views or of opportunities for extensive sightseeing and leisure. The architect therefore chose to create a quaint mini-marina in the style of a small Mediterranean fishing port, offering mooring and an additional gastronomy zone at the edge of a landscaped park with a broad range of building types – including "classic civic references such as fortress walls, palaces and suburbs" – as if to create a persuasively urban ensemble.[24] The heart of the resort was the Hotel Palace. Here Magaš proved himself a virtuoso of gigantic volumes: the staggered heights and offset ground plans of almost all construction elements create a flowing space virtually without scale, whose appeal is further enhanced by fine horizontal slats on facades, the characteristic, slightly offset U-shaped concrete shells, gigantic pergolas enclosing buildings and interstices, and the elaborately landscaped setting. In contrast to the explicitly functional modern idiom of Magaš's first much-appraised hotel project – the Solaris complex in Šibenik –, which emphatically attests to his great admiration for Mies van der Rohe, Le Corbusier and Frank Lloyd Wright – he introduced here several postmodern elements – even associations with the Doge's Palace in Venice suddenly seemed permissible (figs. 9a, b).

Spatial Planning on the Adriatic Coast

Another outstanding characteristic of Yugoslav and Croatian tourist development was the strong tradition of and respect for urban and regional-planning expertise that followed principles of the international modernist avant-garde developed by CIAM architects in the 1930s, at their fifth congress in Paris. Following political calls for annual leave, paid holidays and the introduction of affordable modern holiday camps,[25] the architects and planners in their visionary design and manifestos rejected the binary opposition of rural and urban spheres for the first time, but redefined them as two directly related and mutually dependent spatial categories. The countryside was no longer seen as being inherently antimodern but rather as an additional locus of the genuinely modern practices of leisure and tourism in natural settings.[26]

Admittedly, the dire economic climate of the interwar period left only limited leeway for such ideas. Only after the Second World War did the Fordist segregation of production and reproduction begin to take hold on a significant scale all across Europe: the true "democratization" of travel set in as part of the economic boom of the 1950s but accelerated significantly in the 1960s when mass transportation first became affordable for the majority of people: with a strong effect on both those who traveled and those who benefit or suffer from the influx of tourists. But implementation had proceeded more cautiously in Yugoslavia than in other countries. There, as Mrduljaš argues, it was quickly realized that the success of tourism along the Adriatic coast relied directly on the preservation of spatial and environmental qualities. Each of the larger projects that were realized was preceded by a regional urban-design study.[27]

In 1963, the federal government of Yugoslavia asked the UN to help draft a comprehensive new development plan for the entire Yugoslav Adriatic coast and its hinterlands, which was conducted between 1967 and 1972.[28] International teams of planners from East and West,[29] experienced in large tourism and postcolonial urbanism projects all over the world, were invited to collaborate with local experts of different fields to develop a brilliantly effective toolkit for analyzing and representing the multidisciplinary research findings, then drawing rather optimistic development plans devoted to the dogma of unlimited economic growth, including brand-new resorts of urban size and density. But no large-scale resorts were realized that could compete in size with those built in socialist Bulgaria,[30] for example, or in capitalist France from the 1960s to the 1980s.[31] While both international and Yugoslav architects had been broadly enthusiastic about and inspired by methods and schemes developed over the course of the project, local coastal-region authorities were used to following their own interests, empowered by decentralization policies introduced in 1964–1965 and socialized companies under "self-management." They either downsized proposed designs to match their own needs and budgets or realized their own ideas instead. International planning concepts, inspired by Team 10 ideas of "humanizing" earlier modernist doctrines, were therefore "humanized" a second time.

The development of Babin Kuk, a peninsula northwest of Dubrovnik, is a good example. Had the international planning team led by SWECO and Associates had its way, the largest and most densely built resort on the entire Eastern Adriatic coast would have taken shape there. The concept was to cast a strictly structuralist and metabolist urban fabric across the entire peninsula, composed of huge, canopied connecting axes and gigantic terraced buildings of exposed concrete. This development would have encompassed the peninsula as well as its mountain range, up to the summits of the highest peaks. The installation of a cable-car system to link the peninsula's various levels was even in the plans (figs. 10a–e).[32]

However, financial resources and the political will to realize the scheme was not forthcoming. A renowned American office was nevertheless commissioned: Edward Durell Stone & Associates had a strong track record in

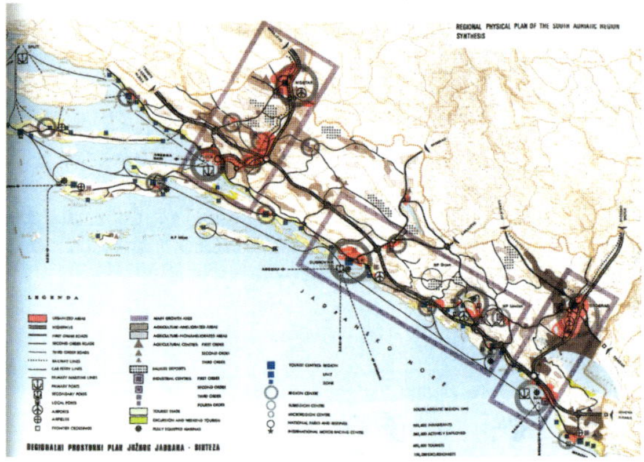

fig. 10a Scheme of the Southern Adriatic plan: Funded by the United Nations, an international team of experts had worked on a comprehensive development plan for the entire Adriatic coast. Source: Vladimir Mattioni, Jadranski projekti (Zagreb: Urbanistički Institut Hrvatske, 2003), 101.

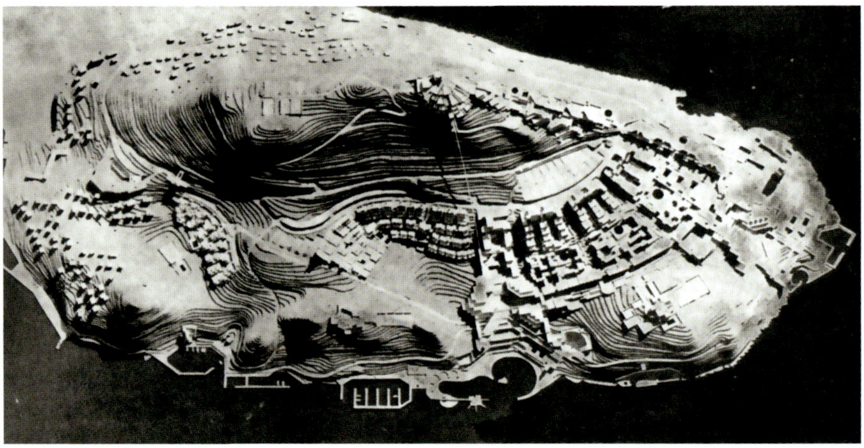

fig. 10b Model of the urban planning scheme for Babin Kuk, a peninsula to the northwest of Dubrovnik, displaying a structuralist urban fabric, including a cable car system, architects: SWECO and Associates, Sweden, 1963–69. Source: Vladimir Mattioni, Jadranski projekti (Zagreb: Urbanistički Institut Hrvatske, 2003), 176.

high-profile state projects in India, Pakistan and Puerto Rico, and built hotels in the Caribbean. The choice was a gesture of goodwill towards the US development bank co-funding the project, and was a means of putting Dubrovnik on the map in the US as a novel tourist destination. Durell Stone & Associates and their local associates Arhitektonski Biro Centar 51 retained the idea of a covered pedestrian zone yet developed alongside it a modest, village-like structure composed of various small, densely built, interlocking clusters of two or three-story units. On the highest spot stood Hotel Plakir, a scattering of staggered cubes, the ground plan of which traced an inverted Y-shape, a well-tested type for hotels in parkland settings, while Hotel President, a large terraced structure barely visible from the road, was perched on the edge of a cliff.

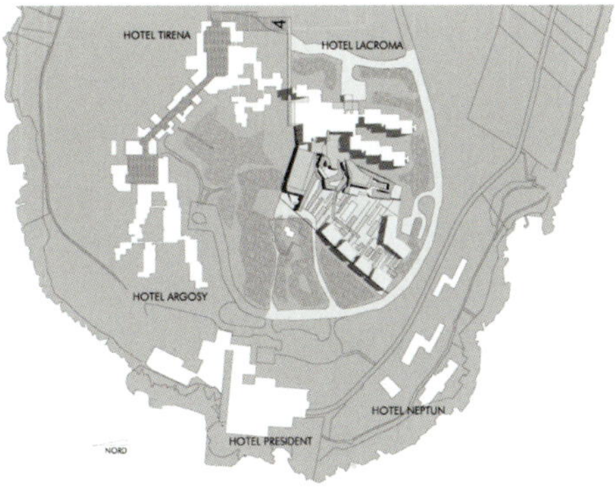

fig. 10c Site plan of realized design of Babin Kuk resort. Architects: Edward Durell Stone Associates (USA), 1976 addition by Boris Podrecca, 2011. Source: Archive of Valamar Dubrovnik.

fig. 10d Areal view of realized design of ... to the left hotel Plakir (today Valamar Lacroma), to the right village style hotels Tirena and Argosy. Source: Archive of Valamar Dubrovnik.

fig.10 e Terraced structure of the sea-shore hotel president. Source: Archive of Valamar Dubrovnik.

Unexpected Side Effects

On the other hand, although not implemented 1:1, these large-scale tourism projects provoked a rather harsh critique due to their mono-cultural character and Taylorist calculations for optimizing tourist capacities, which questioned the socialist dogma of growth that had generally remained undisputed in Yugoslavia. Mass tourism in general was called to task, arguing that the cultural exchange between hosts and guests was dismissed for the benefit of an alienated mass industry of tourism, following almost literally arguments of the Frankfurt School's critique of *Kulturindustrie* (cultural industry) and especially Enzensberger's theory of tourism.[33] On the other hand, favoring tourism facilities against communal infrastructures when it came to large public investments was considered antisocial: everything that seemed to be unavailable for the local population elsewhere was financed for the tourism sector.[34]

Despite all this criticism, these facilities – originally designed as monocultural attractors for tourists, rationalized to maximize profit and representing modernist urban juxtapositions with fishing villages and Venetian harbor towns – unexpectedly but successfully became constituent elements of the local coastal-region public's highly vital everyday life. Except for camping sites and marinas, tourist facilities had never been fenced or walled off, but remained accessible to the public and well-connected to existing networks. Promenades linked these with one another: the fishing village; the harbor and ancient-town centers; private homes of the local population; well-maintained leisure, sport and entertainment facilities at beaches and in the shadows of pine forests (playgrounds, mini-golf, *boccia*, table tennis and tennis); the semi-public spaces of hotels. Even some of the more expensive facilities – bars, clubs, pools, conference and ballrooms, halls for indoor sport – soon became quite naturally appropriated for the needs of the local population, hosting celebrations, sports and cultural events. For local authorities and managers, there was no way to even think about exclusively reserving them for foreign guests. These facilities were considered consensually to be supplements of the local public space and infrastructure – to be "public property," as they had been deemed by law.[35]

Summary

Architecture for seaside tourism calls for a humanization of design language, both in urban scale and in building and interior design: it has to offer stages for people to gaze, meet and mingle, to feel comfortable, to enjoy the landscape. Architects in Yugoslavia and Croatia had been very successful in creating resorts on smaller scales, downsized from international models, very well adapted to the local landscape. The close interconnection between artist, architects and engineers even supported the creation of monumental lyrical expressions in many designs. This effort was supported by the self-confidence of both architects and artists, local managers and politicians who wanted to display their own successes and that of the nation's Third Way – as well as the respect that planners therefore enjoyed in that era.

Endnotes

With special thanks to Maroje Mrduljaš and Norbert Mappes-Niediek.

1 Igor Tchoukarine, "The Yugoslav Road to International Tourism," in *Yugoslavia's Sunny Side: A History of Tourism in Socialism (1950s–1980s)*, eds. Hannes Grandits and Karin Taylor (Budapest and New York: Central European University Press, 2010), 107–138 (p. 114).

2 Vladimir Kulić, "East? West? Or Both? Foreign Perceptions of Architecture in Socialist Yugoslavia," *Journal of Architecture*, 14:1 (2009), 129–147. See also Vladimir Kulić, Maroje Mrduljaš and Wolfgang Thaler, *Modernism In-between: The Mediatory Architectures of Socialist Yugoslavia* (Berlin: Jovis, 2012).

3 Several state institutions, most importantly the Yugoslav Peoples' Army, had built their own tourism facilities accessible to families of staff only. In parallel, private people were tolerated in running small-scale business like bars, grills and restaurants. From 1954, the renting of rooms in weekend homes and bed-and-breakfasts had been permitted as well, and soon covered up to 30 percent of total overnight capacities. See Karin Taylor, "From Trips to Modernity to Holidays in Nostalgia – Tourism History in Eastern and Southeastern Europe," *Tensions of Europe / Inventing Europe* (Working Paper Nr. WP_2011_01, March 2011), 20.

4 Interview with Franco Palma, with Rivijera Hotels Poreč since 1970, where he was general director from 1984 to 2007. For more, see Norbert Mappes-Niediek, "A Thorny Thicket: The Singular Case of Workers' Self-management and Long-drawn-out Privatization in Croatian Tourism," in *Holidays after the Fall: Seaside Architecture and Urbanism in Bulgaria and Croatia*, eds. Elke Beyer, Anke Hagemann, Michael Zinganel (Berlin: Jovis, 2013), 209–221 (pp. 211–212).

5 Croatian tourism journals and architecture magazines regularly published newly planned or realized tourism developments from all over the world.

6 To acknowledge wartime attainments, for example, or for the Party, or to raise Yugoslavia's reputation with exceptional contributions to international exhibitions.

7 For details of the competition entries for Palace and Libertas hotels in Dubrovnik, for example, see *Arhitektura*, 104 (1969), 59–65.

8 Punta Skala, a resort north of Zadar, is one example: founded by Iadera, a subsidiary of a Zadar shipping company, with planning and execution entrusted to Soko Metalworks in Mostar – renowned as the country's leading manufacturer of combat aircraft – Punta Skala was then operated by Oböna, the popular German nudist agency. Haludovo, a resort north of Malinska on the island of Krk that also opened in 1972, was founded by Brodokomerc, an important trading company based in Rijeka, and was operated in a joint venture with *Penthouse* magazine.

9 Igor Duda, "Escaping the City: Leisure Travel in Croatia in the 1950s and 1960s," *Ethnologia-Balkanica*, 9 (2005), 285–304 (p. 289).

10 See Maroje Mrduljaš, "Building the Affordable Arcadia: Tourism Development on the Croatian Adriatic Coast under State Socialism," in *Holidays after the Fall*, 117–207 (p. 117).

11 Božo Lazar, "Neki principi i rješenja kod osnivanja i projektiranja 'Plave lagune' u Poreču," *Arhitektura*, 95–96 (1967), 23–30.

12 Even a "visual-arts supervisor" was commissioned: Boris Vižintin, then director of the prestigious Gallery of Modern Art in Rijeka. Mrduljaš, "Building the Affordable Arcadia," 201.

13 In almost every flagship hotel then built on the Croatian Adriatic coast, visitors found prominently installed paintings or murals, including work by Edo Murtić, who had visited the US in 1951 on a Fulbright grant to study abstract expressionism and later represented Yugoslavia at the Venice Biennale of 1958 and Documenta 2 in Kassel of 1959.

14 This policy refers to the glamorous first period of Hilton International Hotels, built from 1949 to 1965 in parallel with the worldwide expansion of US political influence and allowed the consideration of privately run "cultural programs" of hotels to promote the American lifestyle and "the fruits of the free world" at strategically important international destinations, e.g. in San Juan in Puerto Rico opened in 1949, Istanbul 1945, Berlin 1958, Teheran 1963, and Tel Aviv 1965 See Conrad Hilton, *Be My Guest* (Englewood Cliffs, NJ: Prentice-Hall, 1957), 237; Annabel Jane Wharton, *Building the Cold War: Hilton International Hotels and Modern Architecture* (Chicago: University of Chicago Press, 2001).

15 For parallel developments in other coastal regions, see Zinganel and Beyer, "'Beside the Seaside ...': Architectures of a Modern Global Longing," in *Holidays after the Fall*, 35–53.

16 José Luis Sert, Fernand Léger and Sigfried Giedion, "Nine Points on Monumentality" (1943), first published in Giedion, *Architektur und Gemeinschaft* (Hamburg: Rowohlt, 1956), 40–42; English edition: *Architecture, You and Me* (Cambridge, Mass.: Harvard University Press, 1958) 48–52.

17 See monuments by Bogdan Bogdanović, Dušan Džamonja, et al., in Jan Kempenaers, *Spomenik: The End of History* (Amsterdam: Roma, 2010).

18 An outstanding example of the productive collaboration is the design of Hotel Libertas in Dubrovnik (1968–1974) by architect Andrija Čičin-Šain with artist Raul Goldoni. Vana Gović, *Andrija Činčin-Šain* (Rijeka: Muzej Grada Rijeke, 2009).

19 Vladimir Kulić, "An Avant-Garde Architecture for an Avant-Garde Socialism: Yugoslavia at EXPO '58," *Journal of Contemporary History*, 47:1, special issue "Sites of Convergence – The USSR and Communist Eastern Europe at International Fairs Abroad and at Home" (January 2012), 161–184.

20 Ljiljana Kolešnik, "New Tendencies" in *Hrvatska umjetnost: povijest i spomenici, ed.* Milan Pelc (Zagreb: Institut za povijest umjetnosti; Školska knjiga, 2010) 681–685. Armin Medosch, *New Tendencies: Art at the Threshold of the Information Revolution (1961–1978)* (Cambridge and London: MIT Press 2016).

21 Eva Ceraj, "Bernardo Bernardi – The Spiritus Movens of Early Design in Croatia," *Croatian Academy of Sciences and Arts, Fine Art Archives Art Bulletin*, 63 (2013); Ivana Nikšić Olujić, *Zdravko Bregovac – Arhiv Arhitekta* (Zagreb: Hrvatski muzej arhitekture 2015).

22 Interview with Boris Magaš (architect of the resorts Solaris in Šibenik and Haludovo in Malinska) by the author, Kraljevic, August 24, 2012.

23 See, for example, Julie De Luca's projects in Poreč (1968–1970): Hotel Neptun was so much adapted to the historic town center that it was hardly recognizable as a brand new structure; Pical Apartments in a pine forest

represented the condensed Mediterranean-village type; and the ensemble of three large-scale hotels – Diamant, Kristal and Rubin – at the Brulo resort formed a terraced landscape in a structuralist style. Andrija Čičin-Šain's designs for the hotels Libertas (1968–1974) and Palace (1969–1972) in Dubrovnik represent brilliant examples of terraced structuralist hotel complexes, while the resort Polari/Villas Rubin (1969–1979) south of Rovinj is literally a colorful interpretation of the village type. See Vana Gović, *Andrija Činčin-Šain*.

24 Magaš interview by the author.

25 Paid holidays had been widely discussed by labor movements all over Europe but were first implemented in the Soviet Union in 1922: all workers with at least five-and-a-half months' work tenure were entitled to an annual two-week vacation – and what had hitherto been aristocratic bathing resorts were nationalized and made accessible for general recreation. Entirely new resorts started to be built in the Soviet Union, but also in fascist Italy and Germany from the 1930s: most famously the never-accomplished bathing resort for twenty-thousand tourists on the German island of Rügen, off the eastern Baltic coast, launched by "Kraft durch Freude," the arm of the National Socialist German Labor Front (DAF), awarded a Grand Prix at the 1937 World Expo of Paris.

26 Tom Avermaete, *Another Modern: The Post-War Architecture and Urbanism of Candilis-Josic-Woods* (Rotterdam: NAi, 2005), 332–378 (pp. 338–339). For CIAM details, see *Logis et loisirs: 5e congrès CIAM, Paris, 1937* (Nendeln: Kraus Reprint, 1980).

27 See Mrduljaš, "Building the Affordable Arcadia," 173–179.

28 See Vladimir Mattioni, *Jadranski projekti: projekti Južnog i Gornjeg Jadrana 1967–1972*, (Zagreb: Urbanistički institut Hrvatske, 2003).

29 Most notably Polish architect Adolf Ciborowski, engaged in UN projects including the reconstruction of Skopje, as well as Tekne (Milan), CEKOP (Warsaw), Shankland Cox & Associates (London), SWECO and Vattenbyggnadsbyrån (Stockholm), O.T.A.M. Tourconsult and Urban (Paris/Rome).

30 For details about Bulgaria, see Elke Beyer and Anke Hagemann, "Sun, Sea, Sand… and Architecture: How Bulgaria's Black Sea Coast Was Turned into a Tourist Product," in *Holidays after the Fall*, 57–118.

31 The French development scheme for the 180-kilometer coastline between Montpellier and the Spanish border, known as Mission Racine, ranked among the largest regional- and urban-planning operations ever undertaken in Europe. The scheme included six resort towns, the most famous of which is Jean Balladur's La Grande Motte, with its striking truncated pyramid structures, accommodating a hundred thousand guests, mainly in holiday apartments for sale. Ellen Furlough and Rosemary Wakeman, "Composing a Landscape: Coastal Mass Tourism and Regional Development in the Languedoc-Roussillon, 1960s–1980s," *International Journal of Maritime History*, 9:1 (1997), 187–211.

32 For details of the envisioned Babin Kuk development, see *Arhitektura*, 104 (1969), 25–30; Mattioni, *Jadranski projekti*, 176.

33 Hans Magnus Enzensberger's 1958 essay – published even before mass tourism started – became the most influential source for tourism critique in German-speaking academia. Enzensberger, "A Theory of Tourism," *New German Critique*, 68 (1996), 117–135. There is evidence for a close relation-

ship between Frankfurt School philosophers and Yugoslav critical-leftist intellectuals who met each other from 1963 to 1974 at the annual Summer School of Korčula, organized by the Zagreb-based philosophical journal *Praxis* to discuss new methods of emancipation and a more humanistic Marxism. See Boris Kanzleiter, "Das Praxis-Experiment. Wie jugoslawische Philosophen versuchten, die Welt zu verändern, und ihre Hoffnungen in der Negation verschwanden," *Jungle World*, 4 (January 26, 2005), accessed July 27, 2013, <http://jungle-world.com/artikel/2005/04/14528.html>.

34 See Grgo Gamulin, the influential art critic, referring to Marxist sociologists and philosophers Georges Friedmann and Henri Lefebvre, quoted in Mrduljaš, "Building the Affordable Arcadia," 184, 187.

35 Ibid., 206–207.

Appendix

Notes on Contributors

Wojciech Bałus is full professor at the Institute of Art History of the Jagiellonian University. He studied art history and philosophy. His field of study includes the theory and history of art from the nineteenth century until today, as well as the interface between art and philosophy, cultural anthropology and literary studies. Bałus is editor of the *Ars Vetus et Nova* series, President of the Polish National Committee of Corpus Vitrearum and member of the Polish Academy of Letters and Sciences in Krakow, and of the AICA. His latest publications include *Krakau zwischen Traditionen und Wegen in die Moderne. Zur Geschichte der Architektur und der öffentlichen Grünanlagen im 19. Jahrhundert* (2003) and *Gotik ohne Gott? Die Symbolik des Kirchengebäudes im 19. Jahrhundert* (2016).

Elke Beyer is a historian and urban researcher for the project "Transnational Spaces of Production" at the Habitat Unit, Technical University Berlin. She graduated in History and East European Studies, and was a research associate in the project "Shrinking Cities", Berlin, and at the IRS in Erkner. From 2006–2010, she taught at the Institute for the History and Theory of Architecture, ETH Zurich, followed by a SNF fellowship in Moscow for her dissertation project on town planning in the USSR in the 1960s. She is the co-editor and co-author of *Holidays After The Fall. Seaside Architecture and Urbanism in Bulgaria and Croatia* (Berlin: Jovis, 2013). Her most recent fields of study include global knowledge transfer in architecture and urbanism.

Susana Constantino is a Ph.D. candidate at the Department of Architecture at University of Coimbra with a doctoral grant from the Fundação para a Ciência e Tecnologia (FCT). She is developing a dissertation on the paradigm shift in Portuguese architecture of cultural buildings in the 1960s. She graduated as an architect and received her Master in Rehabilitation of the Built Environment from the University of Coimbra, Portugal. From 2010 through 2013 she taught at the Department of Architecture of the University of Coimbra. She published the book *Arquitectura de Cine Teatros: Evolução e Registo* [1927–1959] (2010).

Nikolas Drosos specializes in art and architecture from postwar Eastern Europe in its global context. He holds a PhD in art history from the Graduate

Center, City University of New York. His dissertation, "Modernism with a Human Face: Synthesis of Art and Architecture in Eastern Europe, 1954–1958," examines the theory and practices relating to the "synthesis of the arts," the integration of art into architecture in the Soviet Union, Poland and Yugoslavia. He has been the recipient of a Fulbright scholarship, a pre-doctoral fellowship at the Center for Advanced Study in the Visual Arts at the National Gallery of Art in Washington, and a post-doctoral fellowship at Columbia University's Harriman Institute.

Karin Hallas-Murula is a professor at Tallinn University of Technology (TUT) in Estonia, Institute of Architecture and Urban Studies, and Head of the Chair of Art and Architecture History. She graduated from St. Petersburg Academy of Arts, studied at the Central University in Prague, and holds a doctoral degree from the Art History Institute in Moscow. In 1991, she founded the Museum of Estonian Architecture where she was first Director until 2010. She has authored more than ten architecture monographs (four of them have won awards in Estonia) and has published widely on architecture and urbanism of the twentieth and twent-first century. She has curated more than 30 architecture exhibitions in Estonia on Estonian architecture, among them the international project "Architecture 1900."

Marcela Hanáčková is an art historian specializing in CIAM and Team 10's relations with Eastern Europe during the Cold War conflict. She is currently submitting her Ph.D. thesis "CIAM and the Cold War. Helena Syrkus in between Architecture and Politics" at the gta/ETH in Zurich. So far she has published on the Czechoslovak CIAM group, Team10 contacts with the East and the Czech architecture studio SIAL. Since her graduation from Charles University in Prague, she has worked as an assistant at the Faculty of Architecture and at the Catholic Theological Faculty in Prague. She has worked for the Centre for Central European Architecture and Research Centre of Academy of Fine Arts in Prague and holds several research scholarships.

Hilde Heynen is full professor at the Department of Architecture at the University of Leuven. Her research focuses on issues of modernity, modernism and gender in architecture. She is the author of *Architecture and Modernity. A Critique* (MIT Press, 1999) and the co-editor of *Back from Utopia. The Challenge of the Modern Movement* (with Hubert-Jan Henket, 010, 2001), *Negotiating Domesticity. Spatial Productions of Gender in Modern Architecture* (with Gülsüm Baydar, Routledge, 2005) and *The SAGE Handbook Architectural Theory* (with Greig Crysler and Stephen Cairns, Sage, 2012). She regularly publishes in journals such as *The Journal of Architecture* and *Home Cultures*.

Judith Hopfengärtner studied architecture at TU Karlsruhe, EPF Lausanne and at the Bartlett School of Architecture, UCL, where she received her Diploma. She taught design at the University of Karlsruhe (KIT) and earned an MAS in History and Theory of Architecture at the Institute gta of the ETH Zurich with research on Aldo Rossi's teachings at the ETH Zurich and his influence on Swiss architects. She was assistant to the Chair for the Theory of Architecture at ETH Zurich 2010–2015 and is co-editor of *Aldo Rossi und die Schweiz. Architektonische Wechselwirkungen* (Zurich, gta, 2011, with Ákos Moravánszky).

Karl R. Kegler is Professor for the History and Theory of Urbanistics and Architecture at the Hochschule München / University of Applied Sciences Munich. From 2011 to 2015, he was postdoc and senior assistant at the Institute gta of the ETH Zurich. Prior to that, Kegler worked as a scientific researcher and lecturer at several university institutions and has co-authored and edited numerous books on the history of architecture and on science and technology studies. Publications and research interests include the intellectual history of planning and architecture, popular culture and literary studies. He has published *Wege zu einer neuen Baukunst* (2000), *Utopische Orte. Utopien in Architektur- und Stadtbaugeschichte* (2004) and *Deutsche Raumplanung* (2015) on the history and theoretical basis of regional planning in Germany.

Béla Kerékgyártó is Associate Professor for Aesthetics and Cultural Theory at the TU Budapest. His main fields of interest are modern history, theory of architecture and urbanism. He has published widely about the philosophical and social background, and about different periods and problems of modern architecture. He edited a comprehensive textbook of architectural theory in the 20th century and the writings of Otto Wagner and Adolf Loos in Hungarian.

Torsten Lange is postdoctoral assistant at the Guest Lectureship for the Theory of Architecture at ETH Zurich. He received his Diploma in Architecture from the Bauhaus University Weimar and his Master in Architectural History from the Bartlett School of Architecture/UCL, and earned his Ph.D. with the thesis "*Komplexe Umweltgestaltung* [complex environmental design]: architectural theory and the production of the built environment in the GDR, 1960–1990" (UCL, 2015). His research focuses on postwar architecture and urbanism, especially in socialist European countries, and examines theories of production, labor, and materiality as well as alternative forms of architectural practice. His work has been published in *ARCH+*, *archimaera*, *The Journal of Architecture*, and *East Central Europe*, and in edited volumes such as *Industries of Architecture* (Routledge, 2016).

Vladimir Kulić teaches architectural history and theory at Florida Atlantic University. He has published *Modernism In-Between: The Mediatory Architectures of Socialist Yugoslavia* (with Maroje Mrduljaš and Wolfgang Thaler, 2012), the exhibition catalog *Unfinished Modernisations* (with Maroje Mrduljaš, 2012), and the collection of essays *Sanctioning Modernism: Architecture and the Making of Postwar Identities* (edited in collaboration with Monica Penick and Timothy Parker, 2014). He is currently working on an exhibition about architecture in socialist Yugoslavia at the Museum of Modern Art in New York (with Martino Stierli, 2018), and on an edited collection about postmodernist architecture in former communist-bloc countries.

Martin Maleschka is an architect and photographer working and living in Cottbus, Germany. While studying Architecture at Brandenburg University of Technology, he developed a keen interest in photography and in the architectural art of the German Democratic Republic – a passion that stems from having grown up in the socialist model city of Eisenhüttenstadt. In 2006, he began uploading photos of architectural art on various image-hosting websites, and since then has built up the most comprehensive photographic collection of architectural art in East Germany with more than 10,000 images published to this day. His work has been exhibited in a number of solo shows. At the moment, he is working on a guidebook for architectural art in East Germany.

Marijke Martin works as an urban historian. She is associate professor in the field of architecture, cultural and urban studies at the Faculty of Arts at Groningen University. Her research includes the comparative analyzing of modern housing estates in Europe, Latin America and Africa. She acted as curator for the exhibition of the civic culture project of Bogotà that was part of the Venice Biennale 2006, and has published numerous articles on postwar architecture and urbanism. She lives in Groningen and Prague.

Juliana Maxim is Associate Professor of Art and Architectural History at the University of San Diego, California. She was the recipient of the American Council of Learned Societies postdoctoral fellowship in Eastern European Studies. She researches and writes on the architectural culture of communism in Romania. She is currently finishing a book titled *The Socialist Life of Modern Architecture: Bucharest, 1947–1965*, which traces the mechanisms through which modern architecture was invested with political meaning in postwar communist Romania.

Luca Molinari is Associate Professor of History of Contemporary Architecture at the Department of Architecture and Design at the Luigi Vanvitelli Faculty of Architecture at the SUN (Seconda Università degli Studi di Napoli) in Naples. He received his Ph.D. in Architecture at the Faculty of Architecture at the TU Delft. He was curator of the Italian Pavilion for the 12th International Architecture Exhibition at the Biennale of Venice in 2010 and had previously curated for architecture at the Triennale of Milan from 2000 to 2004. The main focus of his researches and studies is the postwar European, and especially the Italian, culture of architecture. His recent publications include: *Continuità: a response to identity crises. Ernesto Nathan Rogers and Italian architectural culture after 1945*. (Delft, 2008); *Le case che siamo* (Milan, 2016).

Stanislaus von Moos is an art historian born in 1940 in Lucerne, Switzerland. He is the author of books on Le Corbusier, Renaissance architecture and 20th century design history. His current projects involve architecture and politics in Europe around 1950, and more generally the interactions of the visual arts and architecture in the 20th century. He was Professor of Modern Art at the University of Zurich (1983–2005) and served as Vincent Scully Visiting Professor at Yale University (2010–2014).

Ákos Moravánszky is Professor Emeritus of the Theory of Architecture at the Institute gta of ETH Zurich, where he taught between 1996 and 2016. He studied architecture in Budapest and received his Ph.D. in Vienna. He was a Research Fellow at the Zentralinstitut für Kunstgeschichte in Munich, and the Getty Center in Santa Monica. From 1991 until 1996 he was appointed Visiting Professor at M.I.T. in Cambridge, Mass. The main areas of his research and publication activities are the history of East and Middle European architecture in the nineteenth and twentieth centuries, the history of architectural theory, and the iconology of building materials and constructions. He is the author of *Competing Visions: Aesthetic Invention and Social Imagination in Central European Architecture, 1867–1918* (Cambridge, Mass., 1998) and *Lehrgerüste. Theorie und Stofflichkeit der Architektur* (Zurich, 2015).

Nelson Mota is a lecturer and researcher at the TU Delft, where he is finishing his Ph.D. on the interlocking relation between modernity and the vernacular in postwar housing design decision-making. He is also a guest scholar at The Berlage Center for Advanced Studies in Architecture and Urban Design. He is member of the editorial board and production editor of the academic journal *Footprint*. He graduated in Architecture and received his Master from the University of Coimbra, Portugal, where he lectured in the period 2004–2009. He was the recipient of the Fernando Távora Prize in 2006 and authored the book *A Arquitectura do Quotidiano* (2010), runner-up in the Iberian FAD Prize 2011.

Annie Pedret is an architect and architectural historian of modern architecture and received her Ph.D. and S.M.Arch.S. degrees from the History, Theory and Criticism program at MIT. She holds a professional degree in architecture from the University of British Columbia, and a B.Sc. from the University of Toronto. She is the author of *Team 10: an archival history* (2013) and has published and lectured internationally about CIAM, Team 10 and the ethical premises of modern architecture. Her research interests are the unacknowledged discourses in the historiography of modern architecture. She has taught architectural history and design at the Illinois Institute of Technology in Chicago, the University of Illinois in Chicago, and is currently an Associate Professor in the Design Department at Seoul National University in Seoul, Korea.

Sven Sterken is assistant professor at the Faculty of Architecture at Leuven University, where he teaches courses in the history of architecture and urbanism. He obtained a Master in architectural engineering from the universities of Paris, Pretoria and Ghent, and a Ph.D. in architectural history from the latter university in 2004 with a dissertation on the composer and architect Iannis Xenakis. His current research focuses on the development of architectural and urban expertise within the Catholic milieu in Belgium and its neighboring countries during the 1950s and 1960s.

Cor Wagenaar is full professor at the chair for Architecture, Urbanism and Health at Groningen University, and associate professor at Delft University of Technology. He specializes in urban history and healthcare architecture and is editor of *Happy: Cities and Public Happiness in Postwar Europe* (NAi Publishers, 2004) and author of *Town Planning in the Netherlands since 1800. Responses to Enlightenment Ideas and Geopolitical Realities* (010 publishers, 2011). He lives in Groningen and Berlin.

Dana Vais is professor at the Faculty of Architecture and Urbanism, the Technical University of Cluj, Romania, where she teaches 20th-Century

Architecture and architecture studio. She earned her Ph.D. at the University of Architecture and Urbanism 'Ion Mincu' in Bucharest. Her visiting appointments include University of Cincinnati (Fulbright fellow), École d'Architecture Paris Belleville, Institut Supérieur d'Architecture Saint-Luc in Liège. Her publications include: "Exporting hard modernity: construction projects from Ceausescu's Romania in the 'Third World'" in *The Journal of Architecture* vol. 17 3/2012; and "Techniques of Happiness: Housing Prefabrication in Romania during the 1960s" in *Centropa* vol.13 1/2013.; "The (in)famous Anca Petrescu: authorship and authority in Romanian communist architecture, 1977–1989", in: M. Pepchinski and M. Simon (eds.), *Ideological Equals. Women Architects in Socialist Europe 1945–1989*, Routledge, 2017.

Domonkos Wettstein is an assistant lecturer at the Department of Urban Planning and Design at the Budapest University of Technology and Economics (BME). He attended the University of Lichtenstein in Vaduz and graduated at the Faculty of Architecture at the BME. His doctoral research theme is: Recreation and regional concepts in the architecture of Lake Balaton. He was a visiting scholar at the Institute for History and Theory (gta) at the ETH, Zurich in 2013/14. As a teacher, he has participated in the education of architecture at the BME for three years.

Eva Weyns is a PhD researcher at the KU Leuven Faculty of Architecture, where she works on the research project *Catholic Territories in a Suburban landscape: Religion and Urbanization in Belgium, 1945–1975*. Since completing her studies in architectural engineering (KU Leuven) and in conservation of monuments and sites (Raymond Lemaire International Centre for Conservation, KU Leuven) she has been involved in the discussion on the future of religious heritage. Her current research focuses on the use of architecture and urban planning in the territorial strategies of the Roman Catholic Church in postwar Belgium.

Michael Zinganel is a co-founder of the independent research institute Tracing Spaces, based in Vienna. He studied at the TU Graz and at the Jan van Eyck Academy Maastricht and obtained a Ph.D. in contemporary history at the University of Vienna. From 2001 to 2010 he was assistant professor at the Institute of Building Typology at the TU Graz. Since 2011/12 he was research adviser at the postgraduate academy of Bauhaus Dessau Foundation. He co-edited *Holiday after the Fall – Seaside Architecture and Urbanism in Bulgaria and Croatia* (with Elke Beyer and Anke Hagemann) (Berlin: jovis 2013). From 2014–16 he has been research fellow at the Academy of Fine Arts Vienna.

Index